:: INTRODUCTION

Welcome to the very first *Rising Stars of Manga: United Kingdom and Ireland!*

I can happily say that bringing the yearly *Rising Stars* competition to The United Kingdom and Ireland has been a huge success. In the United States, *Rising Stars* has become a bit of an institution in the manga community. By the time this book hits the stores, the winners of the sixth U.S. competition will have been chosen, which is really cool. Well over half of all the past winners have gone on to sign publishing deals with TOKYOPOP and other top major companies. Check out the WHERE ARE THEY NOW section at the back of this book to learn a little more about what the U.S. winners have gone on to do with their careers. I'm sure by the time the second *Rising Stars U.K. and Ireland* comes out, many of these winners here will find themselves on that list.

Here's how the competition worked: We put out a call to all manga-ka (manga artists) across the U.K. and Ireland and asked them to create original pieces that were 15-20 pages long. These entries were then sent to our offices and scoured over by our crack editorial staff. Their criteria was strict:

1) Rendering and Finishes: Does this piece have a professional look to it? Can this person draw anatomy and do they have an understanding of perspective? How are their facial expressions? How confident are their inked lines? Can they utilize greyscale toning or screen tones? Toning is an important element in the manga aesthetic.

2) Visual Storytelling: How is the story paced out? Does the artist know how to use panel layout to help move the story along? Varying the number, shape and size of the panels has a big effect on how the reader processes the information on the page. A quick successions of small panels can be used to show action, but too many can be hectic and distracting. However, using a page that has maybe only one or two panels after a busy action scene helps to slow things and give the reader a chance to absorb what they've just read. Another thing we look for is the creator's ability to vary what we call the "camera angle." Like how in a good film or television program the movement and position of the camera helps convey the emotion of a scene, the same can be done in manga. Is the "camera" static throughout the entry—meaning is everything drawn straight on like a comic strip in the newspaper? Or does is move from above to below—or from far off to really close?

3) Artistic Stylization: How interesting and original are the character designs and the world in which the story is set? In Japan, doujinshi (original works of existing characters drawn by fans) is an important part of the manga world. However, the ability to recreate one's favourite characters or to draw characters that have a very similar look or style as an existing character is not really what this competition is about. We're looking for artists who have the ability to envision and invent cool characters we haven't seen before—or who can put an interesting twist on something familiar. One other consideration that falls under this heading is how "manga" the entry is. This is a tricky one because it's not

the RISING STARS of MANGA
United Kingdom and Ireland

Bo
Fa
Fa

the
RISING STARS of
MANGA™
United Kingdom and Ireland

Vol. 1

TOKYOPOP

Rising Stars of Manga United Kingdom and Ireland Vol. 1

Associate Editor - Hope Donovan
Design and Layout - Jason Milligan and James Lee
Cover Design - Christopher Tjaslma

Editor - Rob Valois
Senior Editor - Aaron Suhr
Digital Imaging Manager - Chris Buford
Production Managers - Jennifer Miller and Mutsumi Miyazaki
Managing Editor - Lindsey Johnston
Editorial Director - Jeremy Ross
VP of Production - Ron Klamert
Publisher and E.I.C. - Mike Kiley
President and C.O.O. - John Parker
C.E.O. and Chief Creative Officer - Stuart Levy

A  Manga

TOKYOPOP Inc.
5900 Wilshire Blvd. Suite 2000
Los Angeles, CA 90036

E-mail: info@TOKYOPOP.com
Come visit us online at www.TOKYOPOP.com

ISBN: 1-59816-464-3

First TOKYOPOP printing: April 2006
10 9 8 7 6 5 4 3 2 1
Printed in the USA

something that can really be quantified—and the question has sparked a lot of debate. Following this introduction, TOKYOPOP Senior Editor Aaron Suhr shares his opinions on WHAT IS MANGA?

4) Story: Although the artistic elements of this competition always seem to take a front seat, having a well-written and compelling story is paramount. The thing to keep in mind is that the entrants were limited to no less than 15 pages and no more than 20 pages to tell their tales. That's not a lot of pages, seeing as most of our books have 160 pages of story and can go on for many, many volumes. One main thing we look for is if the entry has a beginning, middle and end. If someone's dream is to tell a 300-volume epic that spans 30 generations and has dozens of characters—they should save it for later. No matter how hard they try, they're not going to fit it into 20 pages.

5) Dialogue: You can have a cool-looking entry, with a compelling story— but if the characters don't have anything interesting to say then it all falls apart. One misstep young manga writers make is that their dialogue is often too expository (basically explaining the plot to the reader). Manga, as a visual medium, has the ability to convey most of the story and action through the art. So, if you have a character pulling a sword out of a rock there is no need for him to say, "Look, I'm pulling this sword out of that big rock." The dialogue should complement the art, not explain it.

6) Lettering: Luckily, this is something we're very forgiving on—because almost no one can get this right. Being able to create professional looking balloons and text is difficult. Most people don't have an extensive font library—and the fonts that come with most home computers just don't work for manga or comics. And hand written text is best reserved for spirited sound effects.

Sounds complicated, right? Well it is. For lots of artists and writers around the world manga is their career—and they got there through hard work and sacrifice. Becoming a manga-ka is probably not going to get you a castle or a speedboat, but if you're persistent and successful you might finally be able to move out of your parent's attic and maybe get a scooter.

This is just the first of many Rising Stars competitions. Please check our website for details on future competitions. www.tokyopop.co.uk/rsom

To everyone who took the time to sit down and write and draw an entry, we congratulate you. For those of you who didn't make the book, please don't give up and don't be discouraged. I've seen artists grow over two or three Rising Stars competitions before they've finally won—and they're some of the most talented manga-ka out there.

—*Rob Valois*
Editor

"WHAT IS MANGA?" That is the question TOKYOPOP has asked thousands of aspiring writers and artists to answer over the course of several *Rising Stars of Manga* competitions in the United States. The answers we've gotten, in the form of so many uniquely creative entries, have painted a broad spectrum of possibilities for the format. One would think that a major manga publisher like TOKYOPOP could tell you exactly what manga is, and could provide strict, detailed guidelines as to what belongs in the category. The fact is, we're still figuring it out ourselves!

As a leader in the localization of Japanese and Korean manga, and the only major company to publish such up-and-coming manga-ka outside of Japan, TOKYOPOP is uniquely positioned to help redefine what manga is. The selections we've made in these competitions and the winners we've decided to sign up and publish have already begun to influence the way manga is viewed by its fans, as well as its casual readers. The response has been varied, and has spawned some controversy in the fan community, but we continue to believe in each and every manga piece we print.

And now for the first time, we have turned outside the borders of the U.S. to spotlight the talents of our neighbors in the United Kingdom and Ireland. This edition of *Rising Stars of Manga* is just another example of how manga continues to grow as a global phenomenon—influenced not only by contemporary Japanese pop culture, but the local flavors and styles of creators across the globe.

So whether you're a die-hard otaku, old school comic book fan or a newcomer to the world of sequential art, we are thrilled to have you along on our continuing journey to answer the question "WHAT IS MANGA?" Enjoy the ride!

—Aaron Suhr
Senior Editor

::

FALLING STAR :: Grand Prize Winner ::

Paul Duffield was born in Winchester, England in 1984. He is currently a student of illustration and animation.
www.spoonbard.com
www.spoonbard.deviantart.com

Favorite manga:
Nausicaa of the Valley of the Wind

Favorite manga artist:
Jiro Taniguchi, Taiyo Matsumoto and Hiroki Mafuyu (and western artist Joshua Middleton should definitely get a mention too!)

Author's Comments:
"Falling Star" started out life 3 years ago as a 24 hour comic (Scott McCloud's idea). Me and some friends drew for 24 hours solid, making a page an hour. My comic was about a guy who has one day left to live, but it made no sense because I was so sleep deprived! I dug it up and re-created it for *RSoM* because I really liked the concept.
—Paul Duffield

::

FALLING STAR
GRAND PRIZE WINNER
RISING.STARS.OF.MANGA.2006

::

FALLING STAR :: Grand Prize Winner ::

....

Judge's Comments:

I knew right away that I wanted to put "Falling Star" into the book—however, things aren't quite that easy. There's a process...judging that needs to happen. And I was only one of seven judges. I was convinced that it was going to be an uphill battle: Paul's art doesn't really look like traditional manga—the lines are loose and the characters have a very indie comics style. I was worried. The panel layout and visual story telling are definitely manga informed—that's a plus. But then there's the story—a surrealist tale of lost love and lost hope. Having worked on several of the U.S. Rising Stars, I knew that the winners usually have more universal themes—they're almost always comedies. This was going to be a hard sell, but I was prepared.

The day of judgment came and I collected the preliminary tally sheets from all the judges... I was amazed, "Falling Star" was at the top of almost everybody's lists. When we got into the meeting room to argue our cases and pick the winners, "Falling Star" was written at the top of the big white board on the wall and that's where it stayed all day.

There was no debate and nobody really questioned its place there. There were many battles won and lost that day, but Paul Duffield's "Falling Star" was a universal victory.
—*Rob Valois*

Judge's Comments:

While most of the manga translated into English are shojo and shonen—comics stylized with a youth appeal, there are a lot of artists who work in a more realistic mode. Some artists, like Jiro Taniguchi, have more in common with French comic artists than they do to their Japanese peers. Paul Duffield's "Falling Star" is a beautiful and touching story in this tradition.

The use of un-inked pencils for the linework is also not a traditional manga style, but it's not unheard of—Hiroaki Samura (*Blade of the Immortal*) sticks with pencils. Some Rising Stars entries come in without inks and suffer for it, but Paul Duffield's work looks finished and has enough contrast thanks to the tones and shading.

One of the most striking things about Paul Duffield's art is the composition. The use of spreads, panels on top of art and irregular shapes really make each page come alive, even though the characters are hardly moving. The shard-shaped panels on the edges of some scenes are a neat effect, but inconsistently used. Sometimes, as in the second spread with the doctor standing over the boy, they are purely stylistic. In the flashback scenes later on, they are used as scene breaks to indicate a change in time and place. In this short story it's not really a problem, but if the inconsistency were continued in a longer work, it could be confusing.

Even more than the technique, what makes this story memorable for me is the emotions. The characters are very expressive, both in the realistically rendered close up and more stylized long shots, so that I share their joy and sorrow. The story leaves a lot of details unexplained, but in the end, the emotions tell the story. Excellent work.
—*Jake T. Forbes*

::

FALLING STAR

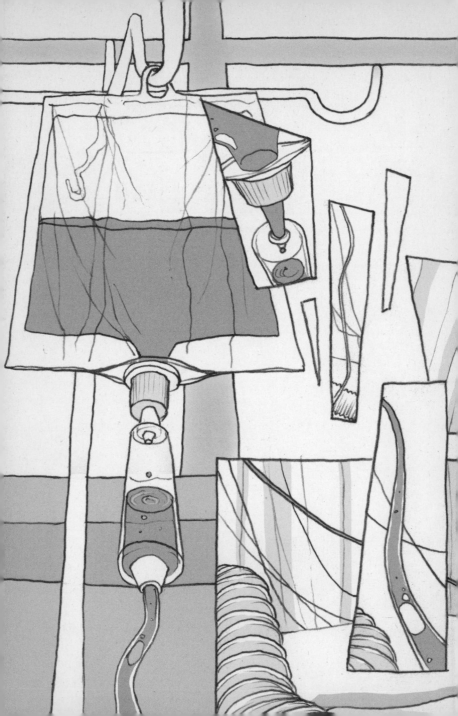

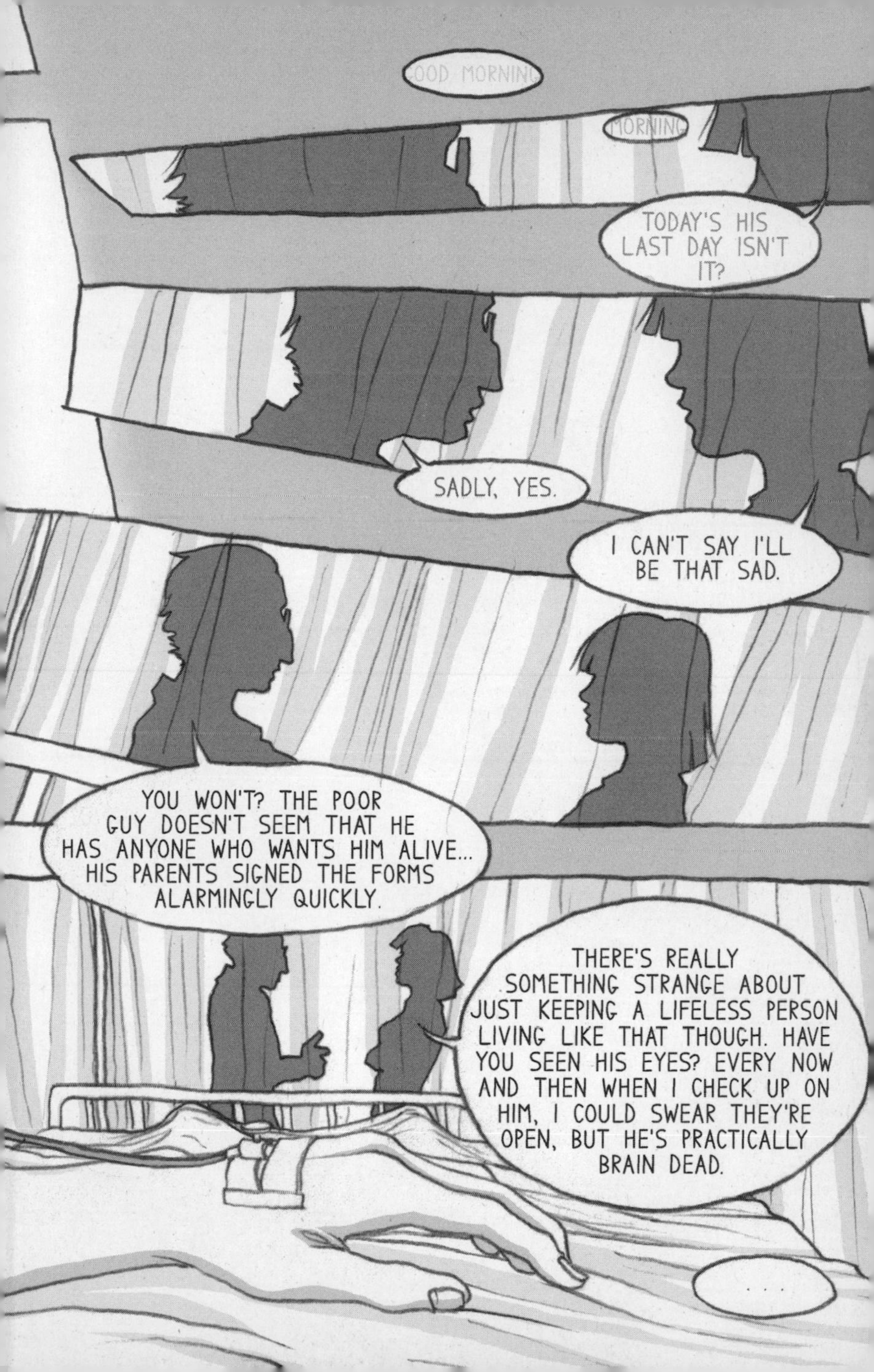
GOOD MORNING
MORNING
TODAY'S HIS LAST DAY ISN'T IT?
SADLY, YES.
I CAN'T SAY I'LL BE THAT SAD.
YOU WON'T? THE POOR GUY DOESN'T SEEM THAT HE HAS ANYONE WHO WANTS HIM ALIVE... HIS PARENTS SIGNED THE FORMS ALARMINGLY QUICKLY.
THERE'S REALLY SOMETHING STRANGE ABOUT JUST KEEPING A LIFELESS PERSON LIVING LIKE THAT THOUGH. HAVE YOU SEEN HIS EYES? EVERY NOW AND THEN WHEN I CHECK UP ON HIM, I COULD SWEAR THEY'RE OPEN, BUT HE'S PRACTICALLY BRAIN DEAD.
. . .

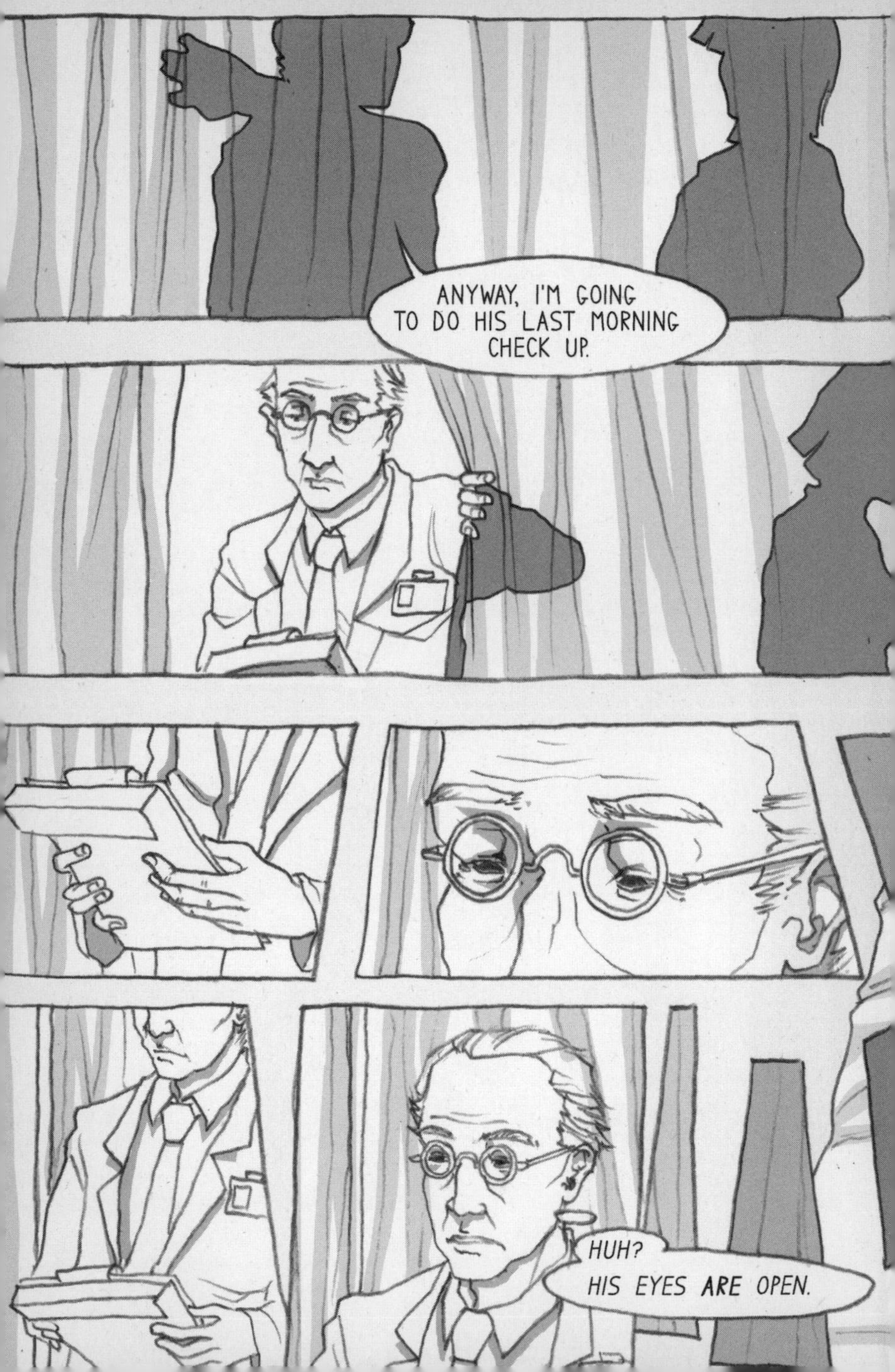
ANYWAY, I'M GOING TO DO HIS LAST MORNING CHECK UP.
HUH?
HIS EYES ARE OPEN.

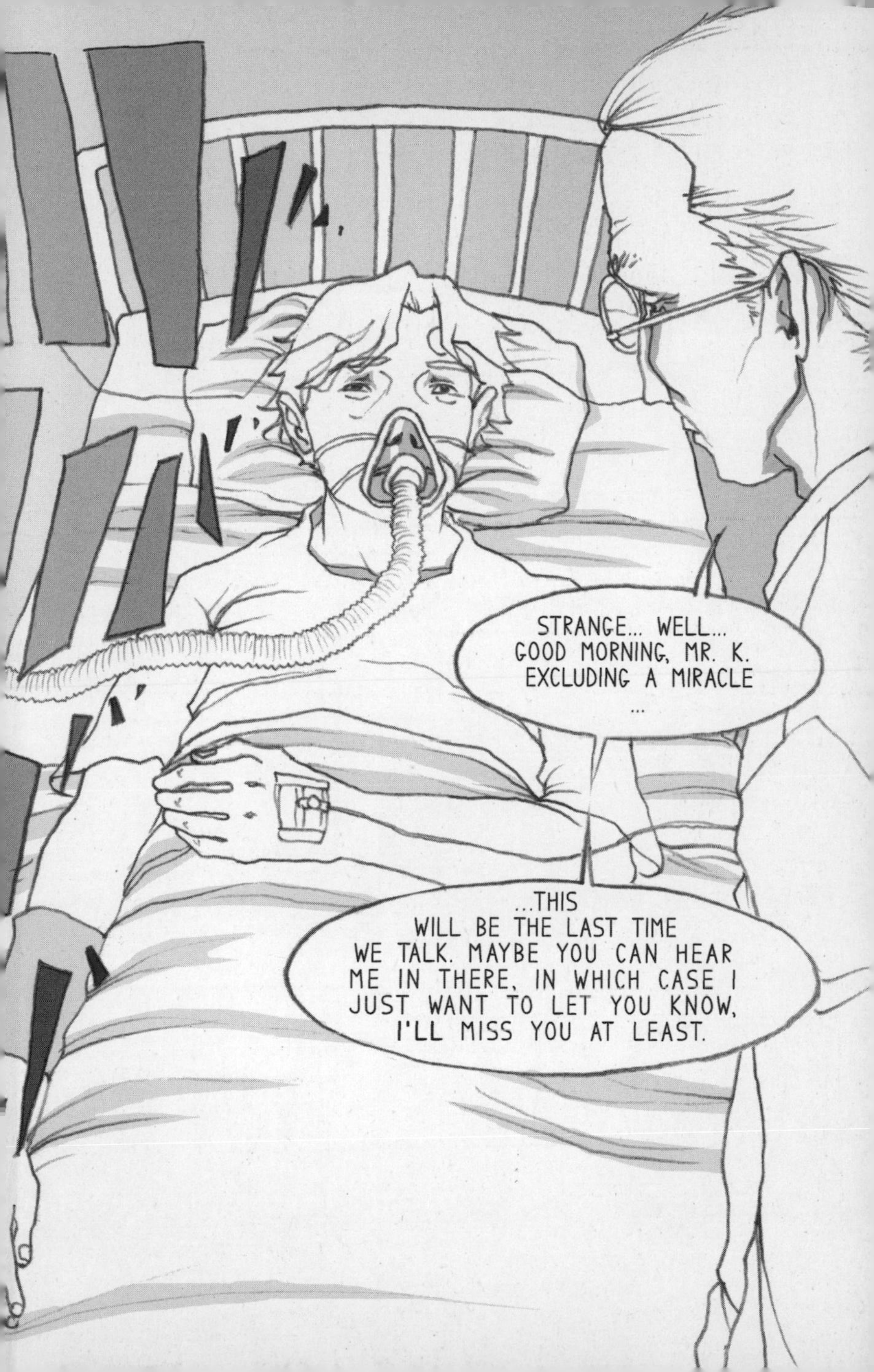
STRANGE... WELL... GOOD MORNING, MR. K. EXCLUDING A MIRACLE ...
...THIS WILL BE THE LAST TIME WE TALK. MAYBE YOU CAN HEAR ME IN THERE, IN WHICH CASE I JUST WANT TO LET YOU KNOW, I'LL MISS YOU AT LEAST.

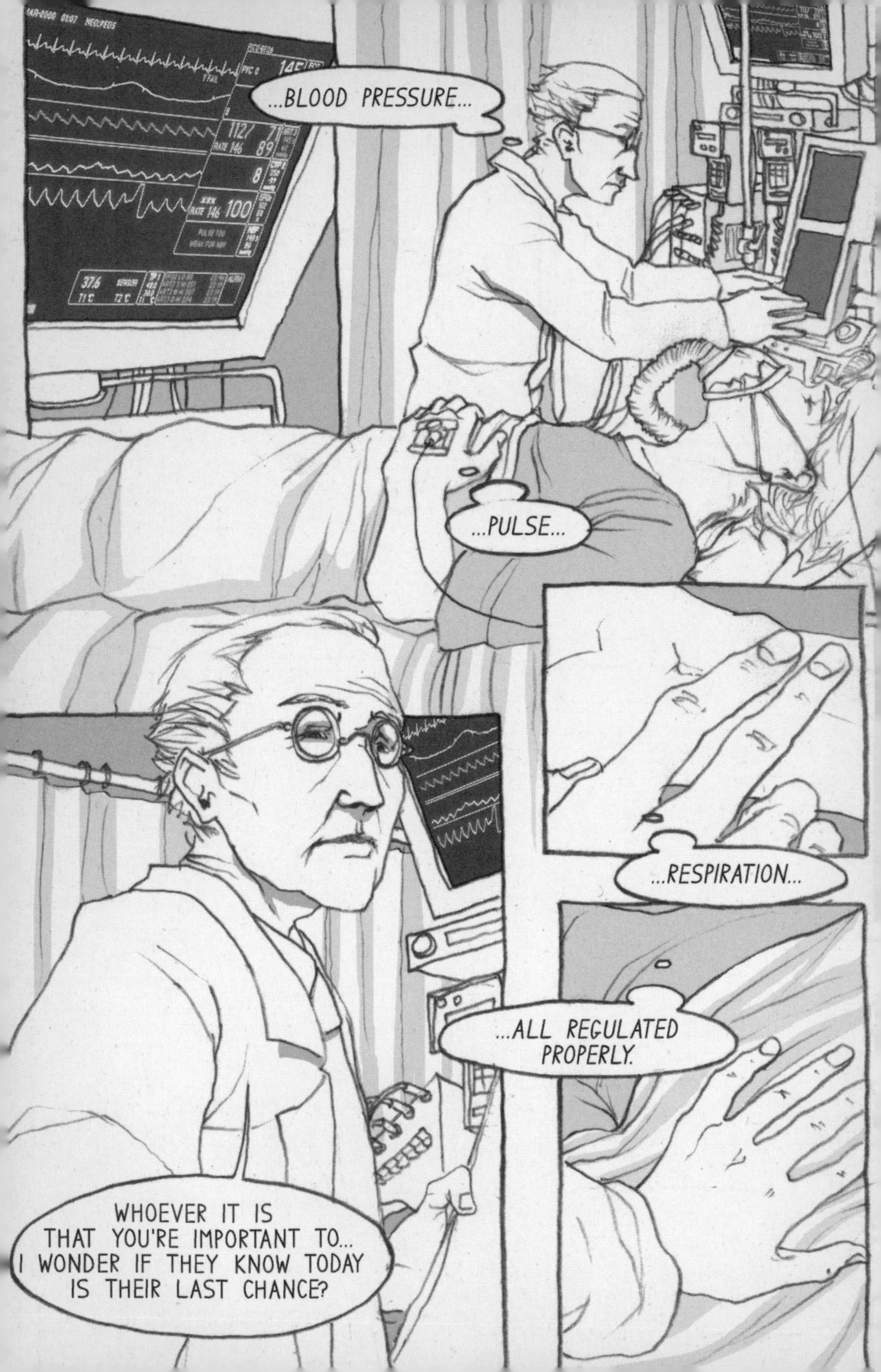
...BLOOD PRESSURE...
...PULSE...
...RESPIRATION...
...ALL REGULATED PROPERLY.
WHOEVER IT IS THAT YOU'RE IMPORTANT TO... I WONDER IF THEY KNOW TODAY IS THEIR LAST CHANCE?

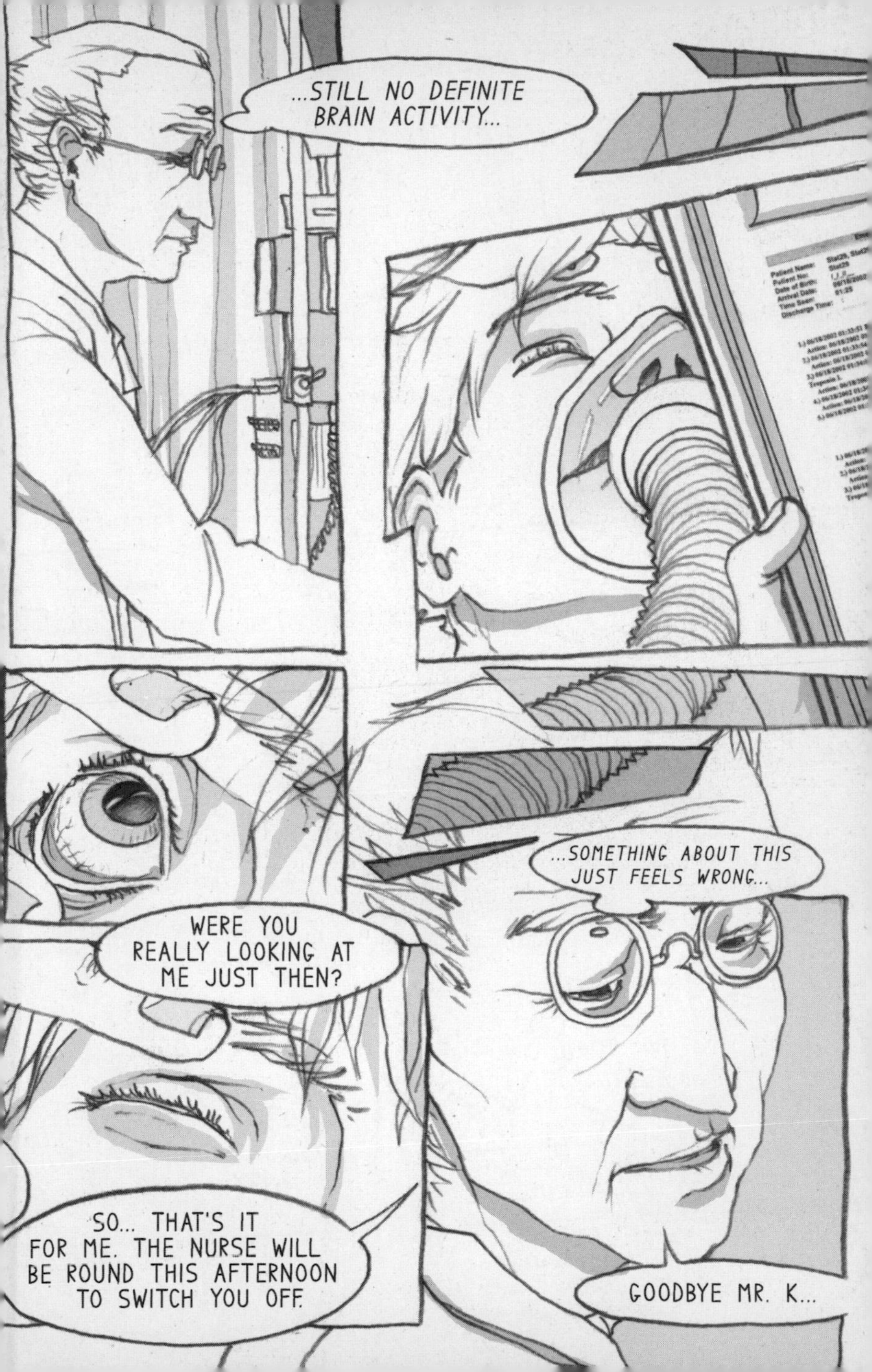
...STILL NO DEFINITE BRAIN ACTIVITY...
WERE YOU REALLY LOOKING AT ME JUST THEN?
SO... THAT'S IT FOR ME. THE NURSE WILL BE ROUND THIS AFTERNOON TO SWITCH YOU OFF.
...SOMETHING ABOUT THIS JUST FEELS WRONG...
GOODBYE MR. K...

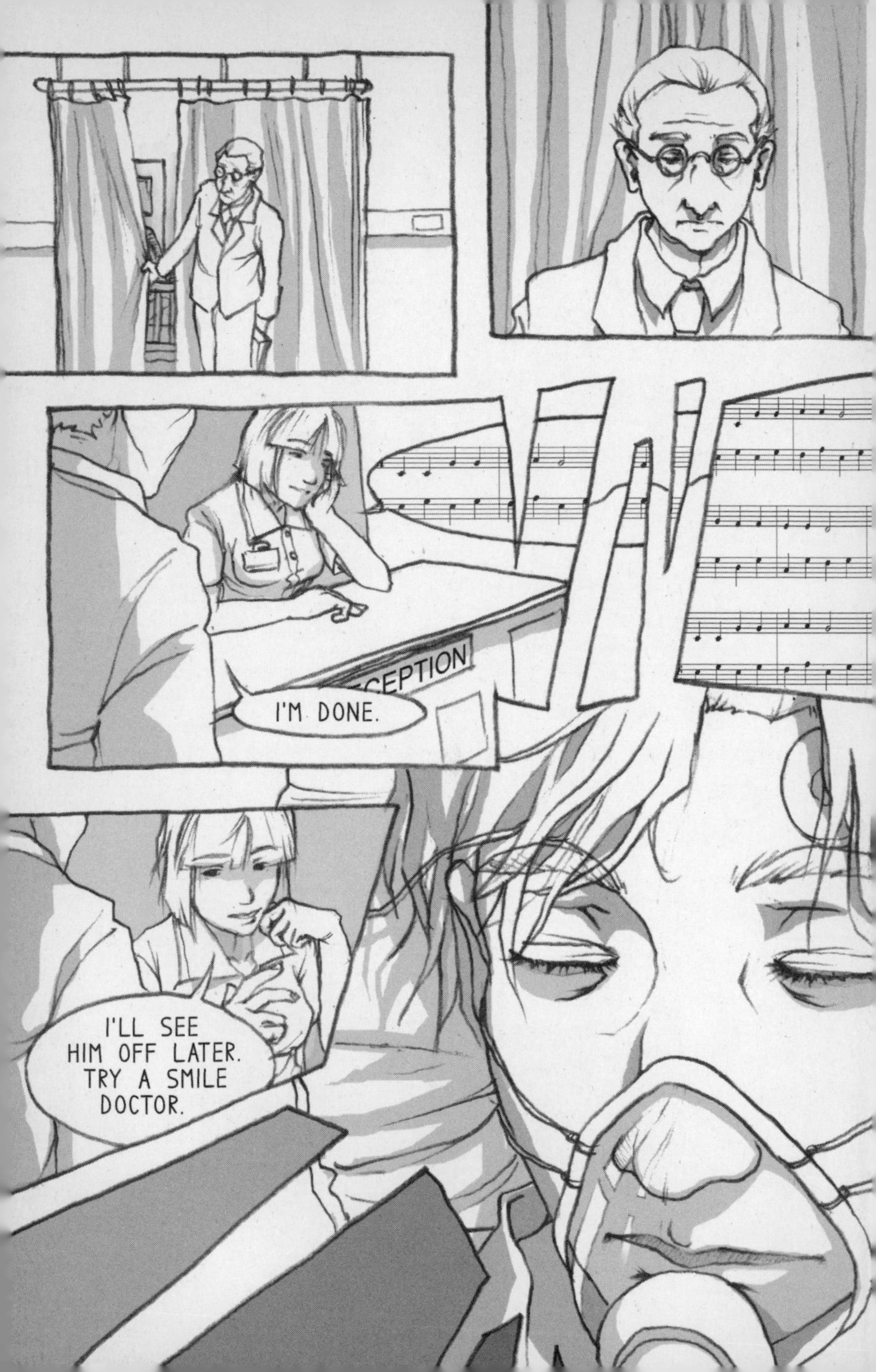
RECEPTION
I'M DONE.
I'LL SEE HIM OFF LATER. TRY A SMILE DOCTOR.

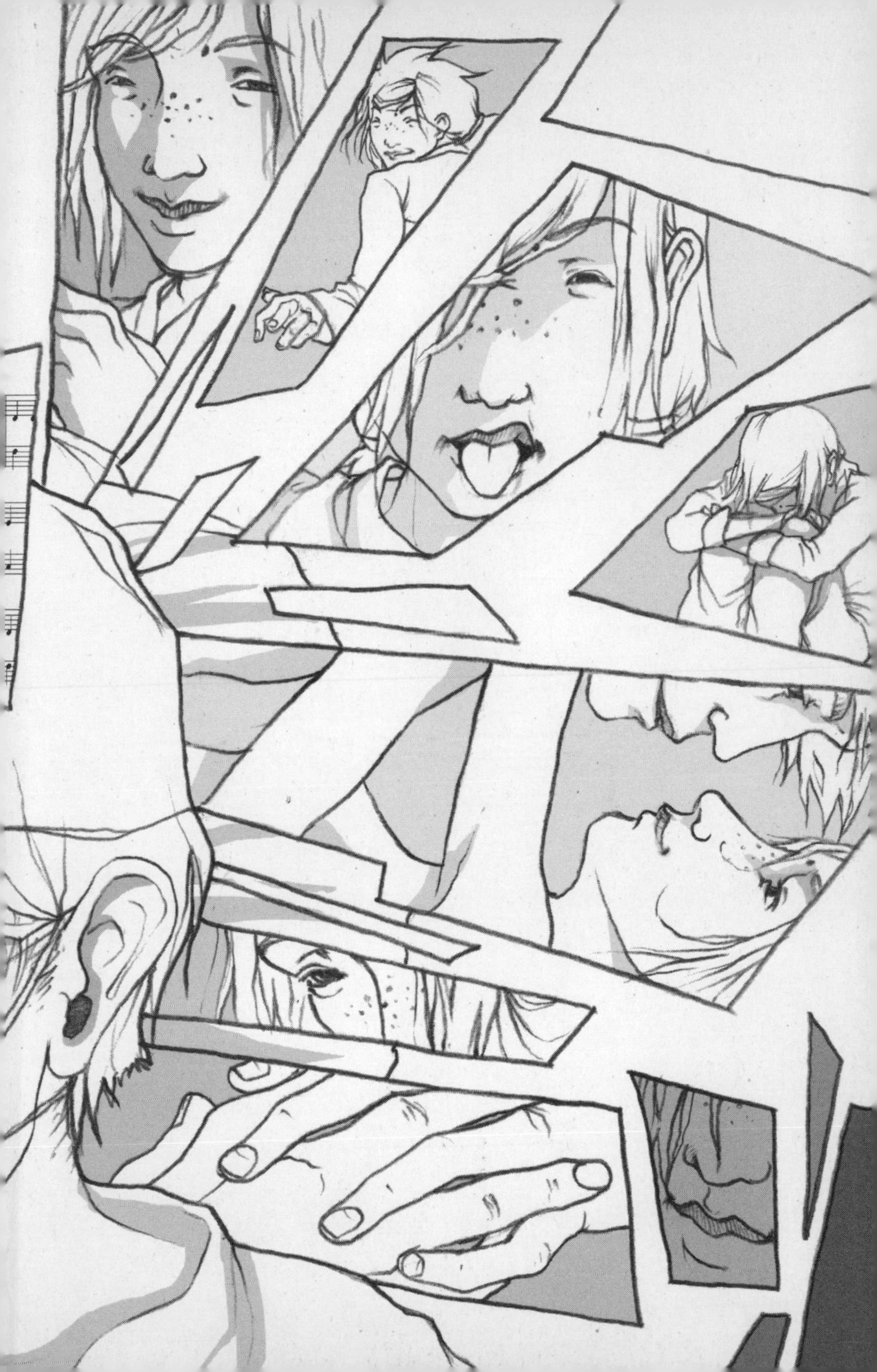

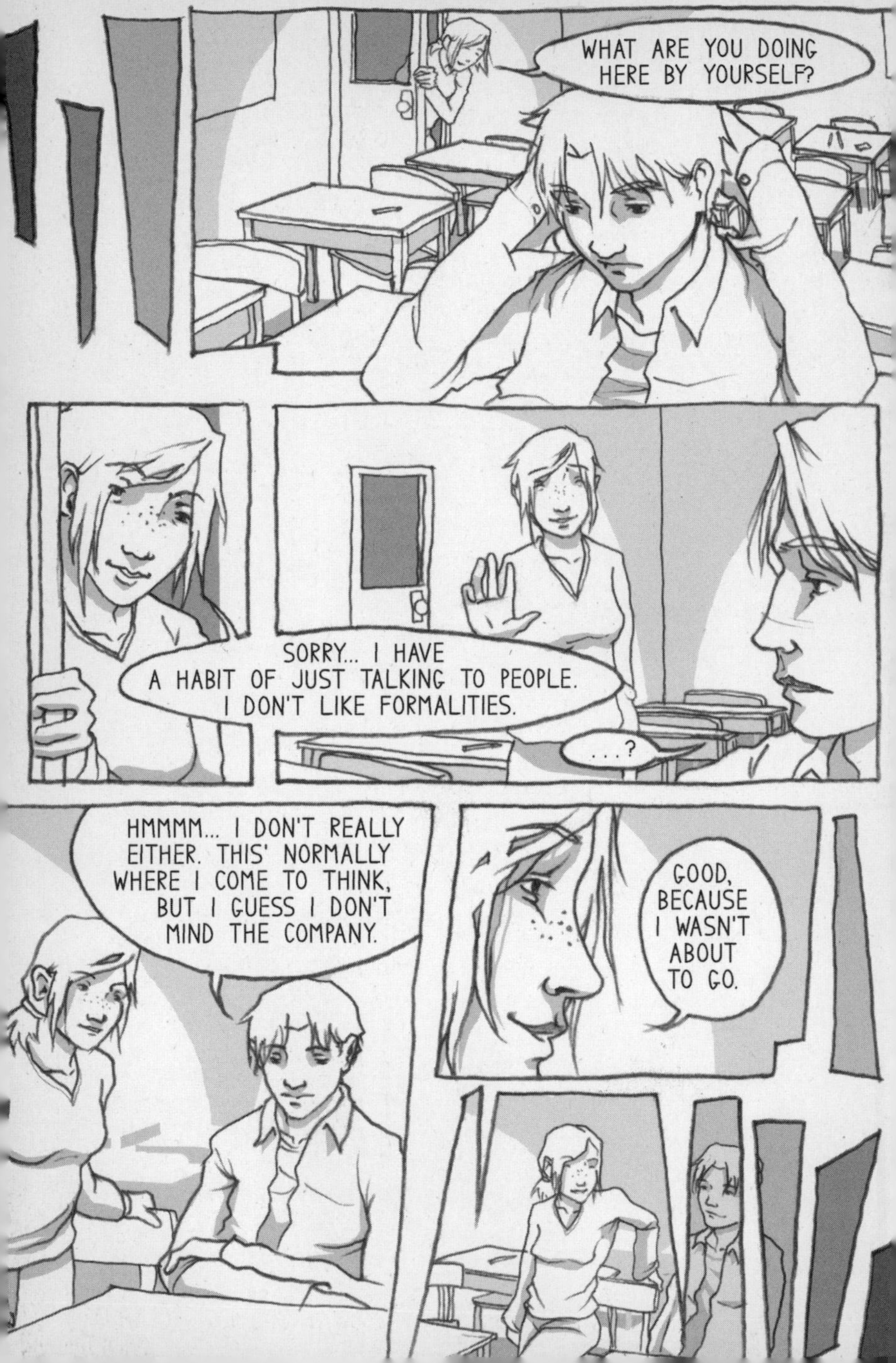
WHAT ARE YOU DOING HERE BY YOURSELF?
SORRY... I HAVE A HABIT OF JUST TALKING TO PEOPLE. I DON'T LIKE FORMALITIES.
. . .?
HMMMM... I DON'T REALLY EITHER. THIS' NORMALLY WHERE I COME TO THINK, BUT I GUESS I DON'T MIND THE COMPANY.
GOOD, BECAUSE I WASN'T ABOUT TO GO.

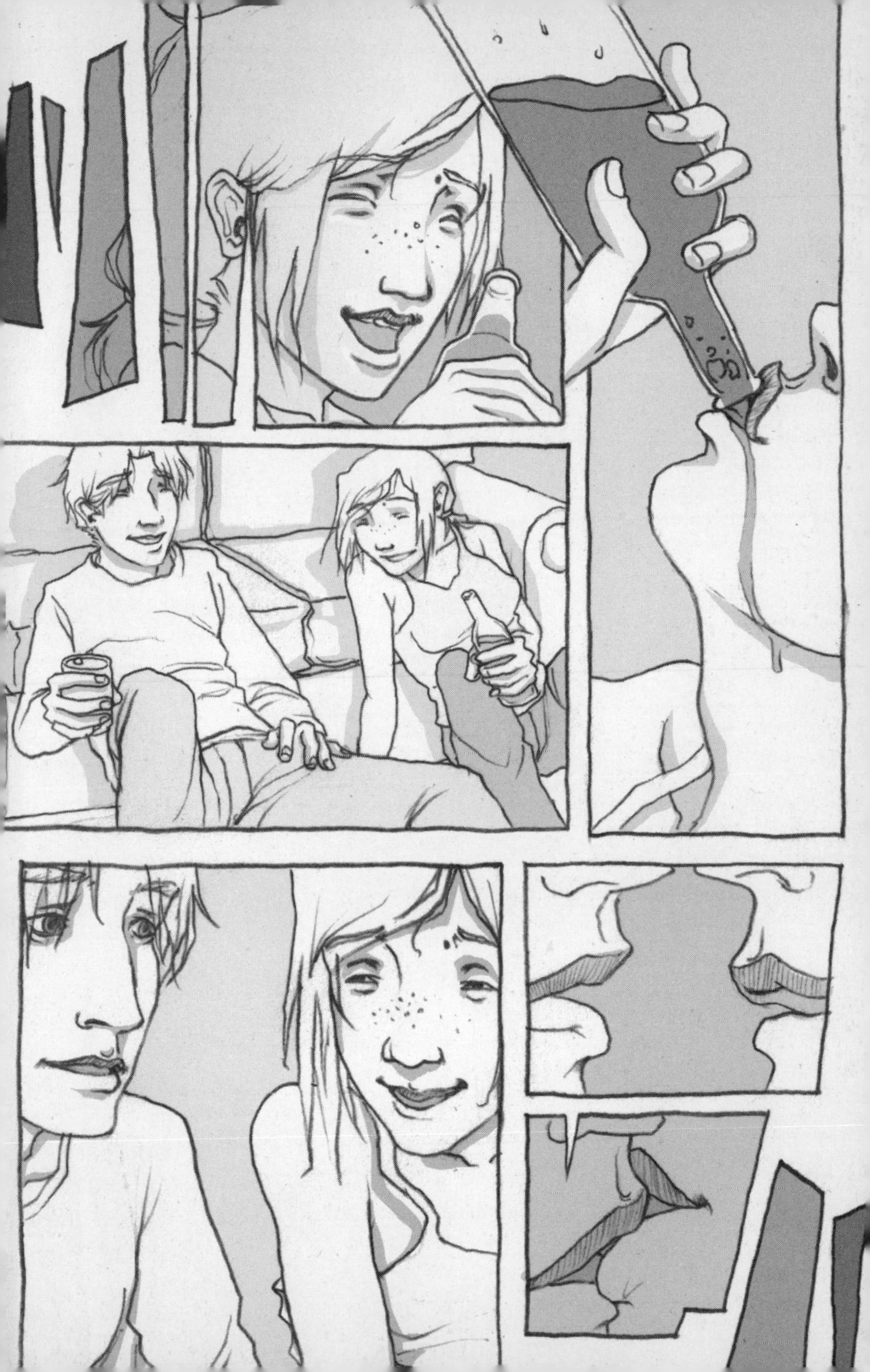

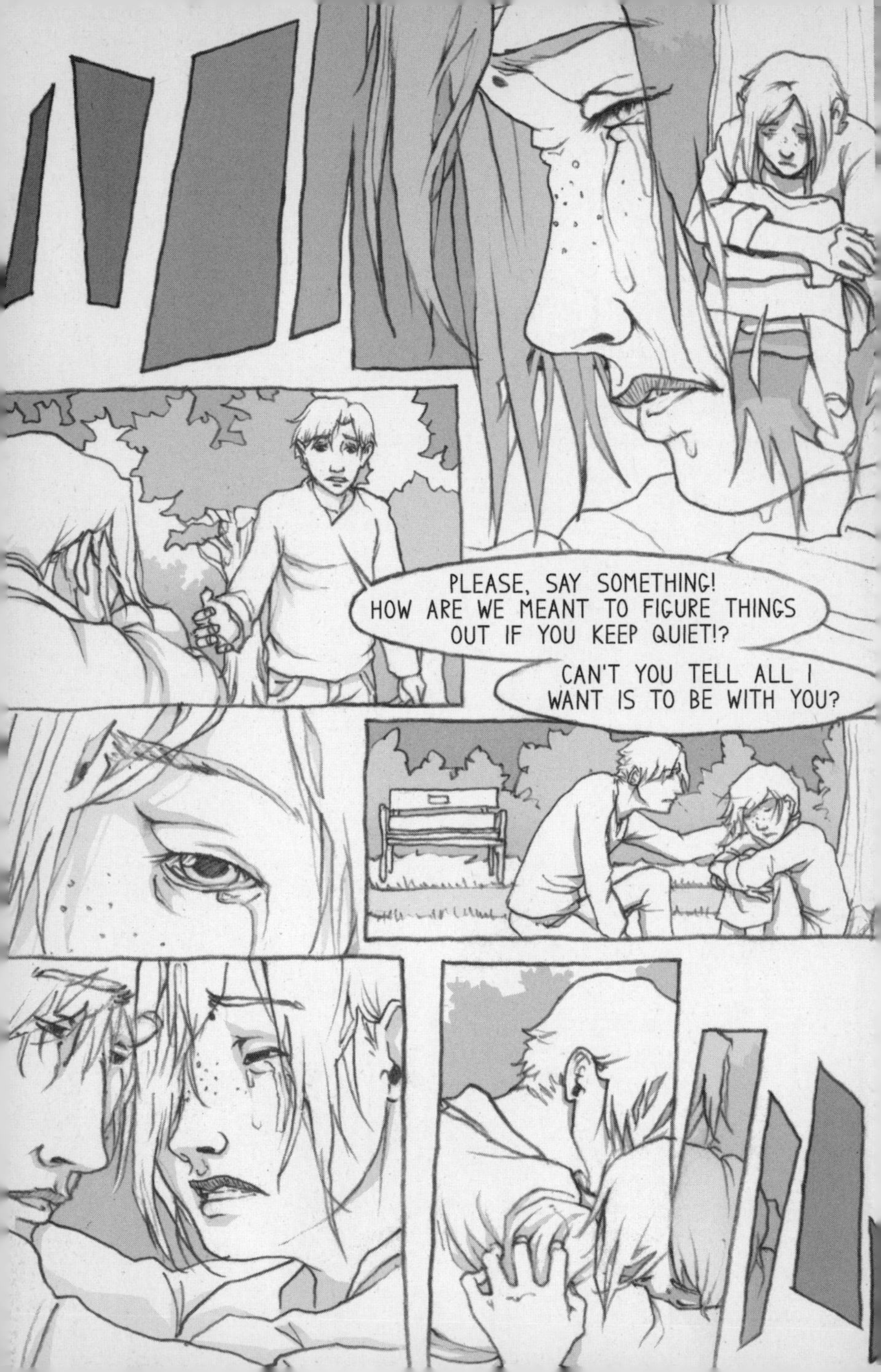
PLEASE, SAY SOMETHING! HOW ARE WE MEANT TO FIGURE THINGS OUT IF YOU KEEP QUIET!?
CAN'T YOU TELL ALL I WANT IS TO BE WITH YOU?

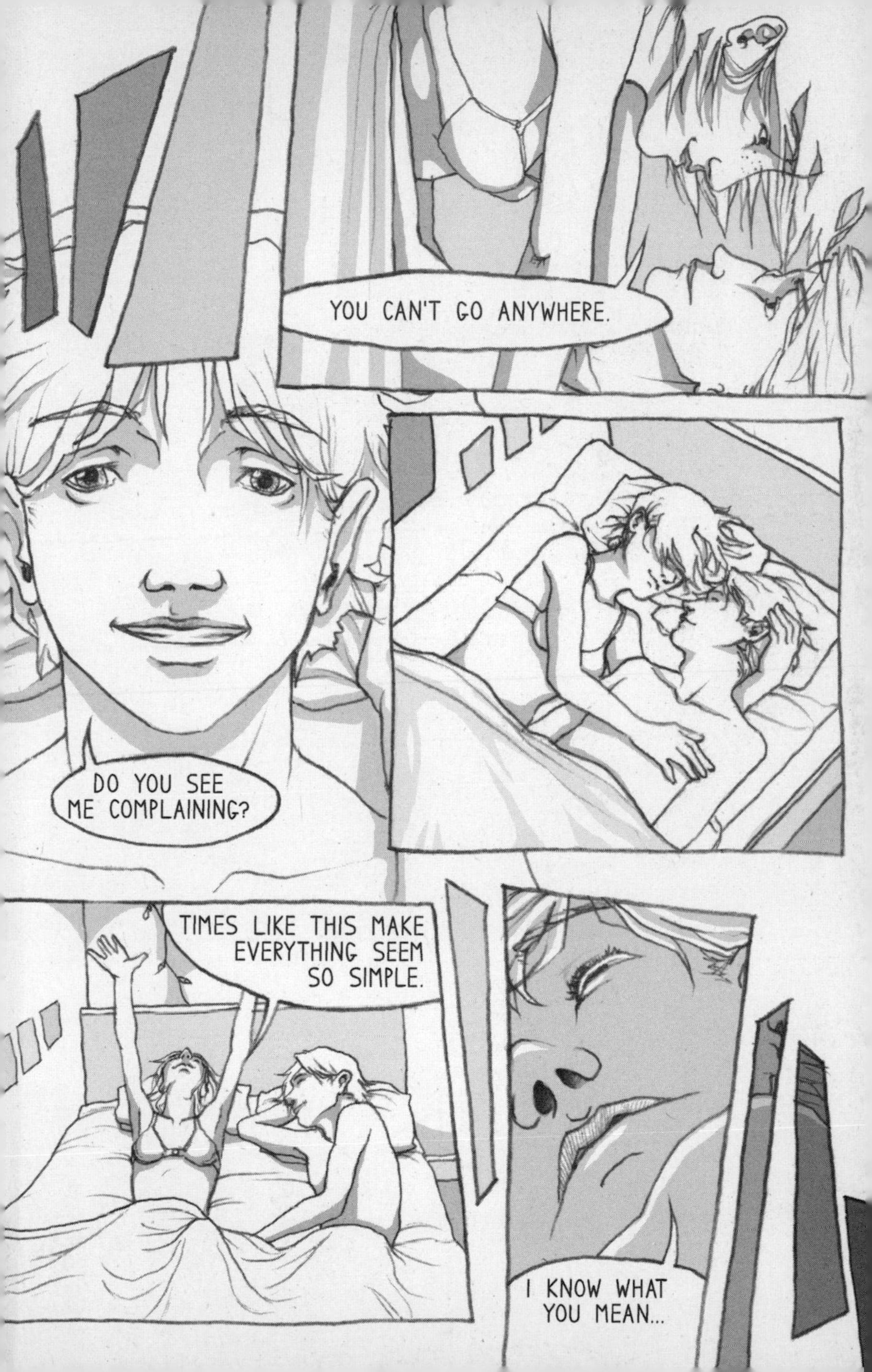
YOU CAN'T GO ANYWHERE.
DO YOU SEE ME COMPLAINING?
TIMES LIKE THIS MAKE EVERYTHING SEEM SO SIMPLE.
I KNOW WHAT YOU MEAN...

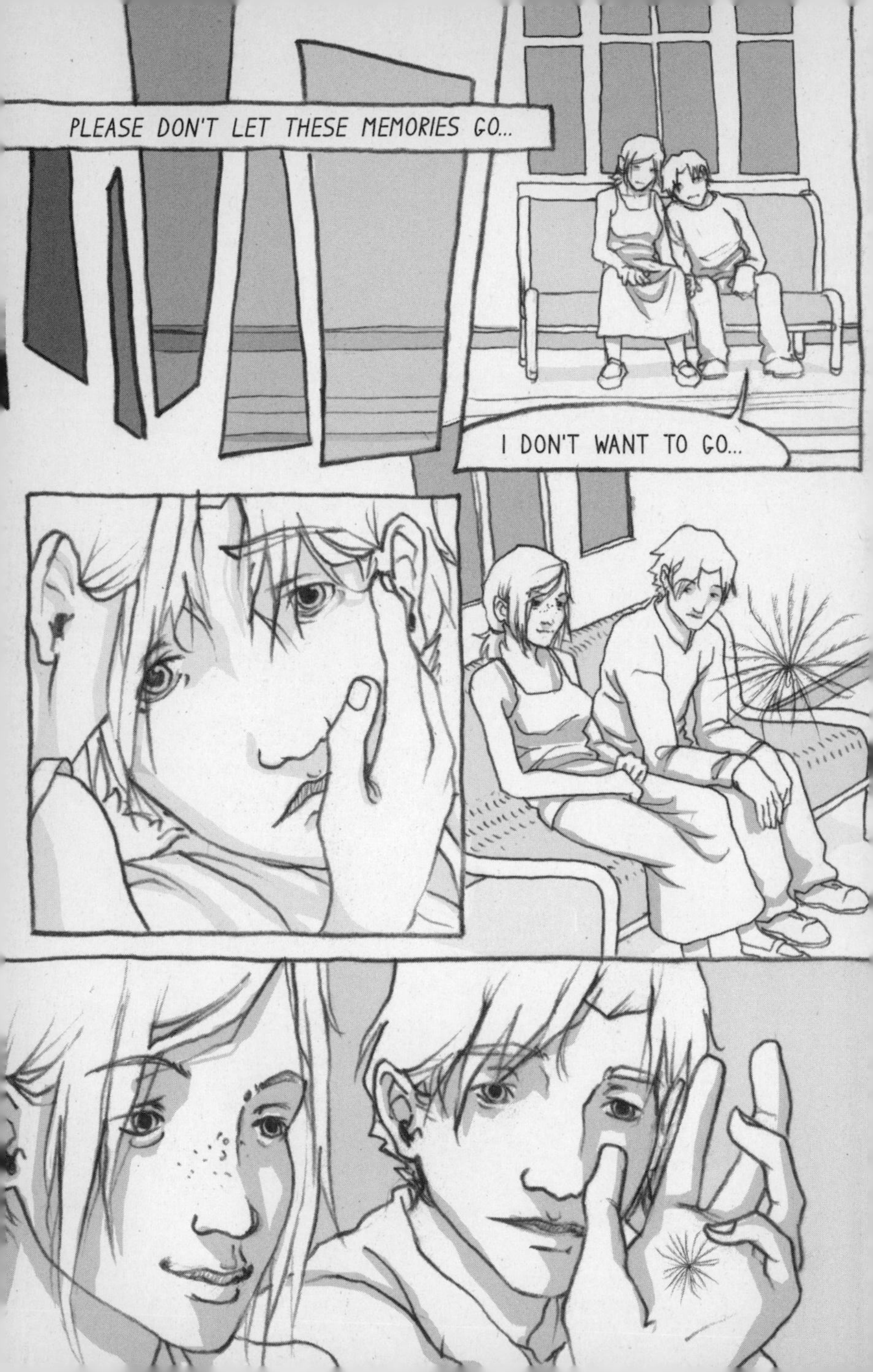
PLEASE DON'T LET THESE MEMORIES GO...
I DON'T WANT TO GO...

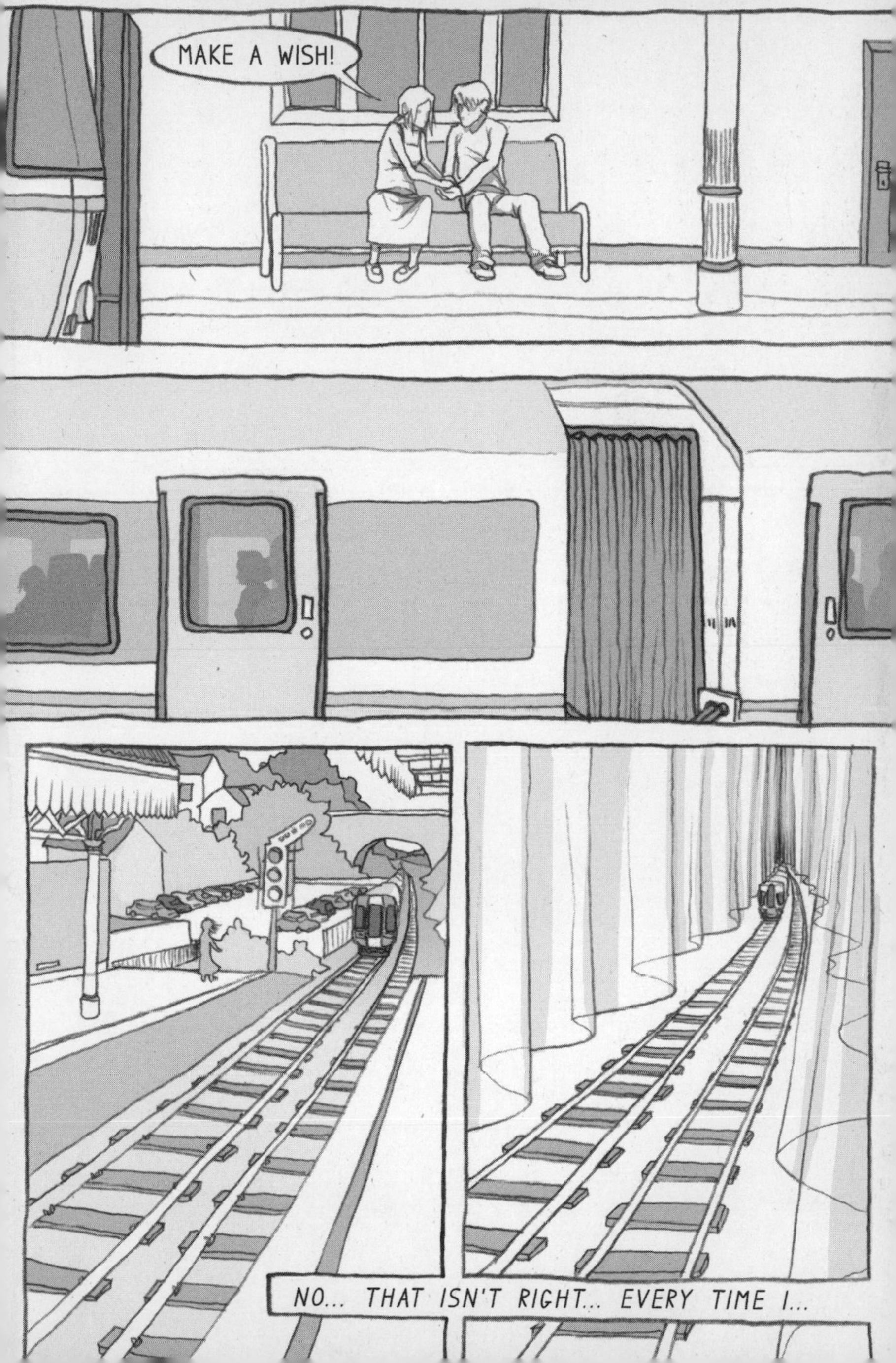
MAKE A WISH!
NO... THAT ISN'T RIGHT... EVERY TIME I...

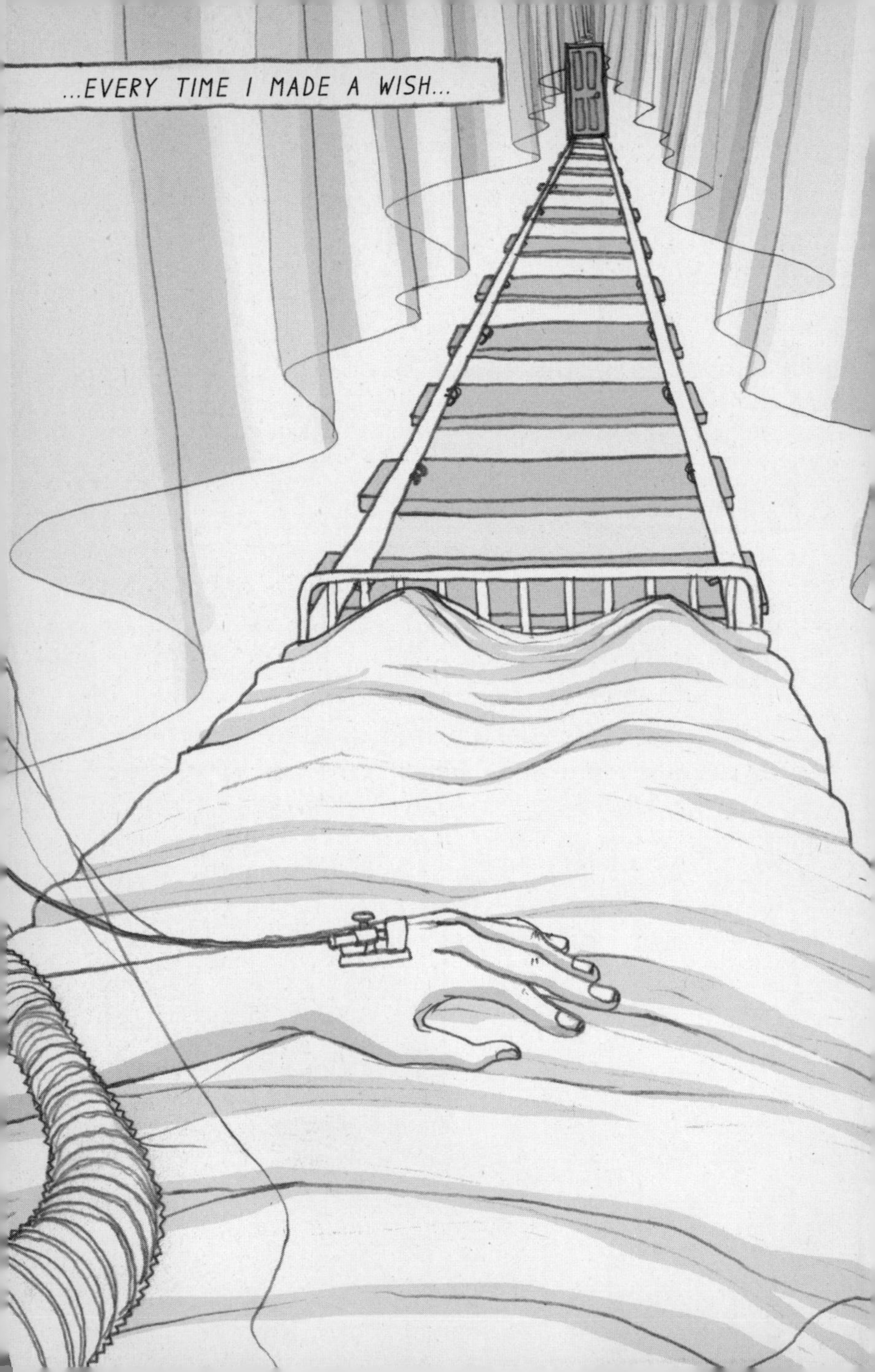
...EVERY TIME I MADE A WISH...

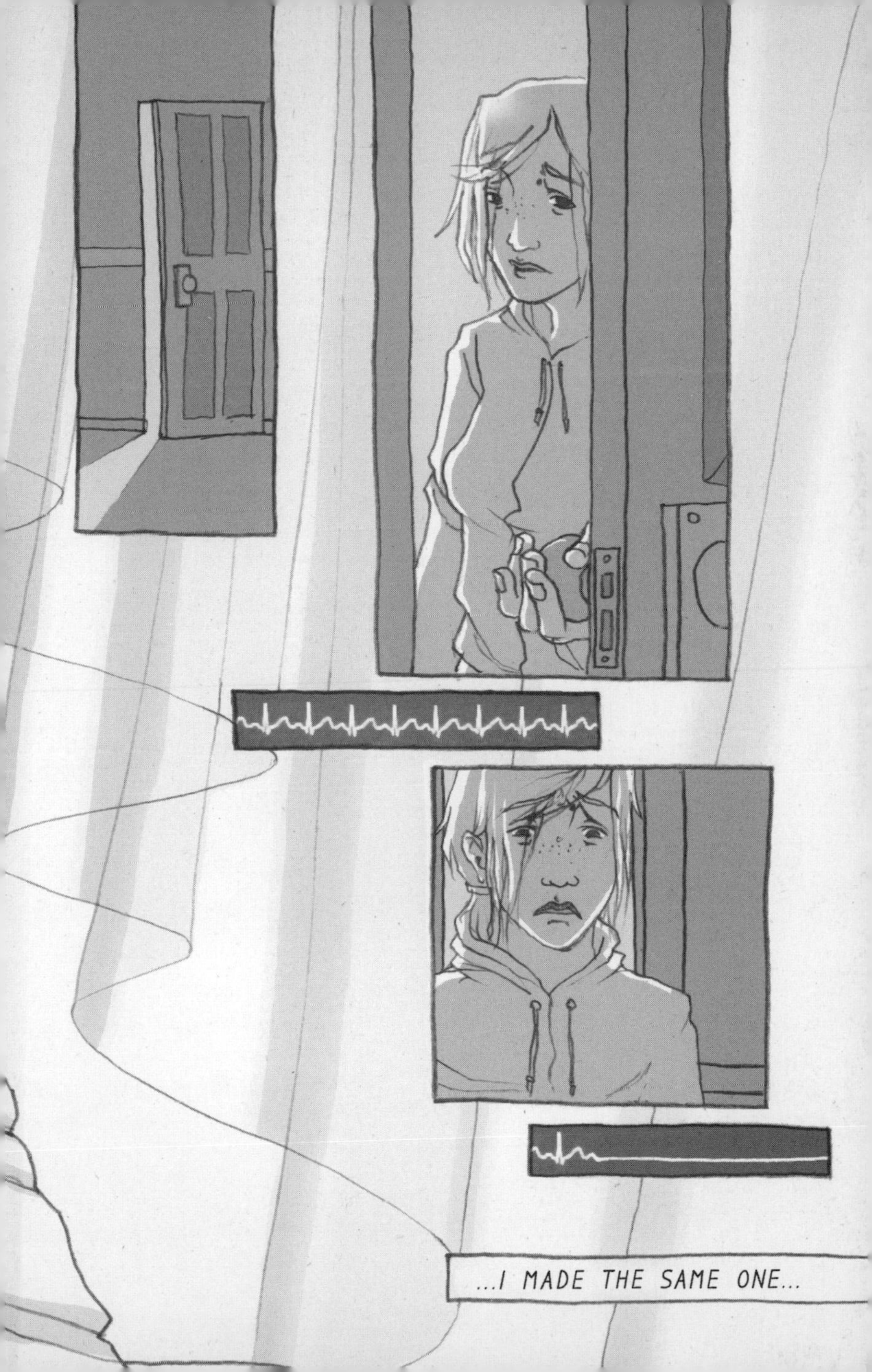
...I MADE THE SAME ONE...

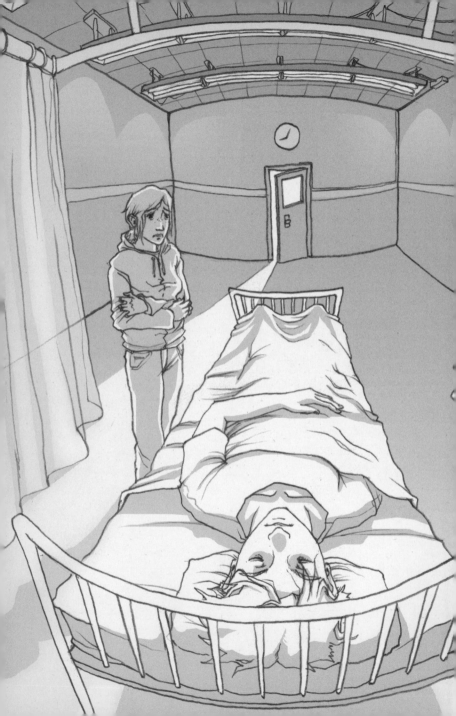

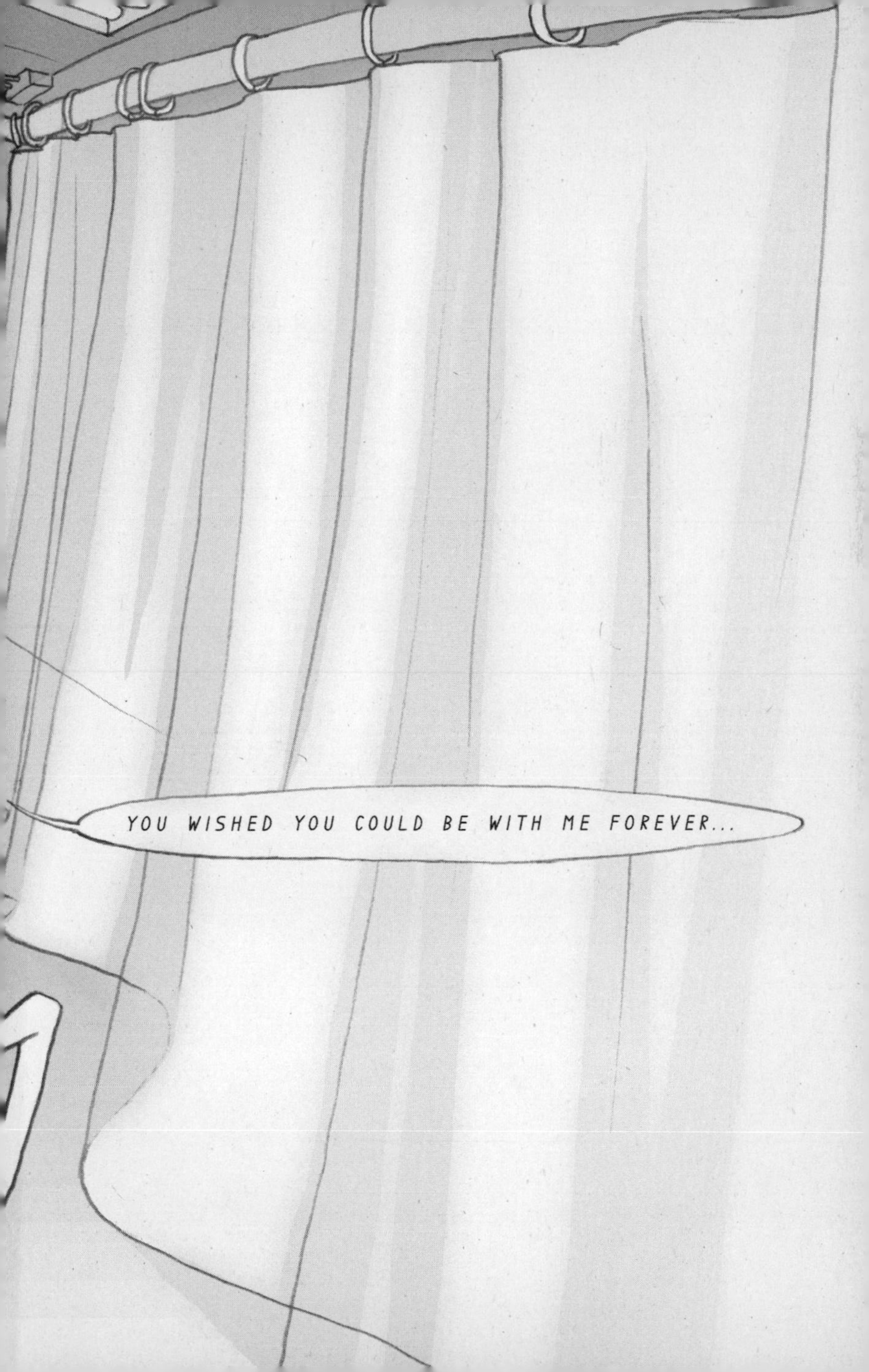
YOU WISHED YOU COULD BE WITH ME FOREVER...

::

FATAL CONNECTION :: Second Place Winner ::

....

Sonia Leong was born in Kuala Lumpur, Malaysia in 1982, but now calls
Cambridge, England home. She works as an illustrator.
www.fyredrake.net

Favorite manga:
Cardcaptor Sakura

Favorite manga artist:
CLAMP, Kei Toumei, Yuji Shiozaki, Peach-Pit, Furumi Soryo, Yukiru Sugisaki

....

Author's Comments:
I created Yanagi as an elite ninja-lady. But I had always wanted her
to die dramatically! She was put aside when other manga projects
took priority, but upon hearing of *RSoM*, I created Nadeshiko as her
opposite and proceeded to make dark plans...left to the last minute, of
course—pages were inked, toned and lettered within five days (without
sleep for the last two nights)!
—*Sonia Leong*

::

::

FATAL CONNECTION :: Second Place Winner ::

Judge's Comments:
Aspiring manga creators take note! Sonia Leong really understands manga composition. She skillfully mixes panel size and shape and uses a variety of angles and perspectives. The text and dialogue balloons are thoughtfully placed, helping guide the reader's eyes across the page. These things might sound trivial, but they make the difference between a good manga and a great manga.

Leong also plays with light and dark in interesting ways. White hair on black backgrounds creates beautiful abstract panels. The use of negative lines (white on black) for the death scenes is classic technique. Most impressively, Leong uses tones to pull of a nighttime scene, which is no easy feat. Only one panel in the entire 20 pages shows the night sky, and yet it is clear throughout that it is night. Great work.

While Leong is clearly versed in manga technique and her anatomy is usually quite good, the end effect feels a little soulless. A lot of new artists are drawn to foreign and fantastic stories, which is only natural—those are reasons why we love manga—but it's harder to create characters that feel real unless they have some grounding in the world we know. The twin sisters in the story strike me as characters the creator thinks are cool, rather than ones she really understands. I would like to see what Leong can do if she brought a little more humanity to her lead characters. The skill is there—it just needs the heart to match. And based on the talent on display here, I'm confident Ms. Leong can do it.
—Jake T. Forbes

Judge's Comments:
This story evoked mixed responses from our judges, although obviously it ranked very highly for all of us, and ended up being a very strong contender for the top prize. On the one hand, we were all impressed with the solidity of the art, and especially the sophistication of visual storytelling. On the other hand, the style was very reminiscent of work we'd seen before. With this much talent, I think some of us were left wishing that Sonia had taken the next step and really started to develop a style all of her own, rather than sticking with a well-rendered but also well-trodden shojo aesthetic.

What really sold the entry for me was the plot twist. It's difficult to create a story with emotional punch in this short a format, and I was both surprised and shocked by the very dark turn the entry takes at the end. We know just enough about the characters and their relationships so that when the unthinkable happens, we as readers actually care about it. If the setting and the look of Sonia's entry seemed a bit derivative, the reader's familiarity with this sort of story worked in its favor in terms of conveying the maximum information in the minimum of space. The use of the two guards as an introduction to the sisters and their relationship was a particularly good storytelling device that helped to establish the setting and the situation without feeling forced. Well done!
—Lillian Diaz-Przybyl

::

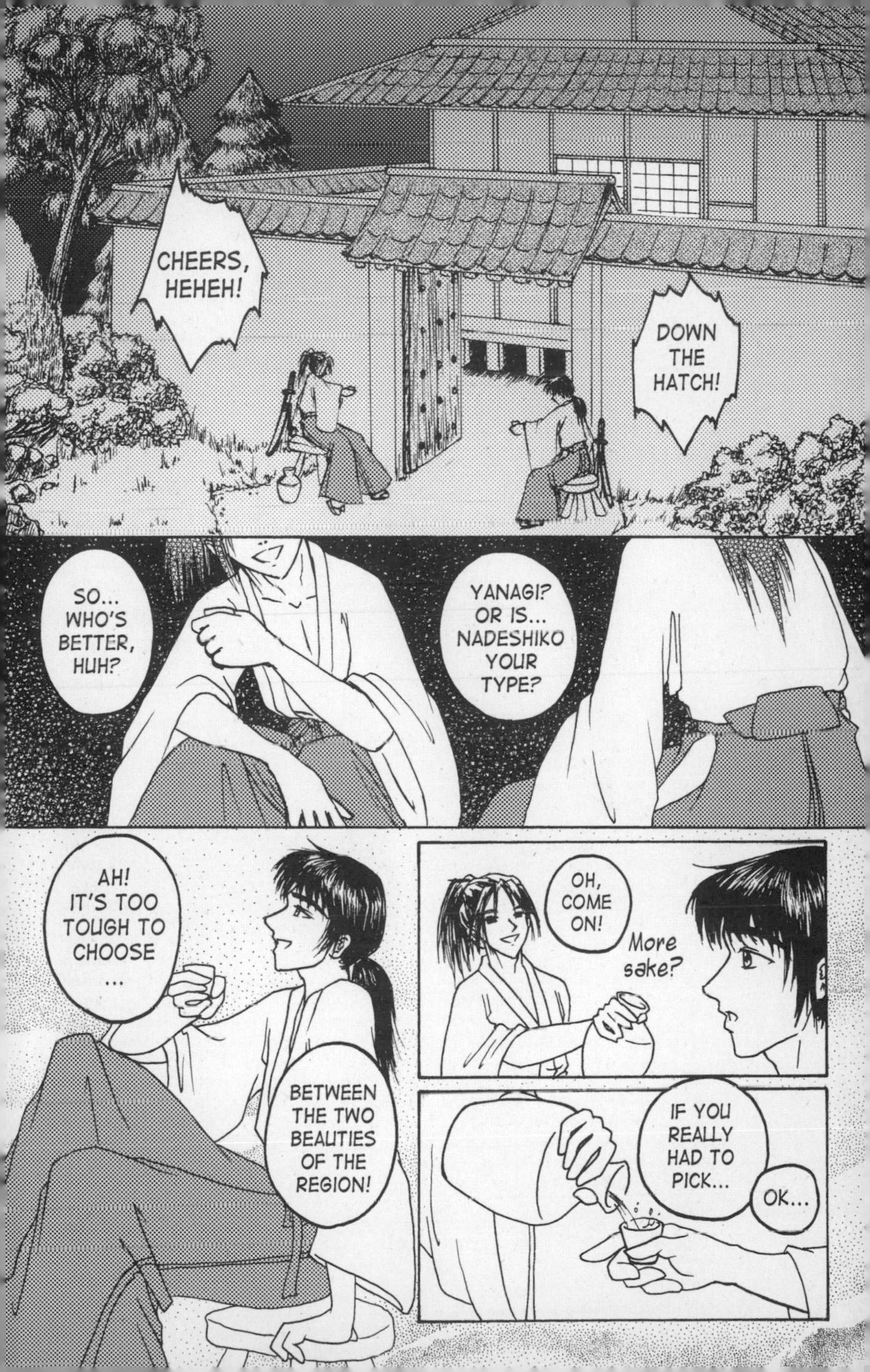
CHEERS, HEHEH!
DOWN THE HATCH!
SO... WHO'S BETTER, HUH?
YANAGI? OR IS... NADESHIKO YOUR TYPE?
AH! IT'S TOO TOUGH TO CHOOSE ...
BETWEEN THE TWO BEAUTIES OF THE REGION!
OH, COME ON!
More sake?
IF YOU REALLY HAD TO PICK...
OK...

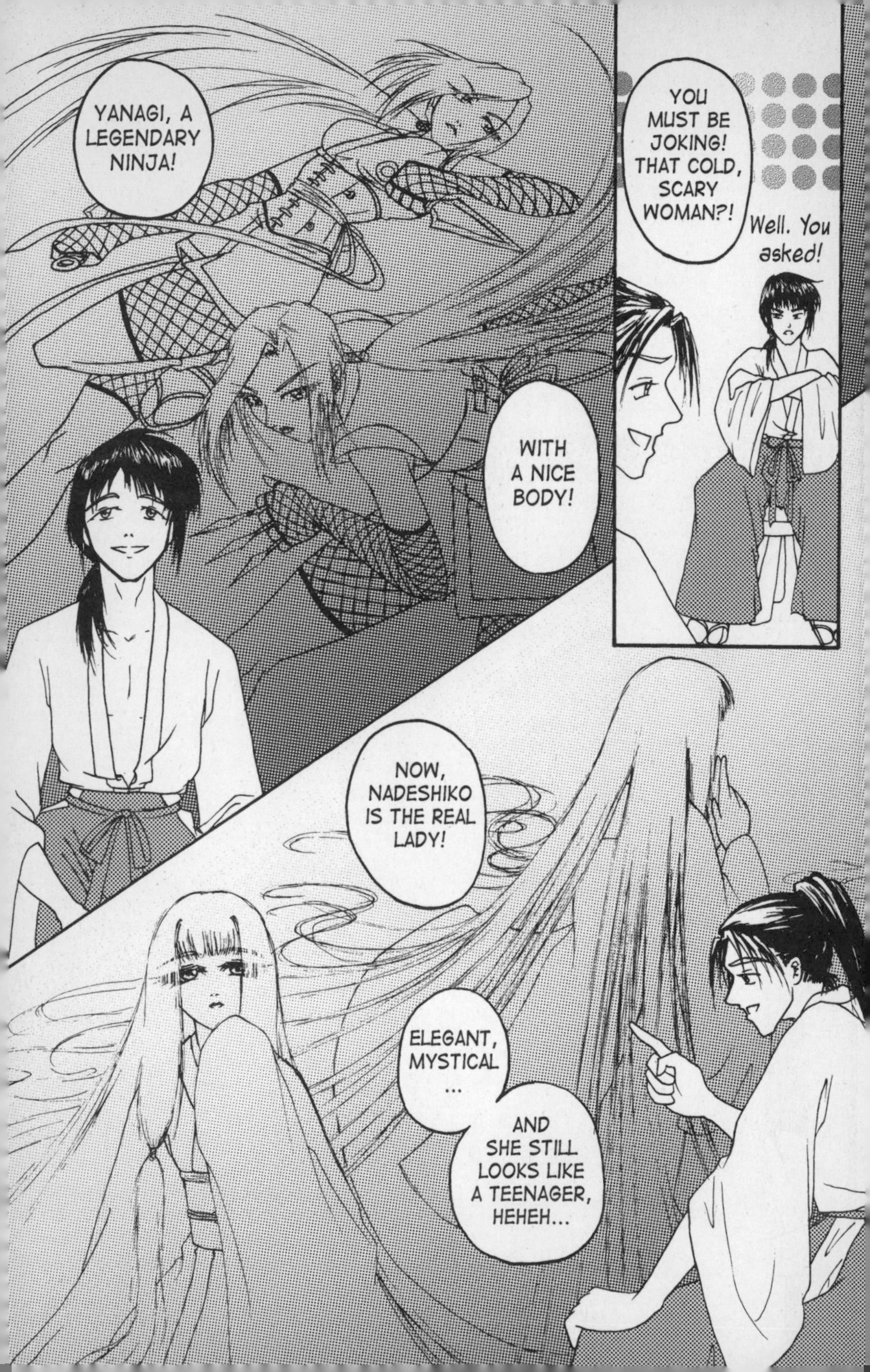
YANAGI, A LEGENDARY NINJA!
WITH A NICE BODY!
YOU MUST BE JOKING! THAT COLD, SCARY WOMAN?!
Well. You asked!
NOW, NADESHIKO IS THE REAL LADY!
ELEGANT, MYSTICAL ...
AND SHE STILL LOOKS LIKE A TEENAGER, HEHEH...

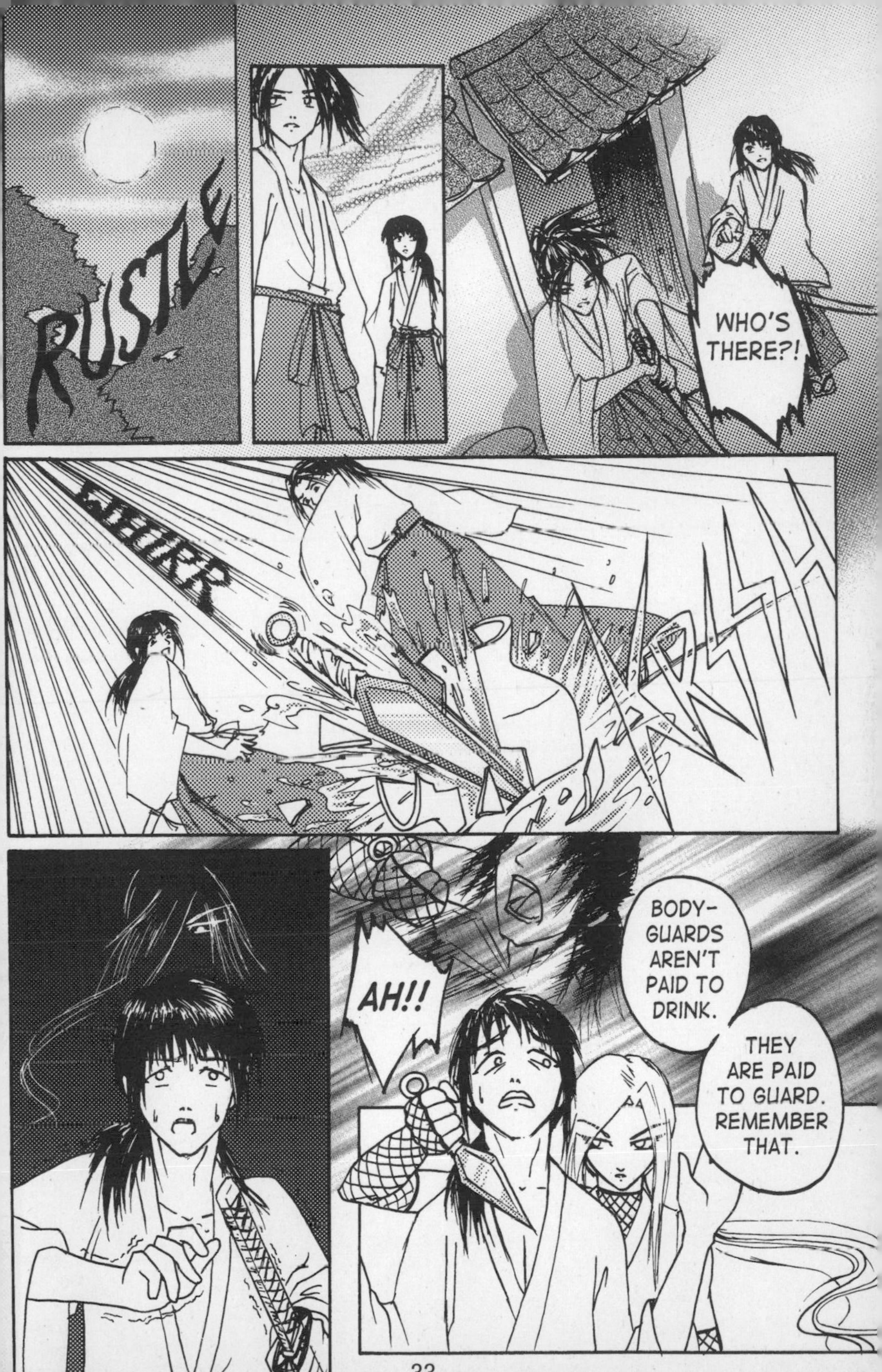
RUSTLE
WHO'S THERE?!
WHIRR
AH!!
BODY-GUARDS AREN'T PAID TO DRINK.
THEY ARE PAID TO GUARD. REMEMBER THAT.

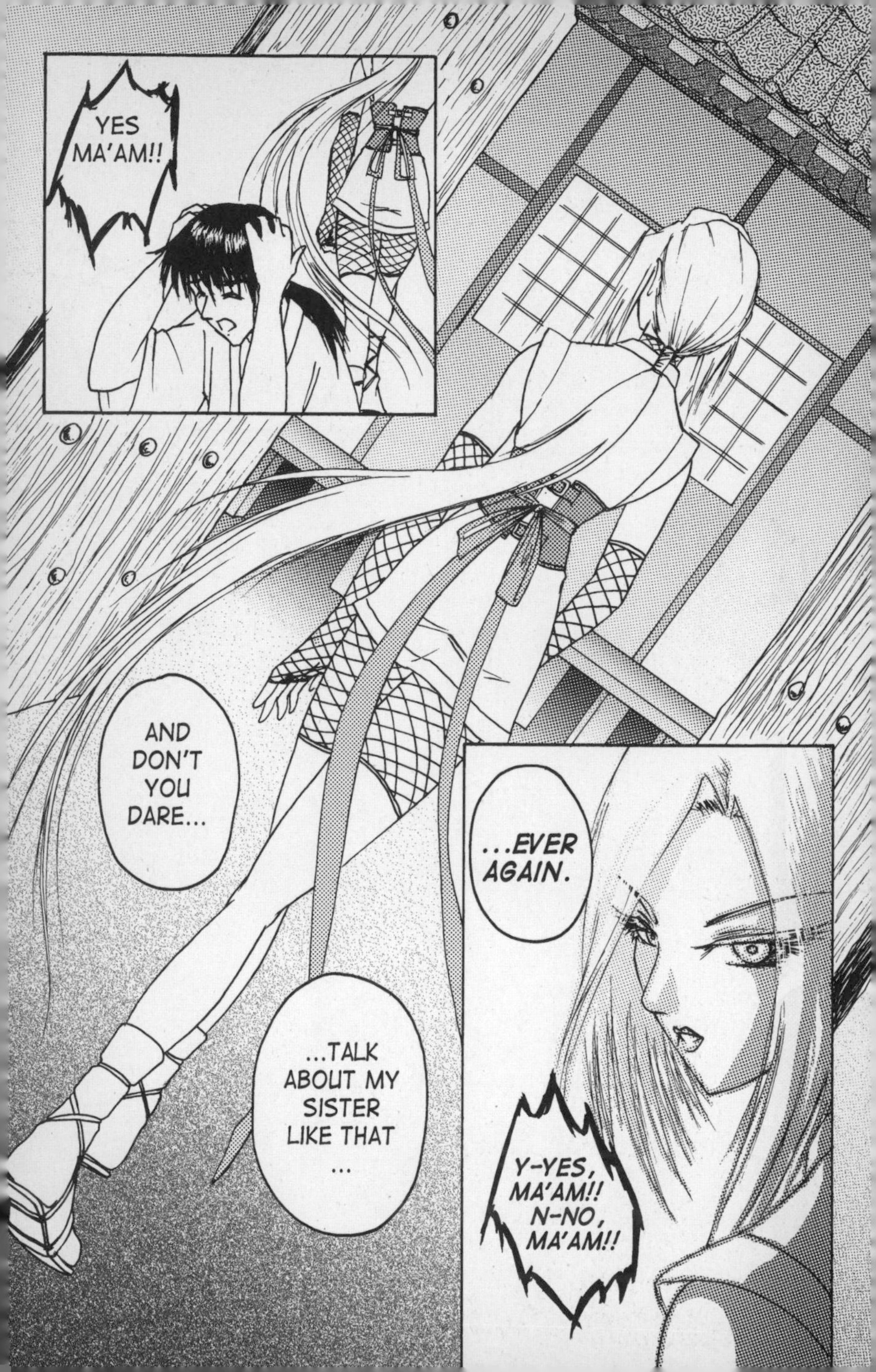
YES MA'AM!!
AND DON'T YOU DARE...
...TALK ABOUT MY SISTER LIKE THAT ...
...EVER AGAIN.
Y-YES, MA'AM!! N-NO, MA'AM!!

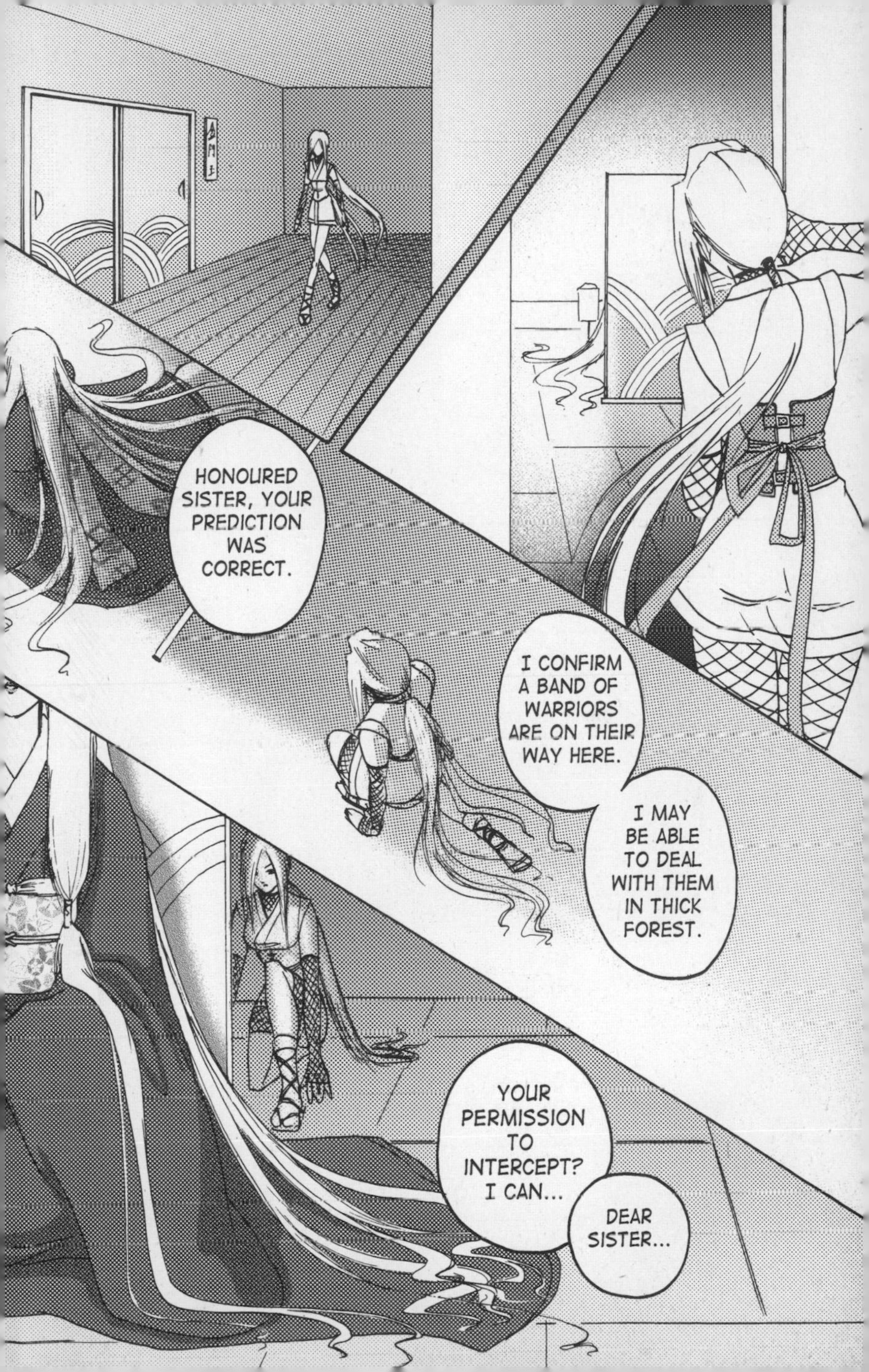
HONOURED SISTER, YOUR PREDICTION WAS CORRECT.
I CONFIRM A BAND OF WARRIORS ARE ON THEIR WAY HERE.
I MAY BE ABLE TO DEAL WITH THEM IN THICK FOREST.
YOUR PERMISSION TO INTERCEPT? I CAN...
DEAR SISTER...

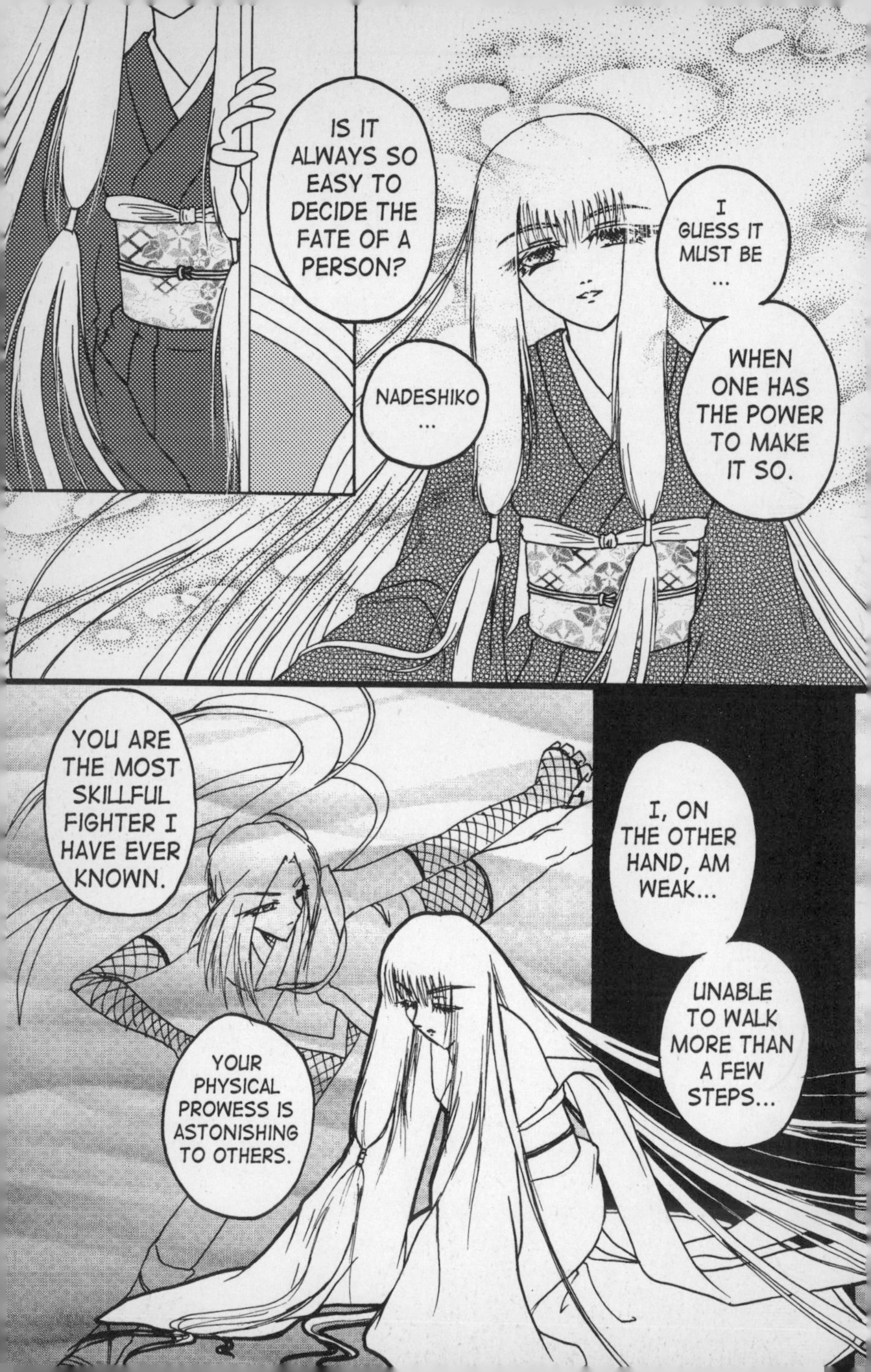
IS IT ALWAYS SO EASY TO DECIDE THE FATE OF A PERSON?
NADESHIKO ...
I GUESS IT MUST BE ...
WHEN ONE HAS THE POWER TO MAKE IT SO.
YOU ARE THE MOST SKILLFUL FIGHTER I HAVE EVER KNOWN.
YOUR PHYSICAL PROWESS IS ASTONISHING TO OTHERS.
I, ON THE OTHER HAND, AM WEAK...
UNABLE TO WALK MORE THAN A FEW STEPS...

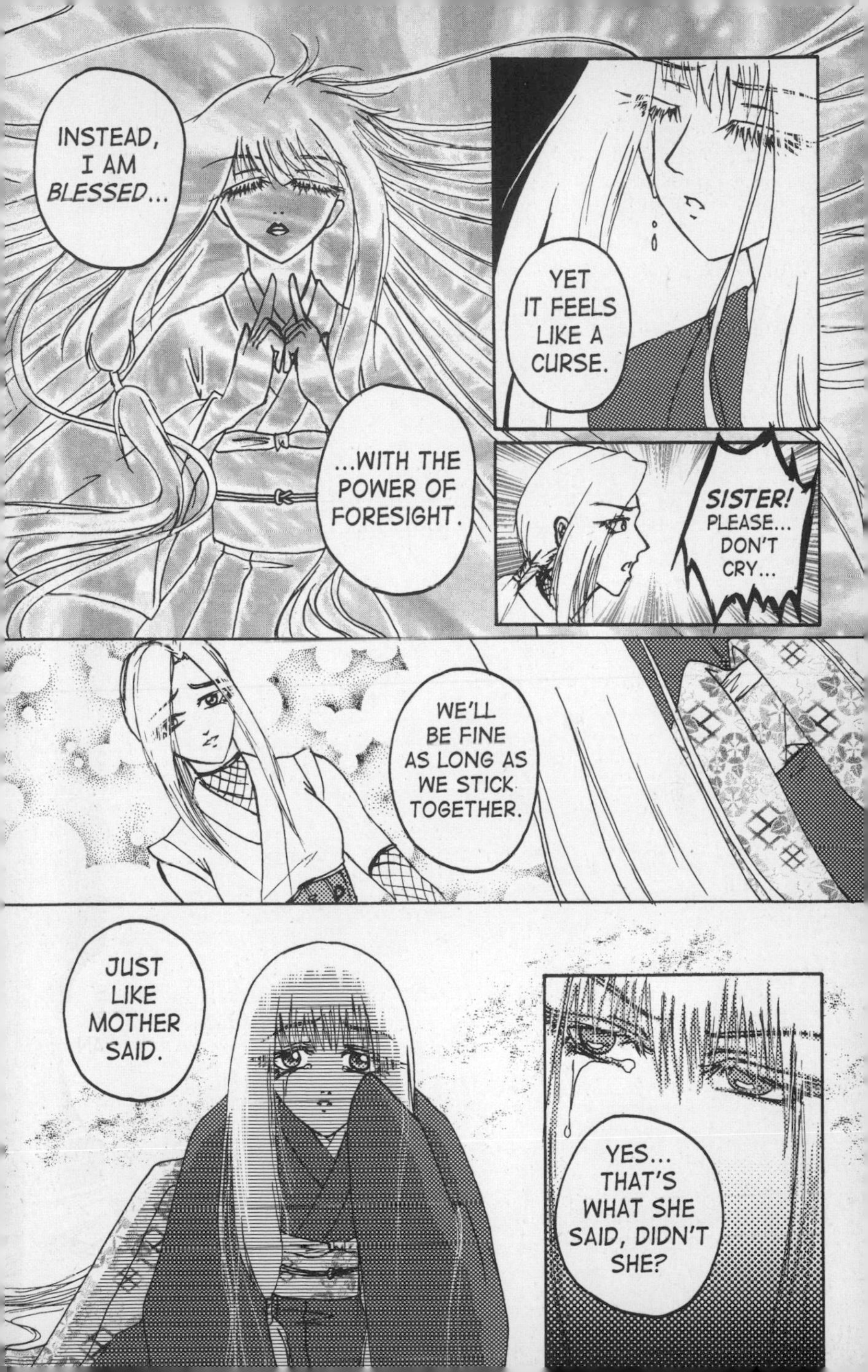
INSTEAD, I AM *BLESSED*...
YET IT FEELS LIKE A CURSE.
...WITH THE POWER OF FORESIGHT.
SISTER! PLEASE... DON'T CRY...
WE'LL BE FINE AS LONG AS WE STICK TOGETHER.
JUST LIKE MOTHER SAID.
YES... THAT'S WHAT SHE SAID, DIDN'T SHE?

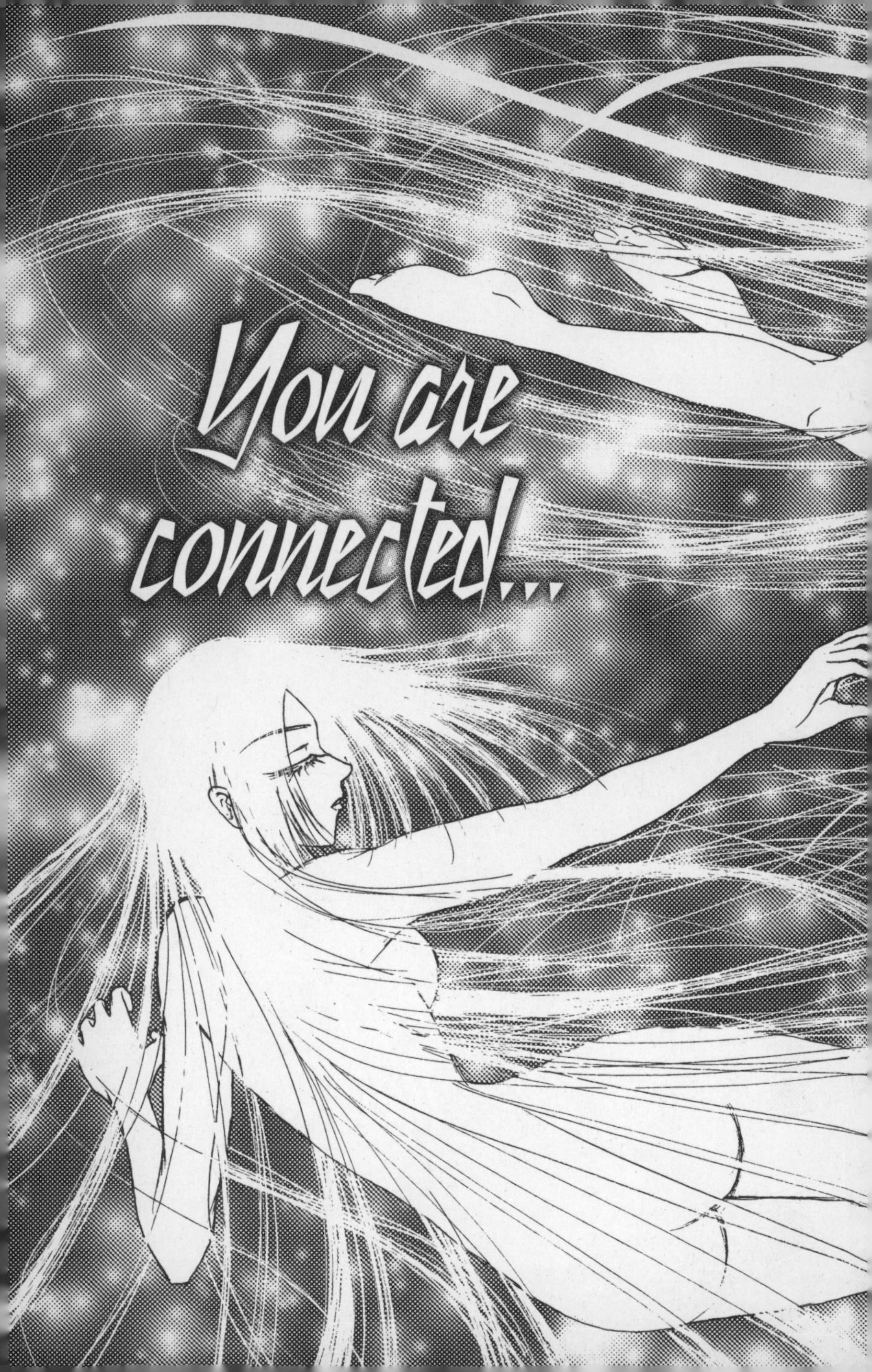
You are connected...

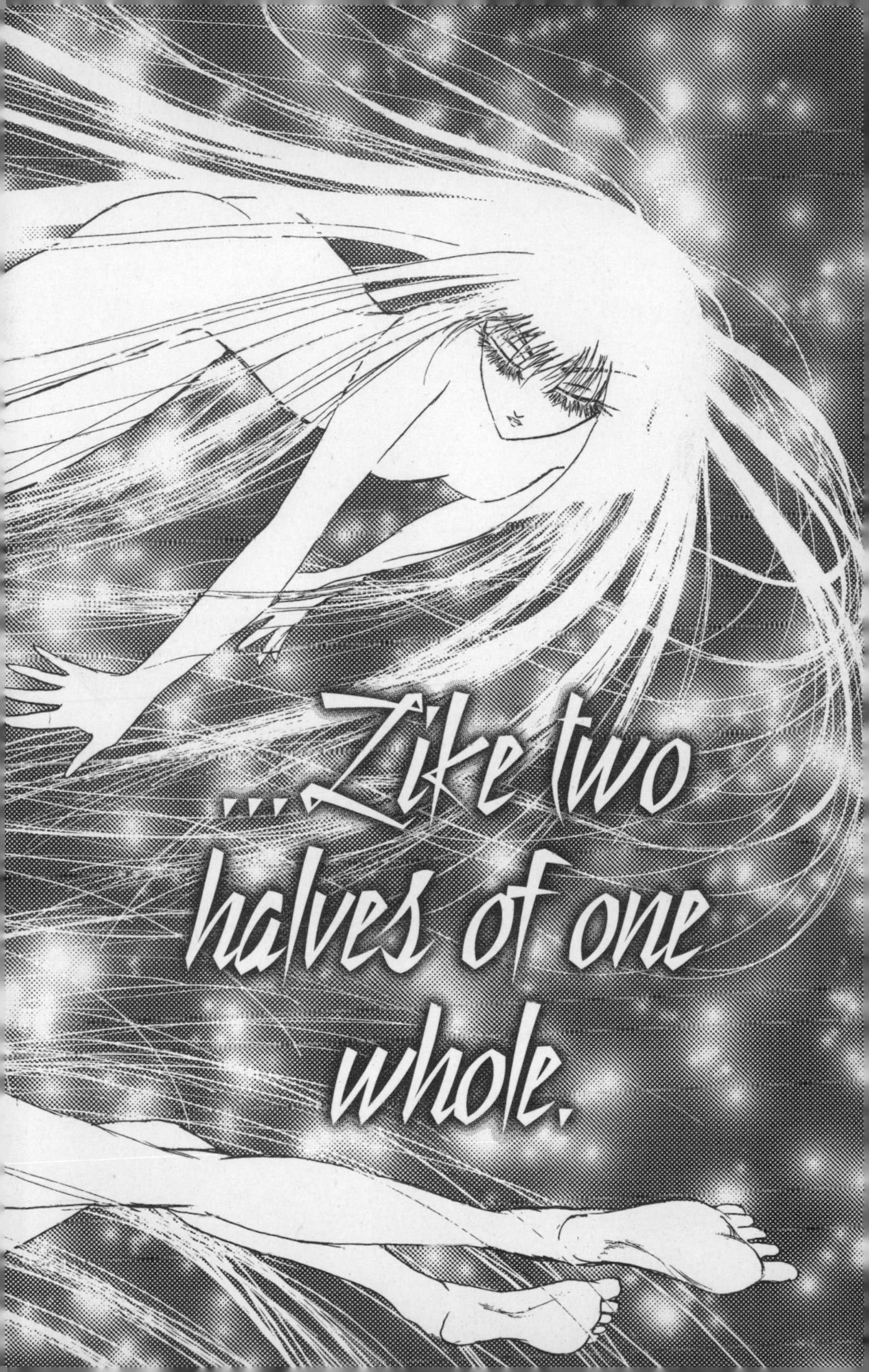
...Like two halves of one whole.

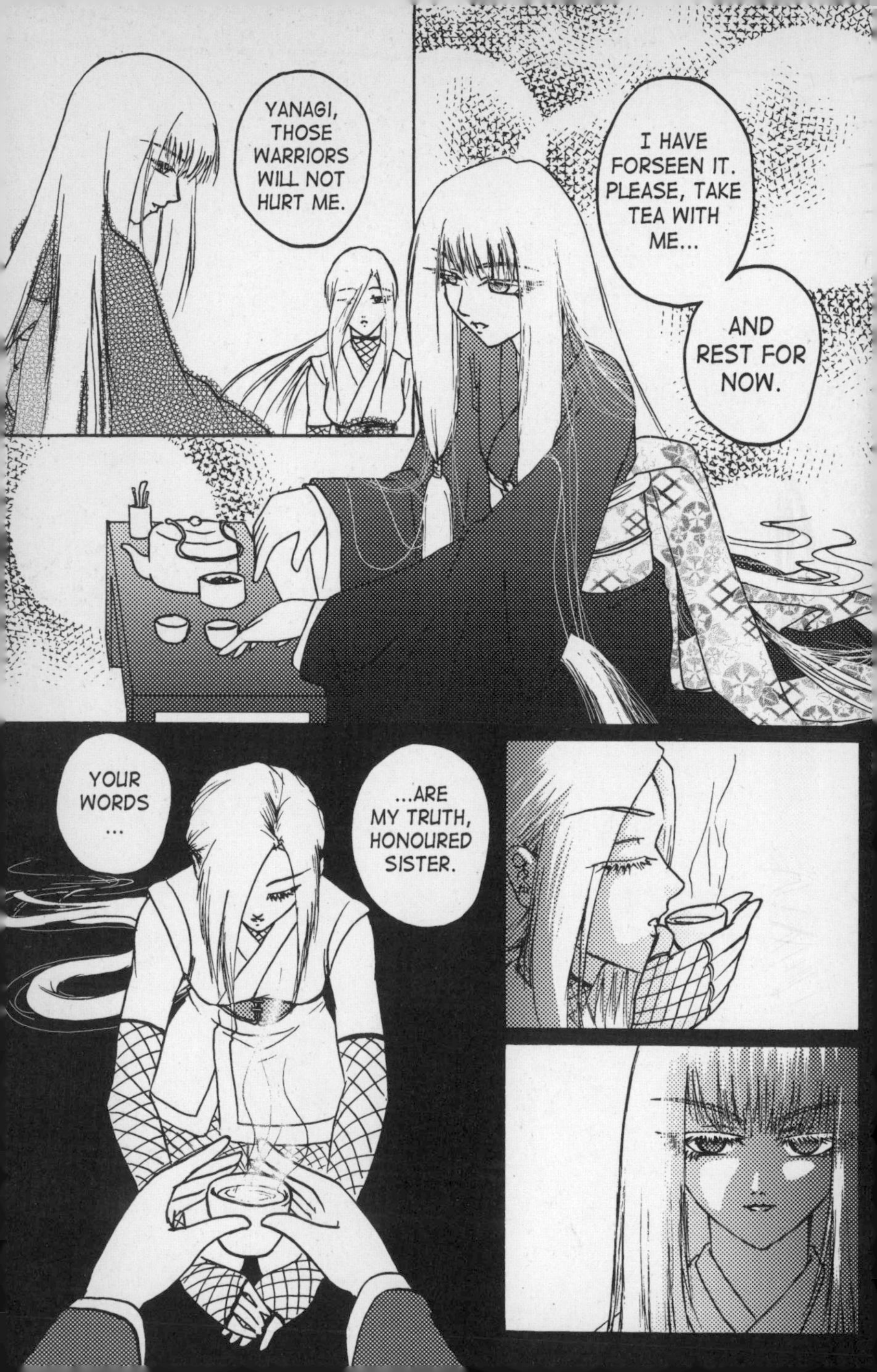
YANAGI, THOSE WARRIORS WILL NOT HURT ME.
I HAVE FORSEEN IT. PLEASE, TAKE TEA WITH ME...
AND REST FOR NOW.
YOUR WORDS ...
...ARE MY TRUTH, HONOURED SISTER.

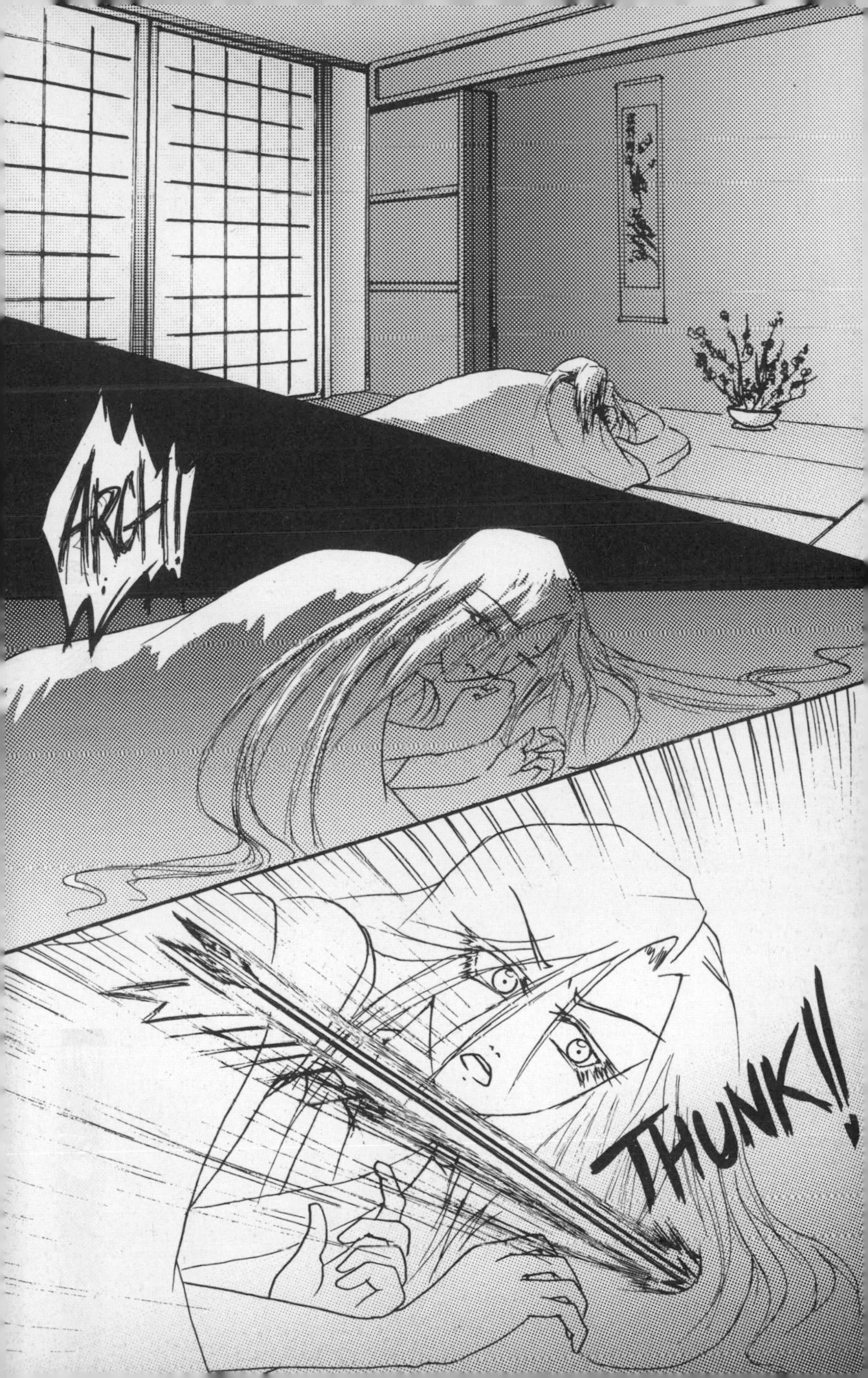
ARGH!!
THUNK!!

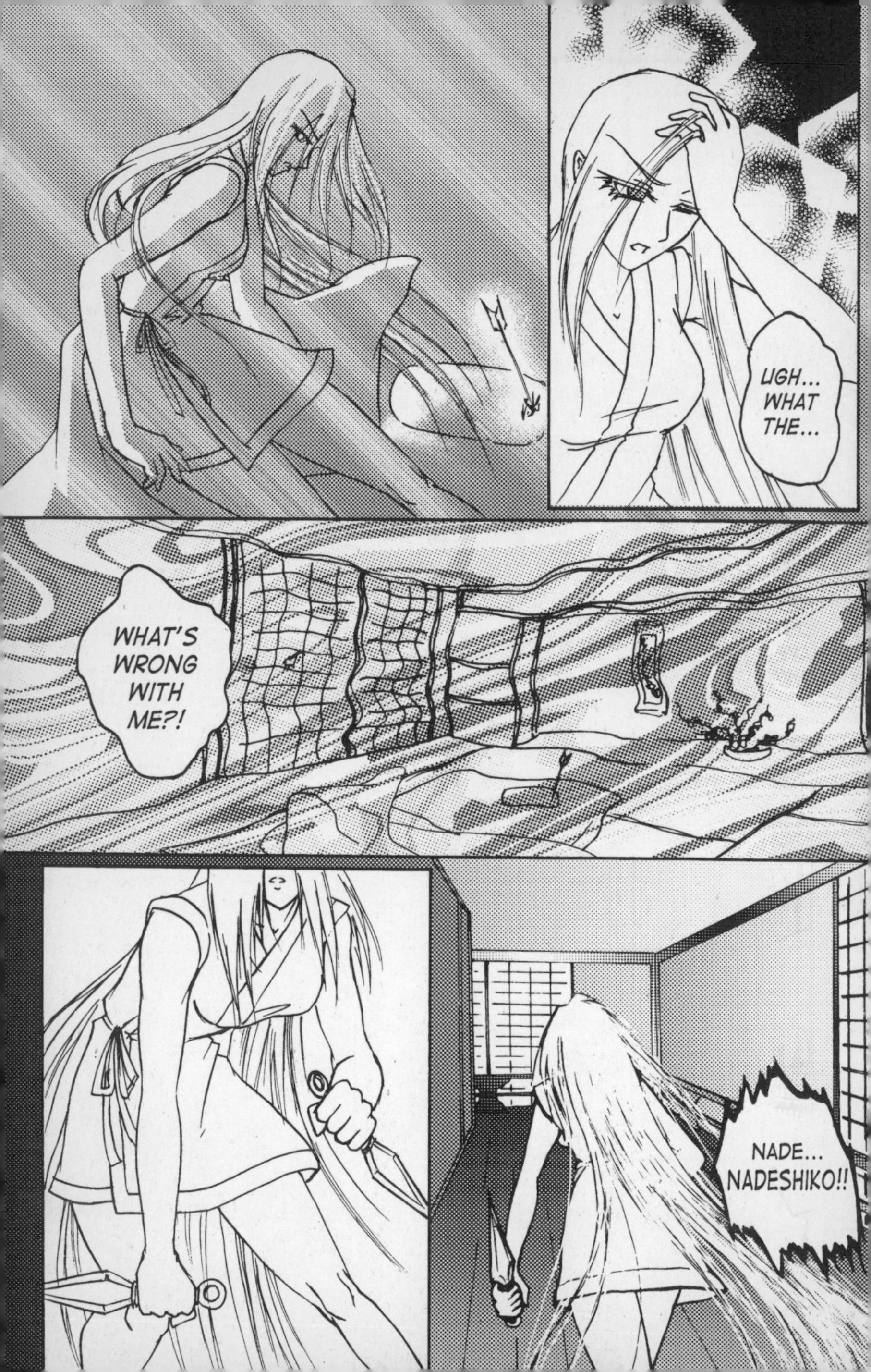
UGH... WHAT THE...
WHAT'S WRONG WITH ME?!
NADE... NADESHIKO!!

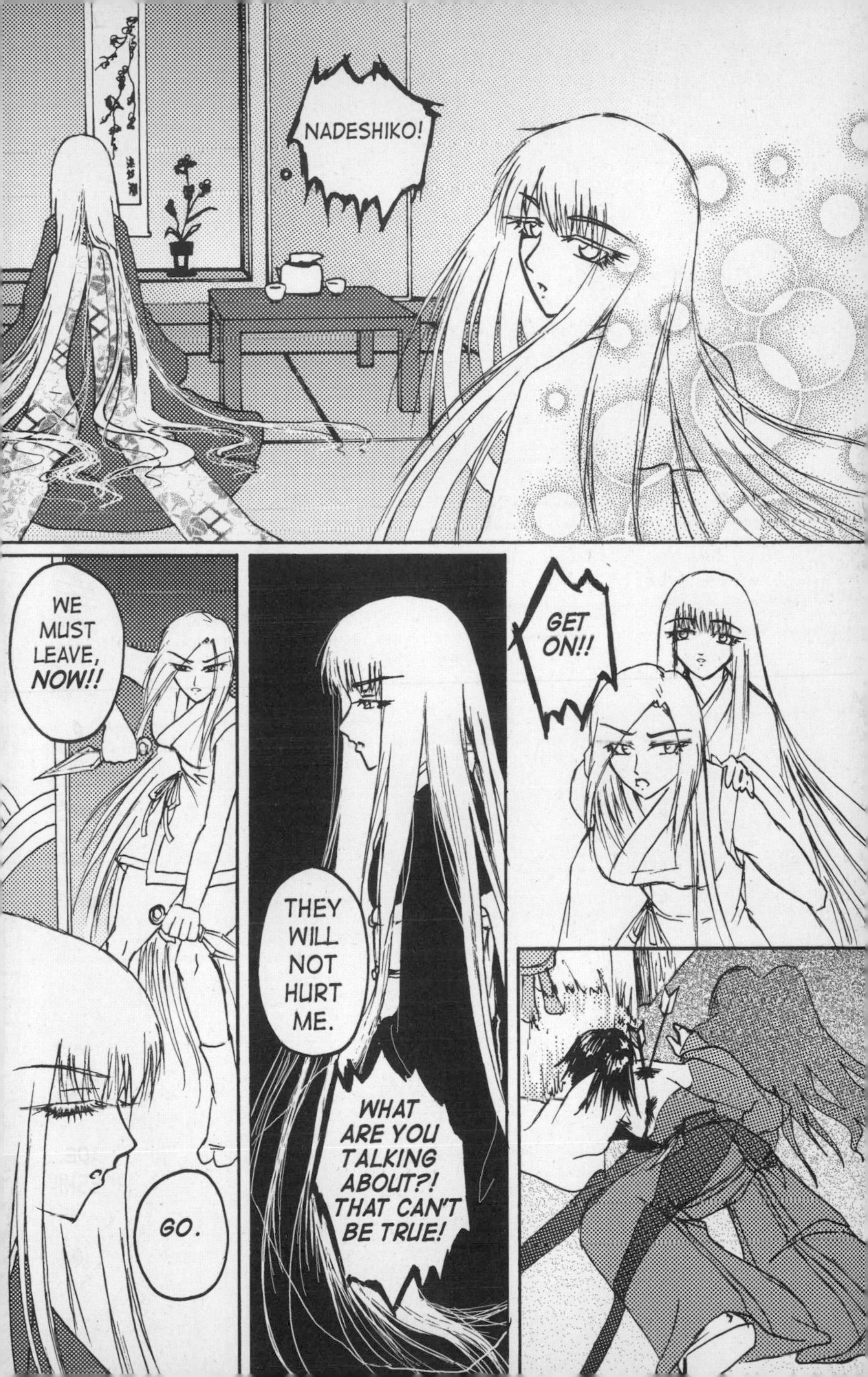
NADESHIKO!
WE MUST LEAVE, NOW!!
GO.
THEY WILL NOT HURT ME.
WHAT ARE YOU TALKING ABOUT?! THAT CAN'T BE TRUE!
GET ON!!

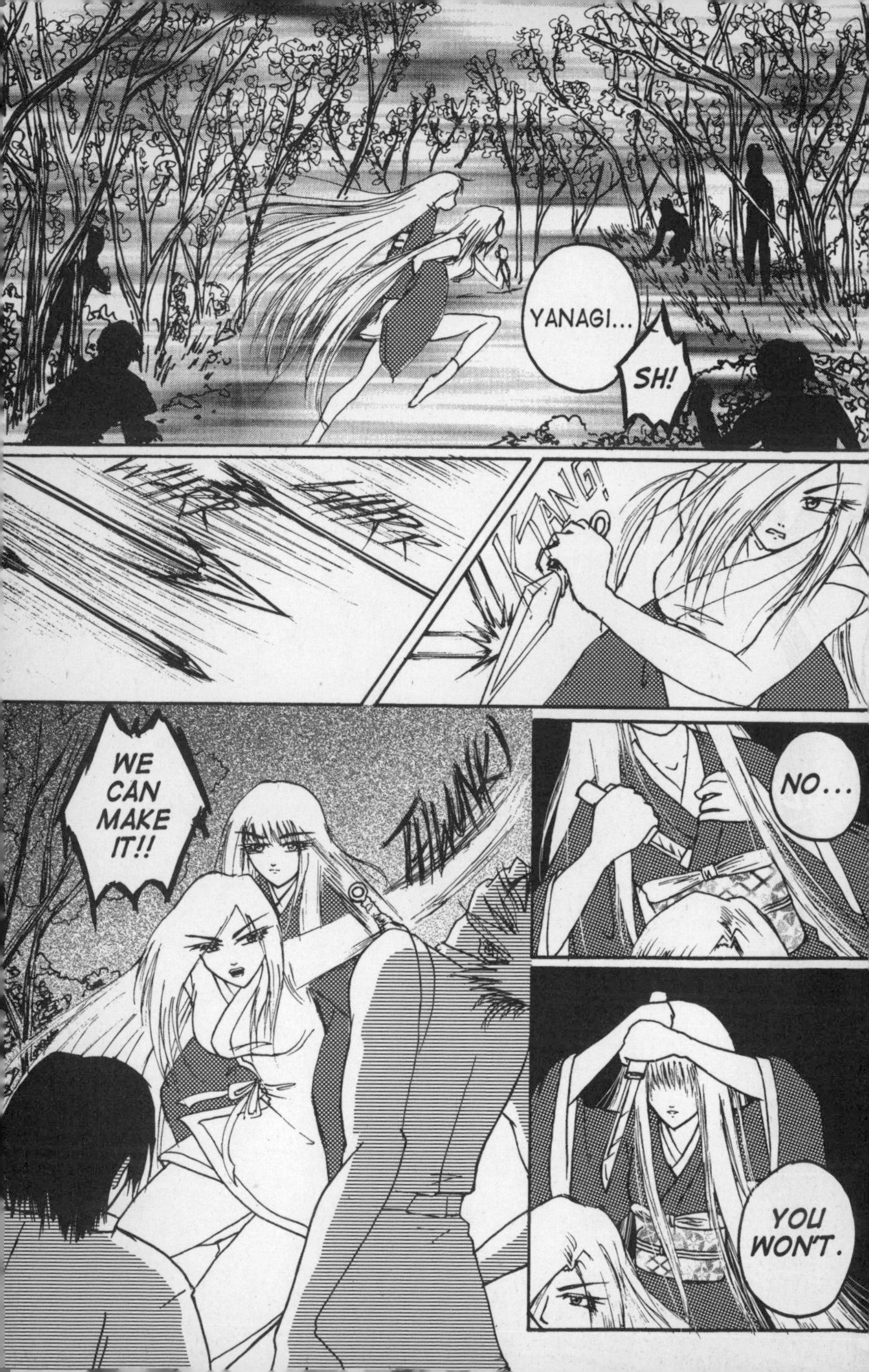
YANAGI...
SH!
KTANG!
WE CAN MAKE IT!!
THWUNK!
NO...
YOU WON'T.

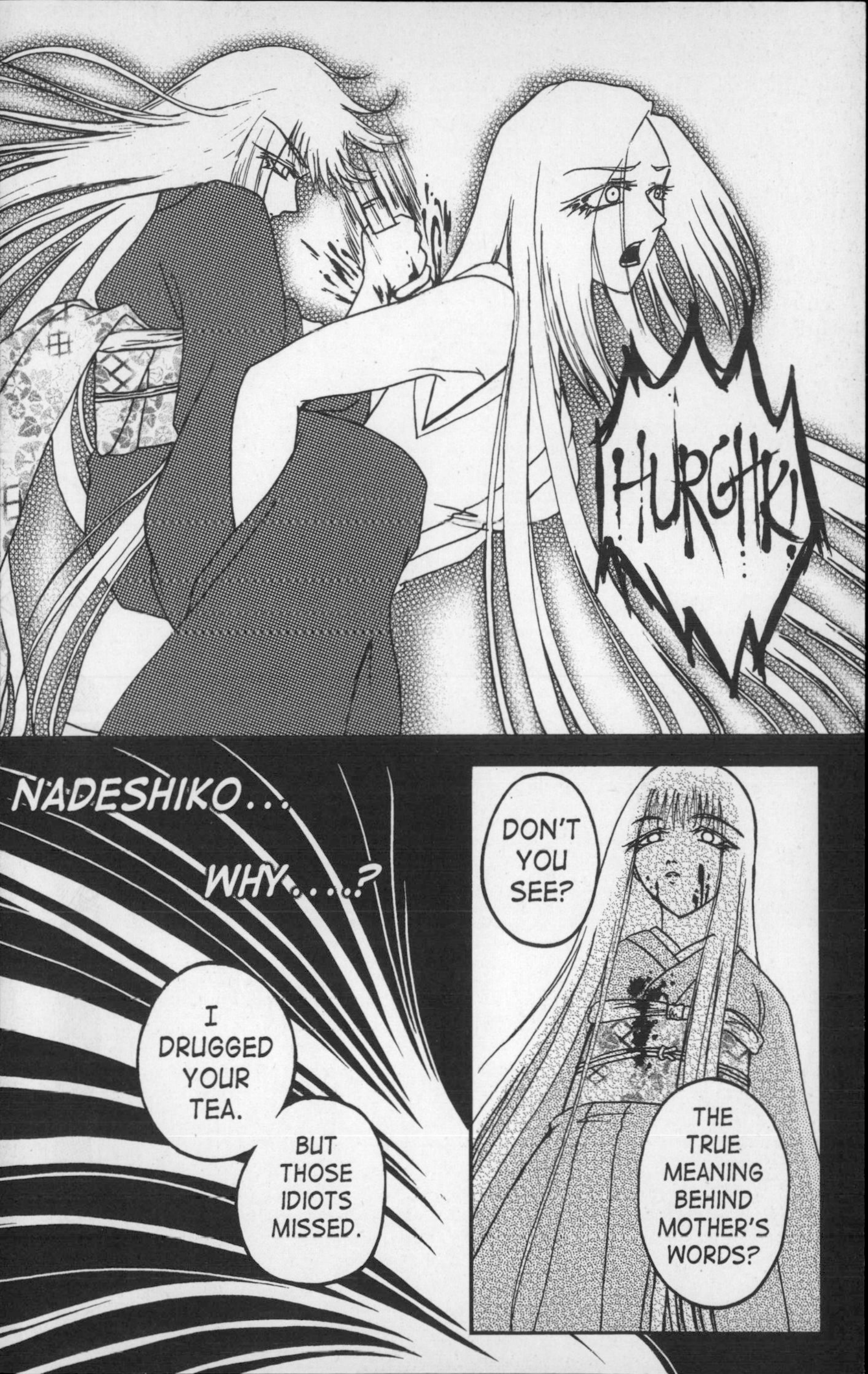
HURGHK!
NADESHIKO...
WHY....?
I DRUGGED YOUR TEA.
BUT THOSE IDIOTS MISSED.
DON'T YOU SEE?
THE TRUE MEANING BEHIND MOTHER'S WORDS?

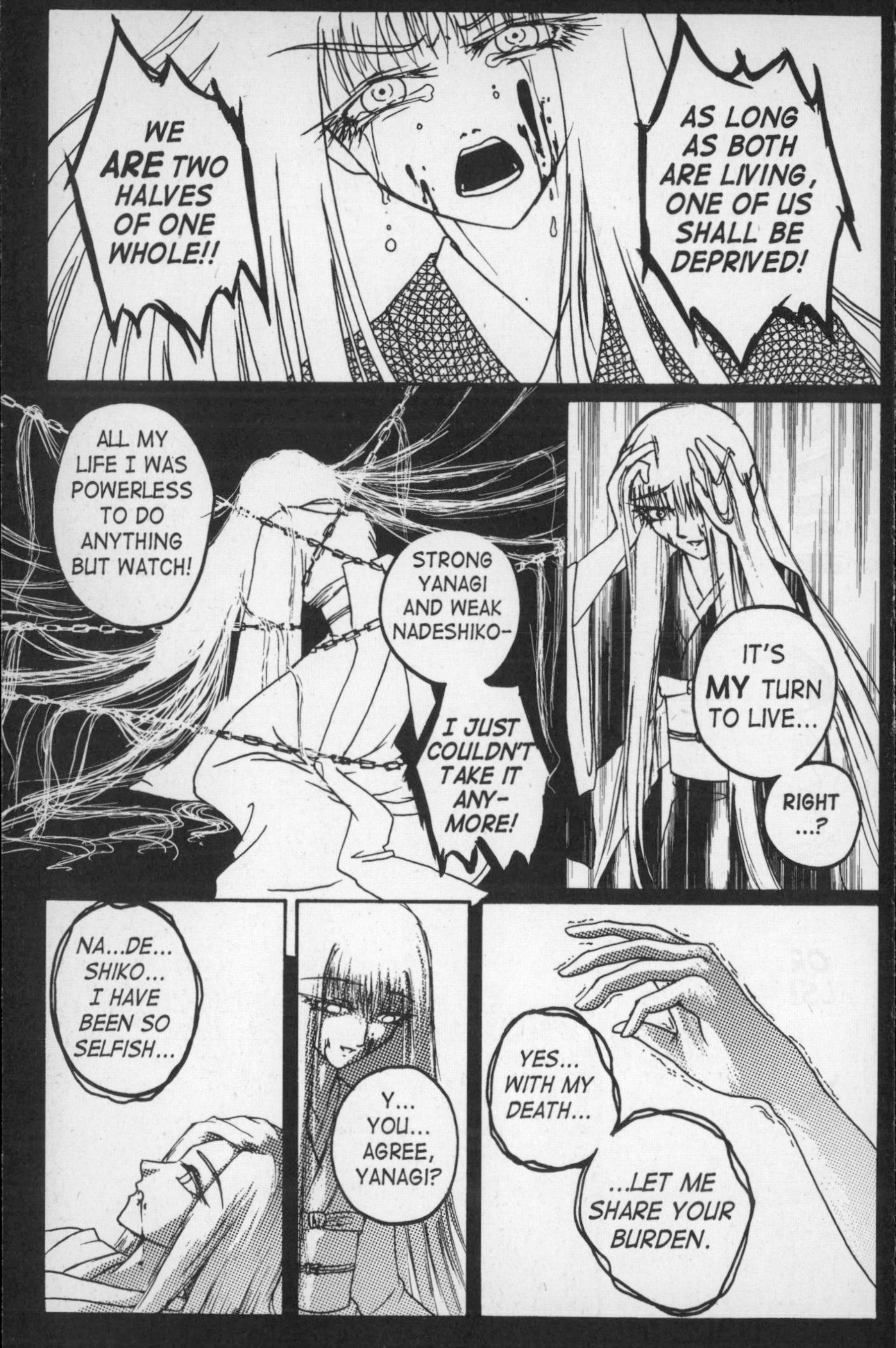
WE ARE TWO HALVES OF ONE WHOLE!!
AS LONG AS BOTH ARE LIVING, ONE OF US SHALL BE DEPRIVED!
ALL MY LIFE I WAS POWERLESS TO DO ANYTHING BUT WATCH!
STRONG YANAGI AND WEAK NADESHIKO-
I JUST COULDN'T TAKE IT ANY-MORE!
IT'S MY TURN TO LIVE...
RIGHT ...?
NA...DE... SHIKO... I HAVE BEEN SO SELFISH...
Y... YOU... AGREE, YANAGI?
YES... WITH MY DEATH...
...LET ME SHARE YOUR BURDEN.

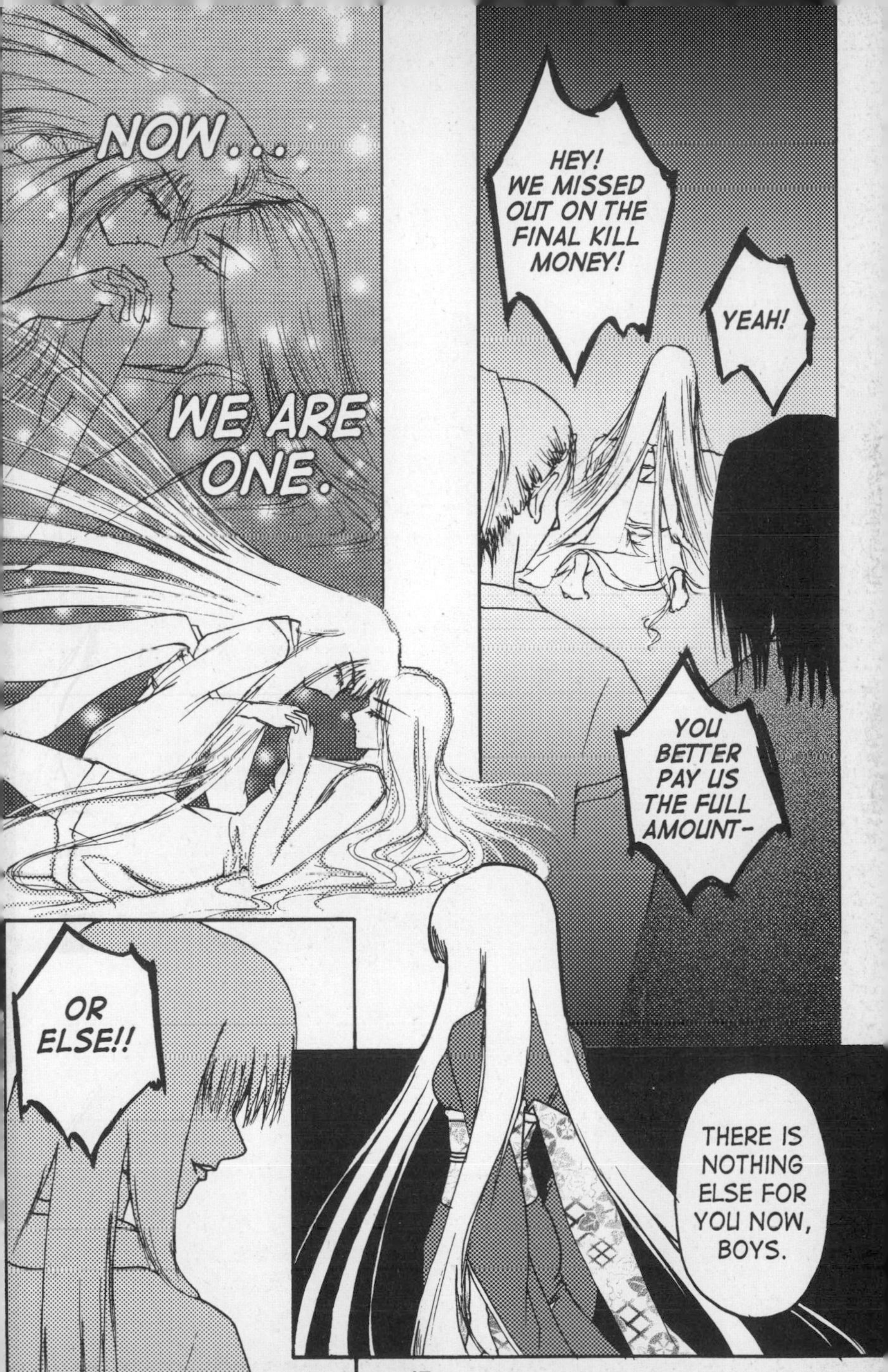
NOW...
WE ARE ONE.
HEY! WE MISSED OUT ON THE FINAL KILL MONEY!
YEAH!
YOU BETTER PAY US THE FULL AMOUNT-
OR ELSE!!
THERE IS NOTHING ELSE FOR YOU NOW, BOYS.

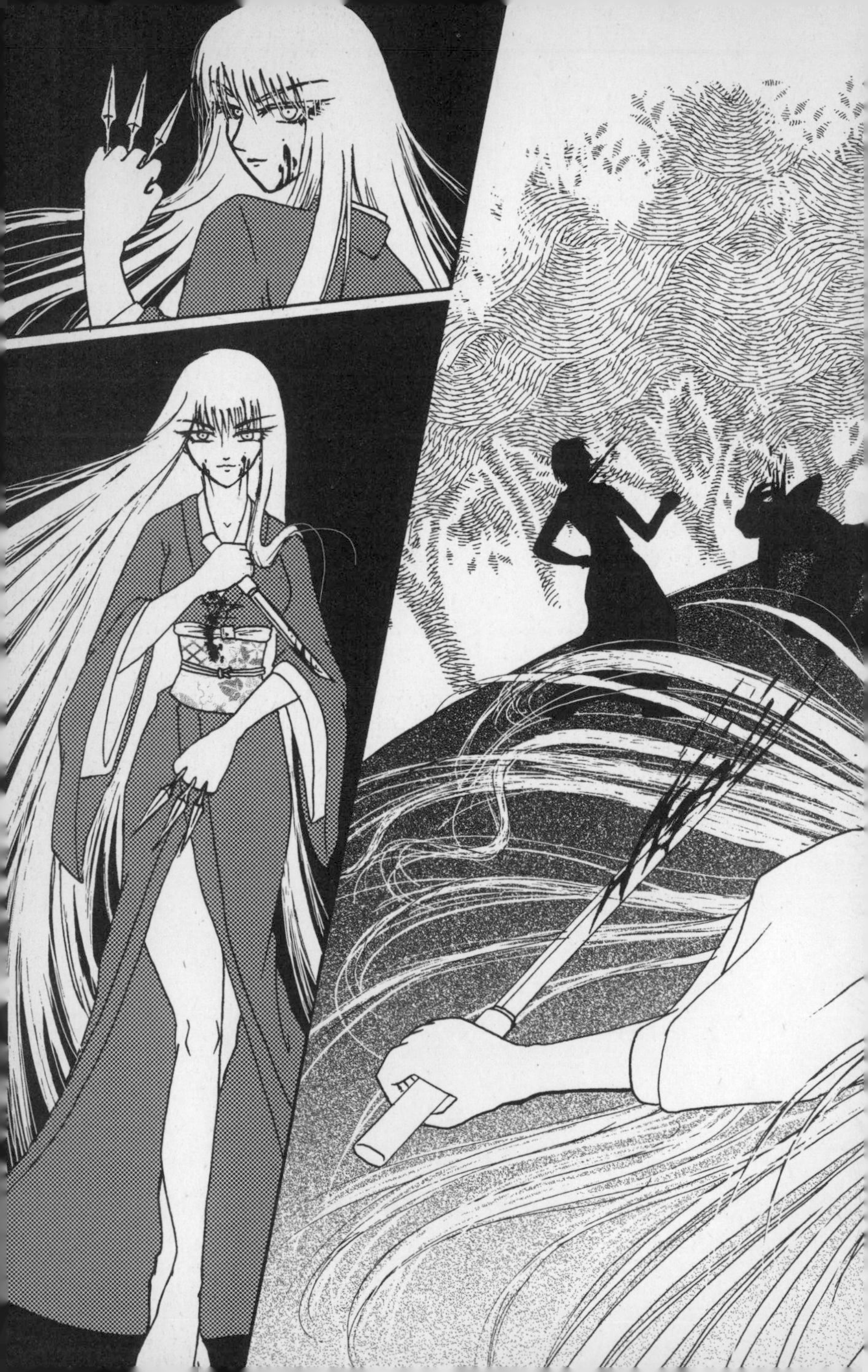

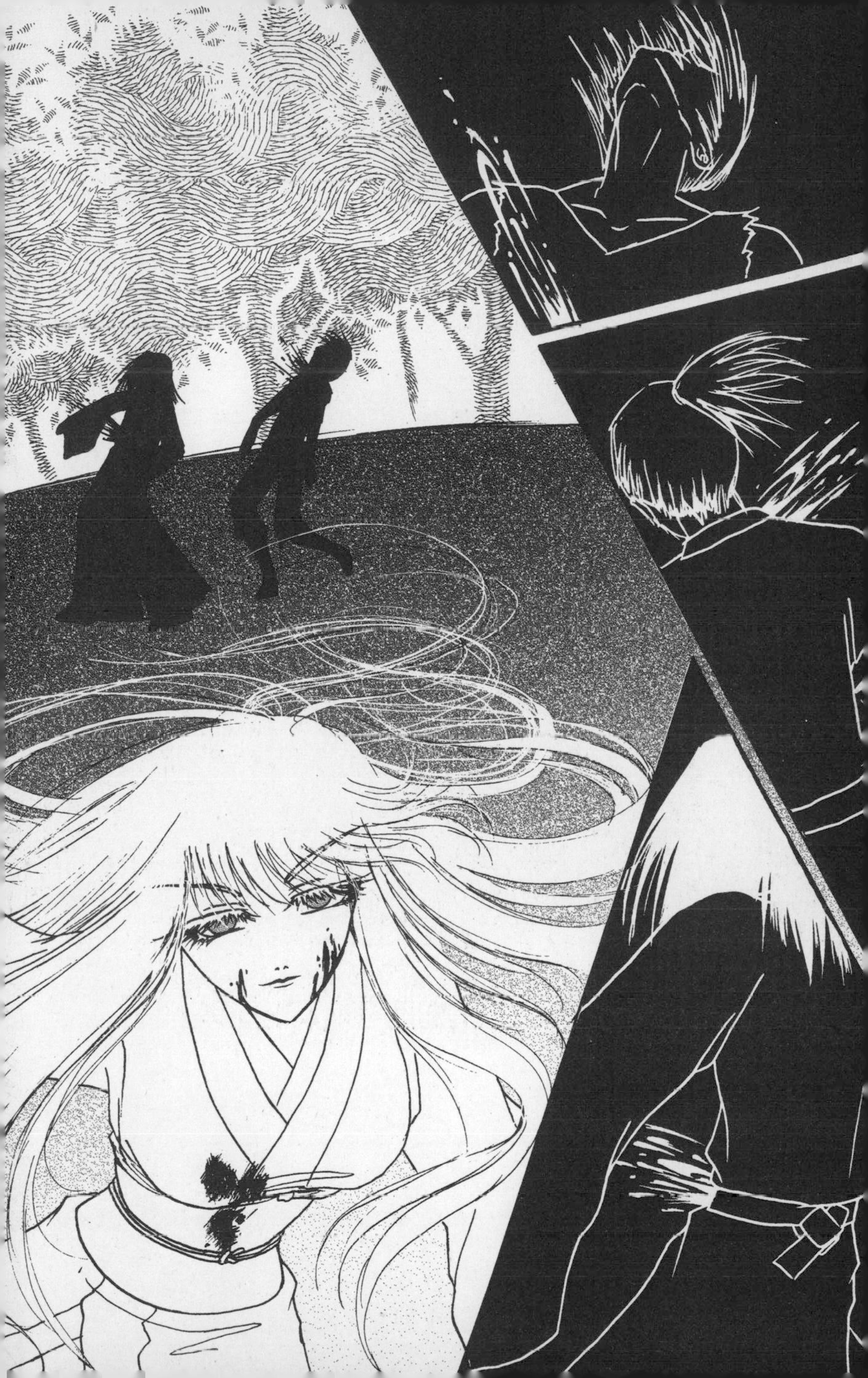

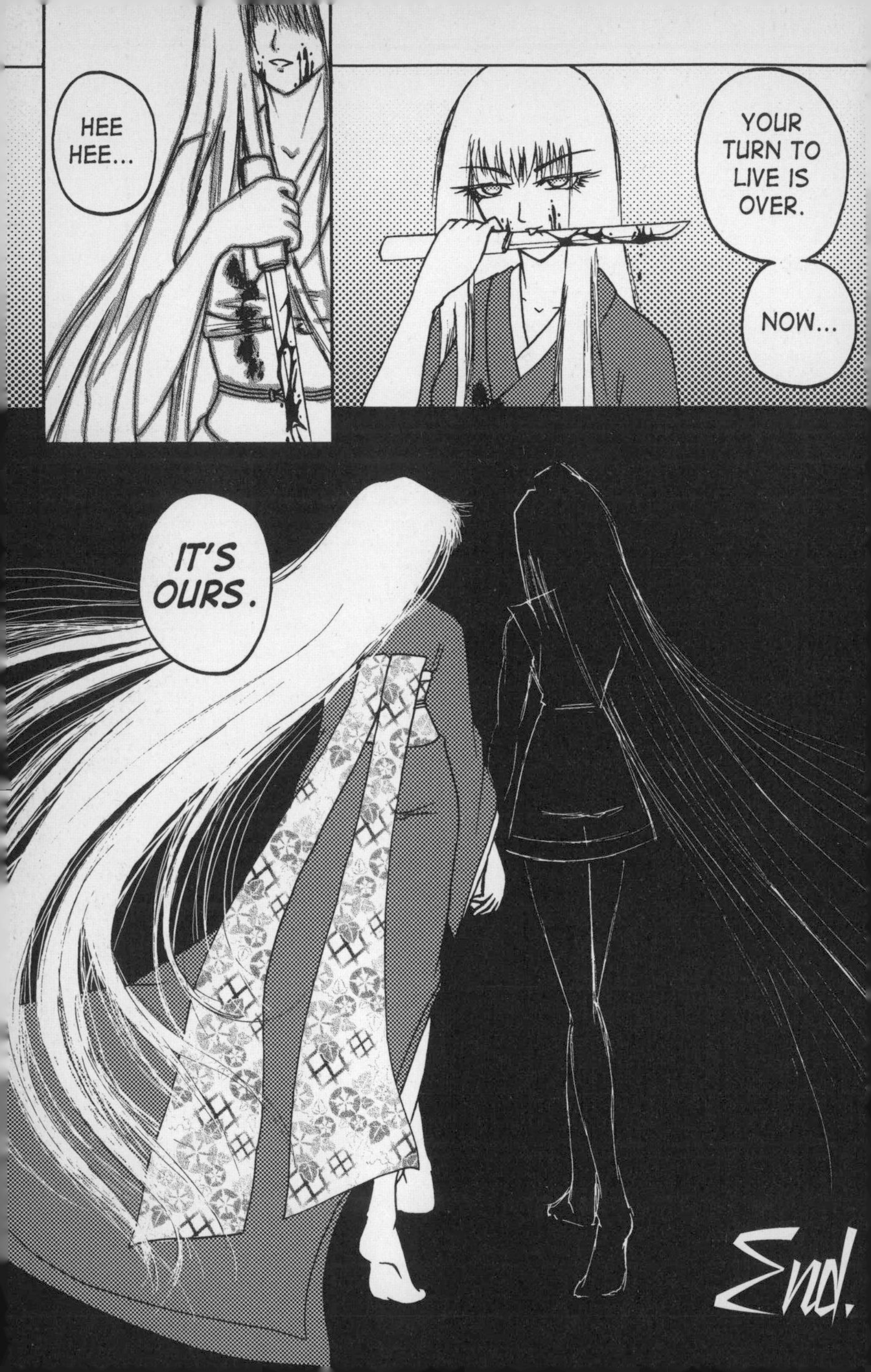
HEE HEE...
YOUR TURN TO LIVE IS OVER.
NOW...
IT'S OURS.
End.

DOJO DYNASTY :: Third Place Winner ::

....

Patrick Warren was born in 1985 in Hammersmith, London. He is
currently a first year student at the University of Westminster, studying
animation.
mrmetallium.deviantart.com/

Favorite manga:
Tenjo Tenge, Bleach, Fullmetal Alchemist

Favorite manga artist:
Oh! Great, Masamune Shirow, Hyung Tae-Kim, Yoshiyuki Sadamoto

....

Author's Comments:
This was my first ever attempt at creating a short manga, so...really It
was just one huge experiment for me. Whatever came into my head, I
just wrote it down and tried drawing it. The hardest thing I found was
fitting everything into 20 pages! (And to be satisfied with what I was
doing—I almost stopped halfway because I hated it!)

I've definitely learnt a lot from doing this.
—*Patrick Warren*

::

DOJO DYNASTY

THIRD PLACE WINNER

RISING.STARS.OF.MANGA.2006

::

DOJO DYNASTY :: Third Place Winner ::

Judge's Comments:
I've always been a huge fan of "gag manga." From classics like *Dr. Slump* to recent stuff like *Bobobo-bo Bo-bobo* and the *RSOM 3* winning entry, "Atomic King Daidogan." "Dojo Dynasty" continues in that tradition with a frantic pace and big laughs on every page. The strength of this entry is the great expressions the characters make as they react to the wacky events taking place. The art is very clean and I had no trouble figuring out what was going on, even on the busiest of pages. Creator Patrick Warren has taken styles from various famous manga series and woven them together to create the funniest entry we saw in this competition. I was very amused by the panels that show the father and daughter reacting together with the same goofy look on their faces. Also impressive was the ability to mix action and comedy and still tell a complete story in the limited number of pages.

There was some criticism about the panel layout being too busy in places but I think it fits for an off-the-wall comedy short such as this. The mixing of more serious shots with super-deformed ones was done very well, making for a lot of hilarious scenes. I particularly liked the scene near the end with characters attacking each other with "spinners." Patrick Warren obviously has a great understanding of manga humor and exploits it to its fullest.
-Alexis Kirsch

Judge's Comments:
This ambitious piece does have a lot in common with "Atomic King Daidogan." It's a take-it-or-leave-it all out effort that attempts to drown the reader in parody and delight with a glittering showcase of absurdity. And for the most part, "Dojo Dynasty" brews a concoction of familiar laughable elements that is enjoyable to read and surprisingly endearing.

The true delight of Patrick's work is his devotion of the smallest detail to the greater cause of comedy. There is no line, sign or character design that hasn't been reconsidered by the artist to maximize its comedic effect to keep you chuckling in a sustained manner throughout the story. And certain lines sparkle like...well, you'll see.

But although this piece shines on the small scale, it rarely takes advantage of the larger imagery and splash pages it is starving for. The overabundance of small panels and miniature text balloons grate on the eyes and choke the piece, making reaching the ending a feat of endurance. Sometimes the piece loses sight of what it is parodying—is it martial arts manga, body builders, or bad dubbing? Inconsistent rendering skills, an overemphasis on similar gradient tones and some boxy yet confusing panel layout contribute the lack of better visual sense that something so funny deserves.
—Hope Donovan

::

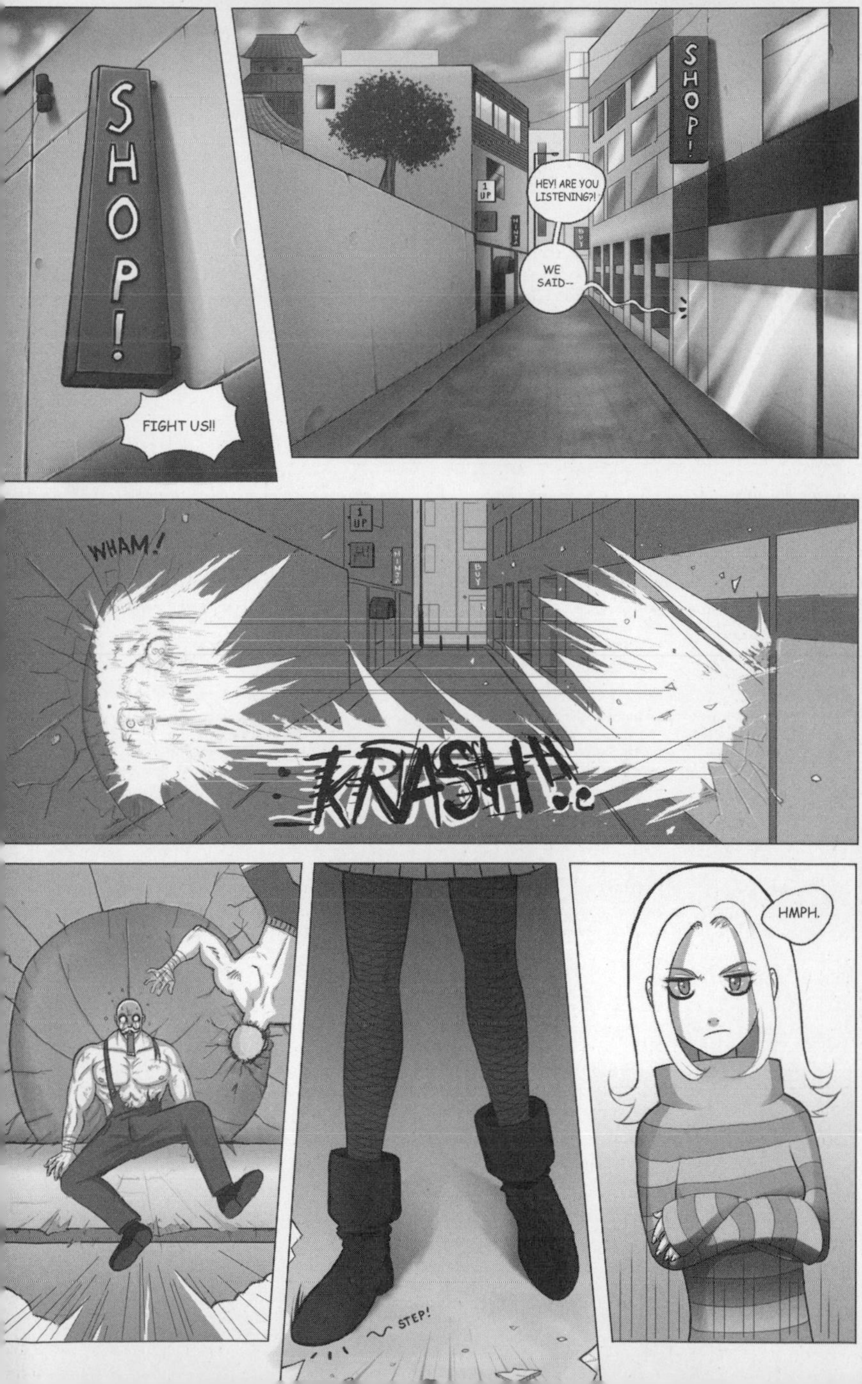
SHOP!
FIGHT US!!
SHOP!
1 UP
HEY! ARE YOU LISTENING?!
WE SAID--
BUY
WHAM!
KRASH!!
HMPH.
STEP!

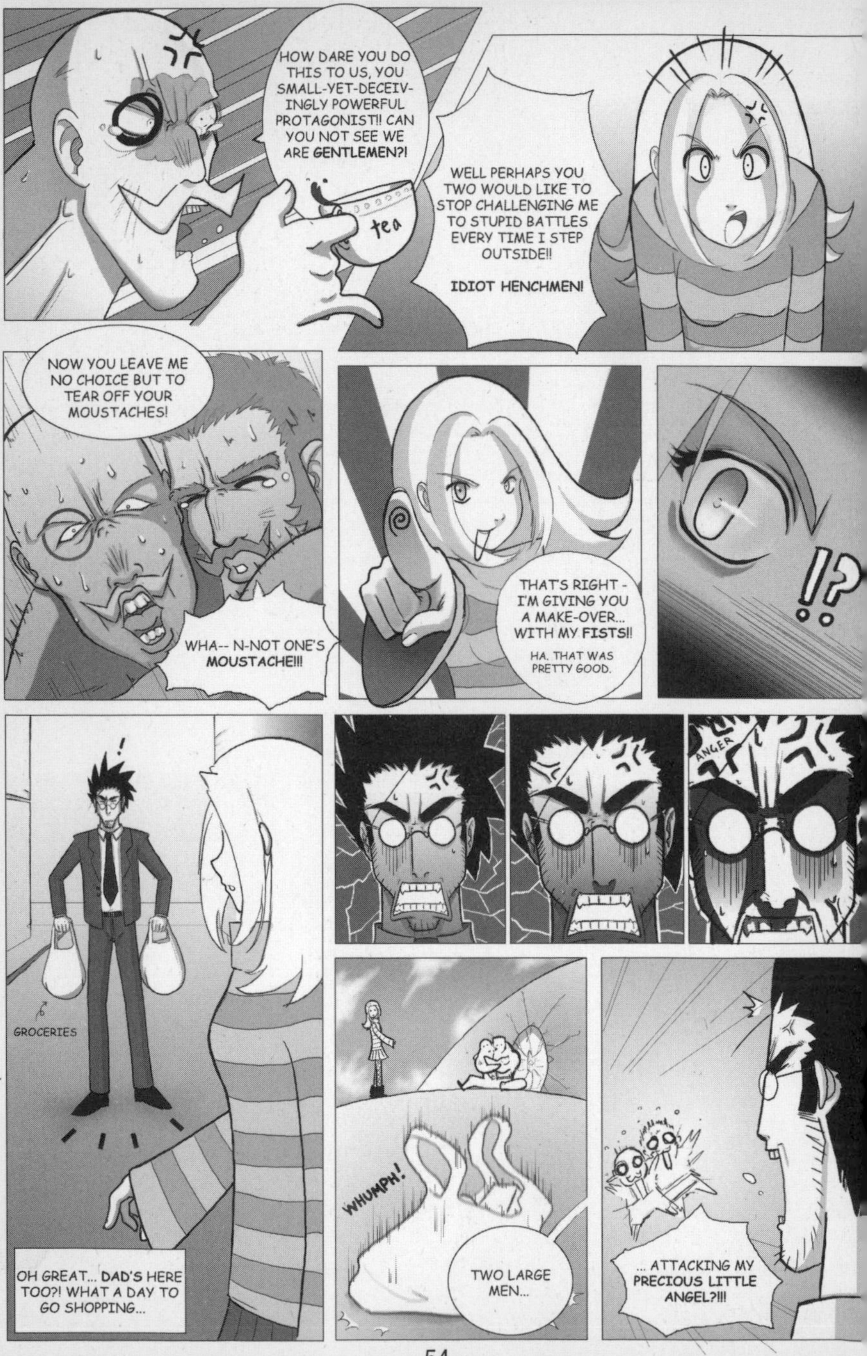
HOW DARE YOU DO THIS TO US, YOU SMALL-YET-DECEIVINGLY POWERFUL PROTAGONIST!! CAN YOU NOT SEE WE ARE GENTLEMEN?!
tea
WELL PERHAPS YOU TWO WOULD LIKE TO STOP CHALLENGING ME TO STUPID BATTLES EVERY TIME I STEP OUTSIDE!!
IDIOT HENCHMEN!
NOW YOU LEAVE ME NO CHOICE BUT TO TEAR OFF YOUR MOUSTACHES!
WHA-- N-NOT ONE'S MOUSTACHE!!!
THAT'S RIGHT - I'M GIVING YOU A MAKE-OVER... WITH MY FISTS!!
HA. THAT WAS PRETTY GOOD.
!?
!
GROCERIES
OH GREAT... DAD'S HERE TOO?! WHAT A DAY TO GO SHOPPING...
ANGER
WHUMPH!
TWO LARGE MEN...
... ATTACKING MY PRECIOUS LITTLE ANGEL?!!!

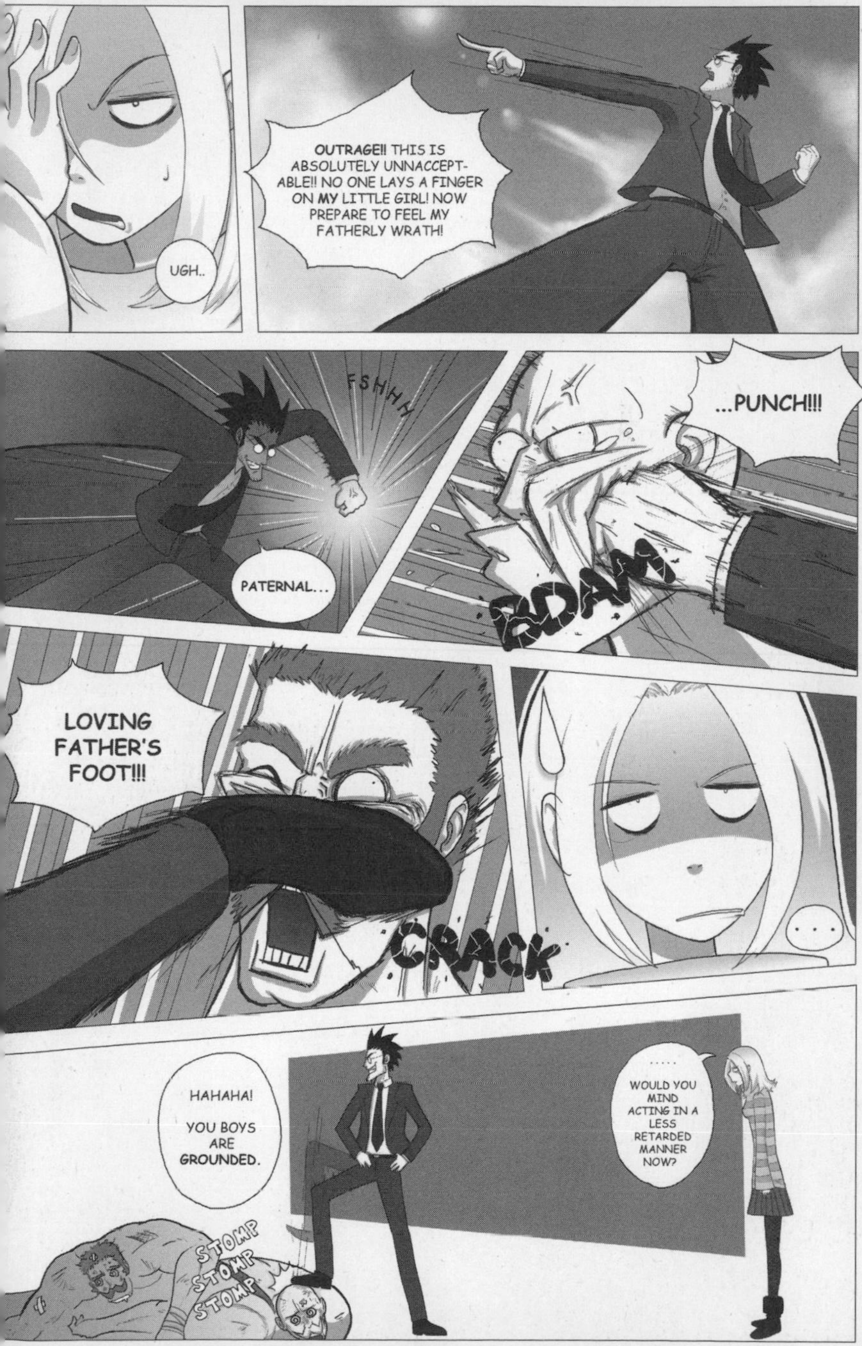

UGH..
OUTRAGE!! THIS IS ABSOLUTELY UNNACCEPT-ABLE!! NO ONE LAYS A FINGER ON MY LITTLE GIRL! NOW PREPARE TO FEEL MY FATHERLY WRATH!
FSHHH
PATERNAL...
...PUNCH!!!
BDAM
LOVING FATHER'S FOOT!!!
CRACK
...
HAHAHA!
YOU BOYS ARE GROUNDED.
STOMP
STOMP
STOMP
.....
WOULD YOU MIND ACTING IN A LESS RETARDED MANNER NOW?

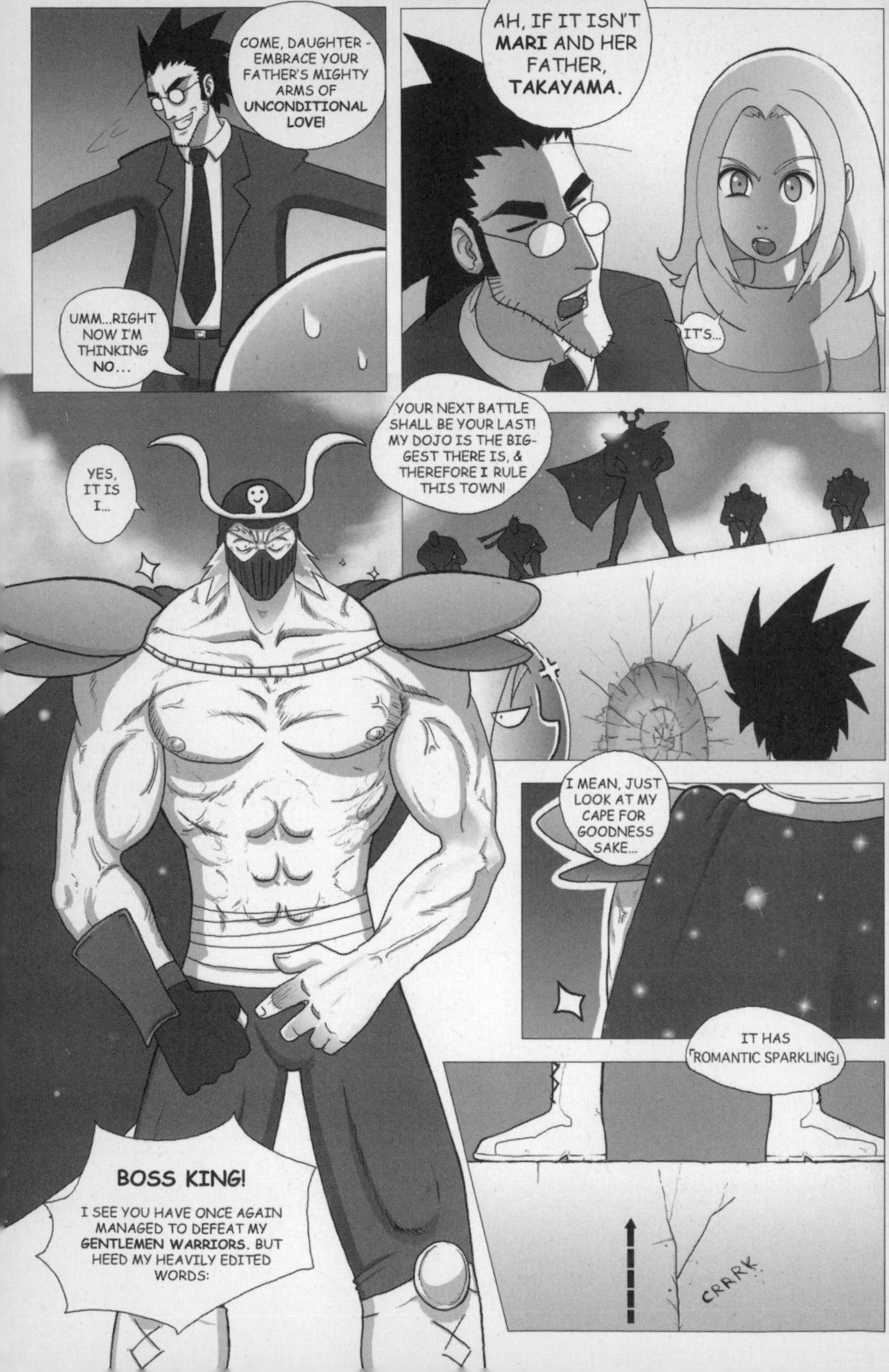
COME, DAUGHTER - EMBRACE YOUR FATHER'S MIGHTY ARMS OF UNCONDITIONAL LOVE!
UMM...RIGHT NOW I'M THINKING NO...
AH, IF IT ISN'T MARI AND HER FATHER, TAKAYAMA.
IT'S...
YES, IT IS I...
BOSS KING!
I SEE YOU HAVE ONCE AGAIN MANAGED TO DEFEAT MY GENTLEMEN WARRIORS. BUT HEED MY HEAVILY EDITED WORDS:
YOUR NEXT BATTLE SHALL BE YOUR LAST! MY DOJO IS THE BIG-GEST THERE IS, & THEREFORE I RULE THIS TOWN!
I MEAN, JUST LOOK AT MY CAPE FOR GOODNESS SAKE...
IT HAS 「ROMANTIC SPARKLING」
CRRRK

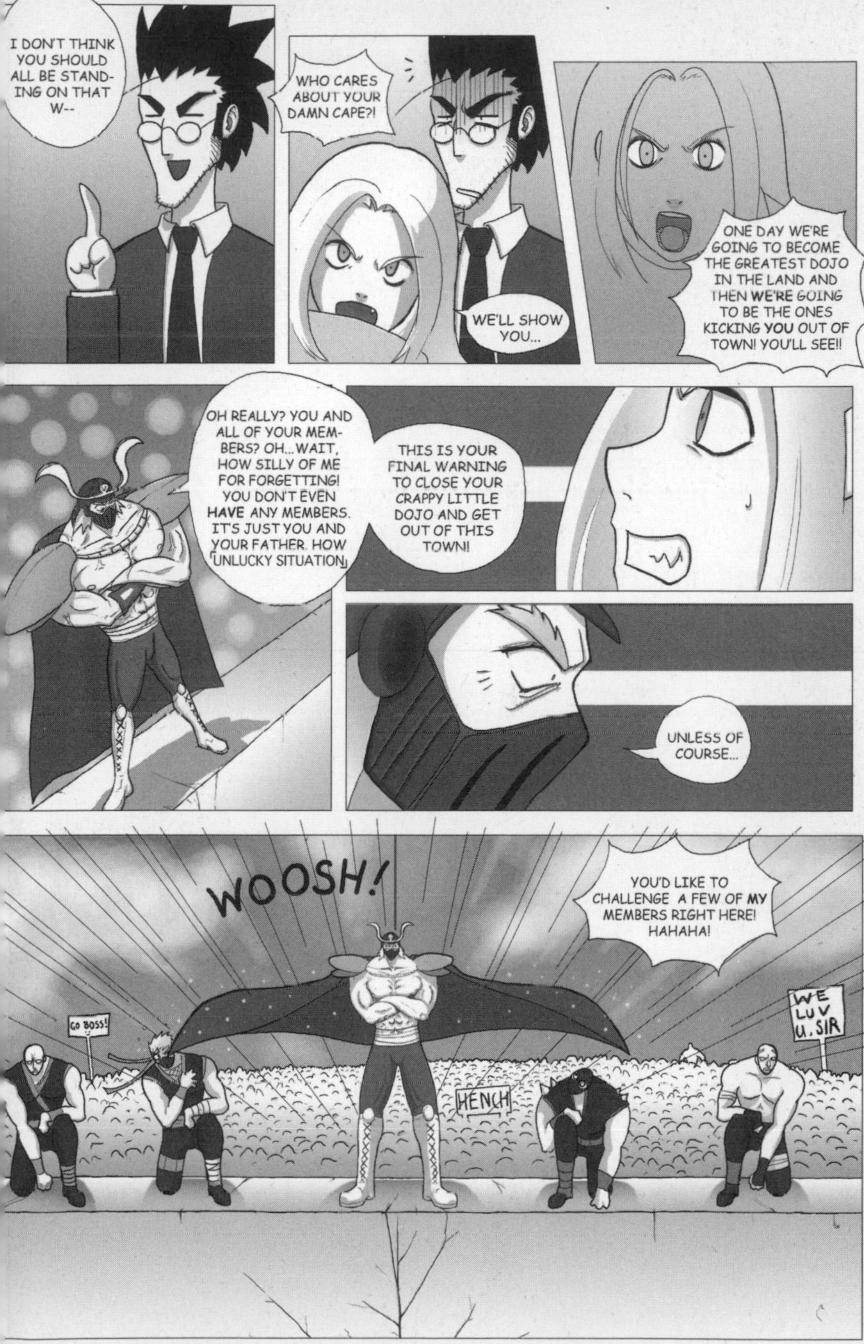
I DON'T THINK YOU SHOULD ALL BE STAND-ING ON THAT W--
WHO CARES ABOUT YOUR DAMN CAPE?!
WE'LL SHOW YOU...
ONE DAY WE'RE GOING TO BECOME THE GREATEST DOJO IN THE LAND AND THEN WE'RE GOING TO BE THE ONES KICKING YOU OUT OF TOWN! YOU'LL SEE!!
OH REALLY? YOU AND ALL OF YOUR MEM-BERS? OH...WAIT, HOW SILLY OF ME FOR FORGETTING! YOU DON'T EVEN HAVE ANY MEMBERS. IT'S JUST YOU AND YOUR FATHER. HOW 「UNLUCKY SITUATION」
THIS IS YOUR FINAL WARNING TO CLOSE YOUR CRAPPY LITTLE DOJO AND GET OUT OF THIS TOWN!
UNLESS OF COURSE...
WOOSH!
YOU'D LIKE TO CHALLENGE A FEW OF MY MEMBERS RIGHT HERE! HAHAHA!
GO BOSS!
HENCH
WE LUV U. SIR

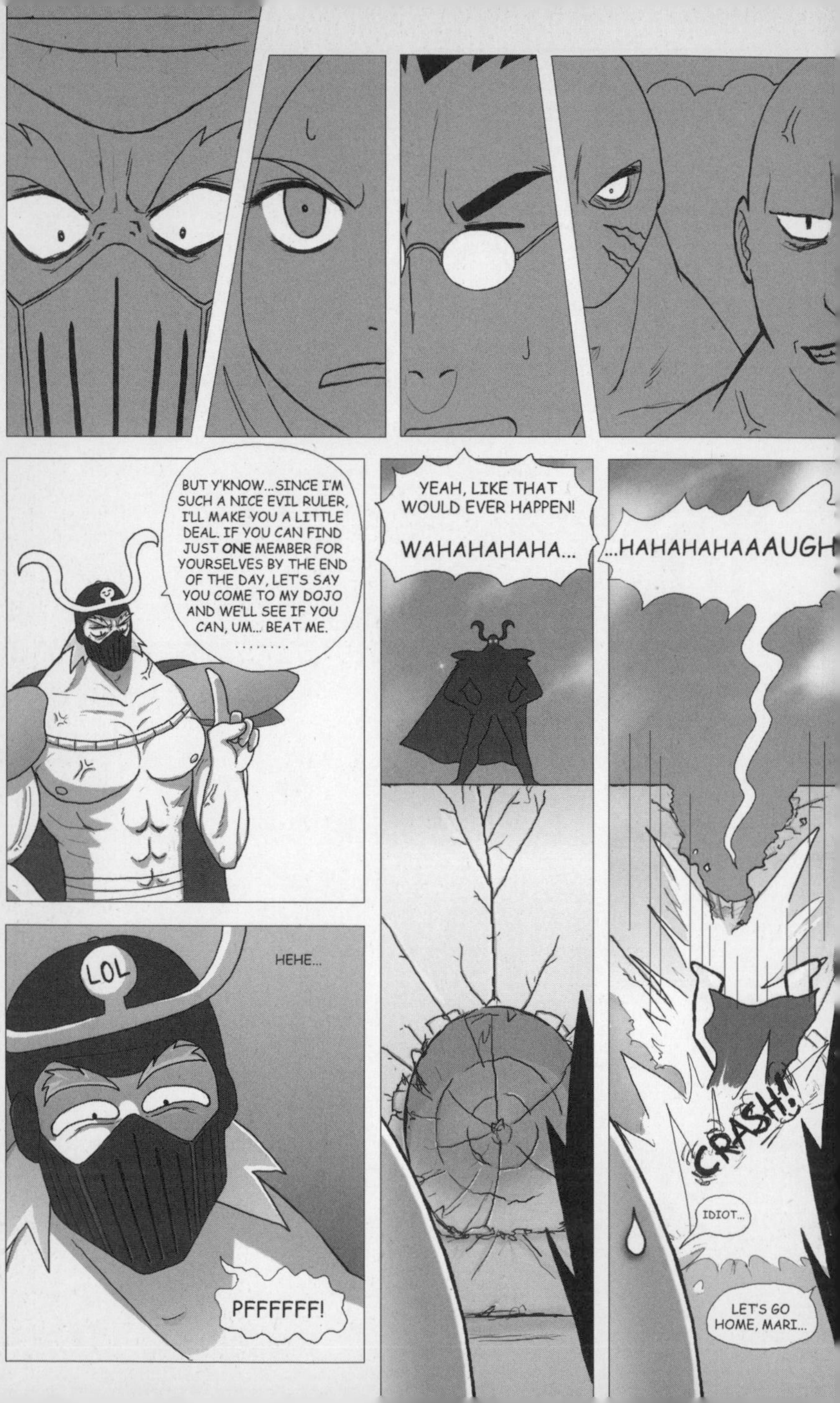
BUT Y'KNOW...SINCE I'M SUCH A NICE EVIL RULER, I'LL MAKE YOU A LITTLE DEAL. IF YOU CAN FIND JUST **ONE** MEMBER FOR YOURSELVES BY THE END OF THE DAY, LET'S SAY YOU COME TO MY DOJO AND WE'LL SEE IF YOU CAN, UM... BEAT ME.
....
YEAH, LIKE THAT WOULD EVER HAPPEN!
WAHAHAHAHA...
...HAHAHAHAAAUGH
HEHE...
PFFFFFF!
CRASH!!
IDIOT...
LET'S GO HOME, MARI...

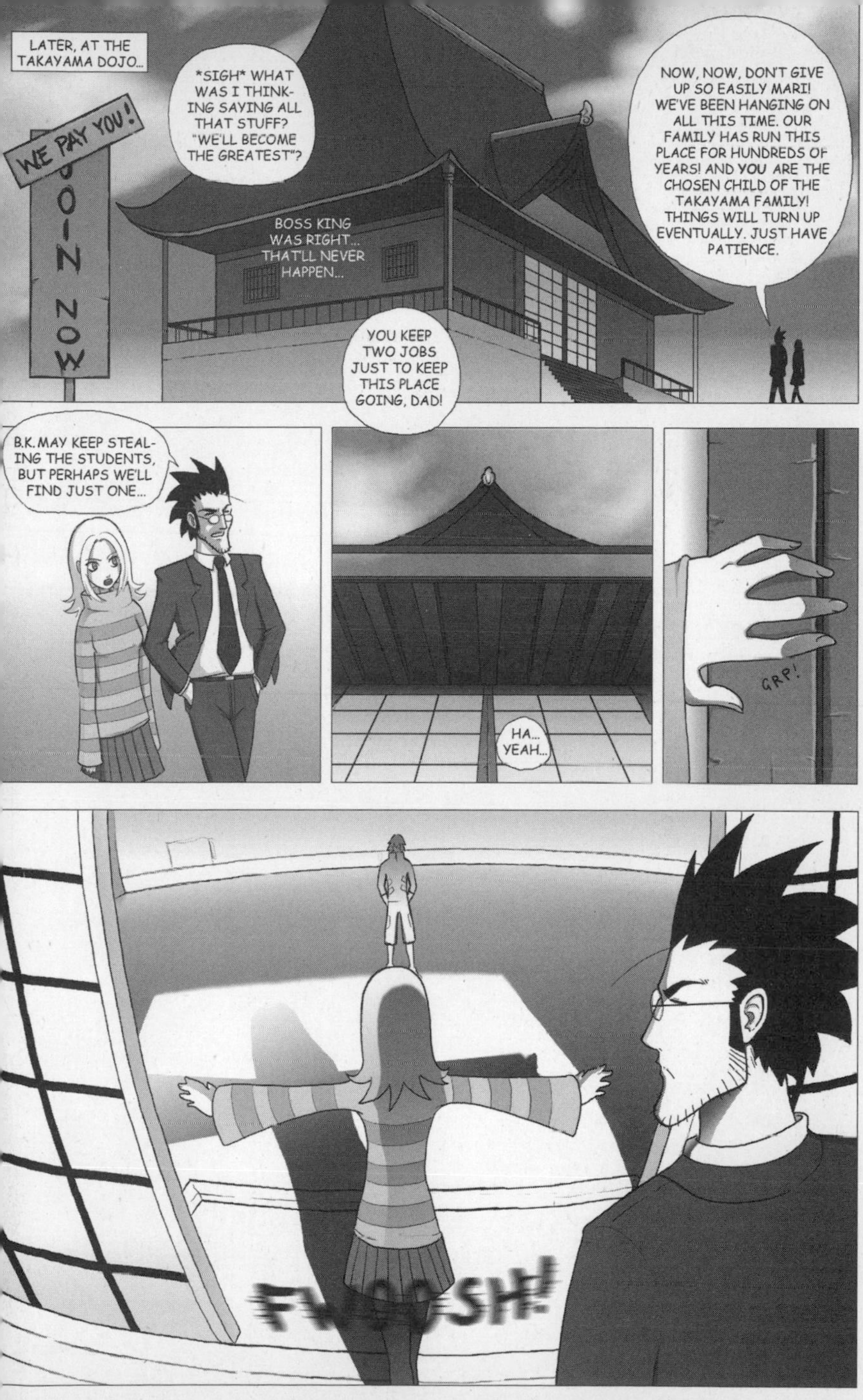
LATER, AT THE TAKAYAMA DOJO...
WE PAY YOU!
JOIN NOW
SIGH WHAT WAS I THINKING SAYING ALL THAT STUFF? "WE'LL BECOME THE GREATEST"?
BOSS KING WAS RIGHT... THAT'LL NEVER HAPPEN...
NOW, NOW, DON'T GIVE UP SO EASILY MARI! WE'VE BEEN HANGING ON ALL THIS TIME. OUR FAMILY HAS RUN THIS PLACE FOR HUNDREDS OF YEARS! AND YOU ARE THE CHOSEN CHILD OF THE TAKAYAMA FAMILY! THINGS WILL TURN UP EVENTUALLY. JUST HAVE PATIENCE.
YOU KEEP TWO JOBS JUST TO KEEP THIS PLACE GOING, DAD!
B.K. MAY KEEP STEALING THE STUDENTS, BUT PERHAPS WE'LL FIND JUST ONE...
HA... YEAH...
GRP!
FWOOSH!

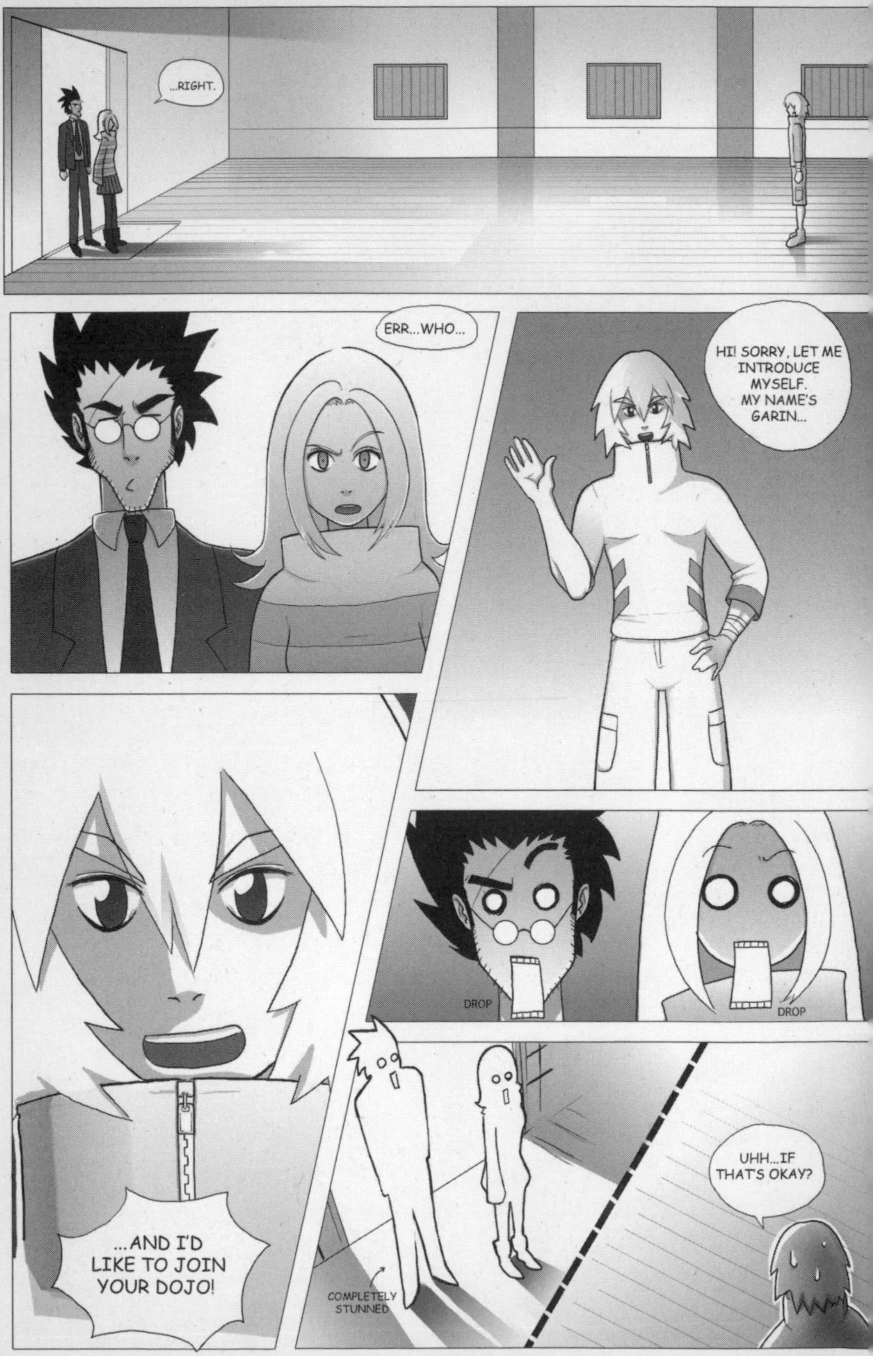
...RIGHT.
ERR...WHO...
HI! SORRY, LET ME INTRODUCE MYSELF. MY NAME'S GARIN...
...AND I'D LIKE TO JOIN YOUR DOJO!
DROP
DROP
COMPLETELY STUNNED
UHH...IF THAT'S OKAY?

WHY ABSOLUTELY!! HERE'S YOUR TRAINING GEAR SO WE CAN START IMMEDIATELY!

ZIP!

W-WHOA...

YOU... ARE SERIOUS, RIGHT? THIS ISN'T A JOKE?

YEAH, YEAH! BUT HOLD ON. FIRST I NEED TO EXPLAIN MY REASONS FOR JOINING YOU TODAY!

REASONS?

I WANT TO HELP YOU DEFEAT BOSS KING!

YOU... HUH?

HA...HAHA! MAN, THIS GUY'S JUST FULL OF SURPRISES! WHAT'S IT GONNA BE NEXT?!

HAHA

OH, BY THE WAY, DID I MENTION THAT BOSS KING IS MY FATHER?

BAMF

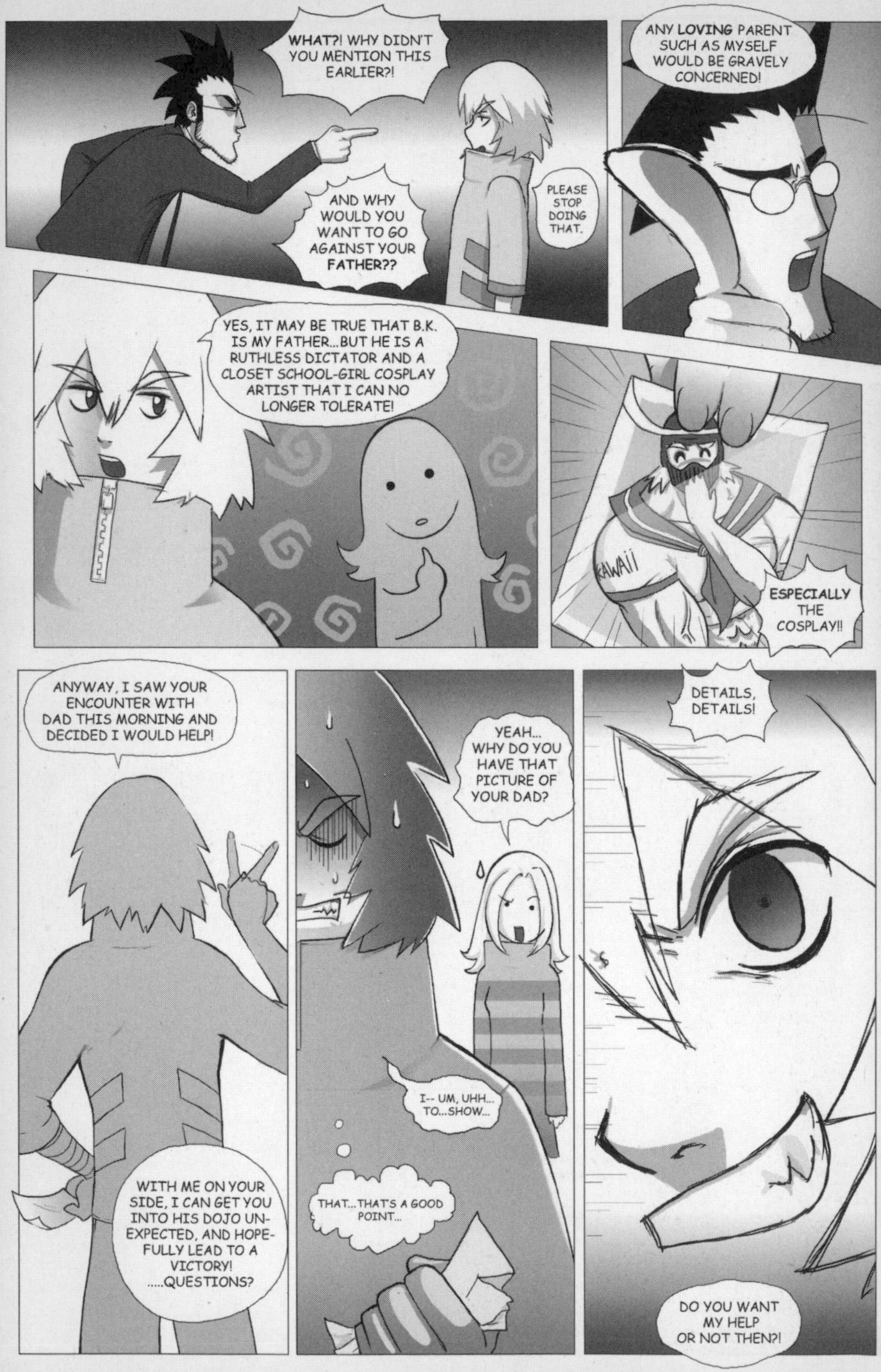
WHAT?! WHY DIDN'T YOU MENTION THIS EARLIER?!
AND WHY WOULD YOU WANT TO GO AGAINST YOUR FATHER??
PLEASE STOP DOING THAT.
ANY LOVING PARENT SUCH AS MYSELF WOULD BE GRAVELY CONCERNED!
YES, IT MAY BE TRUE THAT B.K. IS MY FATHER...BUT HE IS A RUTHLESS DICTATOR AND A CLOSET SCHOOL-GIRL COSPLAY ARTIST THAT I CAN NO LONGER TOLERATE!
KAWAII
ESPECIALLY THE COSPLAY!!
ANYWAY, I SAW YOUR ENCOUNTER WITH DAD THIS MORNING AND DECIDED I WOULD HELP!
WITH ME ON YOUR SIDE, I CAN GET YOU INTO HIS DOJO UN-EXPECTED, AND HOPE-FULLY LEAD TO A VICTORY! .....QUESTIONS?
YEAH... WHY DO YOU HAVE THAT PICTURE OF YOUR DAD?
I-- UM, UHH... TO...SHOW...
THAT...THAT'S A GOOD POINT...
DETAILS, DETAILS!
DO YOU WANT MY HELP OR NOT THEN?!

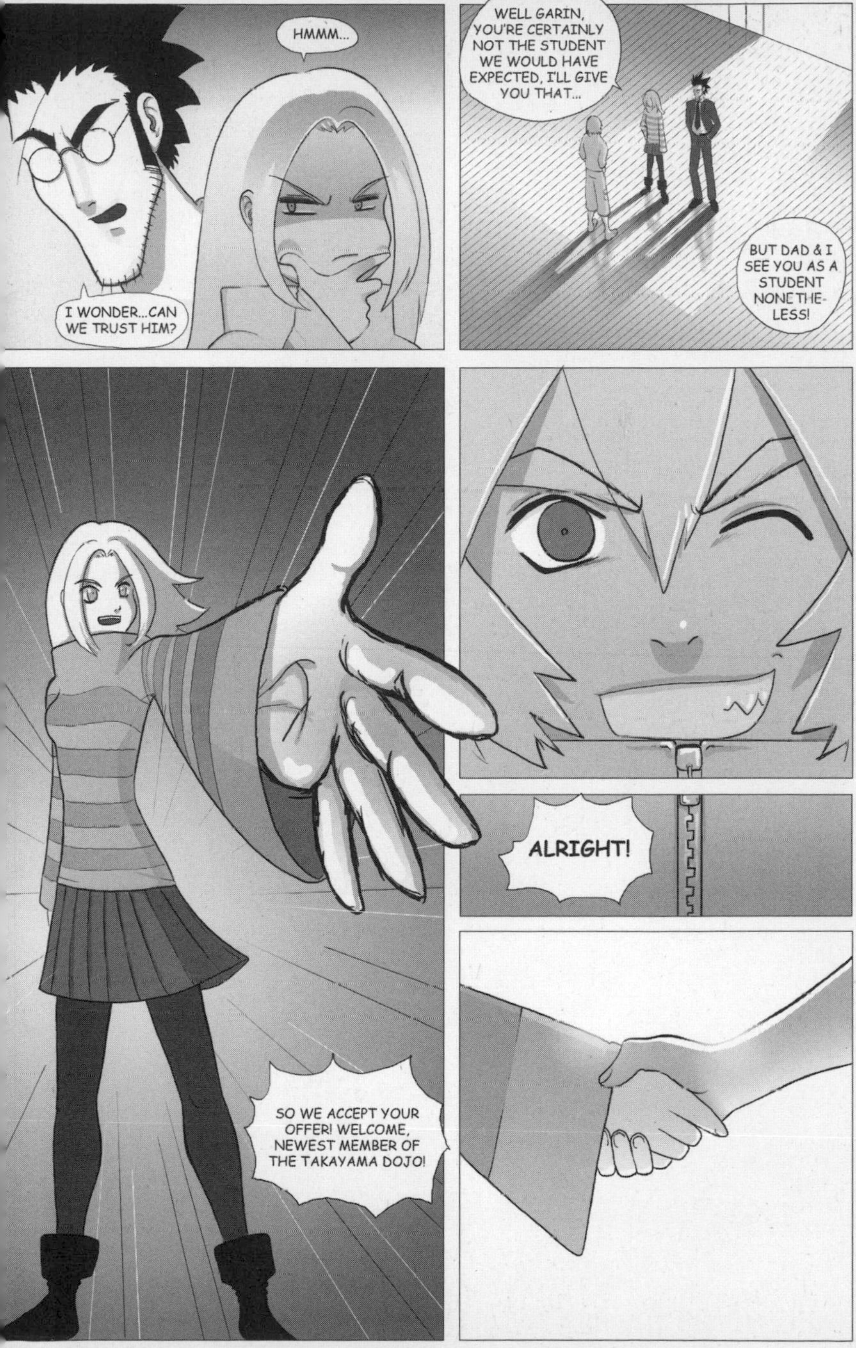
HMMM...
I WONDER...CAN WE TRUST HIM?
WELL GARIN, YOU'RE CERTAINLY NOT THE STUDENT WE WOULD HAVE EXPECTED, I'LL GIVE YOU THAT...
BUT DAD & I SEE YOU AS A STUDENT NONETHE-LESS!
SO WE ACCEPT YOUR OFFER! WELCOME, NEWEST MEMBER OF THE TAKAYAMA DOJO!
ALRIGHT!

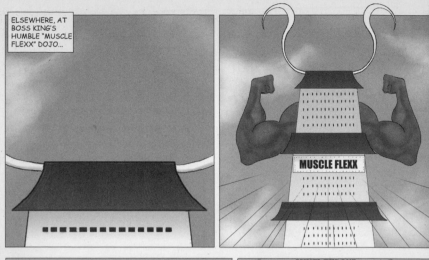

ELSEWHERE, AT BOSS KING'S HUMBLE "MUSCLE FLEXX" DOJO...

MUSCLE FLEXX

COME ON, MEN!! PUSH YOURSELVES HARDER! LIKE ME!

MULTI-THRONE

TNS

TN

IN ORDER TO BE GOOD AT ANYTHING IN LIFE, ONE MUST FIRST ACQUIRE HUGE PECTORIAL MUSCLES! MUCH LIKE THAT OF A LARGE, OILY WHALE!

HUH?

WHALES DON'T HAVE PECTORIAL SIR!

SILENCE WHILE I AM TALKING!!

BRRK!

BADAM!

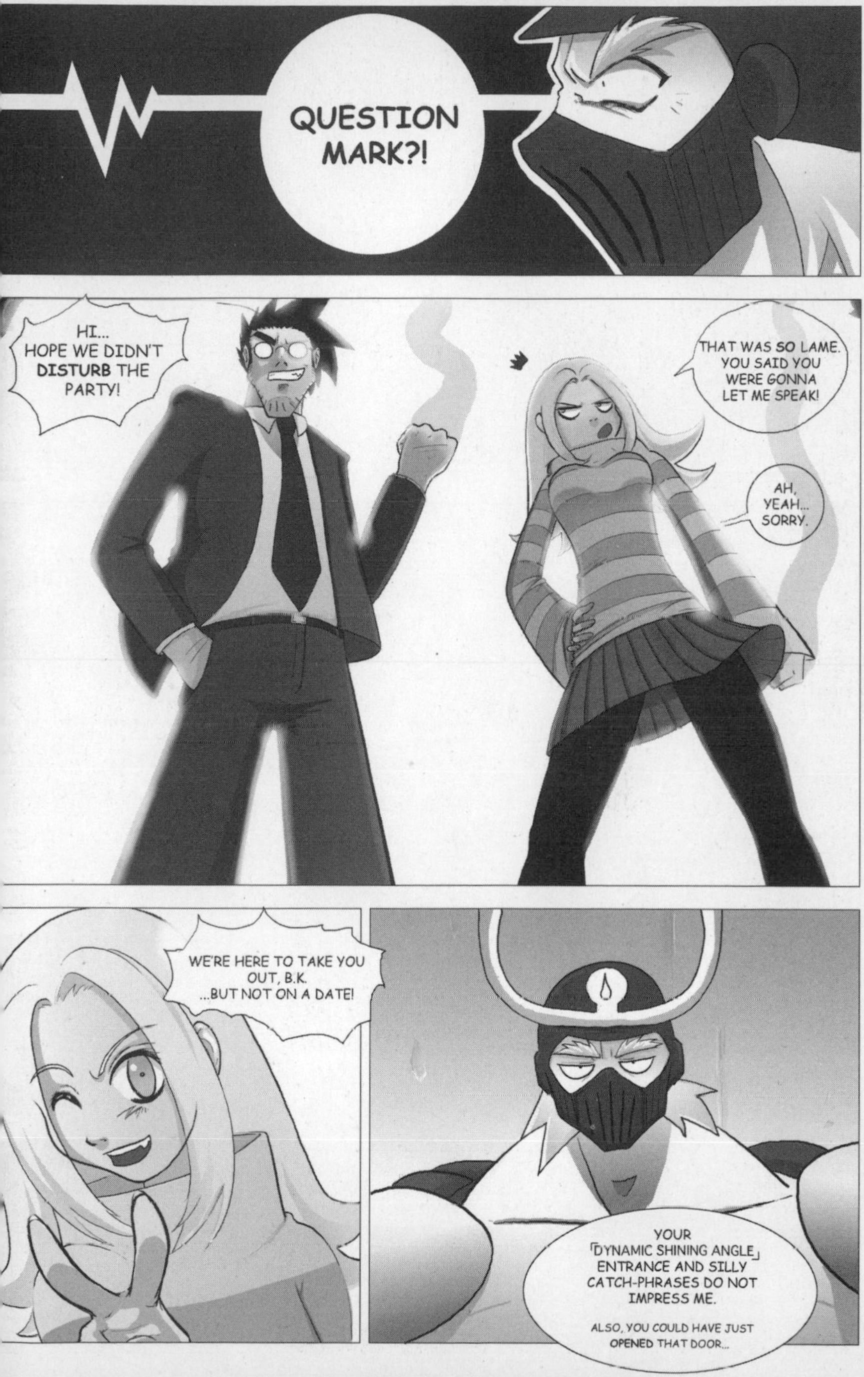
QUESTION MARK?!
HI... HOPE WE DIDN'T DISTURB THE PARTY!
THAT WAS SO LAME. YOU SAID YOU WERE GONNA LET ME SPEAK!
AH, YEAH... SORRY.
WE'RE HERE TO TAKE YOU OUT, B.K. ...BUT NOT ON A DATE!
YOUR 「DYNAMIC SHINING ANGLE」 ENTRANCE AND SILLY CATCH-PHRASES DO NOT IMPRESS ME.
ALSO, YOU COULD HAVE JUST OPENED THAT DOOR...

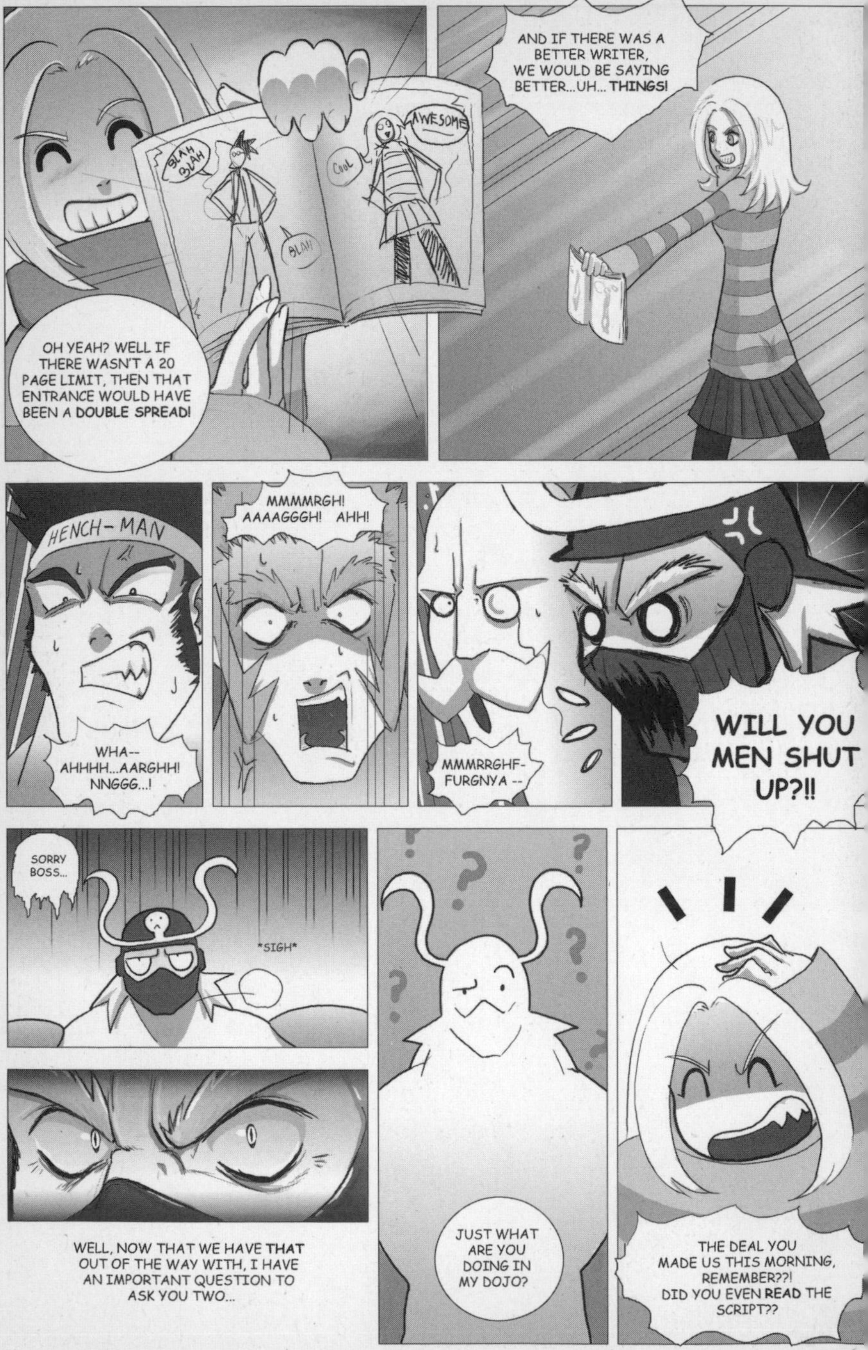
BLAH BLAH
COOL
AWESOME
BLAH
OH YEAH? WELL IF THERE WASN'T A 20 PAGE LIMIT, THEN THAT ENTRANCE WOULD HAVE BEEN A **DOUBLE SPREAD!**
AND IF THERE WAS A BETTER WRITER, WE WOULD BE SAYING BETTER...UH... **THINGS!**
HENCH-MAN
WHA-- AHHHH...AARGHH! NNGGG...!
MMMMRGH! AAAAGGGH! AHH!
MMMRRGHF-FURGNYA --
WILL YOU MEN SHUT UP?!!
SORRY BOSS...
SIGH
WELL, NOW THAT WE HAVE **THAT** OUT OF THE WAY WITH, I HAVE AN IMPORTANT QUESTION TO ASK YOU TWO...
JUST WHAT ARE YOU DOING IN MY DOJO?
THE DEAL YOU MADE US THIS MORNING, REMEMBER??! DID YOU EVEN **READ** THE SCRIPT??

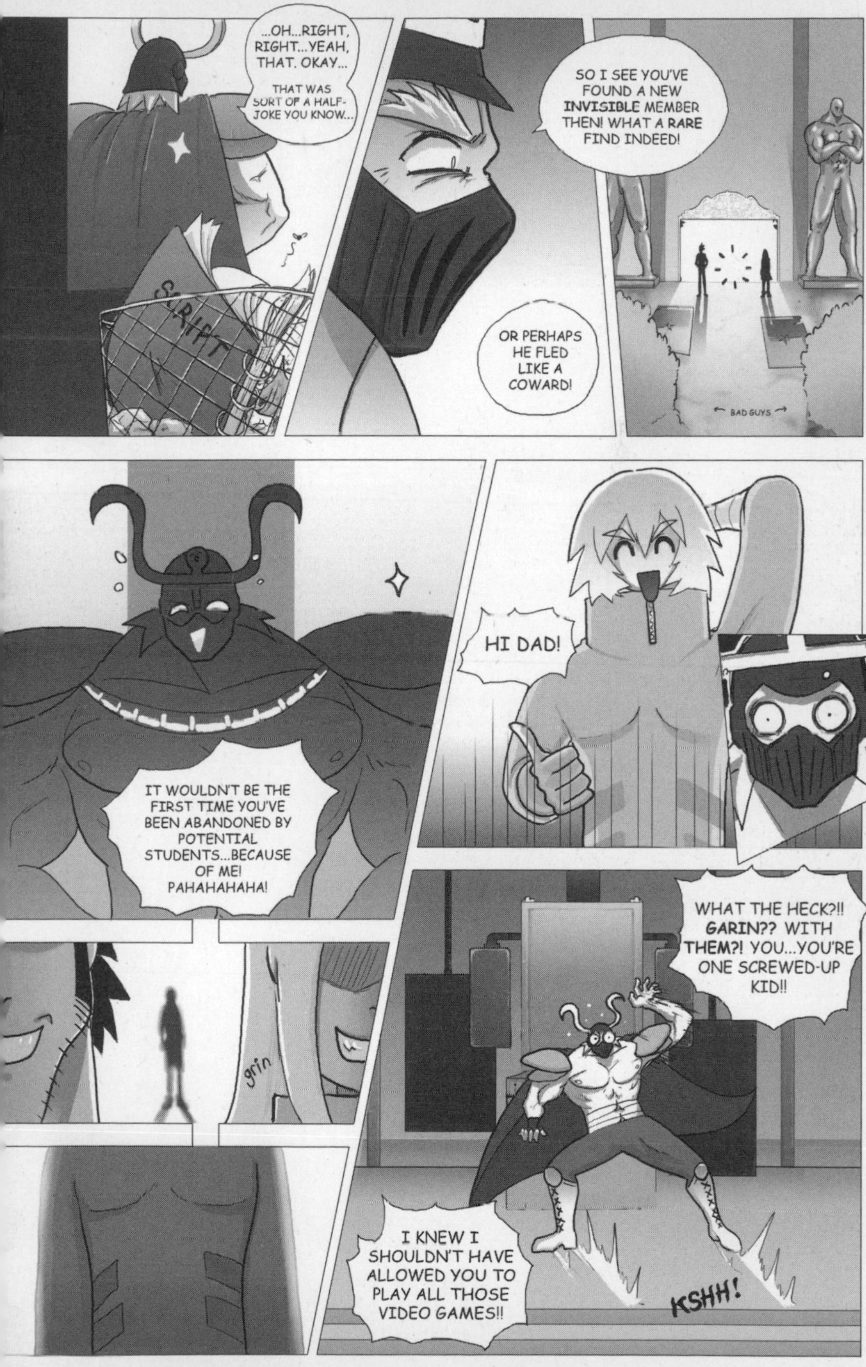
...OH...RIGHT, RIGHT...YEAH, THAT. OKAY...
THAT WAS SORT OF A HALF-JOKE YOU KNOW...
SCRIPT
SO I SEE YOU'VE FOUND A NEW INVISIBLE MEMBER THEN! WHAT A RARE FIND INDEED!
OR PERHAPS HE FLED LIKE A COWARD!
BAD GUYS
IT WOULDN'T BE THE FIRST TIME YOU'VE BEEN ABANDONED BY POTENTIAL STUDENTS...BECAUSE OF ME! PAHAHAHAHA!
HI DAD!
grin
WHAT THE HECK?!! GARIN?? WITH THEM?! YOU...YOU'RE ONE SCREWED-UP KID!!
I KNEW I SHOULDN'T HAVE ALLOWED YOU TO PLAY ALL THOSE VIDEO GAMES!!
KSHH!

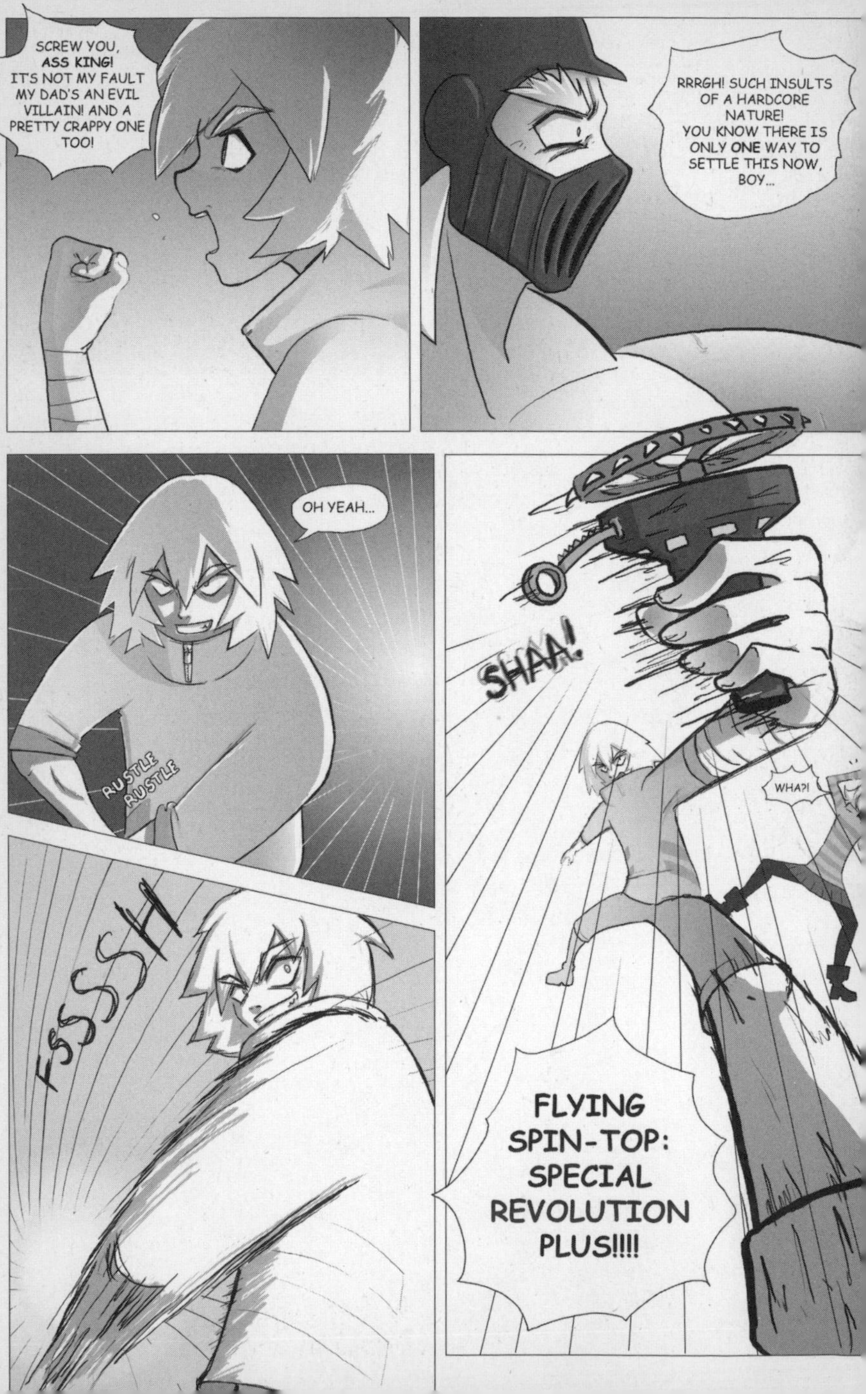

SCREW YOU, ASS KING! IT'S NOT MY FAULT MY DAD'S AN EVIL VILLAIN! AND A PRETTY CRAPPY ONE TOO!
RRRGH! SUCH INSULTS OF A HARDCORE NATURE! YOU KNOW THERE IS ONLY ONE WAY TO SETTLE THIS NOW, BOY...
OH YEAH...
RUSTLE RUSTLE
FSSSSH
SHAA!
WHA?!
FLYING SPIN-TOP: SPECIAL REVOLUTION PLUS!!!!

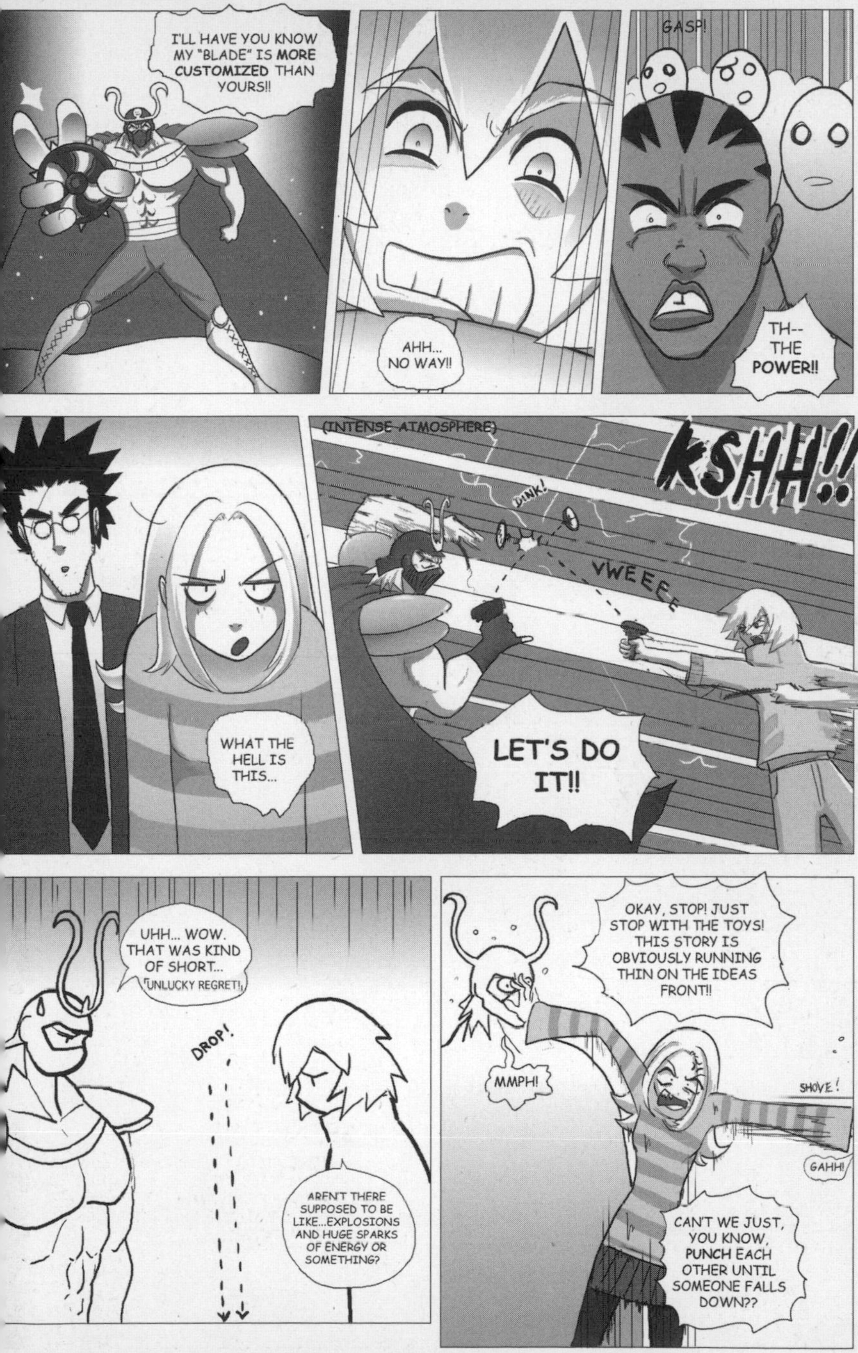
I'LL HAVE YOU KNOW MY "BLADE" IS MORE CUSTOMIZED THAN YOURS!!
AHH... NO WAY!!
GASP!
TH-- THE POWER!!
WHAT THE HELL IS THIS...
(INTENSE ATMOSPHERE)
KSHH!!
DINK!
VWEEEE
LET'S DO IT!!
UHH... WOW. THAT WAS KIND OF SHORT...
「UNLUCKY REGRET!」
DROP!
AREN'T THERE SUPPOSED TO BE LIKE...EXPLOSIONS AND HUGE SPARKS OF ENERGY OR SOMETHING?
OKAY, STOP! JUST STOP WITH THE TOYS! THIS STORY IS OBVIOUSLY RUNNING THIN ON THE IDEAS FRONT!!
MMPH!
SHOVE!
GAHH!
CAN'T WE JUST, YOU KNOW, PUNCH EACH OTHER UNTIL SOMEONE FALLS DOWN??

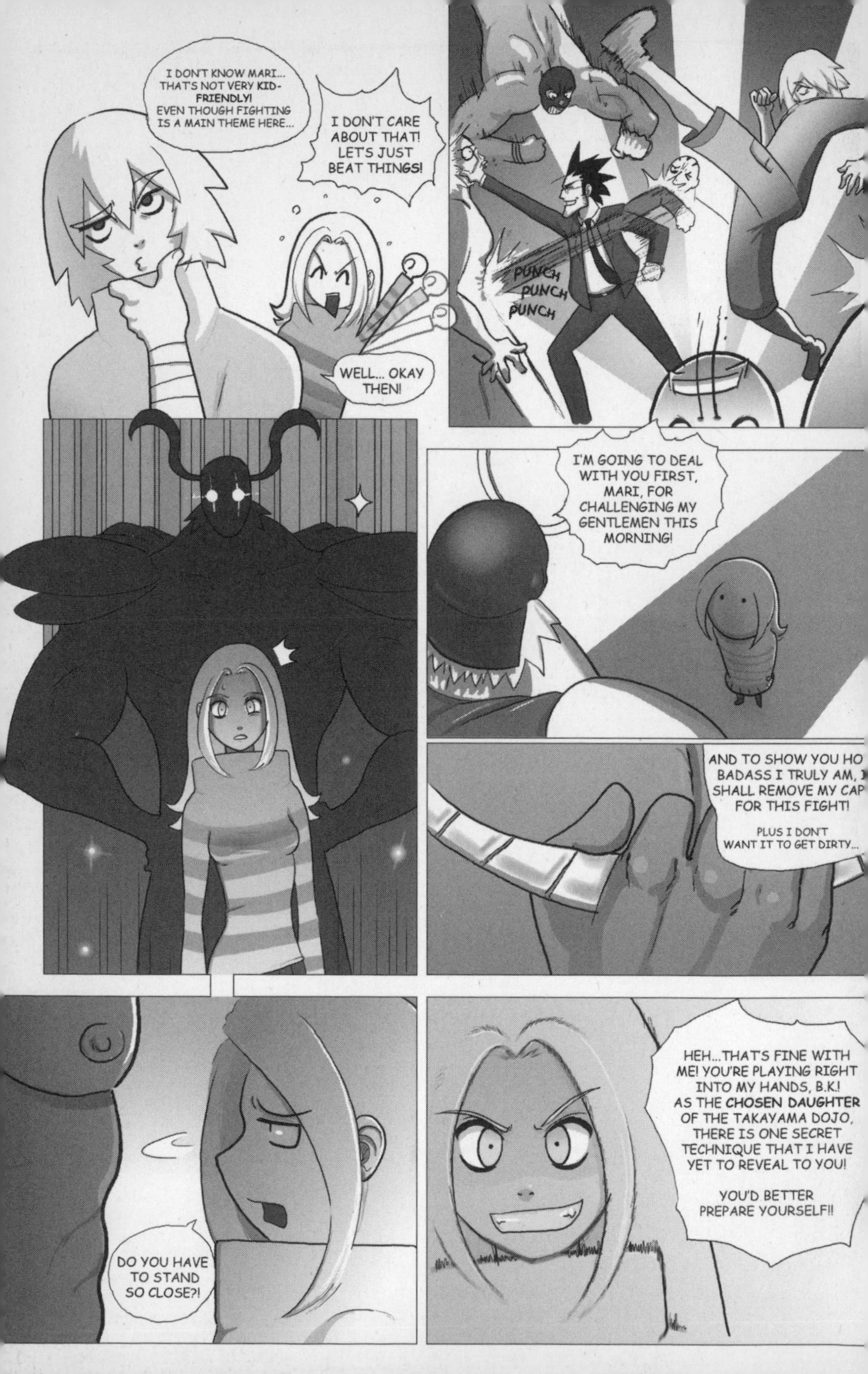

I DON'T KNOW MARI... THAT'S NOT VERY **KID-FRIENDLY!** EVEN THOUGH FIGHTING IS A MAIN THEME HERE...
I DON'T CARE ABOUT THAT! LET'S JUST BEAT THINGS!
WELL... OKAY THEN!
PUNCH PUNCH PUNCH
I'M GOING TO DEAL WITH YOU FIRST, MARI, FOR CHALLENGING MY GENTLEMEN THIS MORNING!
AND TO SHOW YOU HO BADASS I TRULY AM, SHALL REMOVE MY CAP FOR THIS FIGHT!
PLUS I DON'T WANT IT TO GET DIRTY...
DO YOU HAVE TO STAND SO CLOSE?!
HEH...THAT'S FINE WITH ME! YOU'RE PLAYING RIGHT INTO MY HANDS, B.K.! AS THE **CHOSEN DAUGHTER** OF THE TAKAYAMA DOJO, THERE IS ONE SECRET TECHNIQUE THAT I HAVE YET TO REVEAL TO YOU!
YOU'D BETTER PREPARE YOURSELF!!

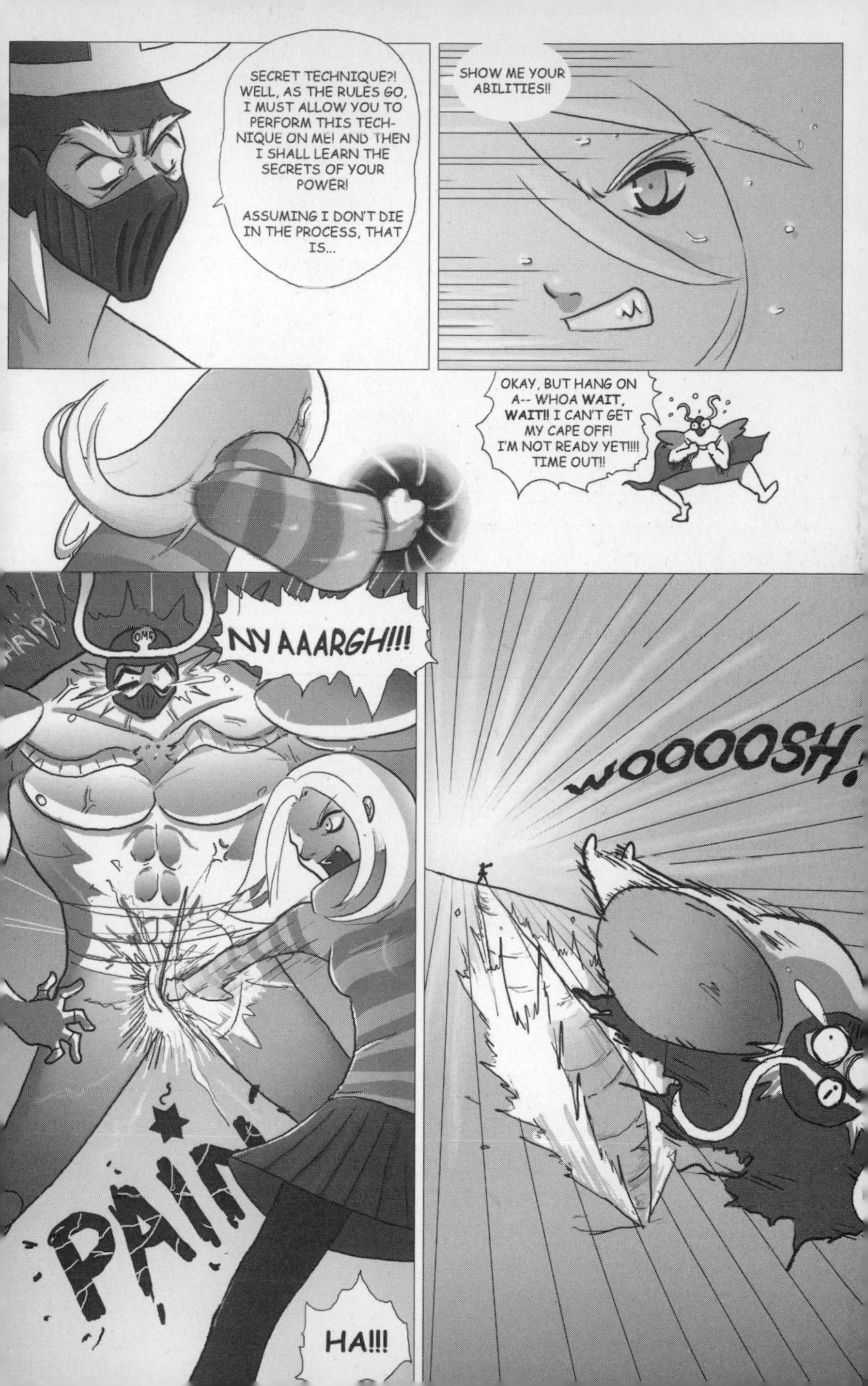
SECRET TECHNIQUE?! WELL, AS THE RULES GO, I MUST ALLOW YOU TO PERFORM THIS TECHNIQUE ON ME! AND THEN I SHALL LEARN THE SECRETS OF YOUR POWER!
ASSUMING I DON'T DIE IN THE PROCESS, THAT IS...
SHOW ME YOUR ABILITIES!!
OKAY, BUT HANG ON A-- WHOA WAIT, WAIT!! I CAN'T GET MY CAPE OFF! I'M NOT READY YET!!!! TIME OUT!!
RIP!
OMG
NYAAARGH!!!
PAIN
HA!!!
WOOOOSH!

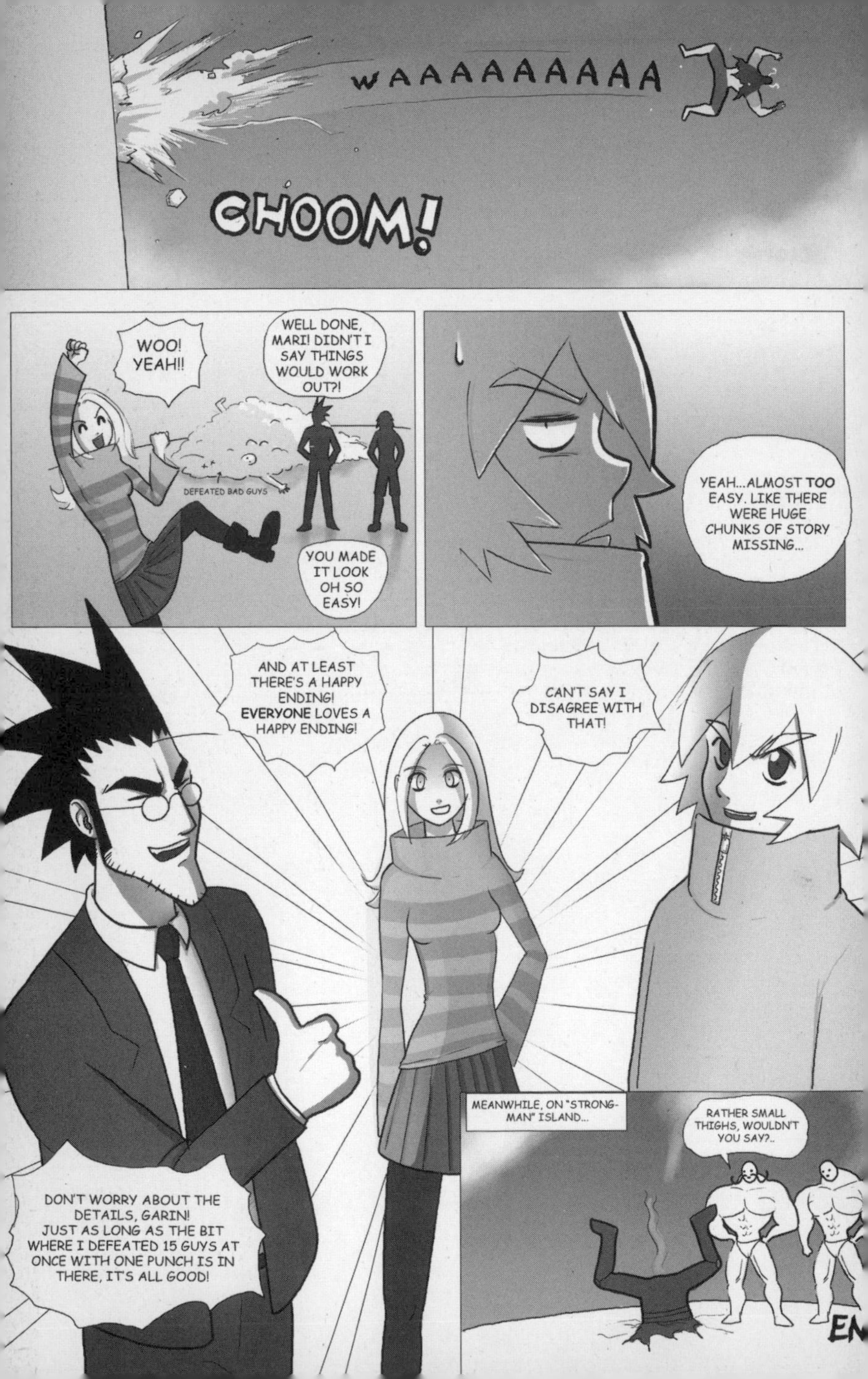
WAAAAAAAAAA
CHOOM!
WOO! YEAH!!
WELL DONE, MARI! DIDN'T I SAY THINGS WOULD WORK OUT?!
DEFEATED BAD GUYS
YOU MADE IT LOOK OH SO EASY!
YEAH...ALMOST **TOO** EASY. LIKE THERE WERE HUGE CHUNKS OF STORY MISSING...
AND AT LEAST THERE'S A HAPPY ENDING! **EVERYONE** LOVES A HAPPY ENDING!
CAN'T SAY I DISAGREE WITH THAT!
DON'T WORRY ABOUT THE DETAILS, GARIN! JUST AS LONG AS THE BIT WHERE I DEFEATED 15 GUYS AT ONCE WITH ONE PUNCH IS IN THERE, IT'S ALL GOOD!
MEANWHILE, ON "STRONG-MAN" ISLAND...
RATHER SMALL THIGHS, WOULDN'T YOU SAY?..

LEGEND OF THE FUTURE :: Runner Up ::

....

Jin Sun Oh was born Seoul, South Korea in 1970. She now lives in Nottingham, England where she works as a freelance illustrator. www.jinsunoh.com

Favorite manga:
Nausicaa and *Conan* by Hayao Miyazaki

Favorite manga artist:
Hayao Miyazaki, Ji-yun Kim, Yumiko Igarashi

....

Author's Comments:
I created this comic after I got inspired by a daydream (believe it or not). Immediately after the dream, I started drawing until I finished the first episode. I've always liked to draw action scenes with dynamic angles, just like in SF/Fantasy movies. I was quite pleased with the result. It was great fun. This is the kind of fun that I want to have more of.
—*Jin Sun Oh*

::

LEGEND OF THE FUTURE

RUNNER UP RISING.STARS.OF.MANGA.2006

::

LEGEND OF THE FUTURE :: Runner Up ::

....

Judge's Comments:
One of the best things about manga is its ability to teleport a reader to a different world with a few key illustrations. In Jin Sun Oh's "Legend of the Future," we're instantly transported to a world of dragons and giant falcons from the very first panel. Look to Jin Sun's art for the reason. The thin, confident line work helps the pages spring to life. Scenes such as our heroine's jubilant leap off the cliff near the end vibrantly capture the moment, allowing us to experience every victory and near-defeat with her. Fully rendered backgrounds help establish the world, while dynamic manga-styled panel layouts and dramatic use of the artist's camera hook us early on and keep us reading to the last page...

...where we discover that this *Rising Stars of Manga* entry is just the beginning of a larger story and lacks a proper ending. This isn't unusual, and it's certainly not the first time that an entry without a satisfying conclusion was chosen as a finalist. However, this may go down as the finalist that was most hurt by its lack of ending. The strength of its art was enough to ensure "Legend of the Future's" place as a finalist, however, if Jin Sun had chosen to tell a complete story, it's likely that she would have made the top three, if not win the Grand Prize.

That said, Jin Sun's accomplishment with "Legend of the Future" is significant, and with any luck, the future will find Jin Sun finishing her great manga.
—*Tim Beedle*

Judge's Comments:
"Legend of the Future" is a very beautiful, fluid manga sequence. This is both its greatest asset and its almost fatal flaw. The visual storytelling, with its fast pace and dynamic panel composition, really makes this piece come alive. Everything has a very animated quality that makes you feel like it's about to jump off the page. From the body language to the line work, each element is quite expressive and clearly moves the reader through the action. In terms of story, however, the work is sorely lacking—so much so that it almost didn't make it into the book. The problem is not so much that the story is bad, it's just not complete. I call it a sequence because that's all it is—a single progression of shots illustrating an action scene. No set up, no motivations and almost no characterization to speak of. It's obvious that the characters know each other, but their relationship remains unclear. That having been said, the piece is still an enjoyable read. Where the story may fail in grabbing the reader's attention, the visuals more than make up for it by really pulling you in and not letting go. Perhaps given more pages, Jin Sun Oh could have spun a far deeper tale. With a strong entry like "Legend of the Future," she may soon get that chance!
—*Aaron Suhr*

::

74

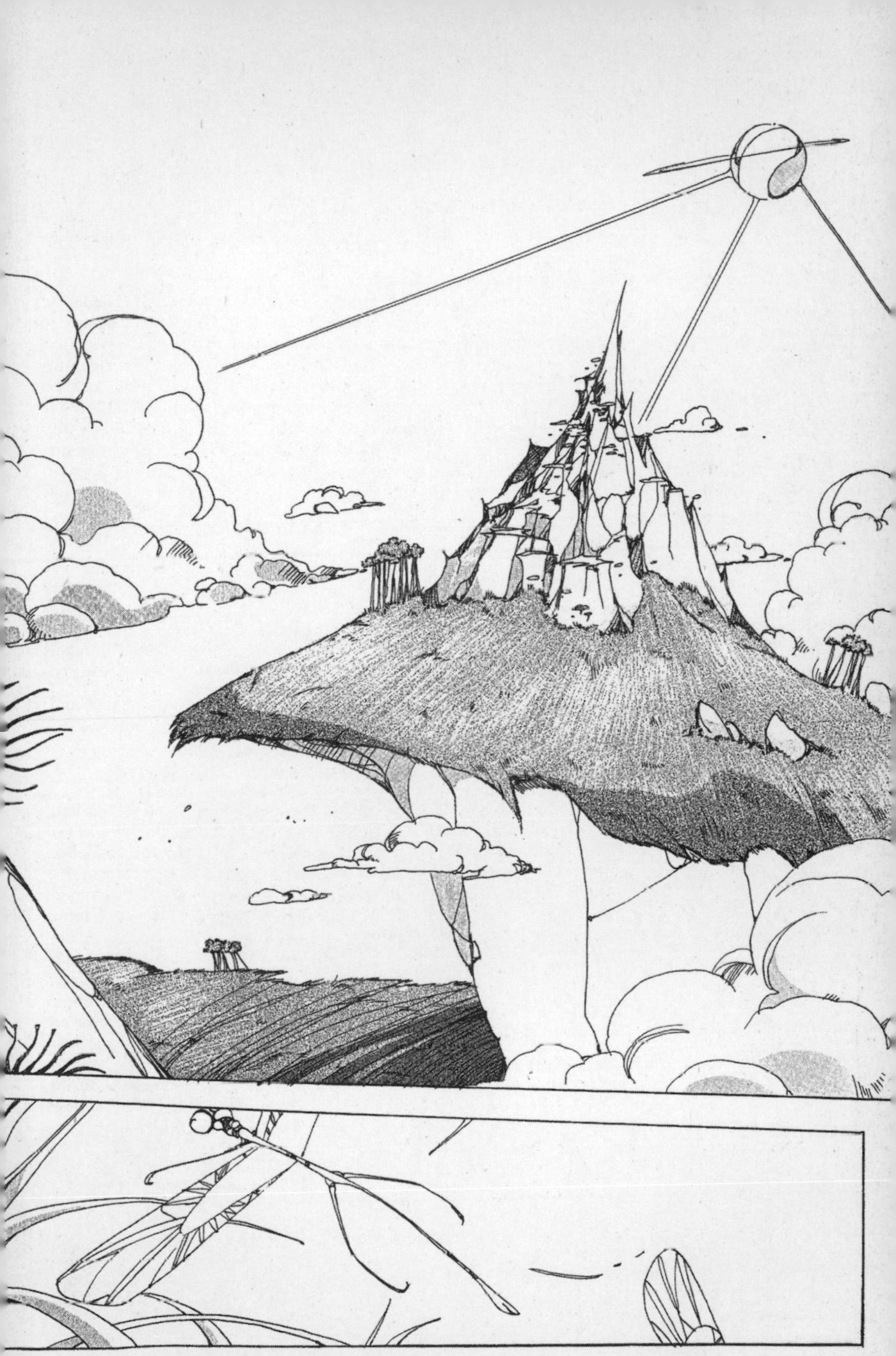

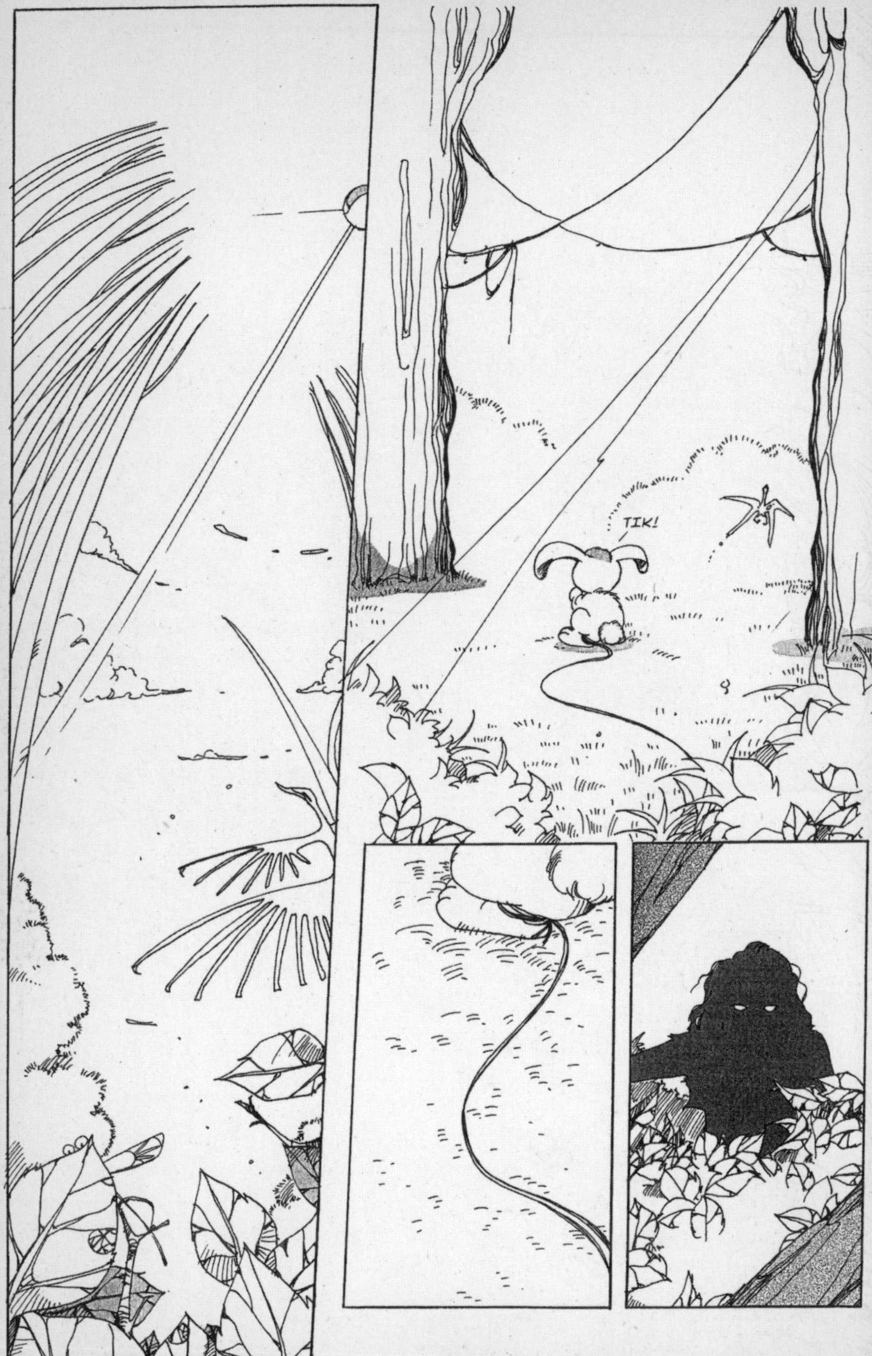
TIK!

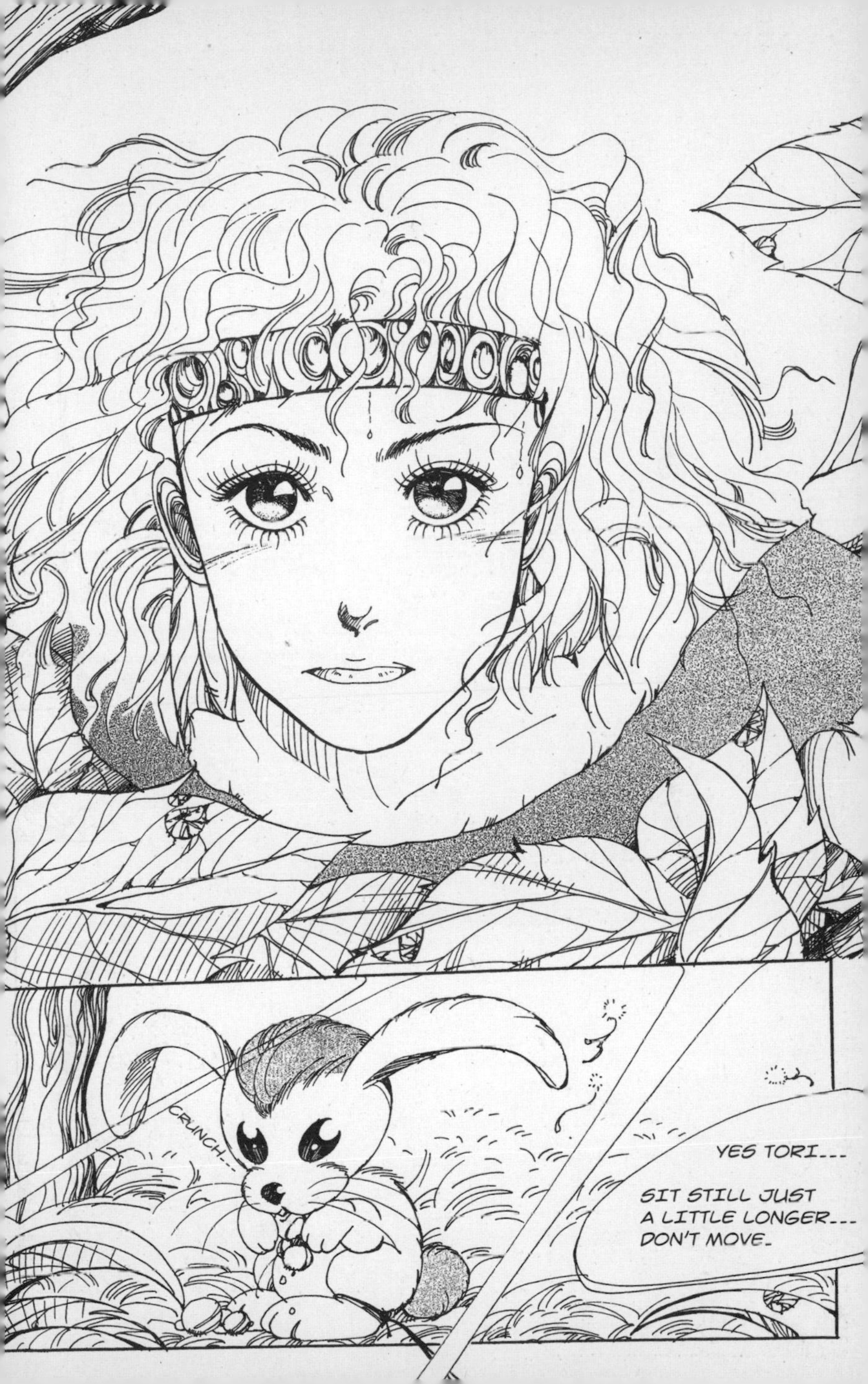
CRUNCH...
YES TORI...
SIT STILL JUST A LITTLE LONGER... DON'T MOVE.

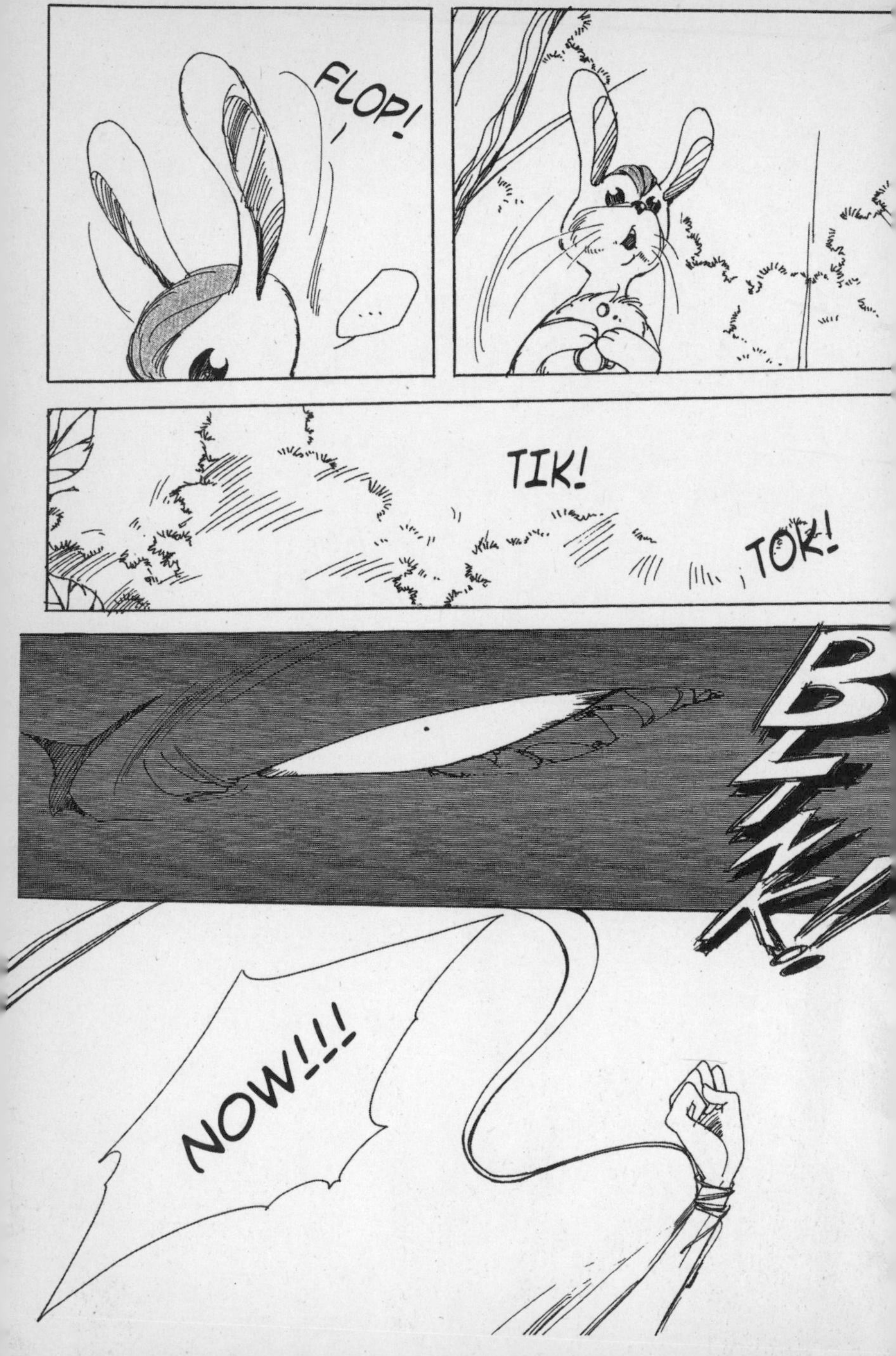
FLOP!
...
TIK!
TOK!
BLINK!
NOW!!!

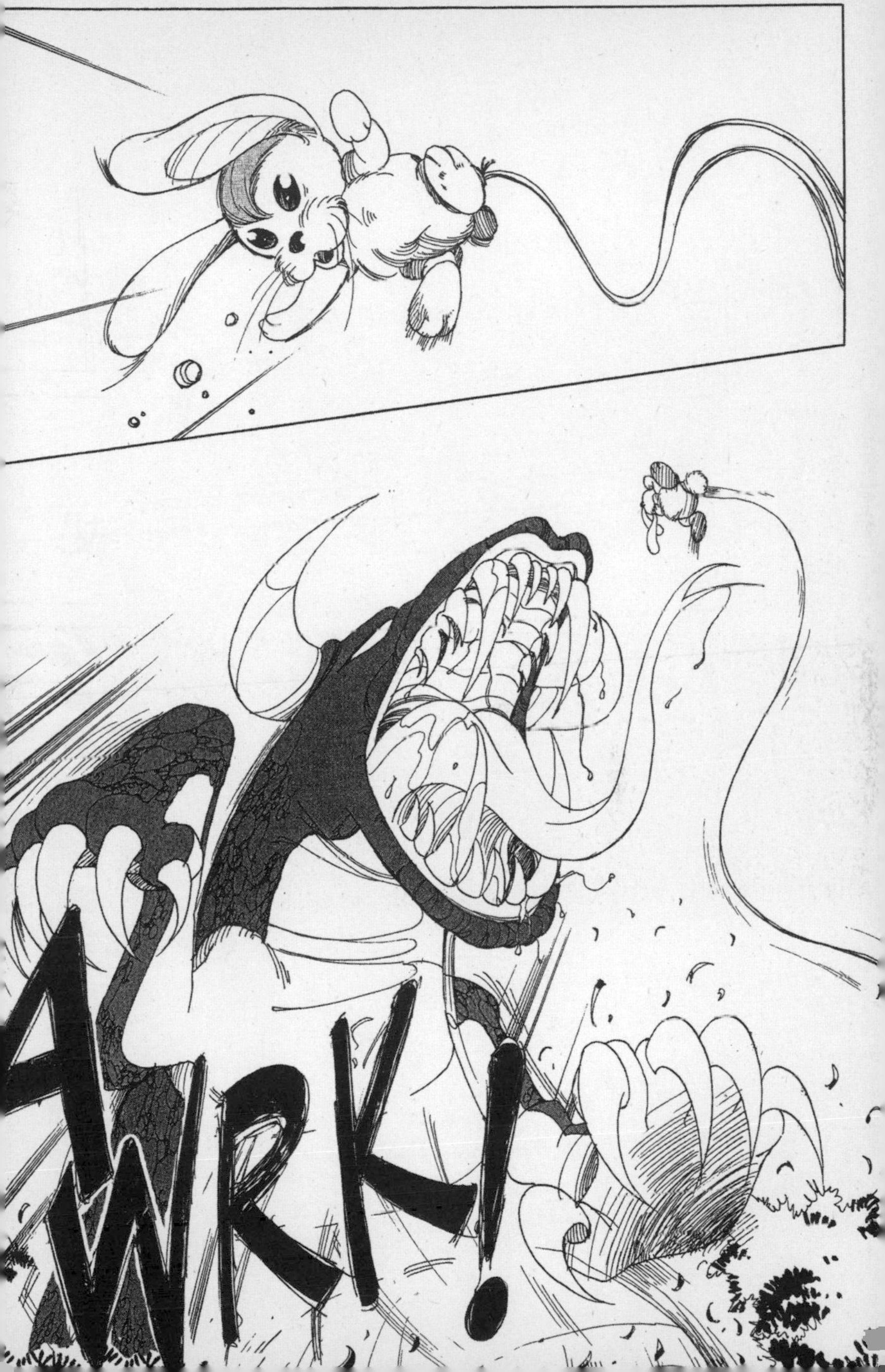
AWRK!

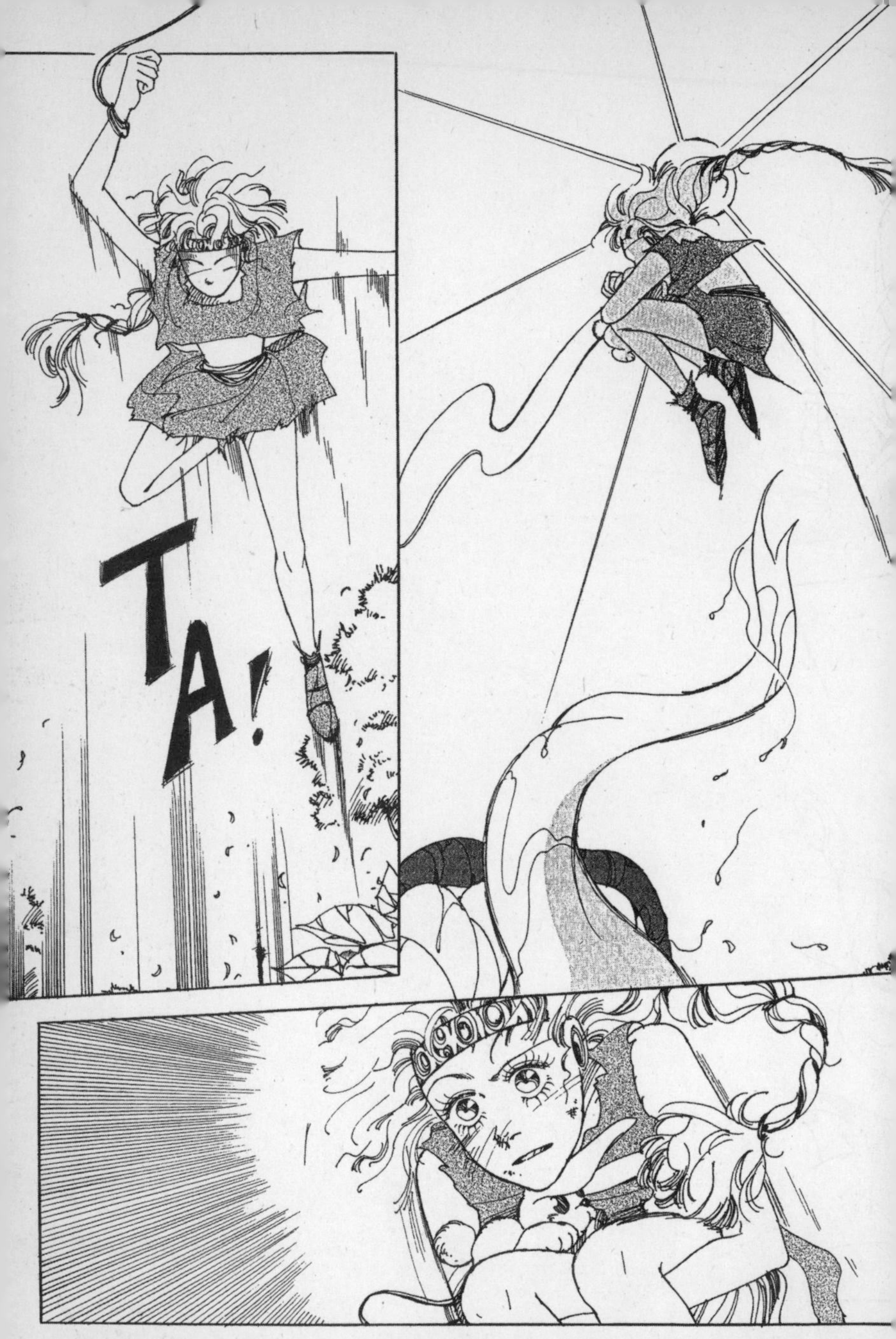
TA!

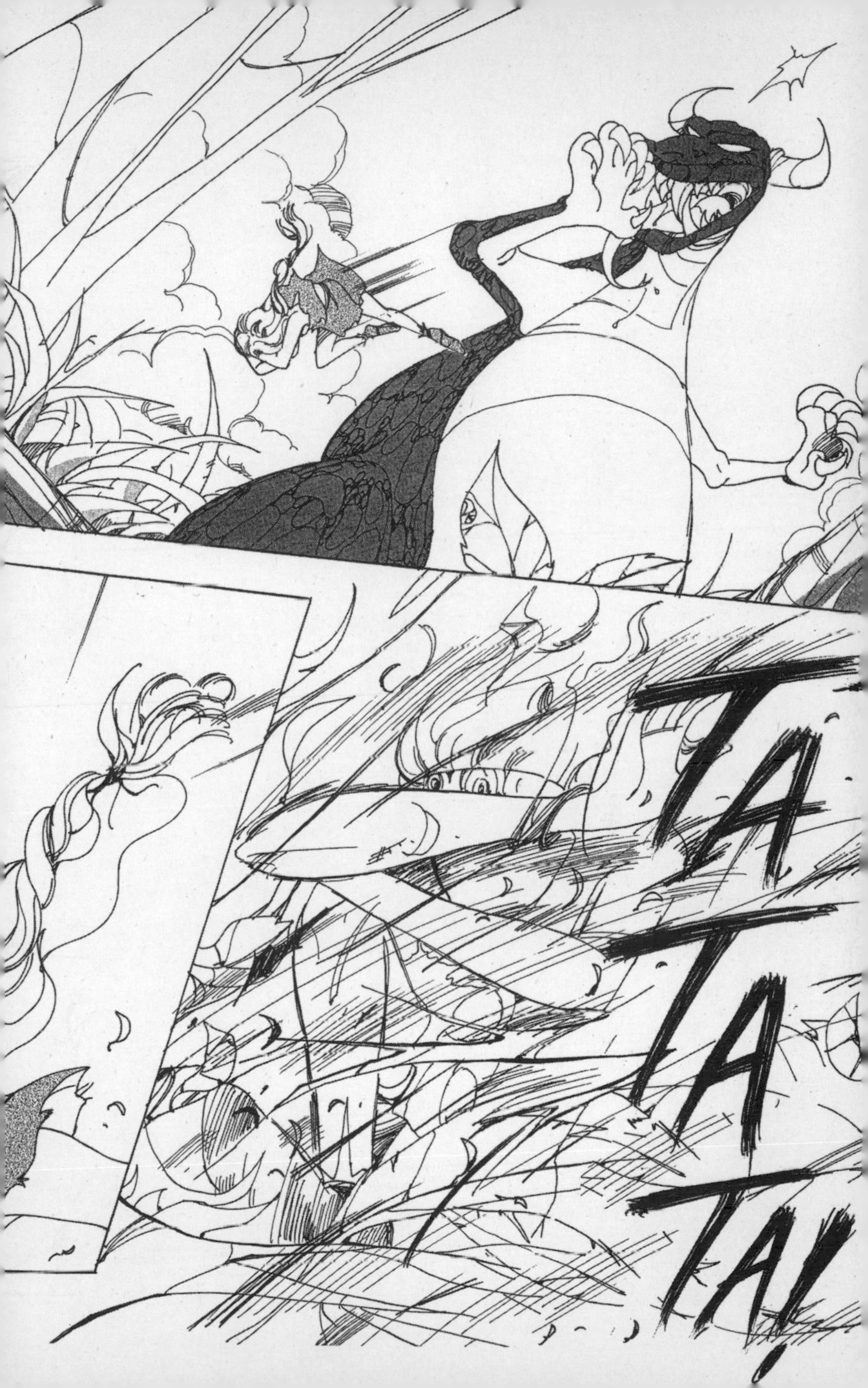
TA TA TA!

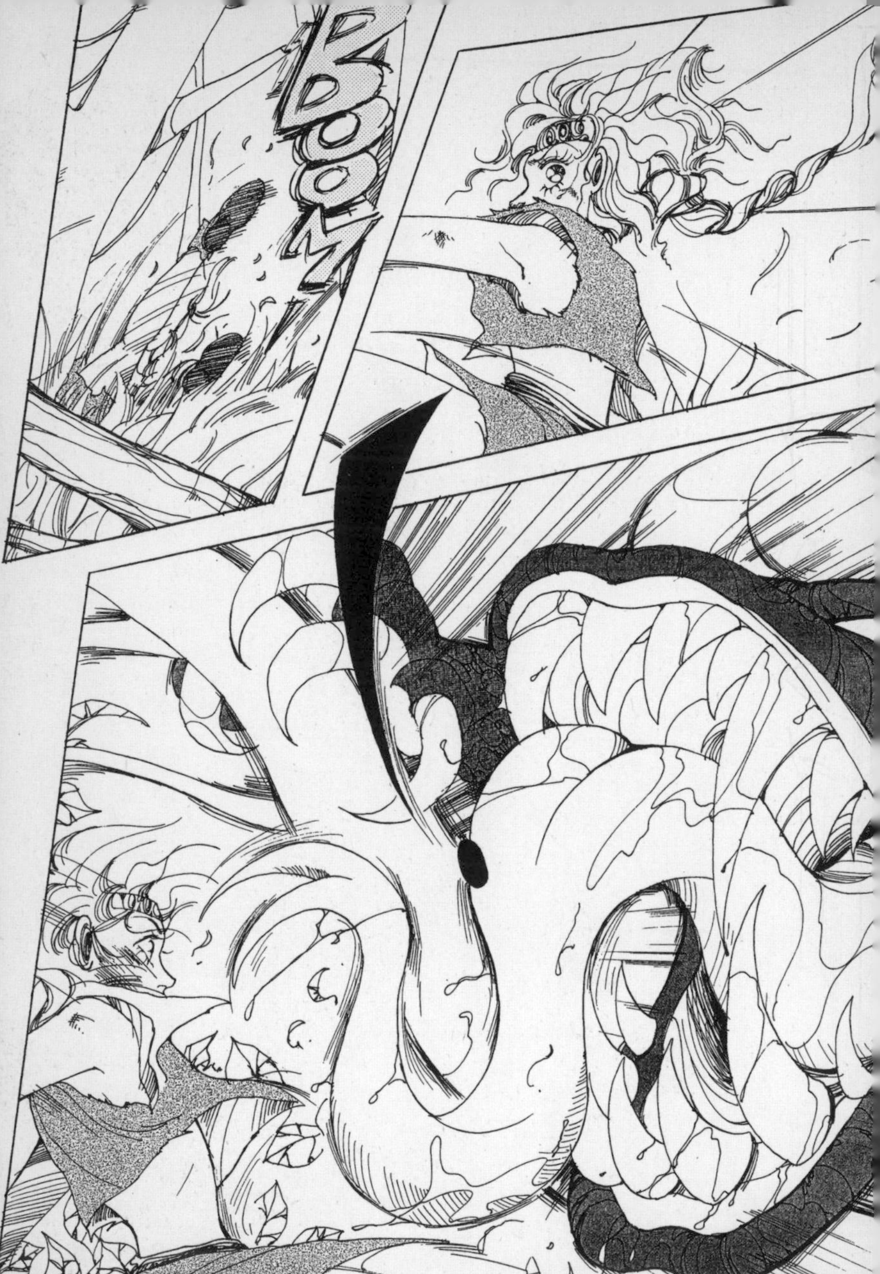
BADOOM

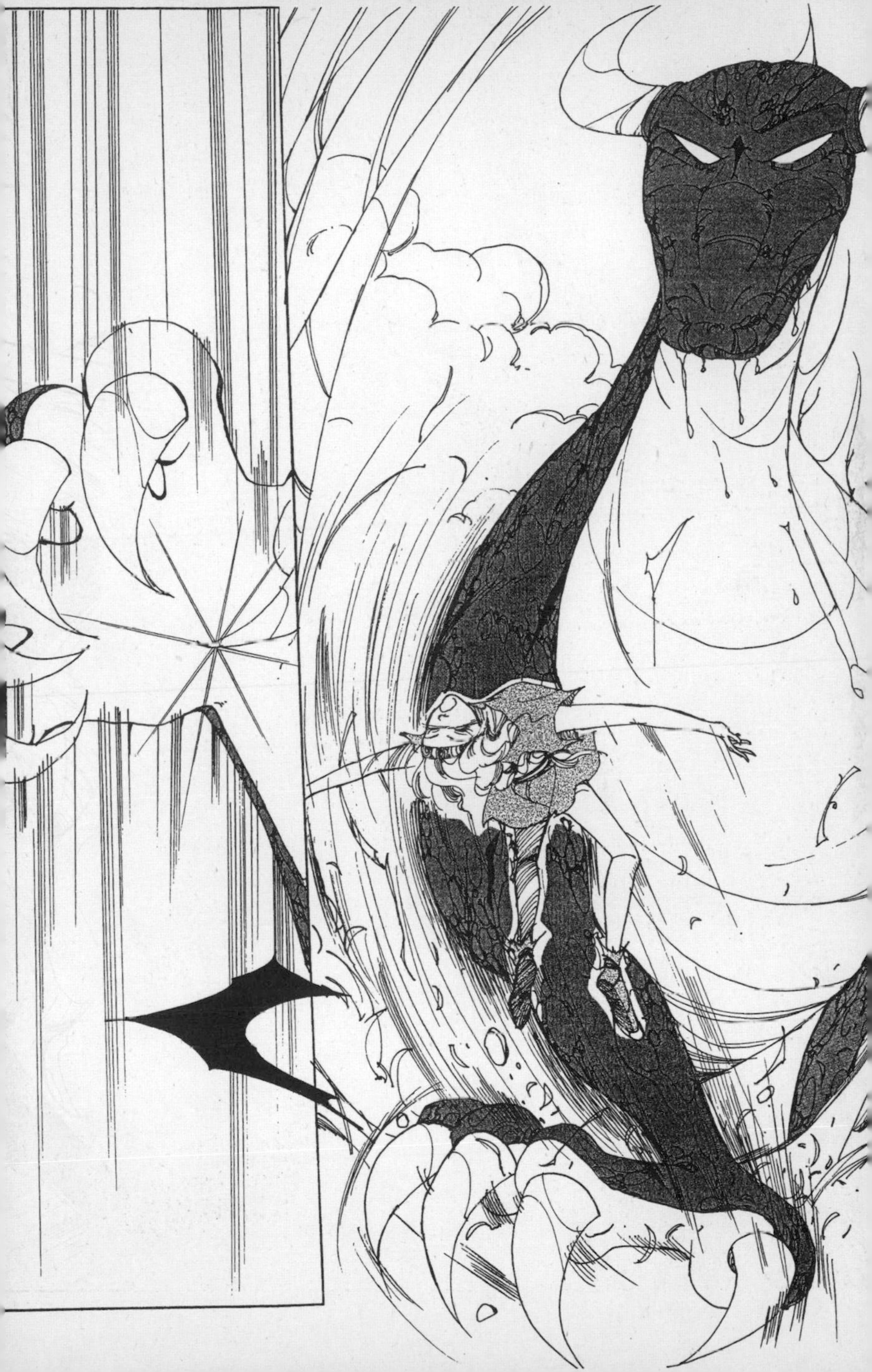

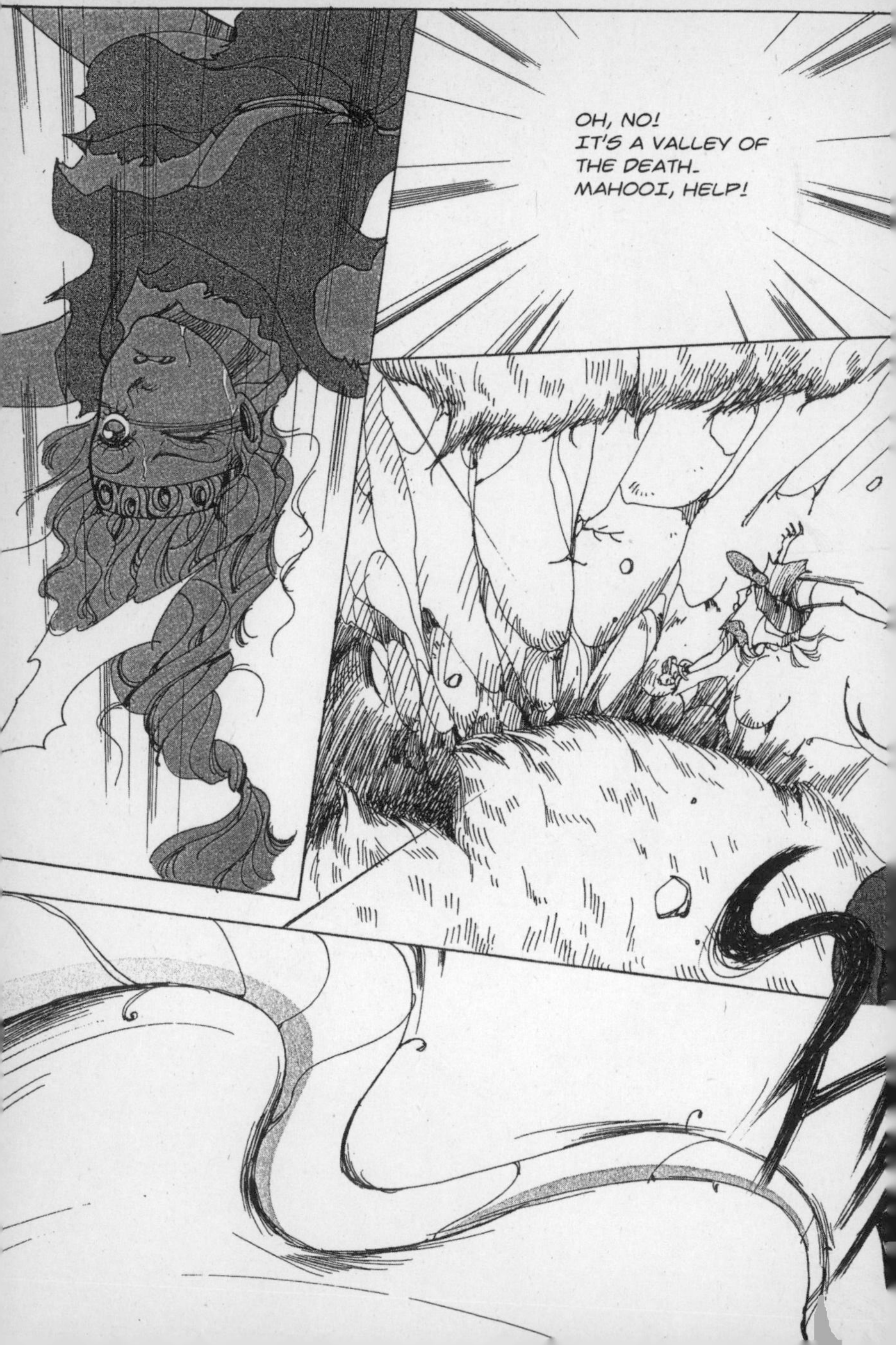
OH, NO!
IT'S A VALLEY OF
THE DEATH.
MAHOOI, HELP!

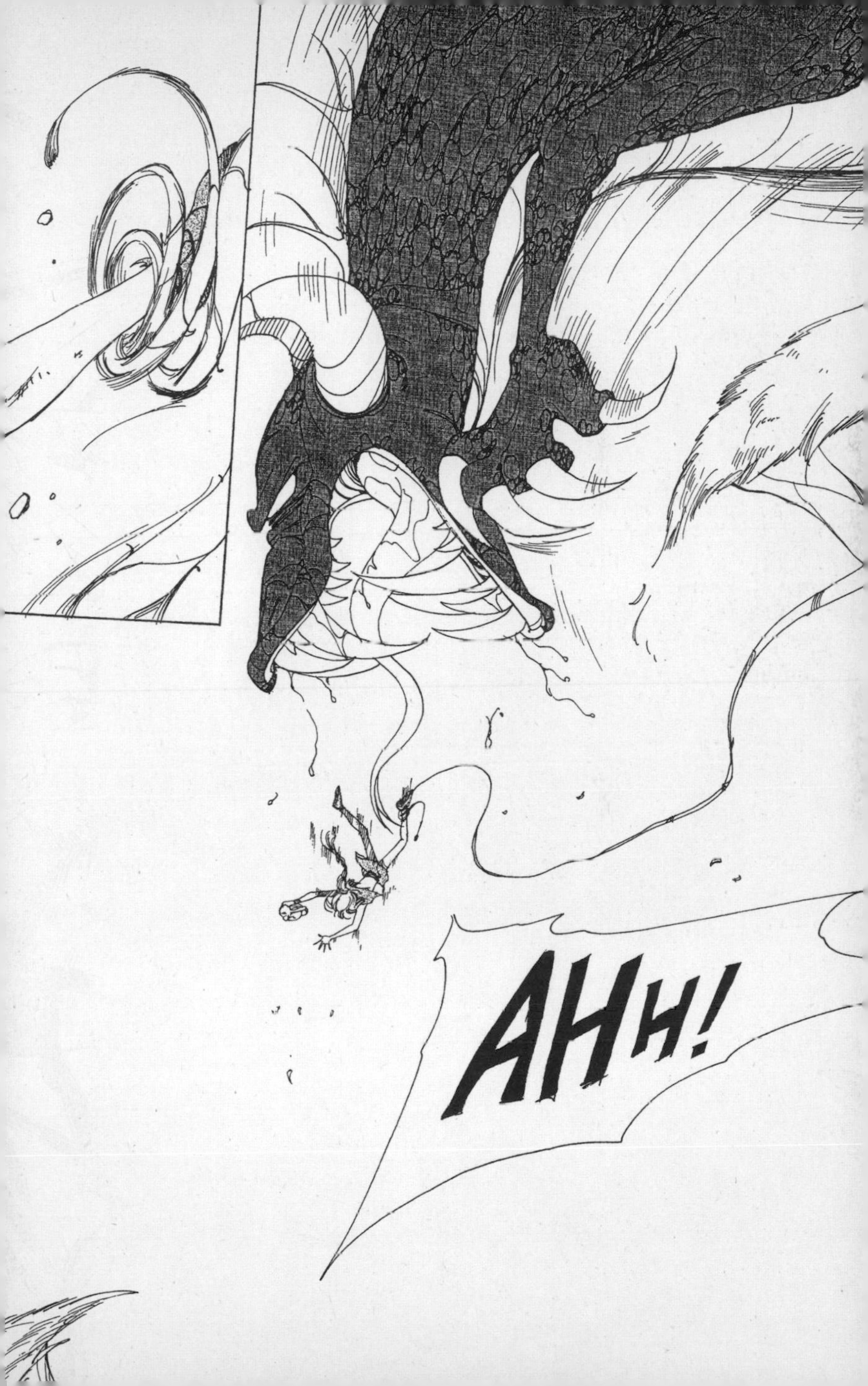
AHH!

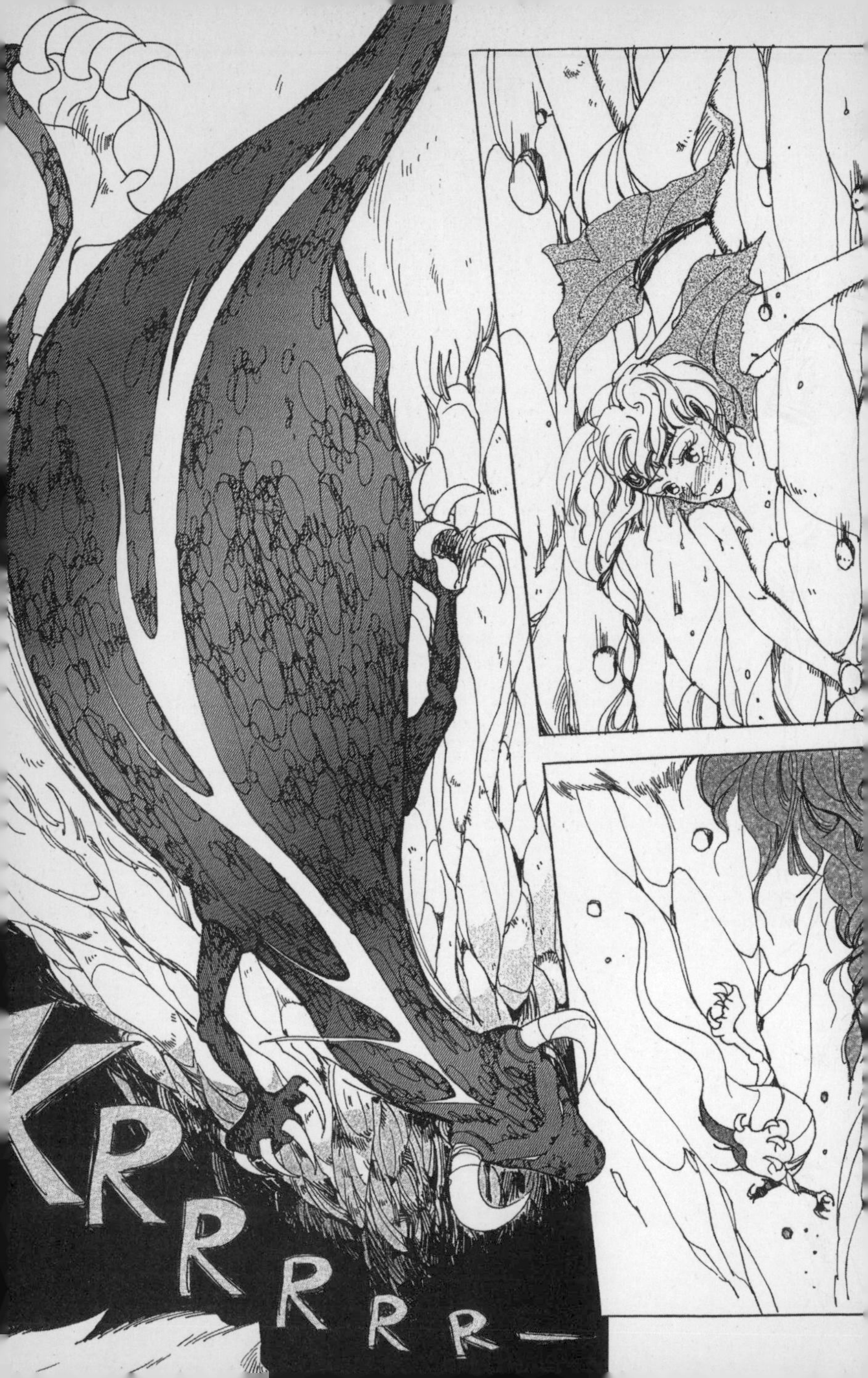
KRRRRR—

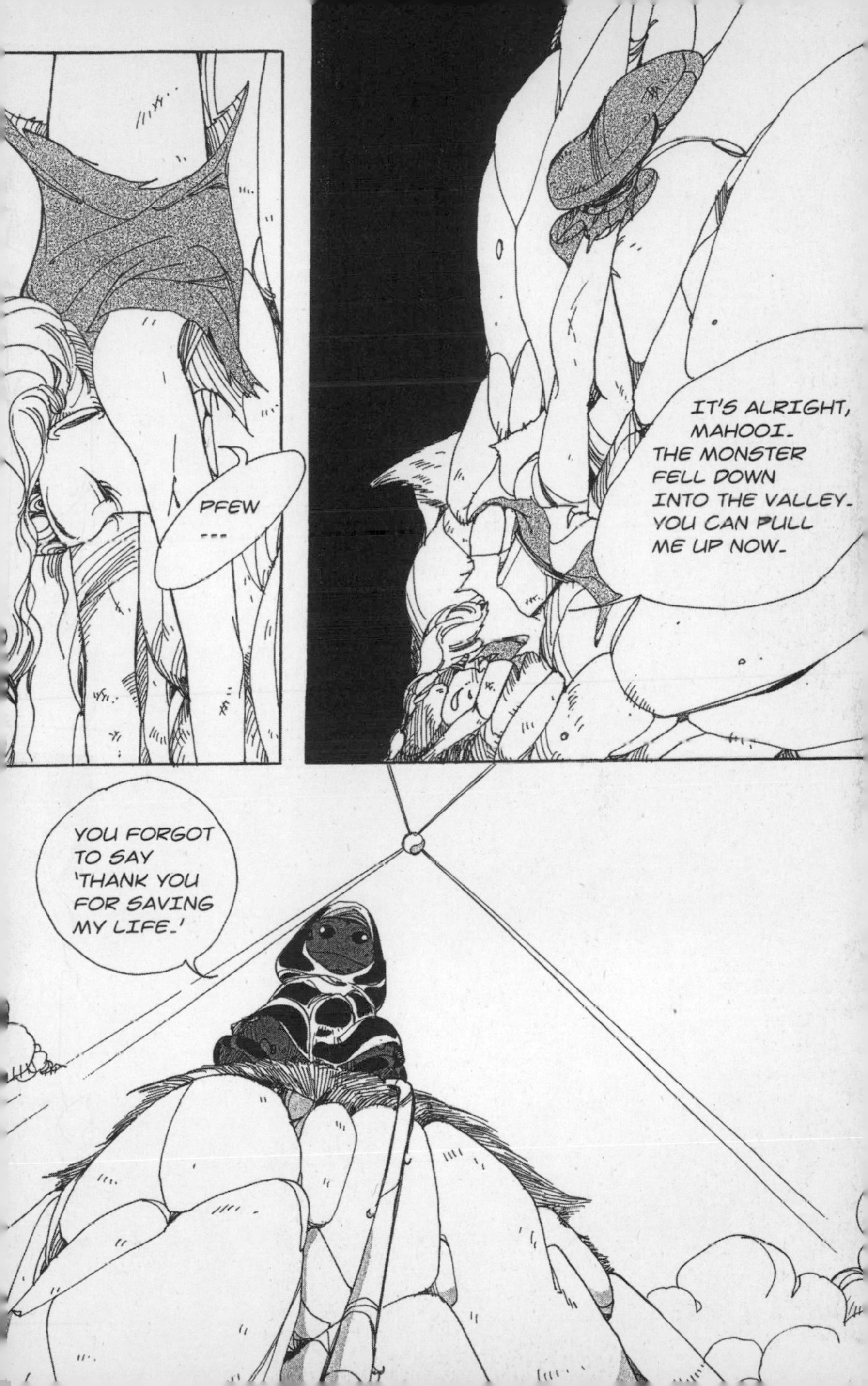
PFEW ---
IT'S ALRIGHT, MAHOOI. THE MONSTER FELL DOWN INTO THE VALLEY. YOU CAN PULL ME UP NOW.
YOU FORGOT TO SAY 'THANK YOU FOR SAVING MY LIFE.'

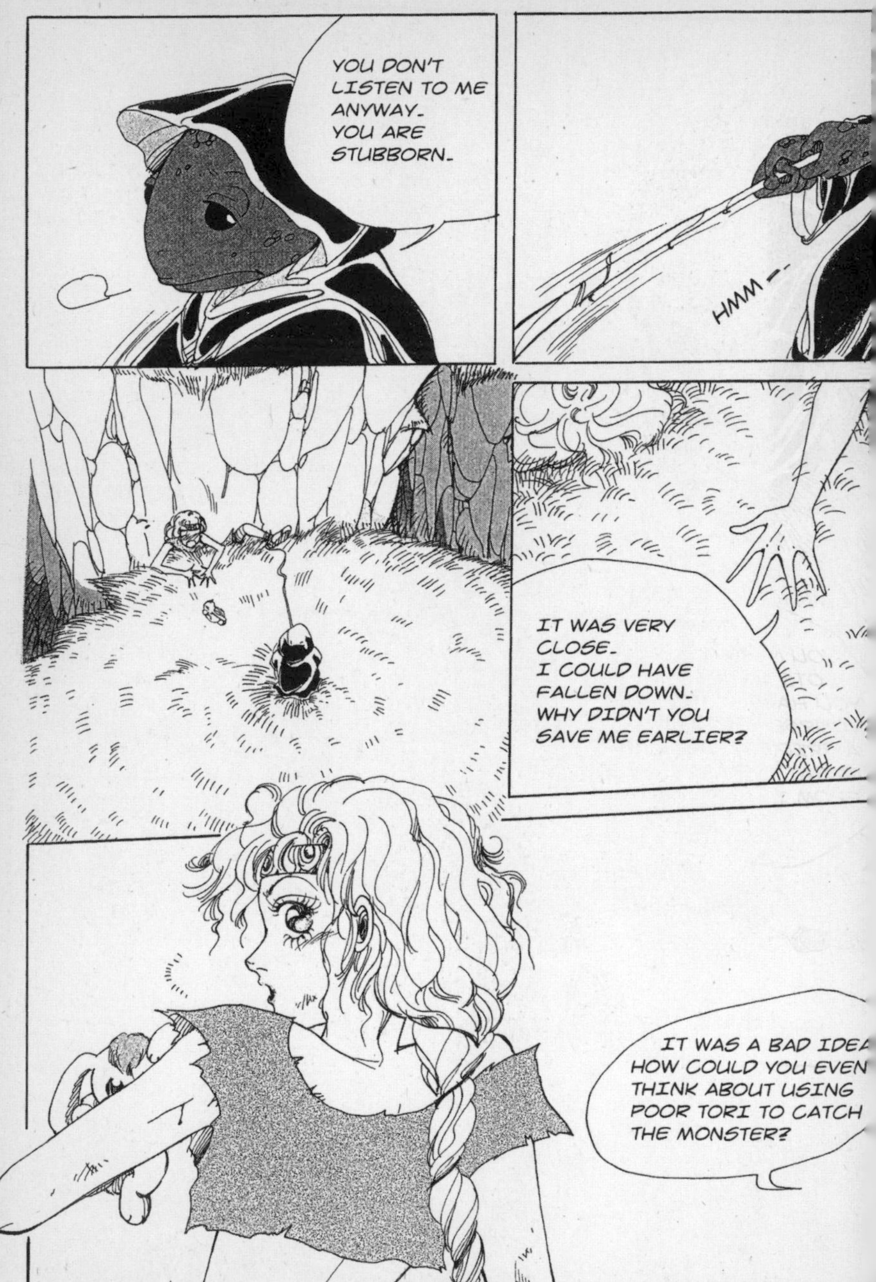
YOU DON'T LISTEN TO ME ANYWAY. YOU ARE STUBBORN.
HMM...
IT WAS VERY CLOSE. I COULD HAVE FALLEN DOWN. WHY DIDN'T YOU SAVE ME EARLIER?
IT WAS A BAD IDEA HOW COULD YOU EVEN THINK ABOUT USING POOR TORI TO CATCH THE MONSTER?

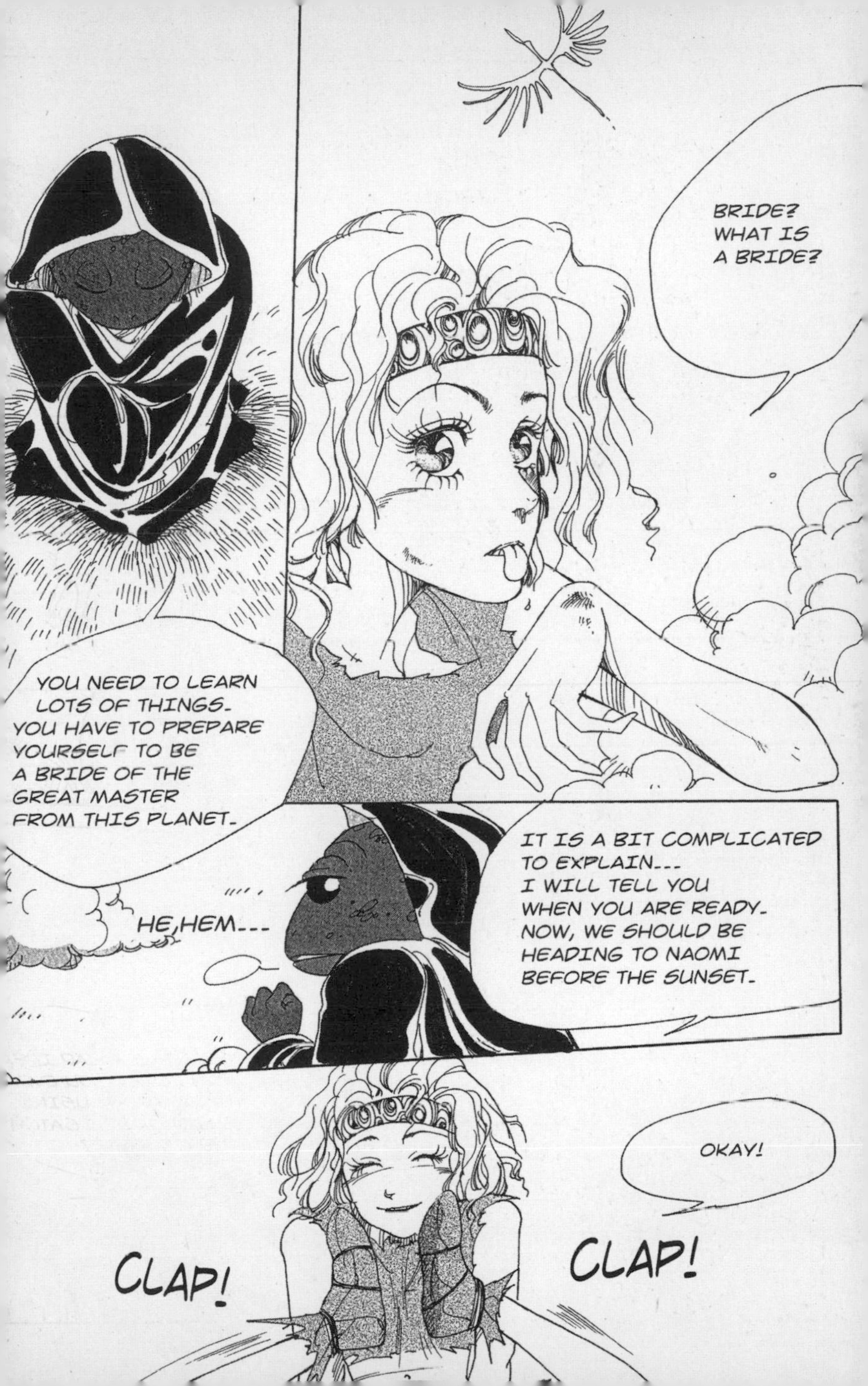

YOU NEED TO LEARN LOTS OF THINGS. YOU HAVE TO PREPARE YOURSELF TO BE A BRIDE OF THE GREAT MASTER FROM THIS PLANET.
BRIDE? WHAT IS A BRIDE?
HE,HEM...
IT IS A BIT COMPLICATED TO EXPLAIN... I WILL TELL YOU WHEN YOU ARE READY. NOW, WE SHOULD BE HEADING TO NAOMI BEFORE THE SUNSET.
CLAP!
OKAY!
CLAP!

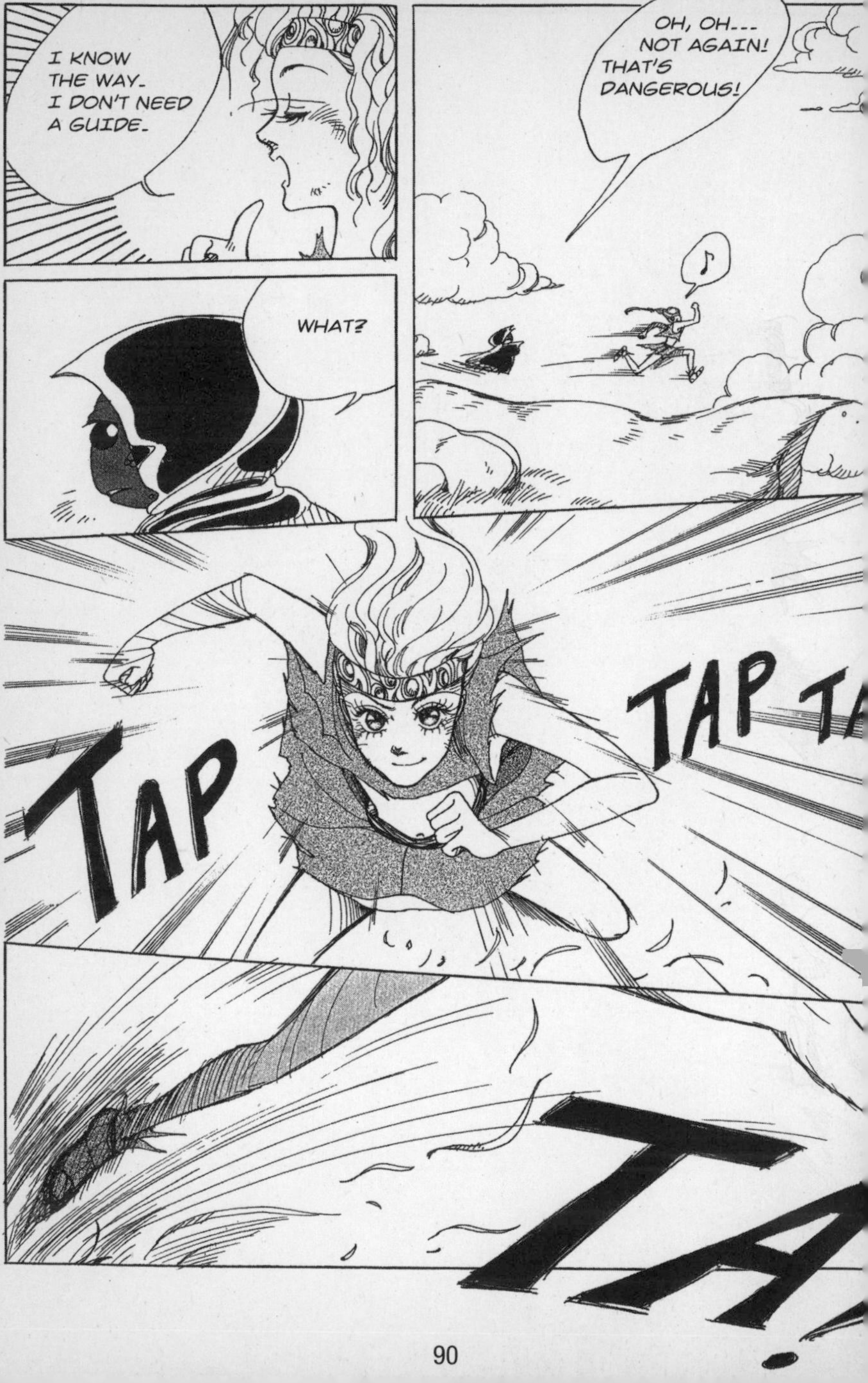
I KNOW THE WAY. I DON'T NEED A GUIDE.
OH, OH... NOT AGAIN! THAT'S DANGEROUS!
WHAT?
♪
TAP
TAP TA
TA

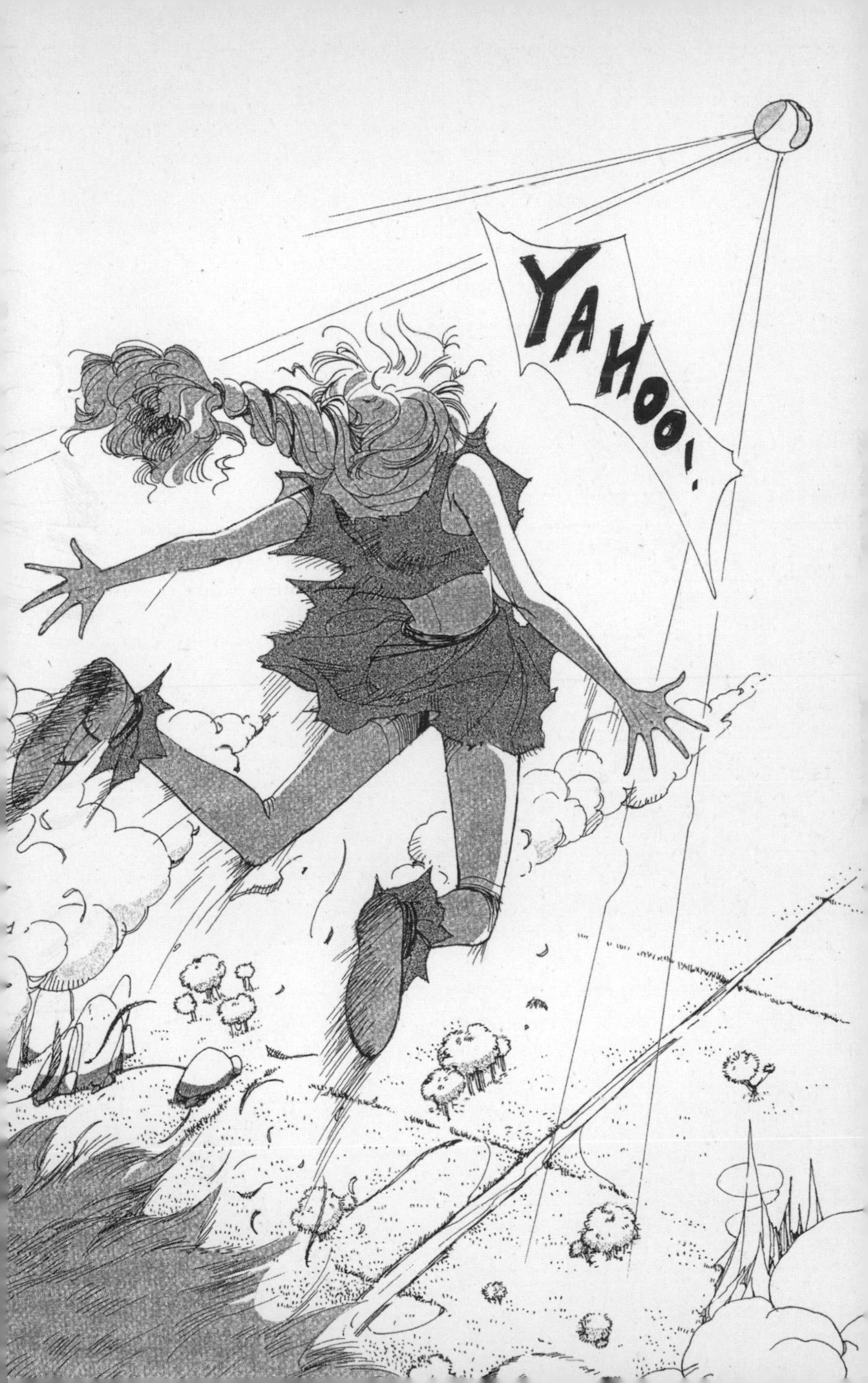
YAHOO!

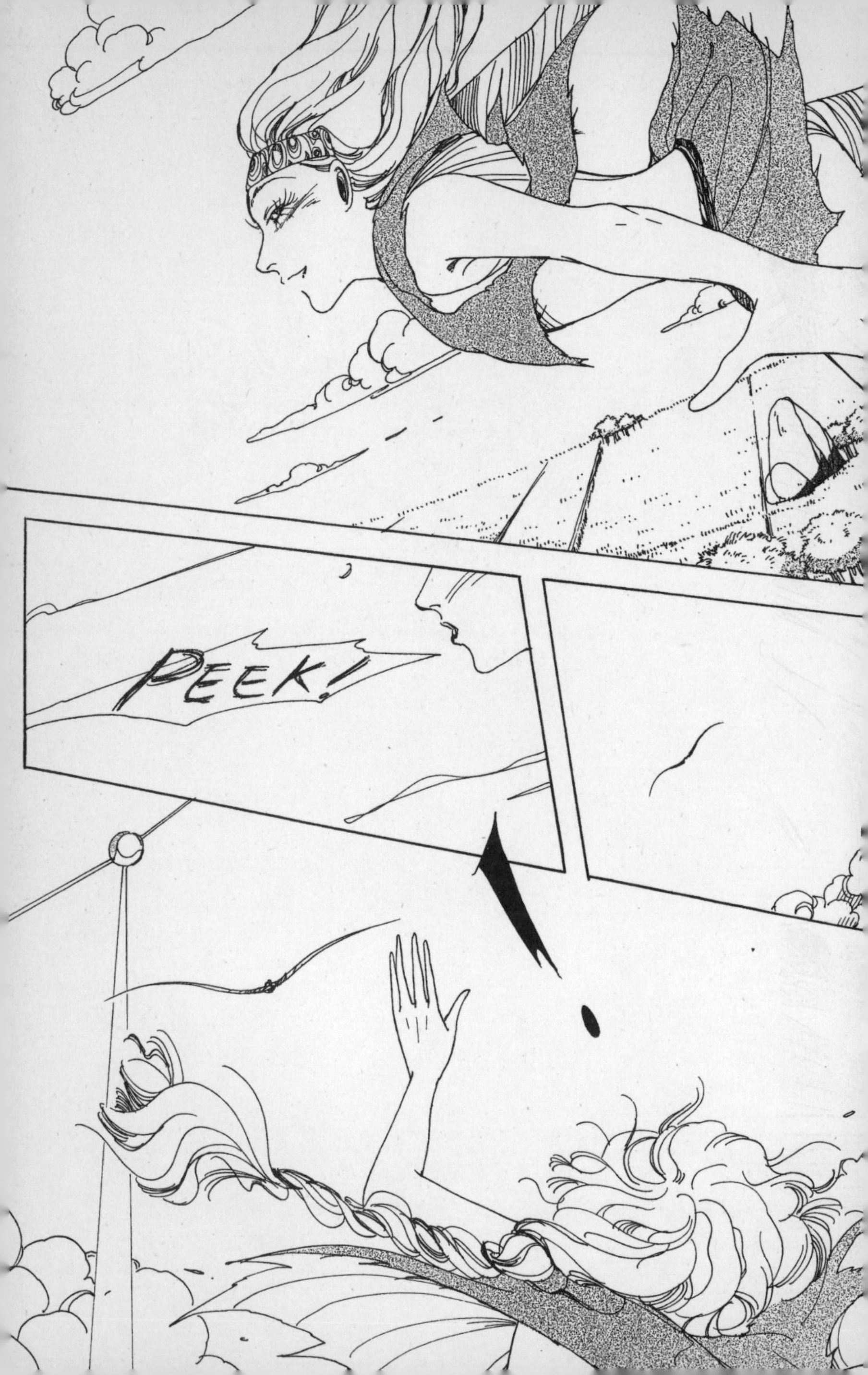
PEEK!

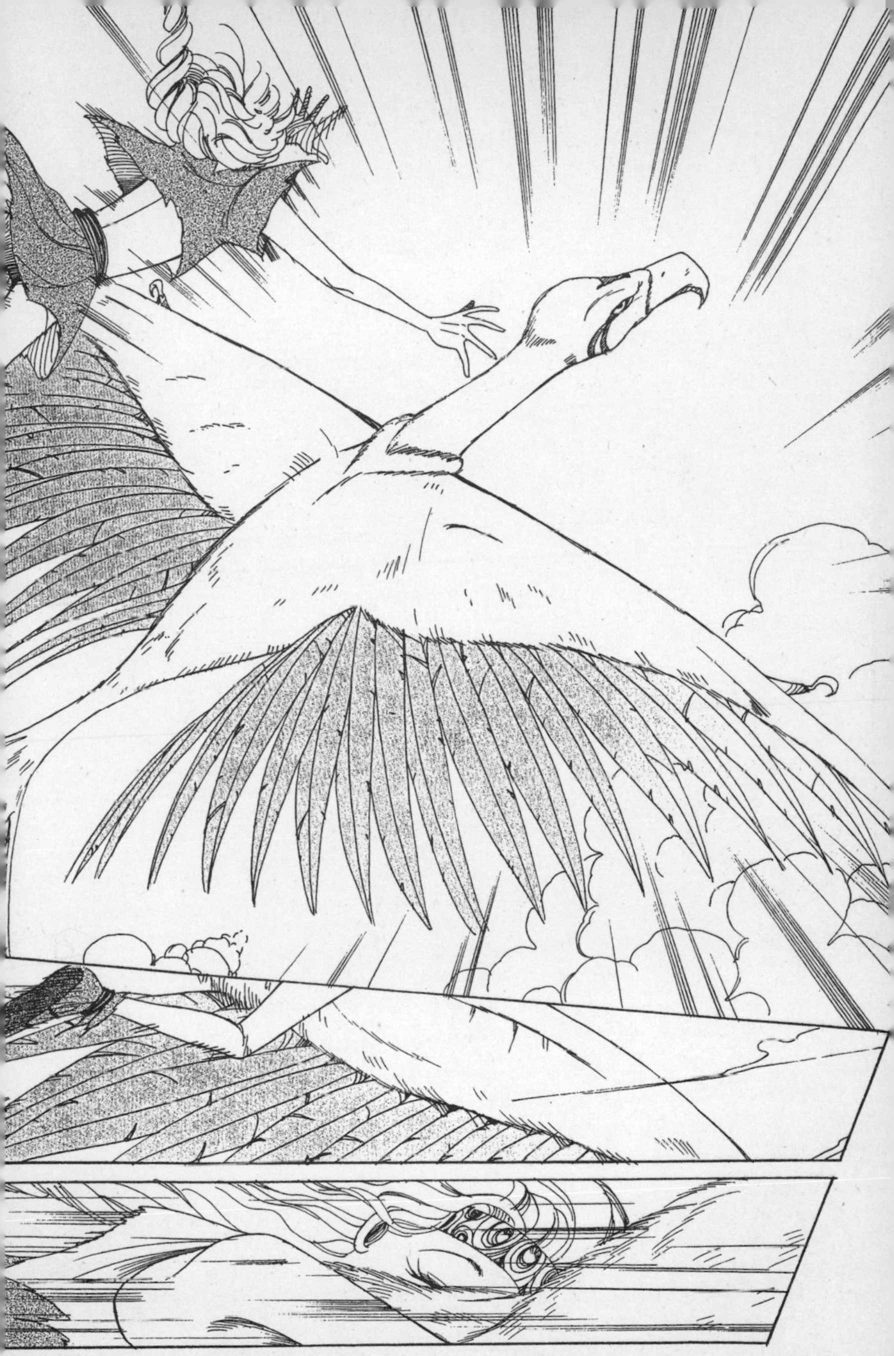

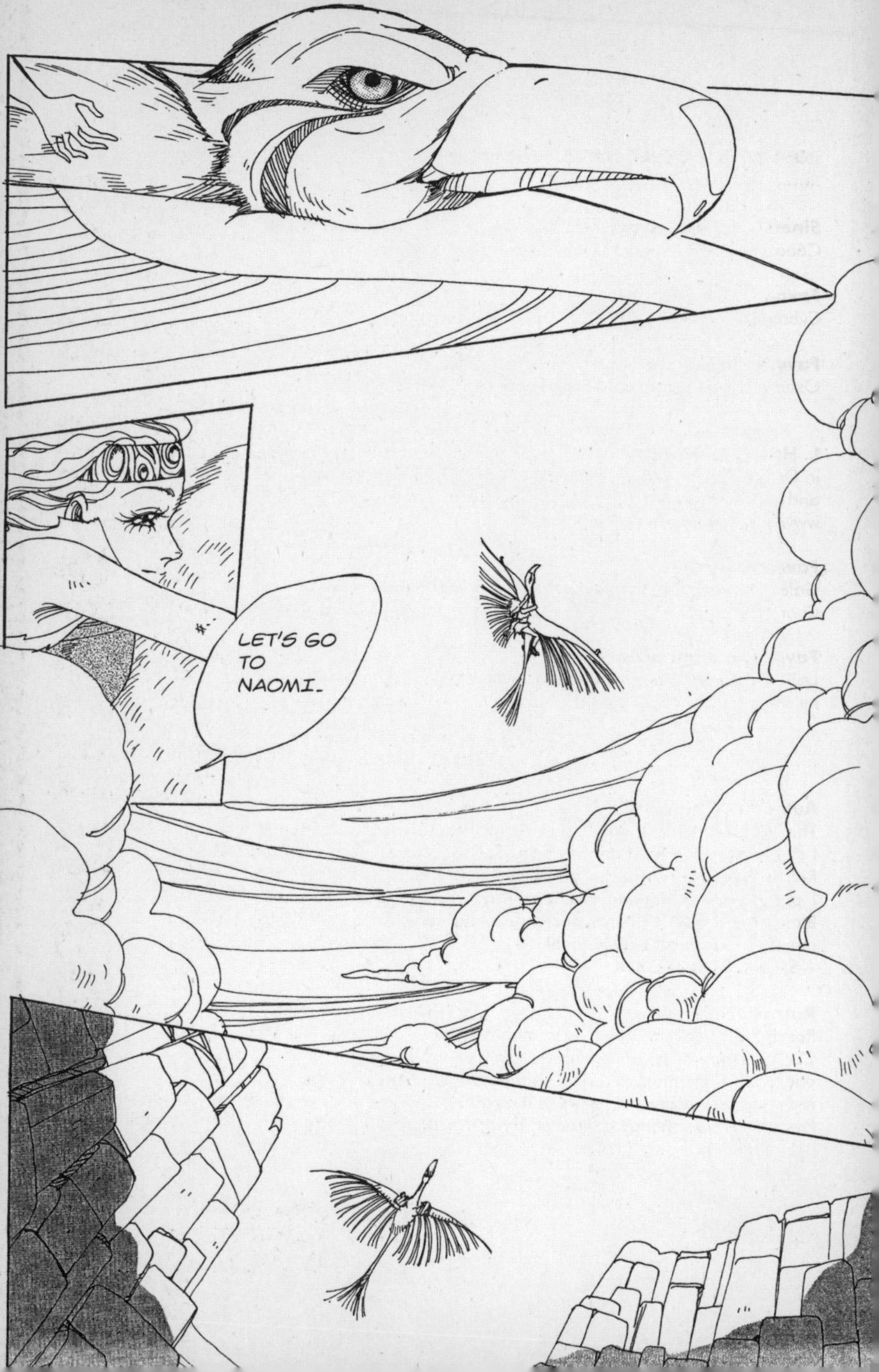
LET'S GO TO NAOMI...

::

ROSE BY ANY OTHER NAME :: Runner Up ::

....

Sinead "Missie" Lynch was born in 1983 in Thunder Bay, Ontario, Canada. She now lives in Dublin and is a childminder.

Favorite manga:
Cyborg 009, Phoenix, Buddha, Azumanga Daioh

Favorite manga artist:
Osamu Tezuka, Masamune Shirow, CLAMP, Keiko Takemiya

L. Hamilton was born in 1985 in Drogheda, County Louth. She now lives in Duleek, County Meath, Republic of Ireland and is an animation student and comic book artist.
www.angelfire.com/art2/leescomics/

Favorite manga:
Galaxy Express 999, Yokohoma Kaidaishi Kikou, Pilgrim Jager, Comic Party

Favorite manga artist:
Leiji Matsumoto, Hitoshi Ashinano, Moto Hagio, Adam Warren (okay, so he's a "pseudomanga" artist...), Yukito Kishiro, Masamune Shirow

....

Author's Comments:
The story for "Rose By Any Other Name" came about in a strange way. I started with the bare bones of an idea for a retelling of the Little Red Riding Hood story. Things got a little crazy after that, the first script I produced was nothing but incoherent scribble with "Is Maith Liom Blathanna" being the only decipherable phrase. I'm surprised Leeann managed to translate it so well!
—*Sinead "Missie" Lynch*

Author's Comments:
Rose, the main character, was meant to have a wacky wardrobe of CLAMP-esque dresses. But when I came round to drawing them, they ended up a lot more ordinary than expected. Yet I have faith that the red and black coat Rose wears to the Flower Children's Park can identify Rose as an unorthodox character, but instantly recognizable.
—*L. Hamilton*

::

95

::

ROSE BY ANY OTHER NAME :: Runner Up ::

Judge's Comments:
This is a science fiction story, but like the best science fiction, it is very human. "Rose By Any Other Name" tells a story that moves like a collection of snapshots, recording the disintegration of a family in the shadow of new technology. It touches on what makes something human, and whether that is which is human can survive under the crushing weight of its own needs.

The best that "Rose By Any Other Name" has to offer is an apocalyptic vision calmly told, of a civilized madness overgrown by a more primal way of life, and of learning about love and appropriate limits too late. Artwise, "Rose By Any Other Name" is at its finest in setting scenes and people within them in ways that reflect their emotional states. Some of the art is also very cute. The panel layouts are pretty satisfying, and nothing is overdone, if not fully consistent.

Let's also not forget the believability of the technology and catastrophes portrayed in this piece. One of its sure strengths is in presenting a plausible, if unhappy, future.
—Hope Donovan

Judge's Comments:
"Rose By Any Other Name" is an interesting entry. The art is good, but not the best of the bunch. The story, while engaging, treads heavily on familiar grounds. Wow...not much of a glowing recommendation, you say. Well, here's what makes this entry so interesting—despite all that, it's really good. See, not everything needs to be groundbreaking or technically perfect to be successful. What Leeann (or L.) and Sinead did was create an intriguing character with strong design elements and placed her in a well thought-out world. For a manga creator, or any kind of storyteller, that's one of the most important skills to have. I was comfortable, in this world through the whole read and by the end I really felt for Rose. For me, this one story evoked more of an emotional response than any of the other hundreds of entries we received...for that alone I felt that this story need to be in the book.
—Rob Valois

::

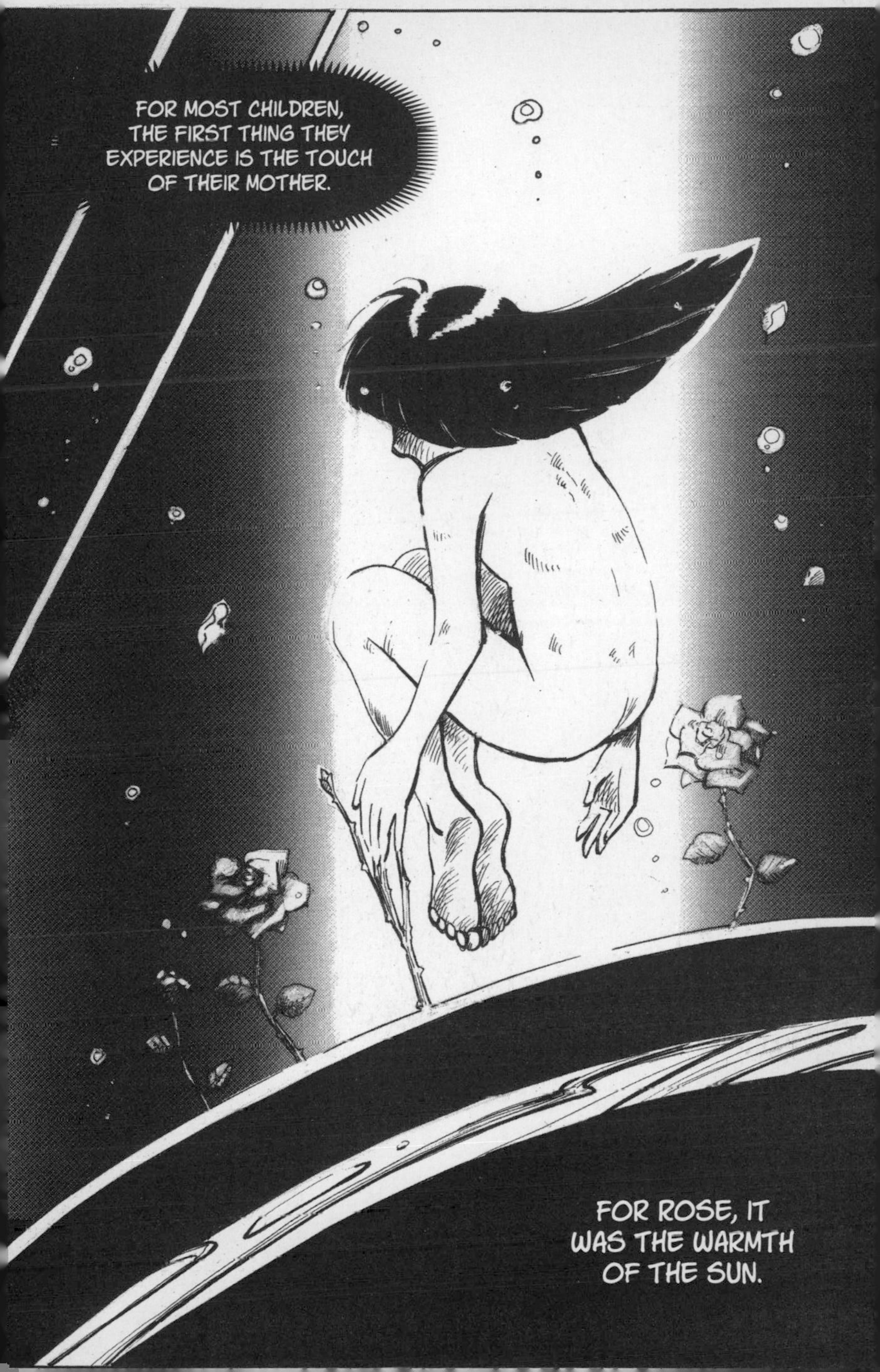
FOR MOST CHILDREN, THE FIRST THING THEY EXPERIENCE IS THE TOUCH OF THEIR MOTHER.
FOR ROSE, IT WAS THE WARMTH OF THE SUN.

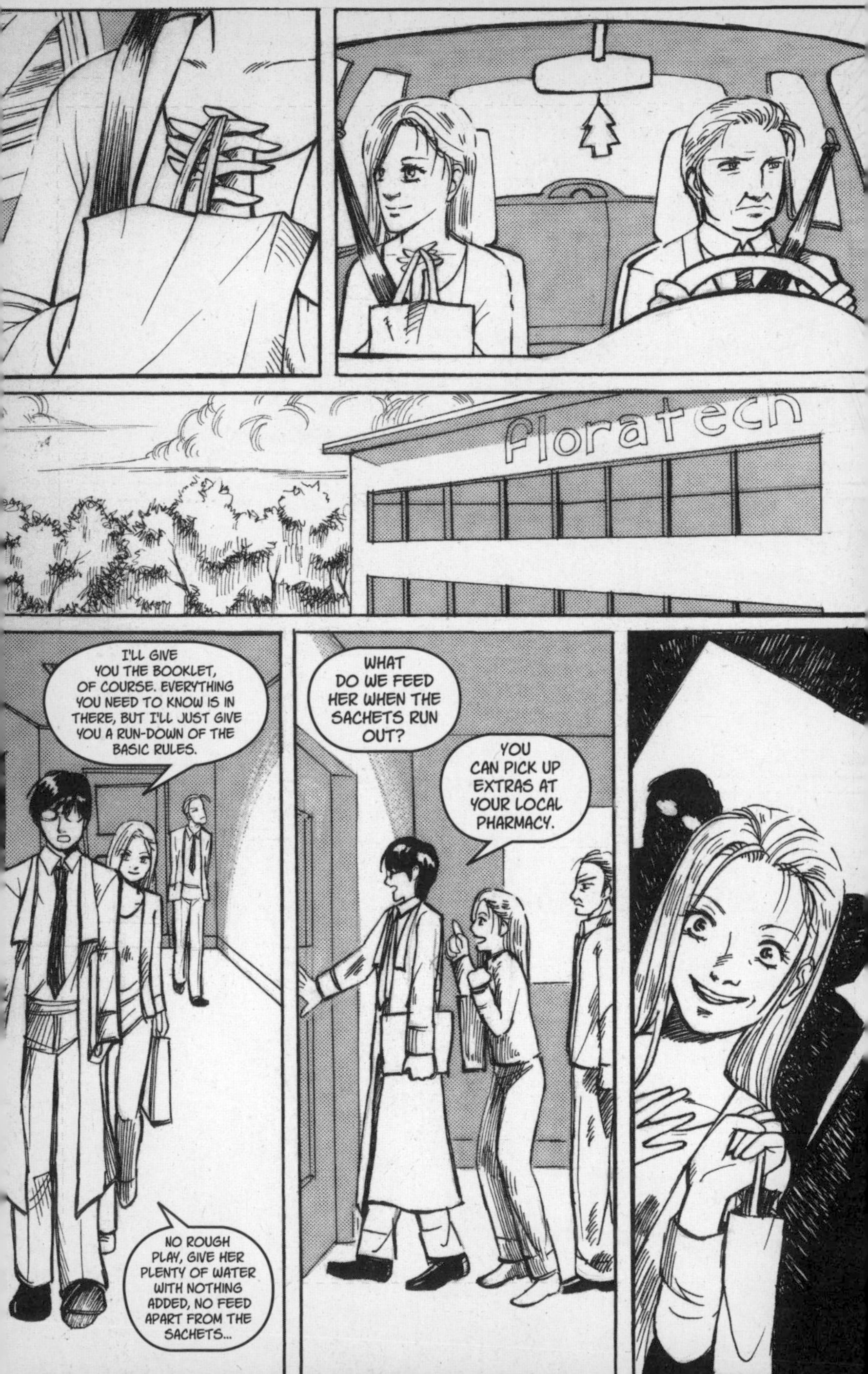
Floratech
I'LL GIVE YOU THE BOOKLET, OF COURSE. EVERYTHING YOU NEED TO KNOW IS IN THERE, BUT I'LL JUST GIVE YOU A RUN-DOWN OF THE BASIC RULES.
NO ROUGH PLAY, GIVE HER PLENTY OF WATER WITH NOTHING ADDED, NO FEED APART FROM THE SACHETS...
WHAT DO WE FEED HER WHEN THE SACHETS RUN OUT?
YOU CAN PICK UP EXTRAS AT YOUR LOCAL PHARMACY.

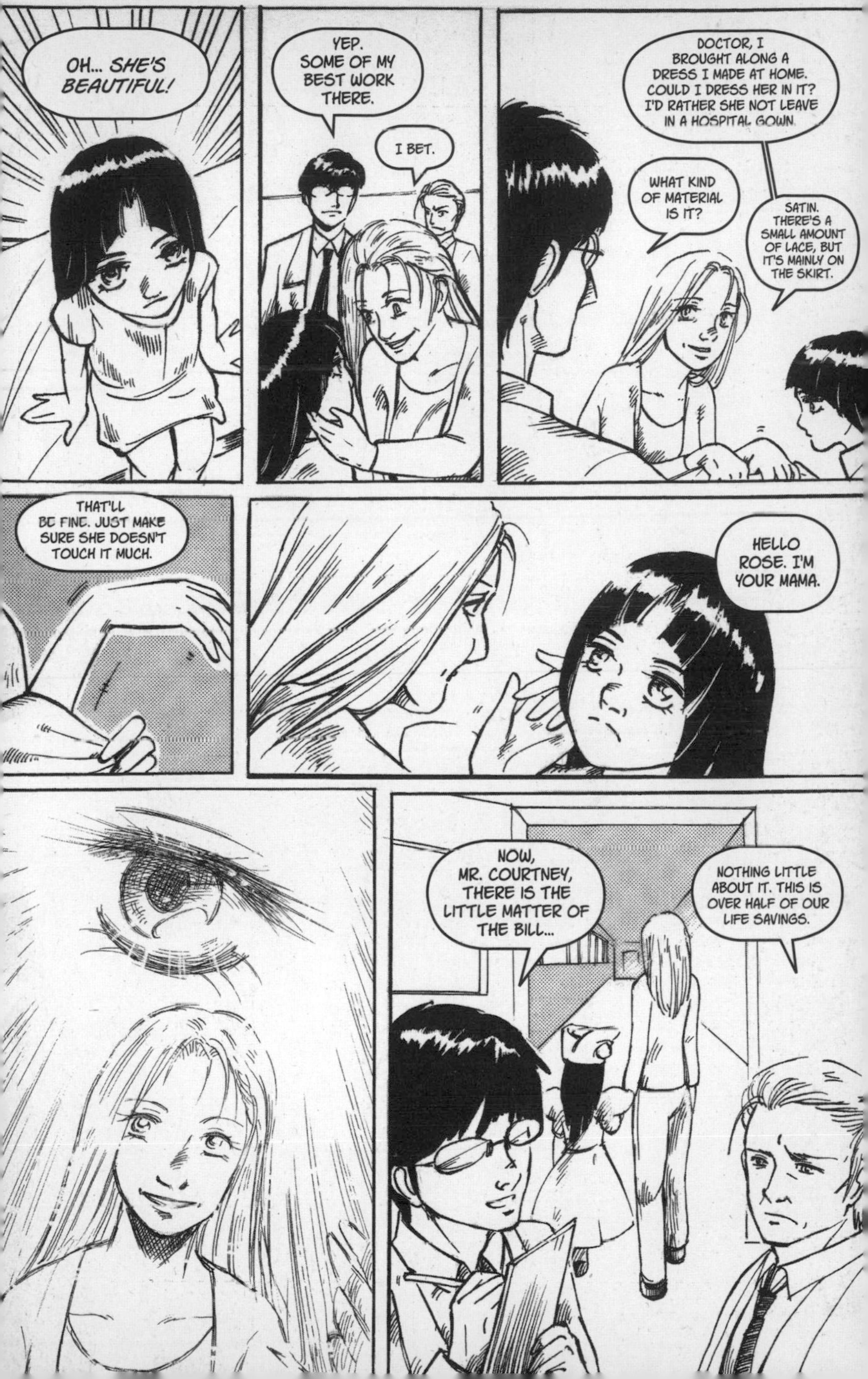
OH... SHE'S BEAUTIFUL!
YEP. SOME OF MY BEST WORK THERE.
I BET.
DOCTOR, I BROUGHT ALONG A DRESS I MADE AT HOME. COULD I DRESS HER IN IT? I'D RATHER SHE NOT LEAVE IN A HOSPITAL GOWN.
WHAT KIND OF MATERIAL IS IT?
SATIN. THERE'S A SMALL AMOUNT OF LACE, BUT IT'S MAINLY ON THE SKIRT.
THAT'LL BE FINE. JUST MAKE SURE SHE DOESN'T TOUCH IT MUCH.
HELLO ROSE. I'M YOUR MAMA.
NOW, MR. COURTNEY, THERE IS THE LITTLE MATTER OF THE BILL...
NOTHING LITTLE ABOUT IT. THIS IS OVER HALF OF OUR LIFE SAVINGS.

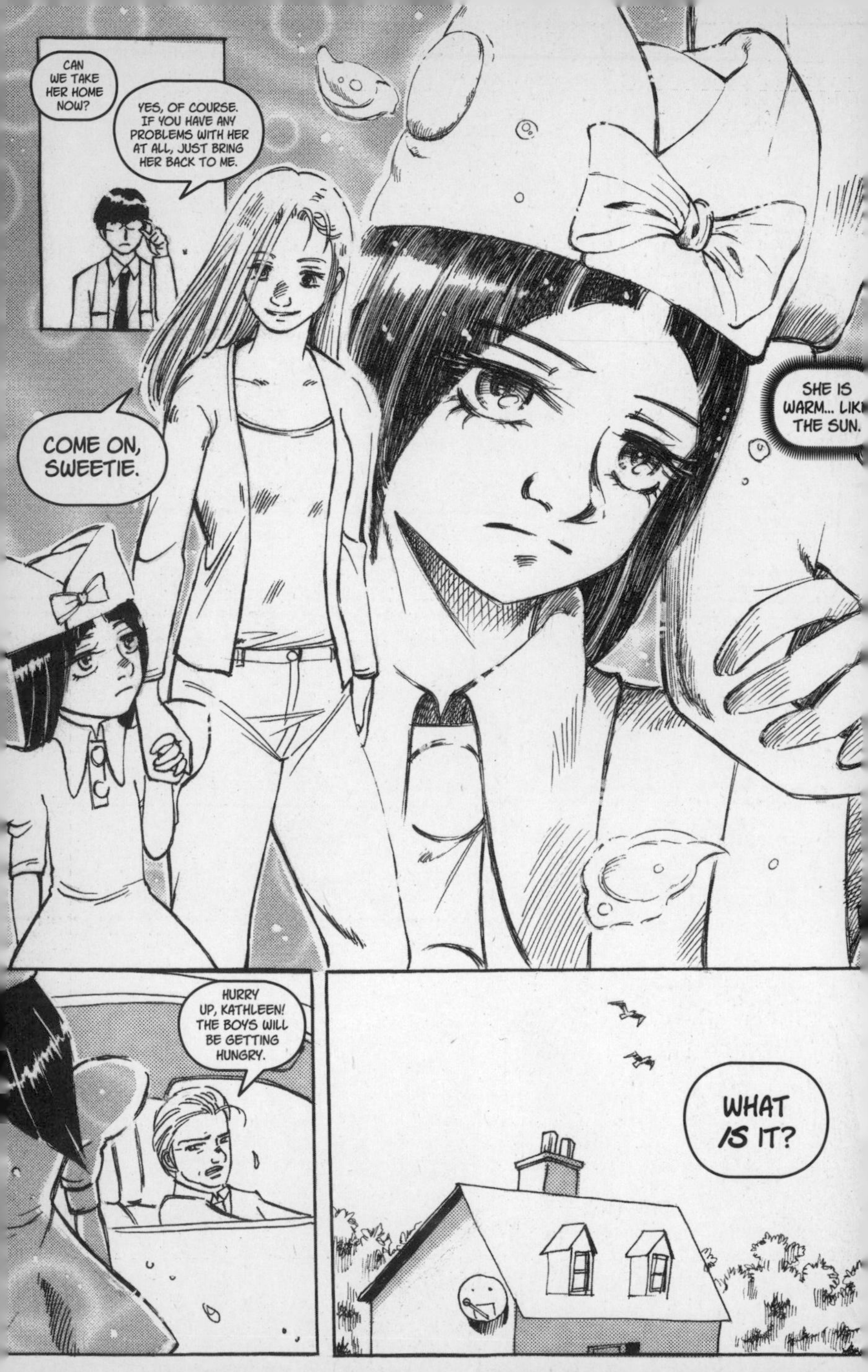
CAN WE TAKE HER HOME NOW?
YES, OF COURSE. IF YOU HAVE ANY PROBLEMS WITH HER AT ALL, JUST BRING HER BACK TO ME.
COME ON, SWEETIE.
SHE IS WARM... LIKE THE SUN.
HURRY UP, KATHLEEN! THE BOYS WILL BE GETTING HUNGRY.
WHAT IS IT?

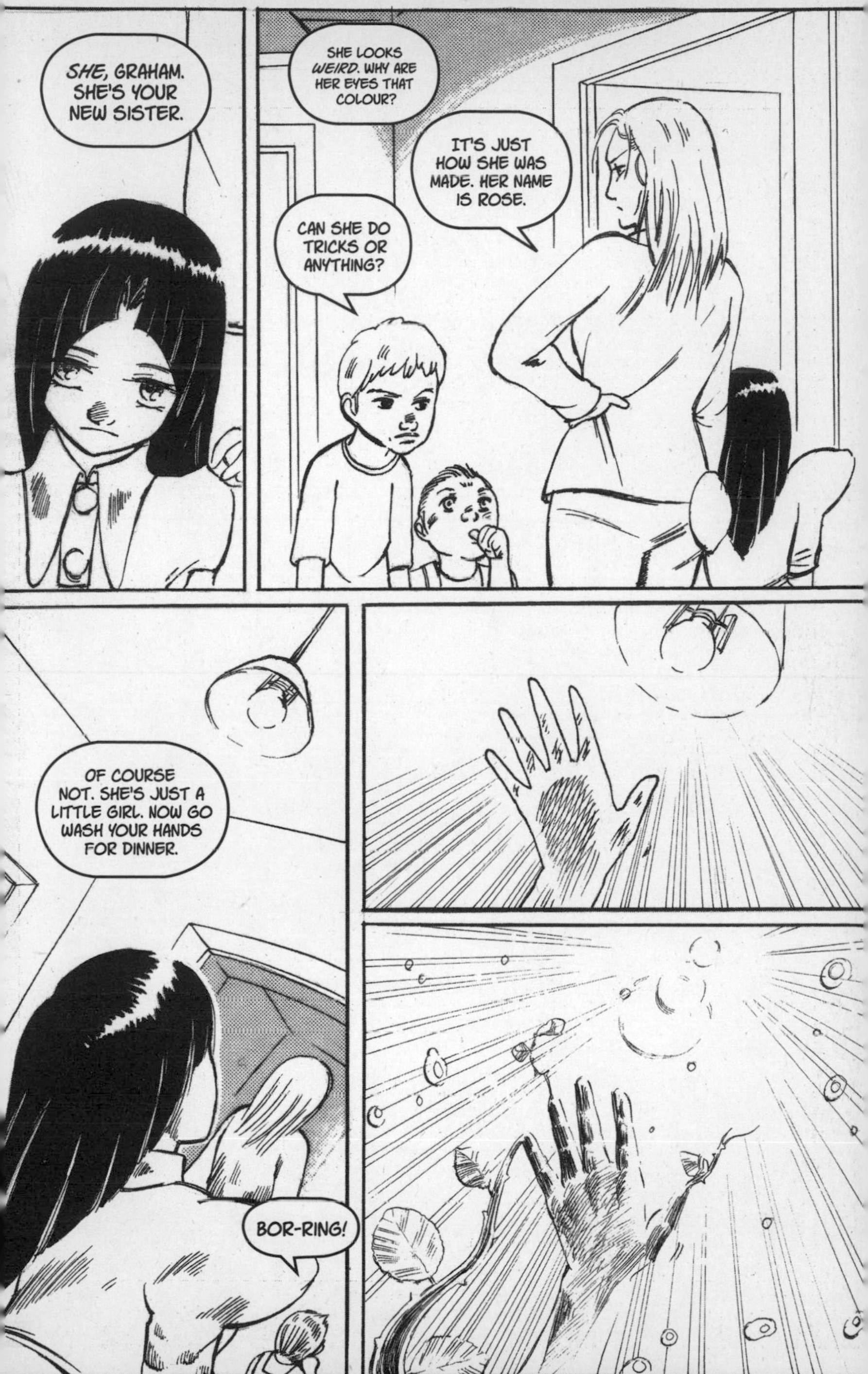
SHE, GRAHAM. SHE'S YOUR NEW SISTER.
SHE LOOKS WEIRD. WHY ARE HER EYES THAT COLOUR?
IT'S JUST HOW SHE WAS MADE. HER NAME IS ROSE.
CAN SHE DO TRICKS OR ANYTHING?
OF COURSE NOT. SHE'S JUST A LITTLE GIRL. NOW GO WASH YOUR HANDS FOR DINNER.
BOR-RING!

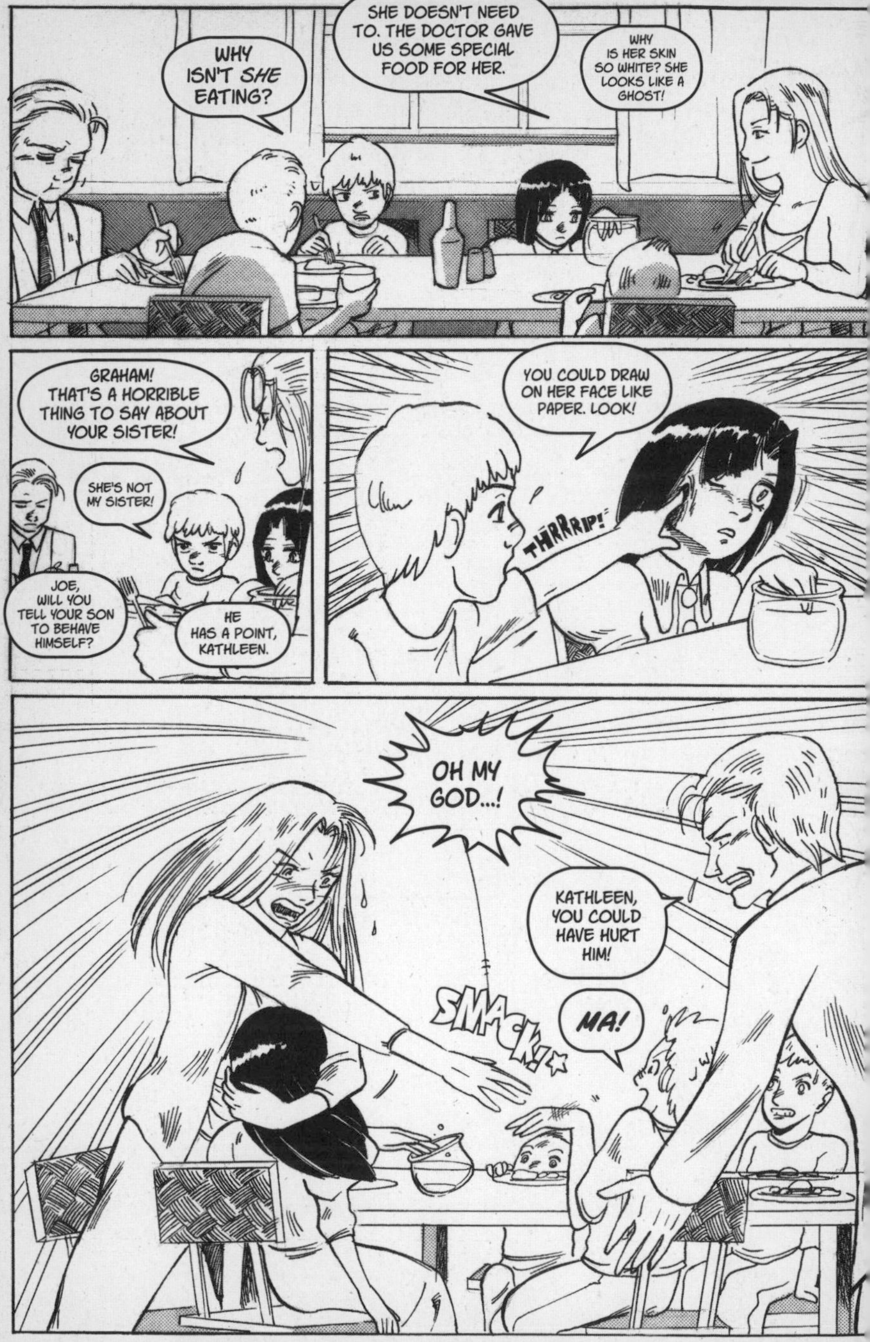
WHY ISN'T *SHE* EATING?
SHE DOESN'T NEED TO. THE DOCTOR GAVE US SOME SPECIAL FOOD FOR HER.
WHY IS HER SKIN SO WHITE? SHE LOOKS LIKE A GHOST!
GRAHAM! THAT'S A HORRIBLE THING TO SAY ABOUT YOUR SISTER!
SHE'S NOT MY SISTER!
JOE, WILL YOU TELL YOUR SON TO BEHAVE HIMSELF?
HE HAS A POINT, KATHLEEN.
YOU COULD DRAW ON HER FACE LIKE PAPER. LOOK!
THRRRIP!
OH MY GOD...!
KATHLEEN, YOU COULD HAVE HURT HIM!
SMACK!
MA!

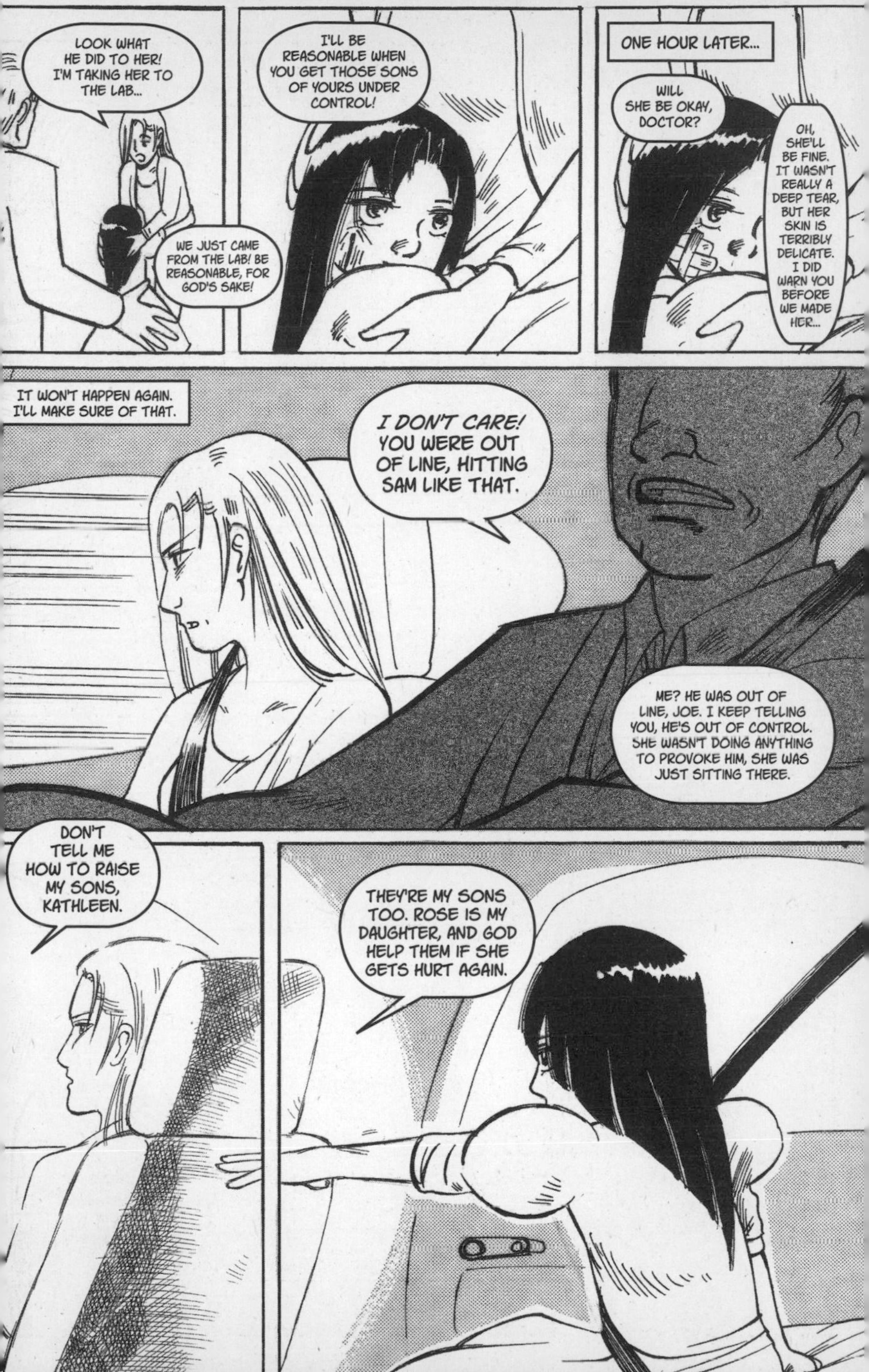
LOOK WHAT HE DID TO HER! I'M TAKING HER TO THE LAB...
WE JUST CAME FROM THE LAB! BE REASONABLE, FOR GOD'S SAKE!
I'LL BE REASONABLE WHEN YOU GET THOSE SONS OF YOURS UNDER CONTROL!
ONE HOUR LATER...
WILL SHE BE OKAY, DOCTOR?
OH, SHE'LL BE FINE. IT WASN'T REALLY A DEEP TEAR, BUT HER SKIN IS TERRIBLY DELICATE. I DID WARN YOU BEFORE WE MADE HER...
IT WON'T HAPPEN AGAIN. I'LL MAKE SURE OF THAT.
I DON'T CARE! YOU WERE OUT OF LINE, HITTING SAM LIKE THAT.
ME? HE WAS OUT OF LINE, JOE. I KEEP TELLING YOU, HE'S OUT OF CONTROL. SHE WASN'T DOING ANYTHING TO PROVOKE HIM, SHE WAS JUST SITTING THERE.
DON'T TELL ME HOW TO RAISE MY SONS, KATHLEEN.
THEY'RE MY SONS TOO. ROSE IS MY DAUGHTER, AND GOD HELP THEM IF SHE GETS HURT AGAIN.

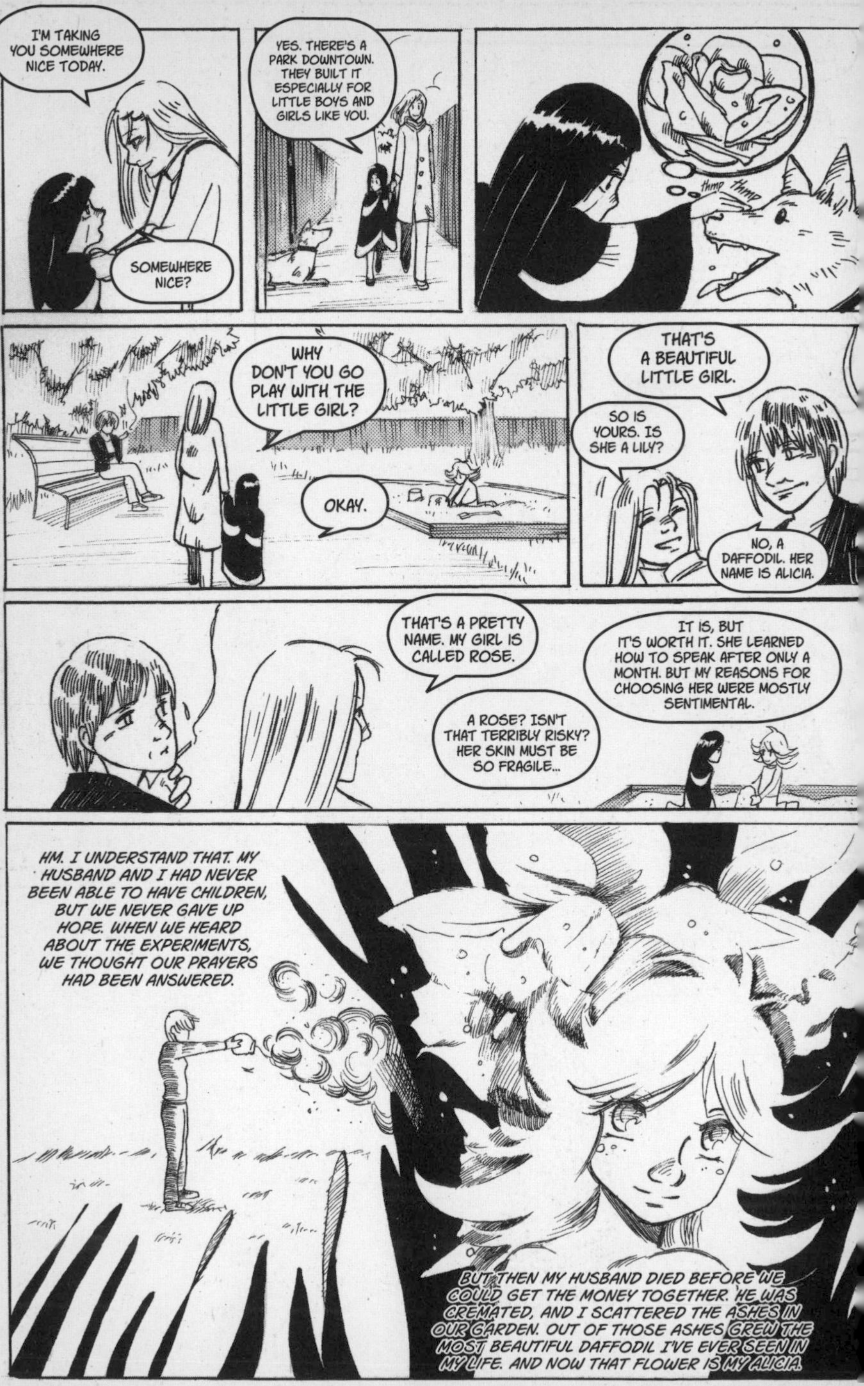
I'M TAKING YOU SOMEWHERE NICE TODAY.
SOMEWHERE NICE?
YES. THERE'S A PARK DOWNTOWN. THEY BUILT IT ESPECIALLY FOR LITTLE BOYS AND GIRLS LIKE YOU.
thmp thmp
WHY DON'T YOU GO PLAY WITH THE LITTLE GIRL?
OKAY.
THAT'S A BEAUTIFUL LITTLE GIRL.
SO IS YOURS. IS SHE A LILY?
NO, A DAFFODIL. HER NAME IS ALICIA.
THAT'S A PRETTY NAME. MY GIRL IS CALLED ROSE.
A ROSE? ISN'T THAT TERRIBLY RISKY? HER SKIN MUST BE SO FRAGILE...
IT IS, BUT IT'S WORTH IT. SHE LEARNED HOW TO SPEAK AFTER ONLY A MONTH. BUT MY REASONS FOR CHOOSING HER WERE MOSTLY SENTIMENTAL.
HM. I UNDERSTAND THAT. MY HUSBAND AND I HAD NEVER BEEN ABLE TO HAVE CHILDREN, BUT WE NEVER GAVE UP HOPE. WHEN WE HEARD ABOUT THE EXPERIMENTS, WE THOUGHT OUR PRAYERS HAD BEEN ANSWERED.
BUT THEN MY HUSBAND DIED BEFORE WE COULD GET THE MONEY TOGETHER. HE WAS CREMATED, AND I SCATTERED THE ASHES IN OUR GARDEN. OUT OF THOSE ASHES GREW THE MOST BEAUTIFUL DAFFODIL I'VE EVER SEEN IN MY LIFE. AND NOW THAT FLOWER IS MY ALICIA.

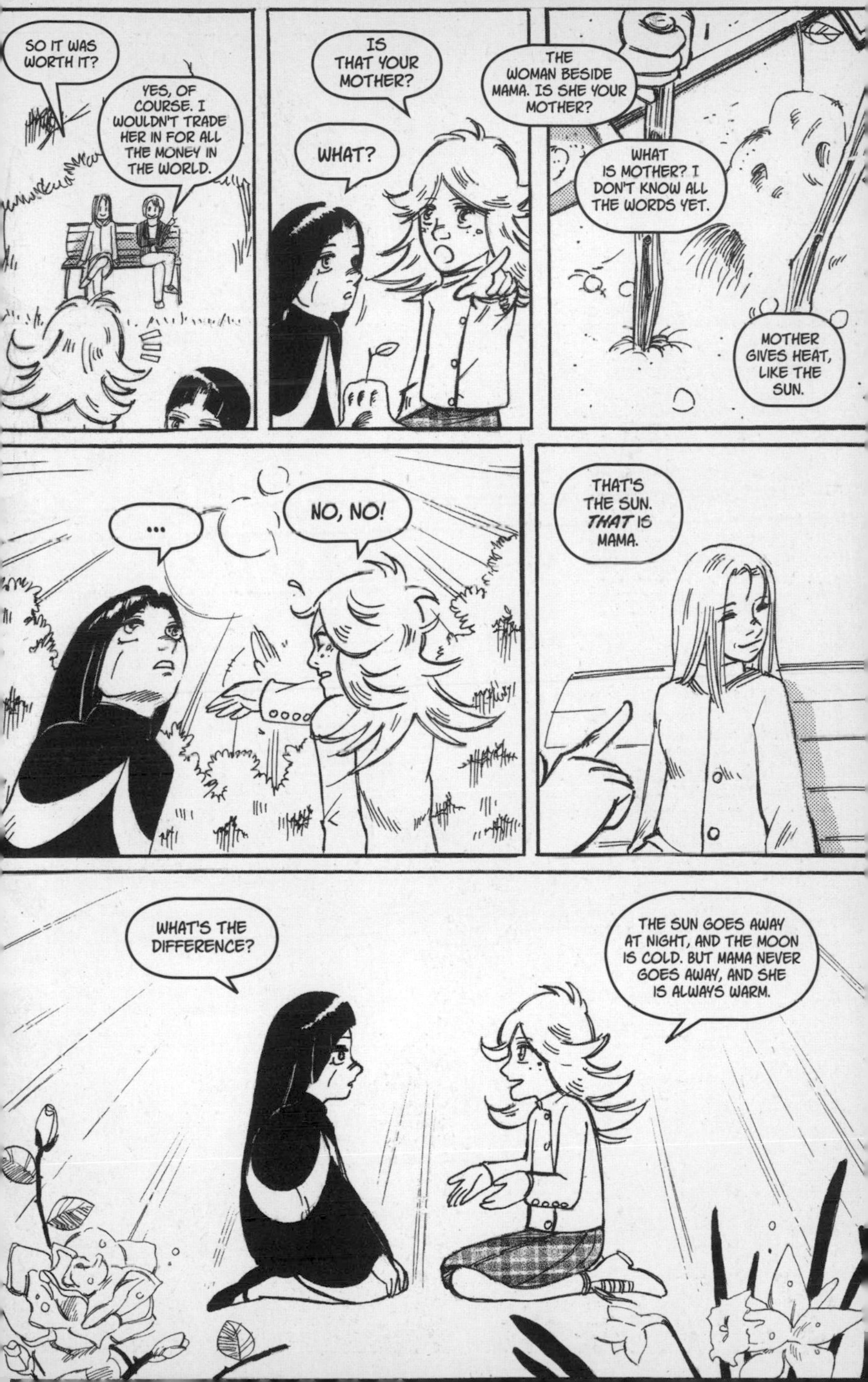
SO IT WAS WORTH IT?
YES, OF COURSE. I WOULDN'T TRADE HER IN FOR ALL THE MONEY IN THE WORLD.
IS THAT YOUR MOTHER?
WHAT?
THE WOMAN BESIDE MAMA. IS SHE YOUR MOTHER?
WHAT IS MOTHER? I DON'T KNOW ALL THE WORDS YET.
MOTHER GIVES HEAT, LIKE THE SUN.
...
NO, NO!
THAT'S THE SUN. *THAT* IS MAMA.
WHAT'S THE DIFFERENCE?
THE SUN GOES AWAY AT NIGHT, AND THE MOON IS COLD. BUT MAMA NEVER GOES AWAY, AND SHE IS ALWAYS WARM.

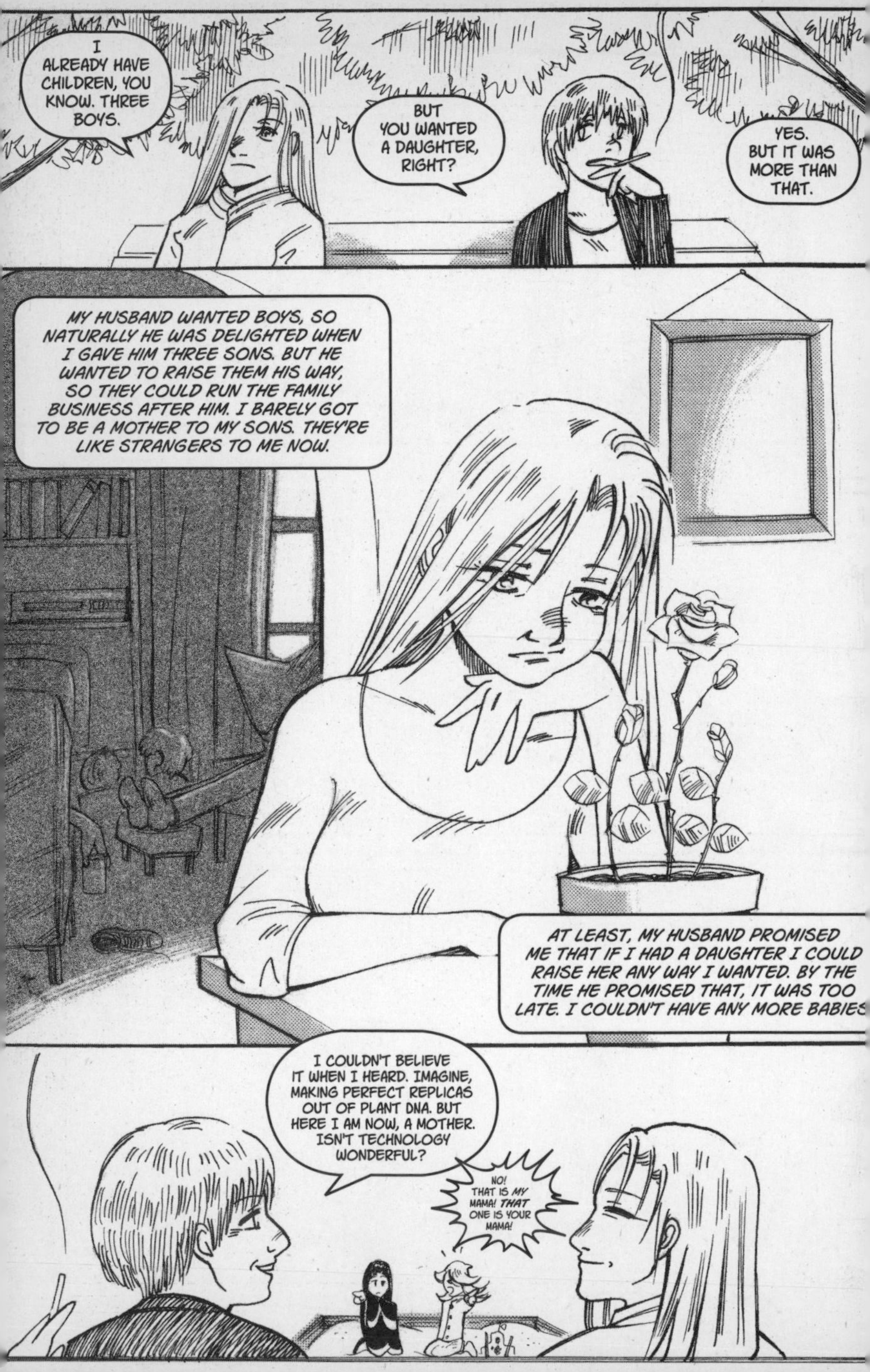
I ALREADY HAVE CHILDREN, YOU KNOW. THREE BOYS.
BUT YOU WANTED A DAUGHTER, RIGHT?
YES. BUT IT WAS MORE THAN THAT.
MY HUSBAND WANTED BOYS, SO NATURALLY HE WAS DELIGHTED WHEN I GAVE HIM THREE SONS. BUT HE WANTED TO RAISE THEM HIS WAY, SO THEY COULD RUN THE FAMILY BUSINESS AFTER HIM. I BARELY GOT TO BE A MOTHER TO MY SONS. THEY'RE LIKE STRANGERS TO ME NOW.
AT LEAST, MY HUSBAND PROMISED ME THAT IF I HAD A DAUGHTER I COULD RAISE HER ANY WAY I WANTED. BY THE TIME HE PROMISED THAT, IT WAS TOO LATE. I COULDN'T HAVE ANY MORE BABIES
I COULDN'T BELIEVE IT WHEN I HEARD. IMAGINE, MAKING PERFECT REPLICAS OUT OF PLANT DNA. BUT HERE I AM NOW, A MOTHER. ISN'T TECHNOLOGY WONDERFUL?
NO! THAT IS *MY* MAMA! ***THAT*** ONE IS YOUR MAMA!

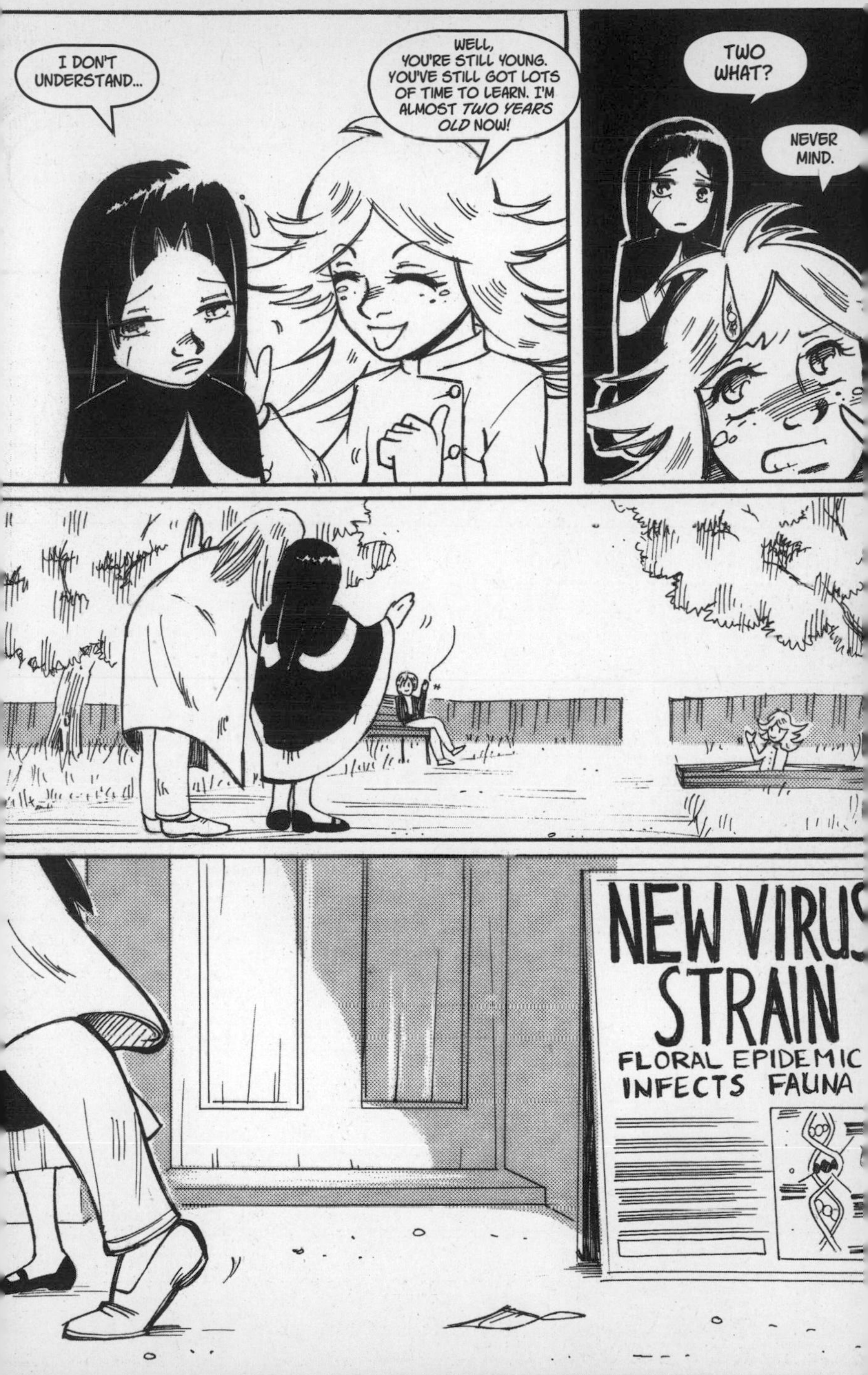
I DON'T UNDERSTAND...
WELL, YOU'RE STILL YOUNG. YOU'VE STILL GOT LOTS OF TIME TO LEARN. I'M ALMOST *TWO YEARS OLD* NOW!
TWO WHAT?
NEVER MIND.
NEW VIRUS STRAIN
FLORAL EPIDEMIC INFECTS FAUNA

YOU FORGOT TO PICK MICHAEL UP FROM SCHOOL *AGAIN!* WHERE WERE YOU?

THE SCHOOL IS A TEN MINUTE WALK AWAY. GOD KNOWS HE COULD USE THE EXERCISE.

THAT'S NOT FOR YOU TO SAY!

I'M HIS MOTHER. OF COURSE I CAN SAY.

EVER SINCE YOU GOT THAT *THING* YOU'VE BEEN NEGLECTING YOUR DUTIES. IT'S NOT RIGHT, KATHLEEN.

DUTIES? I'M THEIR MOTHER, BUT I MIGHT AS WELL BE THEIR COOK OR PERSONAL MAID.

I WAS NEVER REALLY THEIR MOTHER. YOU SAW TO THAT. NOW I SUPPOSE YOU WANT TO TAKE AWAY MY DAUGHTER TOO?

IT'S A *PLANT,* KATHLEEN!

WE CAN HAVE IT DECON- STRUCTED AND YO CAN PLANT IT IN TH GARDEN IF YOU WAN BUT IT WAS A MISTA TO WARP IT LIKE THAT IN THE FIRS' PLACE!

NO. YOU TOOK MY SONS, YOU OWED ME A DAUGHTER.

I KNOW. I HAD MY BAGS PACKED YESTERDAY. WE'LL BE GOING NOW.

NO. I DON'T. BUT I STILL WON'T GIVE HER UP.

LOOK, I'VE HEARD REPORTS. SOME VIRUS OR SOMETHING THAT'S BEING CARRIED BY THE FLOWER CHILDREN. THEY DON'T KNOW HOW SERIOUS IT IS YET, BUT YOU WOULDN'T WANT TO RISK THE HEALTH OF OUR BOYS, WOULD YOU?

I WON'T HAVE HER IN MY HOUSE! NEAR MY SONS!

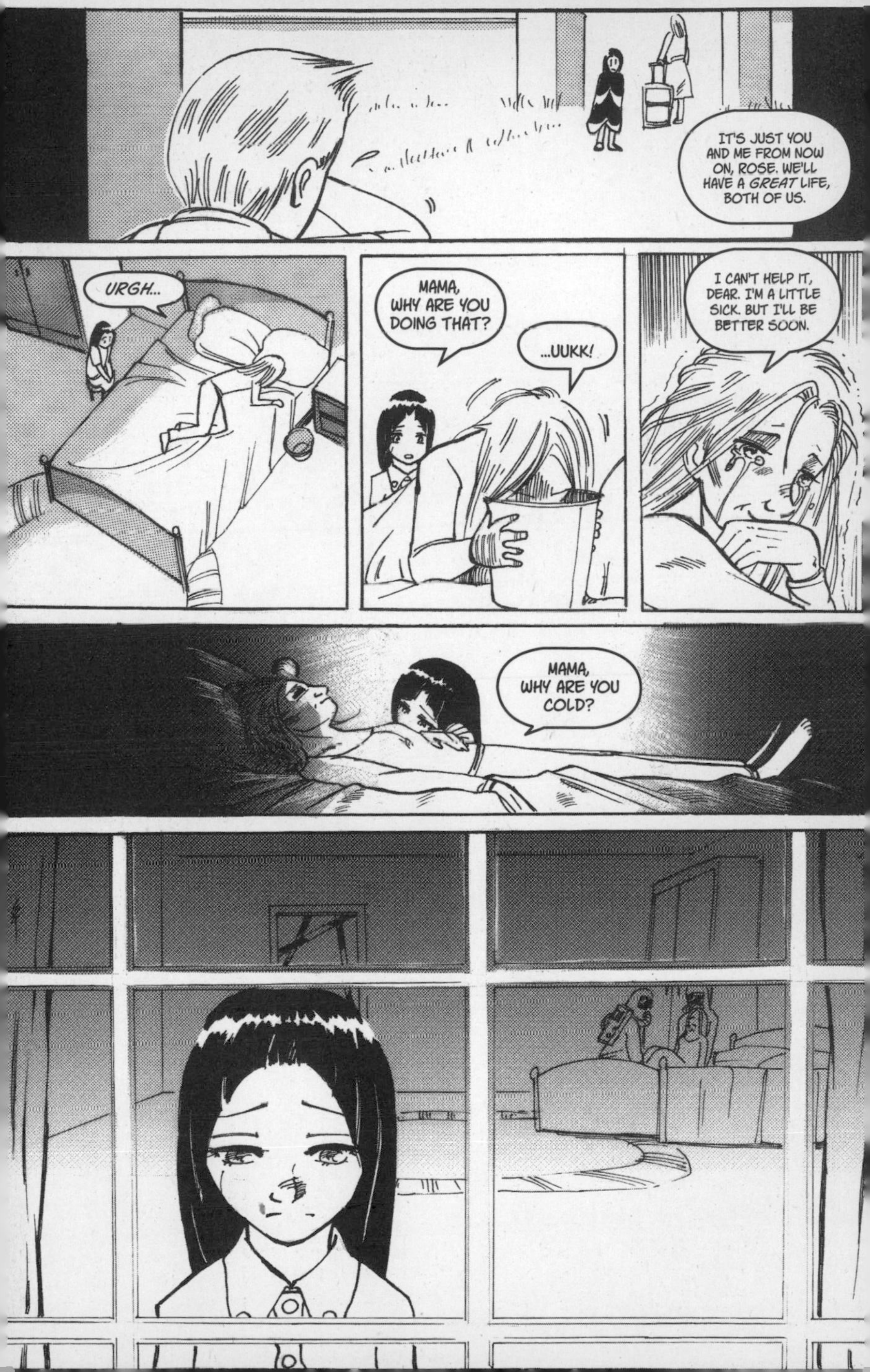
IT'S JUST YOU AND ME FROM NOW ON, ROSE. WE'LL HAVE A *GREAT* LIFE, BOTH OF US.
URGH...
MAMA, WHY ARE YOU DOING THAT?
...UUKK!
I CAN'T HELP IT, DEAR. I'M A LITTLE SICK. BUT I'LL BE BETTER SOON.
MAMA, WHY ARE YOU COLD?

TMP

SNMF!

GRRRAWF!!!

...to the owner by physical contact and may be airborne. The virus causes death by asphyxiation in humans and a (slower neural) liquidation similar to rabies in canine...

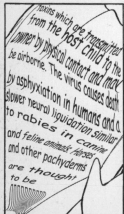

...toxins which are transmitted from the host child to the owner by physical contact and may be airborne. The virus causes death by asphyxiation in humans and a (slower neural) liquidation similar to rabies in canine and feline animals, horses and other pachyderms are thought to be

I KNOW YOU...

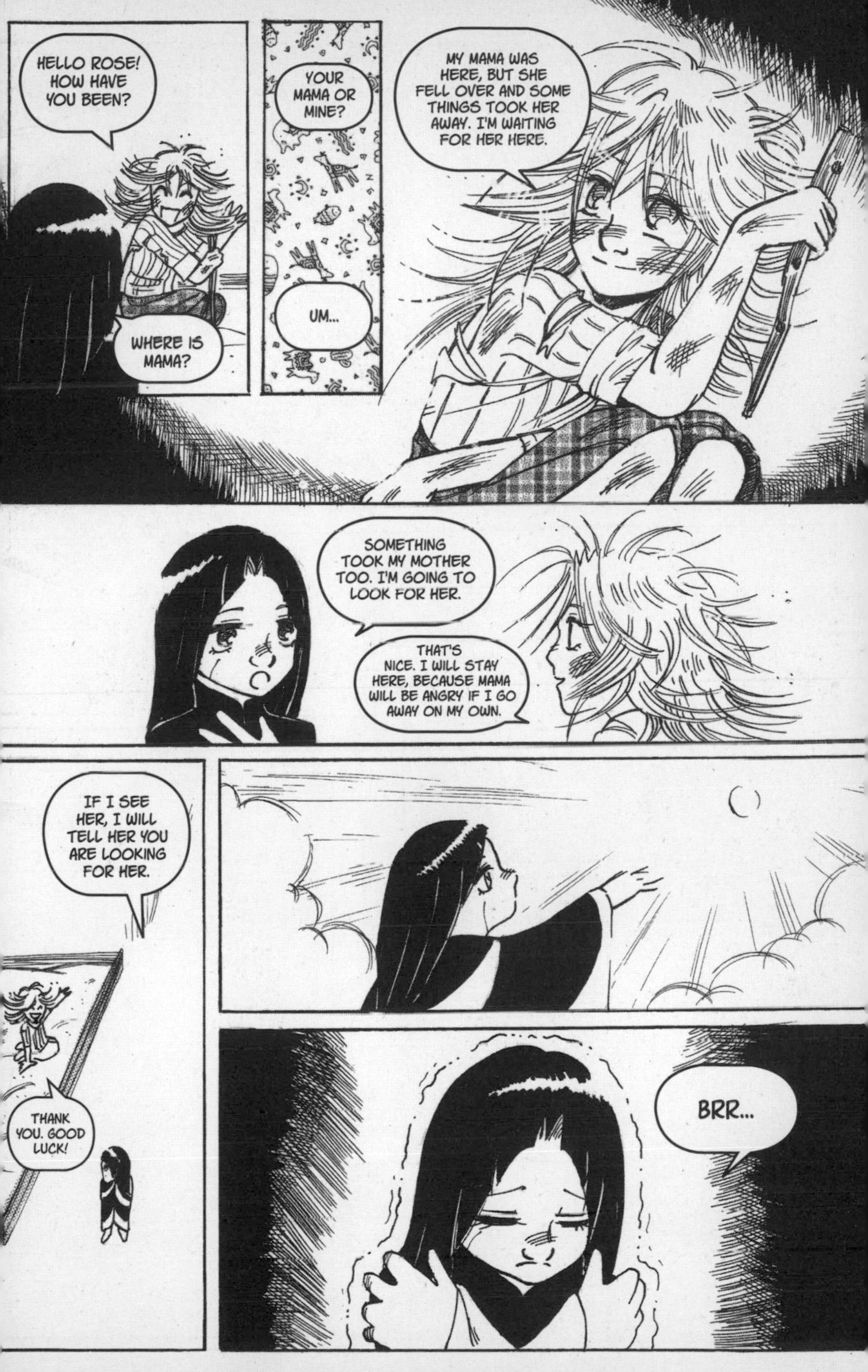
HELLO ROSE! HOW HAVE YOU BEEN?
WHERE IS MAMA?
YOUR MAMA OR MINE?
UM...
MY MAMA WAS HERE, BUT SHE FELL OVER AND SOME THINGS TOOK HER AWAY. I'M WAITING FOR HER HERE.
SOMETHING TOOK MY MOTHER TOO. I'M GOING TO LOOK FOR HER.
THAT'S NICE. I WILL STAY HERE, BECAUSE MAMA WILL BE ANGRY IF I GO AWAY ON MY OWN.
IF I SEE HER, I WILL TELL HER YOU ARE LOOKING FOR HER.
THANK YOU. GOOD LUCK!
BRR...

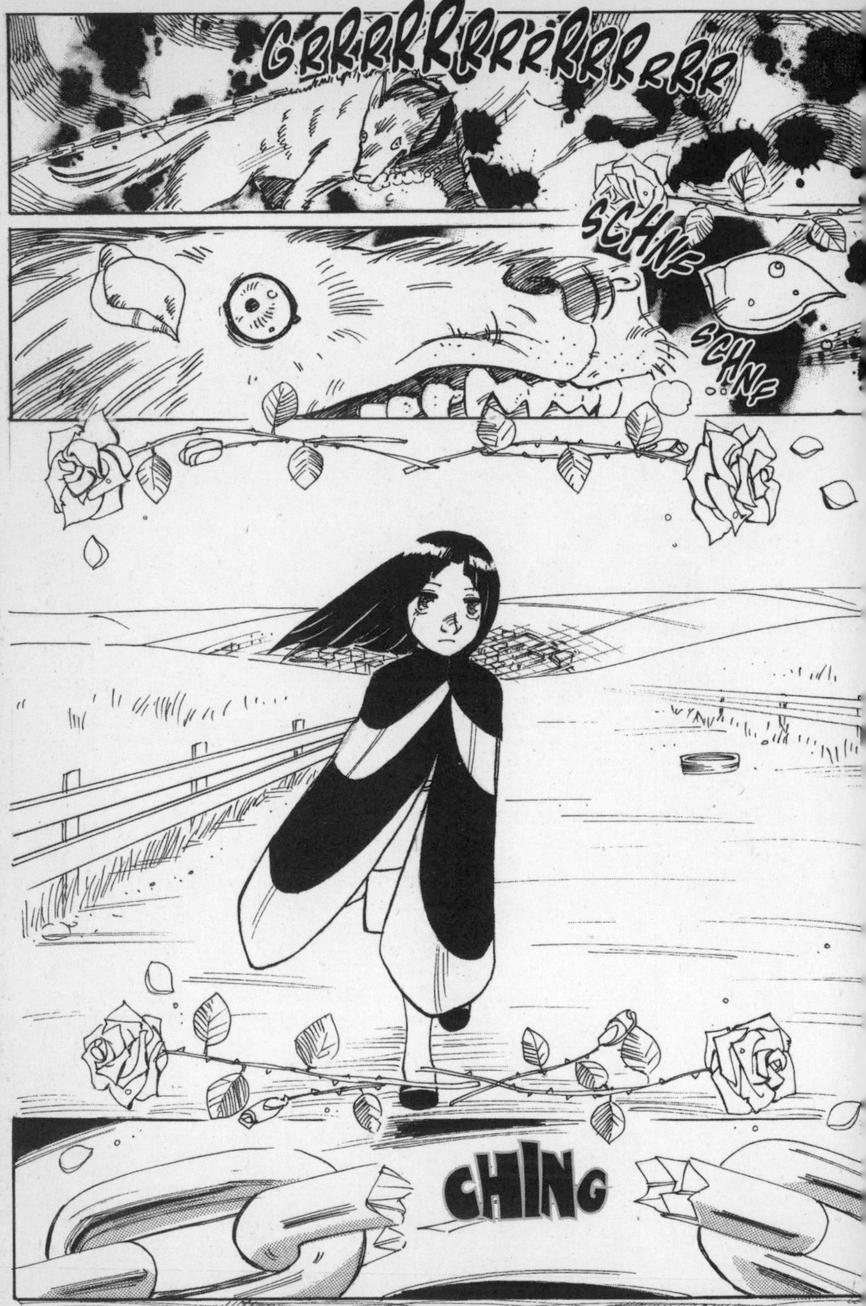
GRRRRRRRRRRRRRRRRR
SCHNF
SCHNF
CHING

BETWEEN THE LINES :: Runner Up ::

....

Emma Vieceli was born in 1979 in Basildon, Essex. She now lives in Cambridge, England and is a moderator and does customer support for an online roleplaying game.
www.toothycat.net/~emsie
www.sweatdrop.com

Favorite manga:
So hard to choose!! Favourites include: *X1999, Kare Kano, Fake, Tarot Café*

Favorite manga artist:
CLAMP, Ryoko Ikeda (she's a pure legend), Sang-Sun Park

....

Author's Comments:
I learned a very important lesson in the creation of this manga. NEVER set a manga in a library!!! It's a lesson that a friend of mine once told me and oh, how I wish I'd listened! *grin*

However, sitting here now, I'm very pleased that I persevered!
My biggest issue with this piece was wondering what on earth was in fact bothering the young man! I spent literally days pondering this and trying to learn his secrets along with the heroine's. Whether I now know the answer will remain a mystery, but I really felt by the end that it just wasn't needed in the comic. My aim was to capture the way in which we can affect the lives of those around us, if only in a small way—I hope that it worked!
—Emma Vieceli

::

::

BETWEEN THE LINES :: Runner Up ::

....

Judge's Comments:
Emma told an extremely simple story and it paid off. This is said not to undermine her storytelling ability, which is quite good, but rather to illustrate an important point: not every manga needs to be an epic—or an excerpt of an epic. So often do we receive RSoM entries or just submissions in general that are so unbelievably dense and sprawling that it becomes painful to even think about them. Manga is a disposable medium that's meant to be read fast...that's a fact. I find that if I have to labour over a story, it's usually not worth it; something's wrong. With "Between the Lines" that was never an issue. The story, in its simplicity, had a main character that was easily relatable and empathic, even with barely a word said. Emma's clean shojo style had a simple, minimalist panel layout that worked to compliment the actions of the main character, rather than overwhelm or distract from the emotions that the story was working to evoke.

The reason this story ended up with a "Runner Up" slot and not higher in the book is that, while Emma has a strong grasp of the aesthetics of manga and has talent, there are some flaws within the art itself, and that was a drawback for some of the judges. There are inconsistencies in characters from panel to panel, her lines lack confidence and their weight is uneven, and she has trouble drawing hands. These are all things fixed with practice... Her skills are there, they just lack refinement. The reason I fought to have this story in the book is that I see amazing potential in Emma, this is someone who in a eight months or a year will be making some of the best shojo manga out there.
—Rob Valois

Judge's Comments:
This was actually my favorite entry out of all the ones I read from this competition. Nothing groundbreaking here and the story isn't very original but I really enjoyed reading "Between the Lines." Creator Emma Vieceli had a simple story she wanted to tell and tells it very well. Many of the entries we read try to stuff too much into 20 pages and suffer from that. This one tried to take something very basic and execute it perfectly. And for the most part, "Between the Lines" succeeded. This was the strongest pure shojo entry that we saw and does a great job of following most shojo conventions. The layout is very strong with close-up shots of the main character's face placed well.

The art can be inconsistent at times and some of the panels could have used more work. This was definitely an entry where it helped to look at it as a whole and not focus on each individual part. But even with that, it had a certain charm that drew in most of the judges. This is an artist with a lot of potential and I'd like to see her try something more challenging in the future.
—Alexis Kirsch

::

114

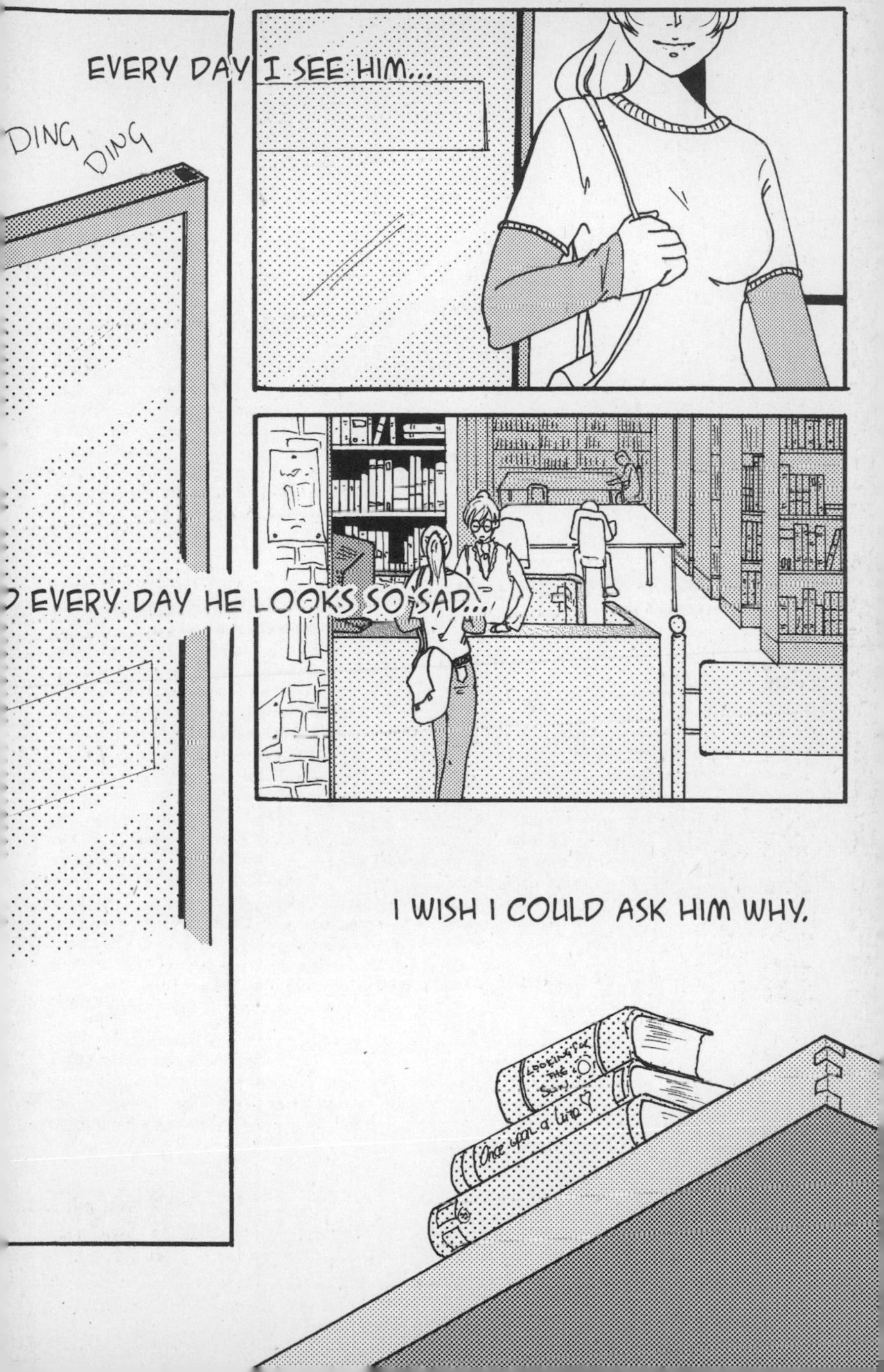
EVERY DAY I SEE HIM...
DING
DING
EVERY DAY HE LOOKS SO SAD...
I WISH I COULD ASK HIM WHY.
LOOKING FOR THE SUN
Once upon a time

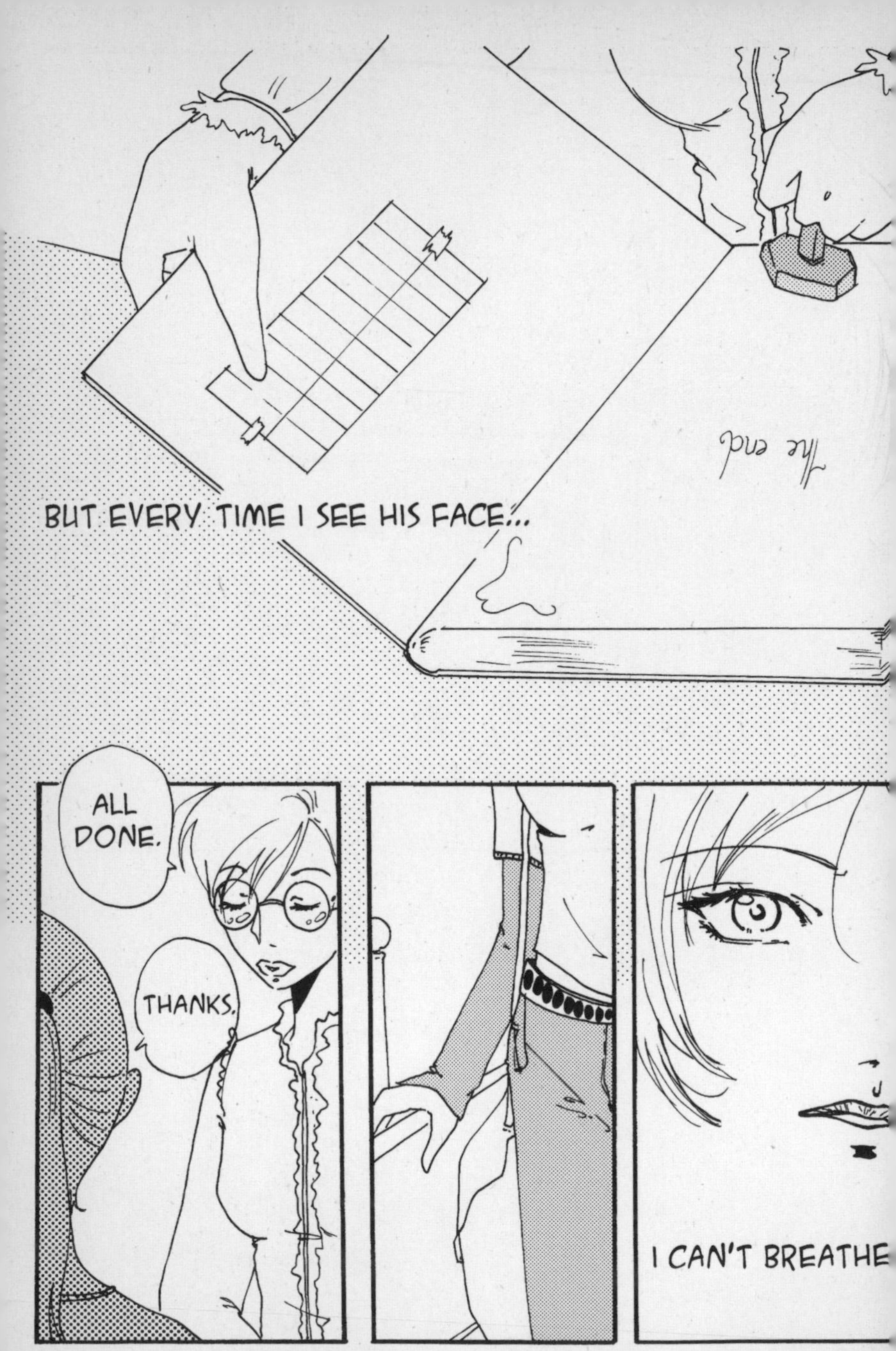

the end
BUT EVERY TIME I SEE HIS FACE...
ALL DONE.
THANKS.
I CAN'T BREATHE

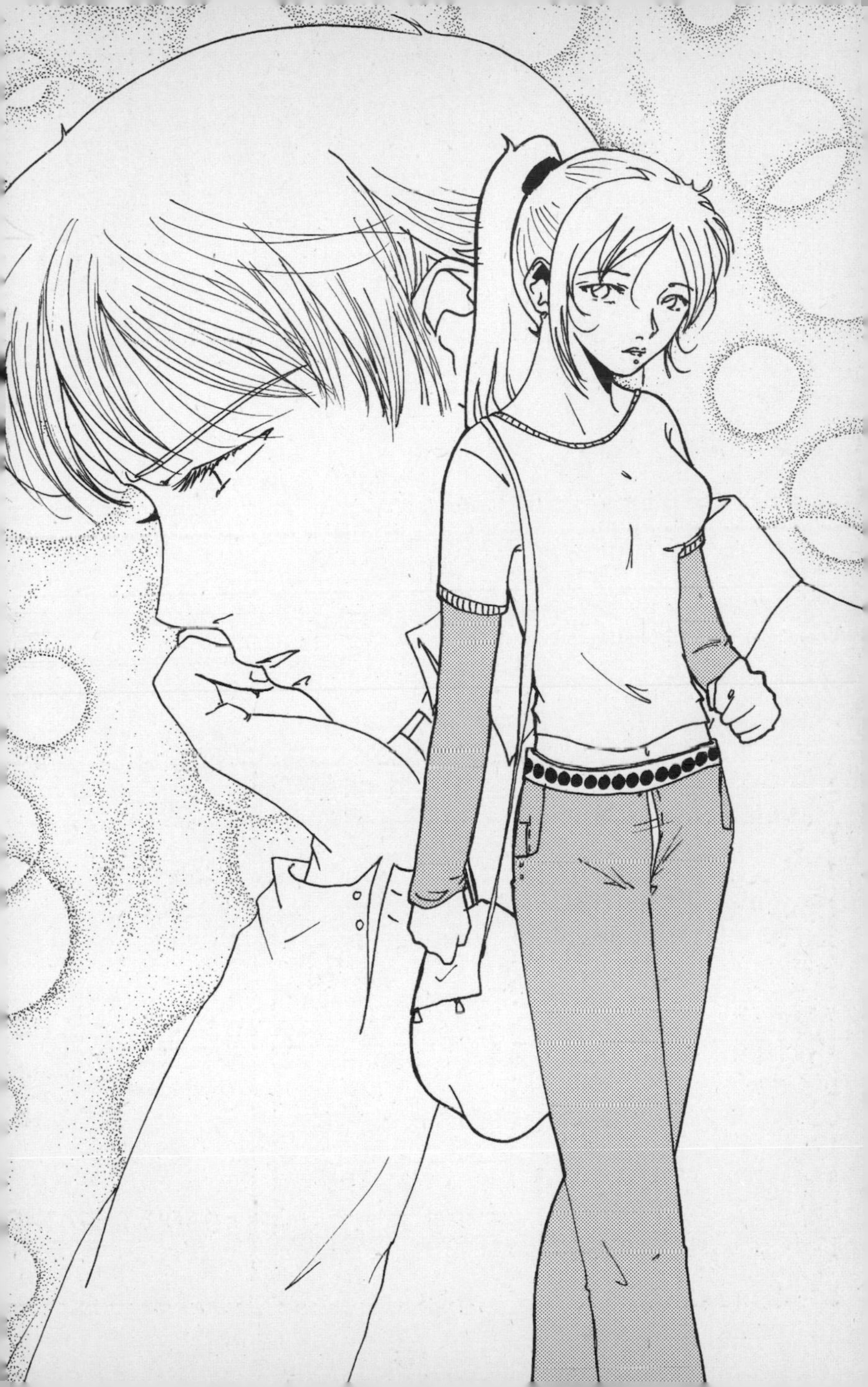

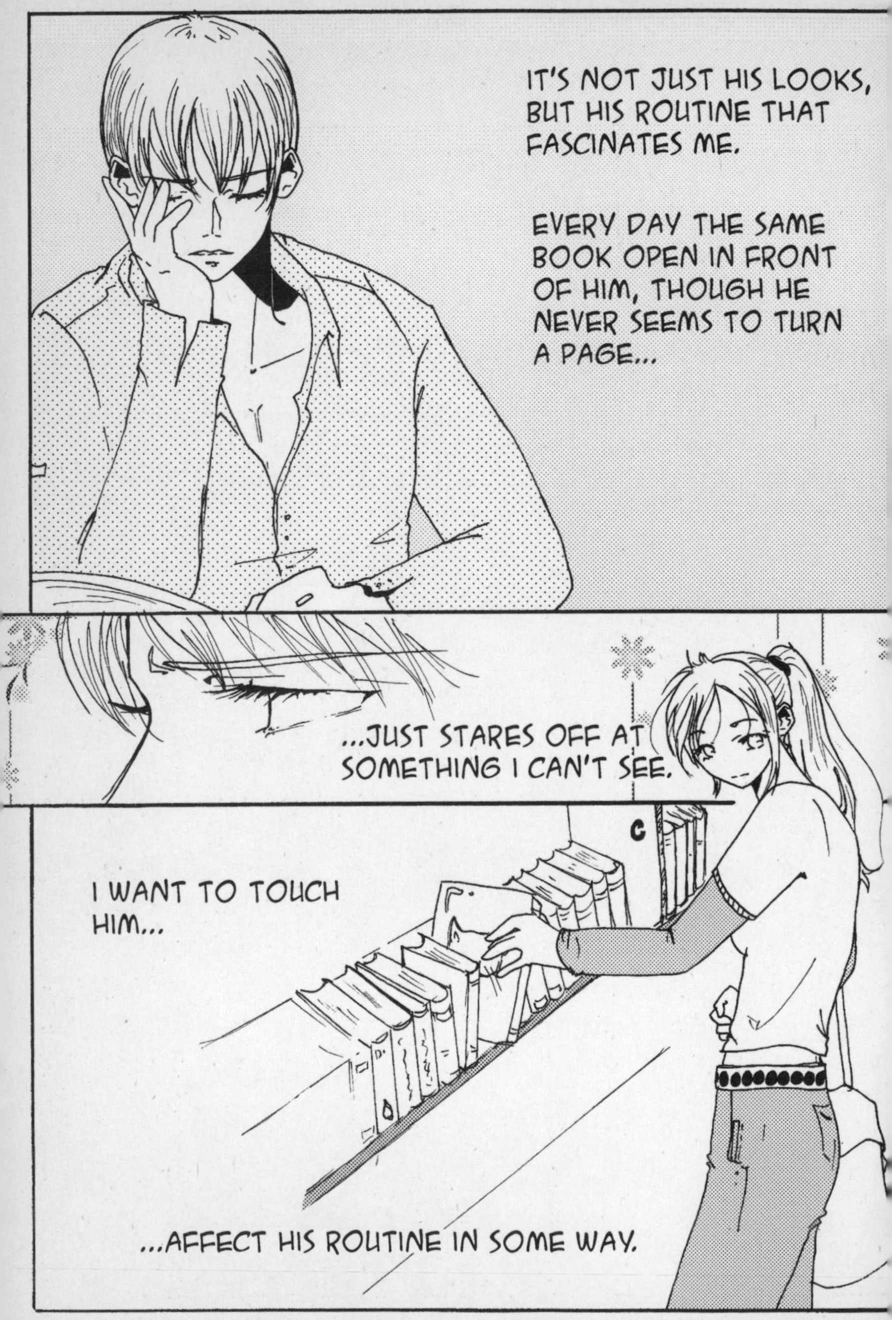
IT'S NOT JUST HIS LOOKS, BUT HIS ROUTINE THAT FASCINATES ME.
EVERY DAY THE SAME BOOK OPEN IN FRONT OF HIM, THOUGH HE NEVER SEEMS TO TURN A PAGE...
...JUST STARES OFF AT SOMETHING I CAN'T SEE.
I WANT TO TOUCH HIM...
...AFFECT HIS ROUTINE IN SOME WAY.

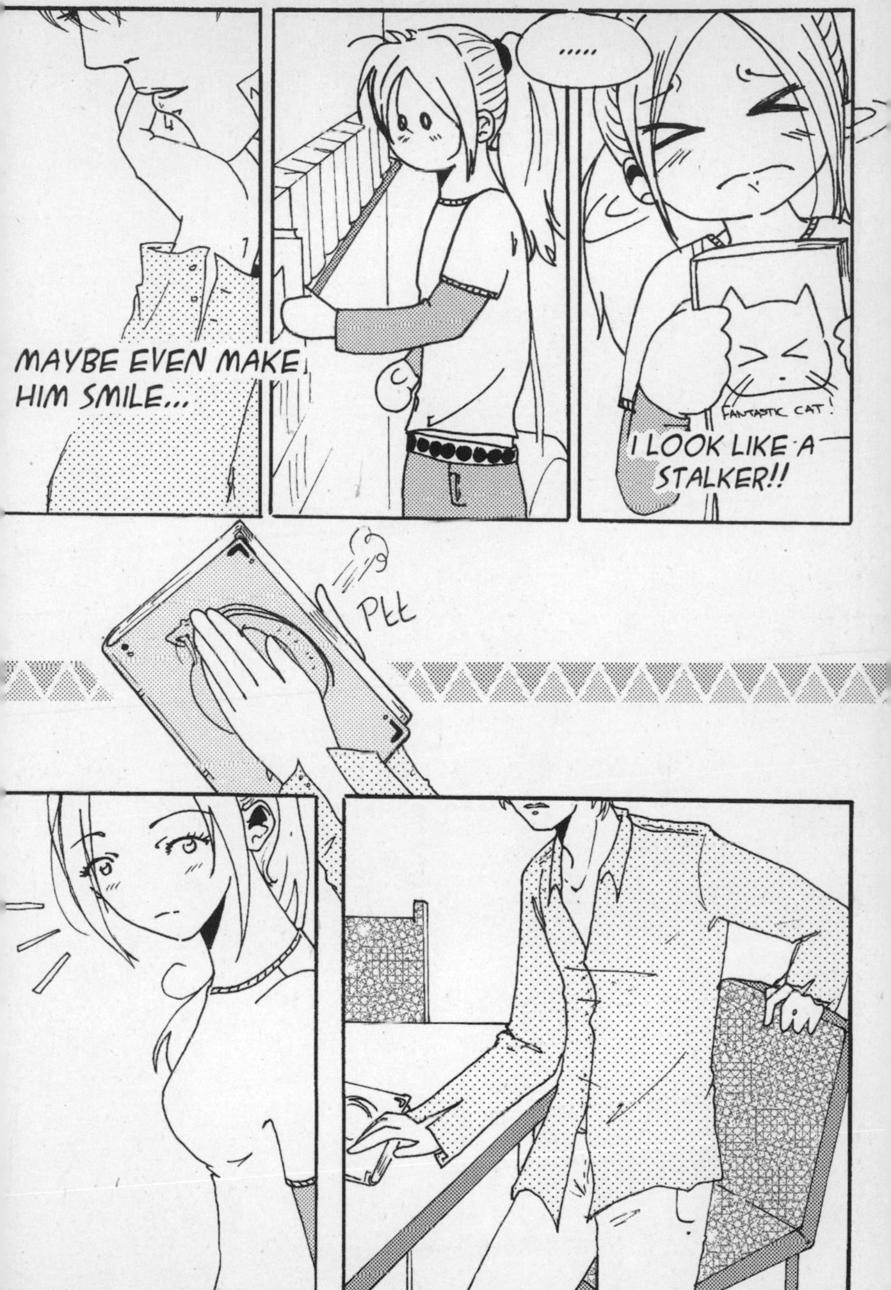
MAYBE EVEN MAKE HIM SMILE...
.....
FANTASTIC CAT!
I LOOK LIKE A STALKER!!
PLE

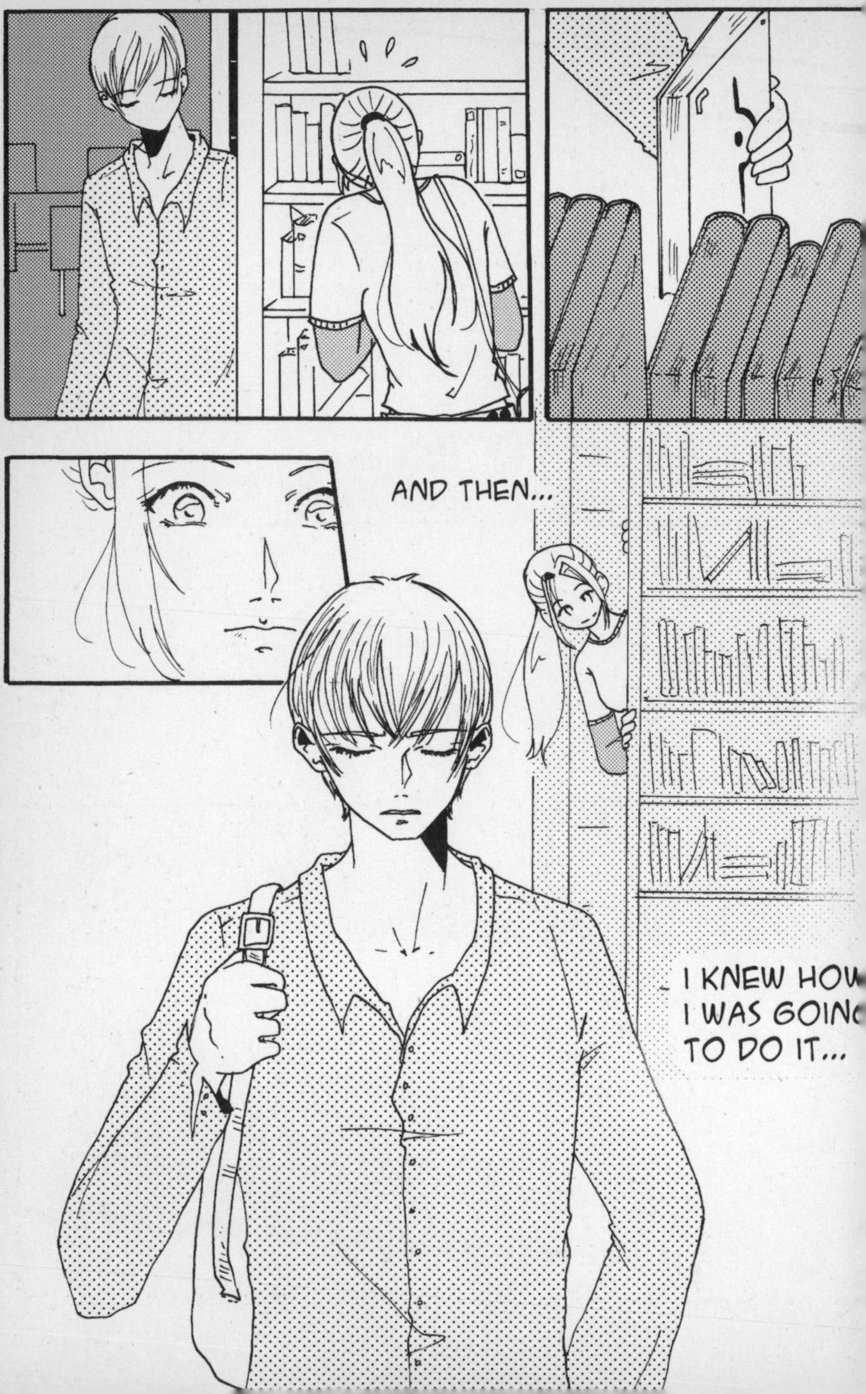
AND THEN...
I KNEW HOW I WAS GOING TO DO IT...

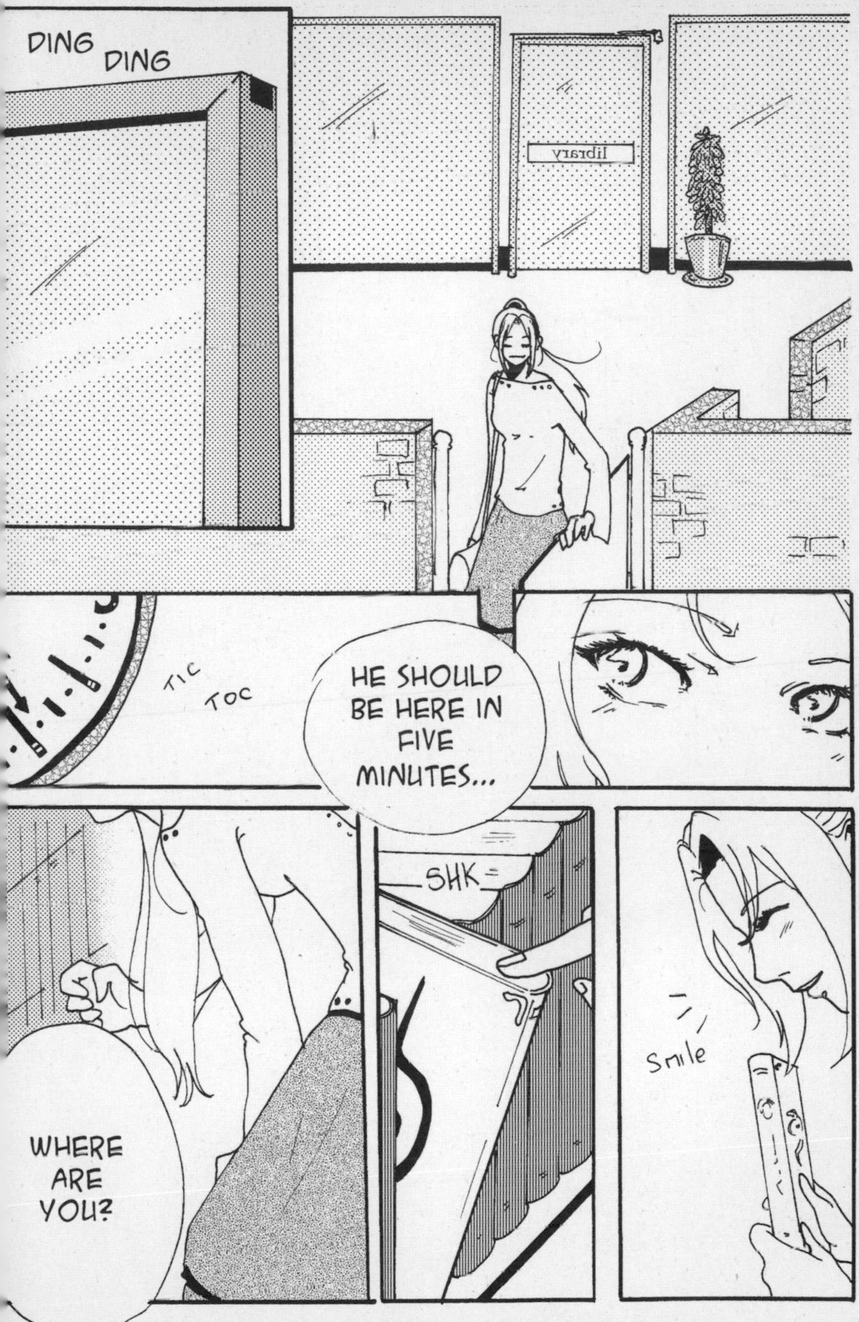
DING
DING
library
TIC
TOC
HE SHOULD BE HERE IN FIVE MINUTES...
WHERE ARE YOU?
SHK
Smile

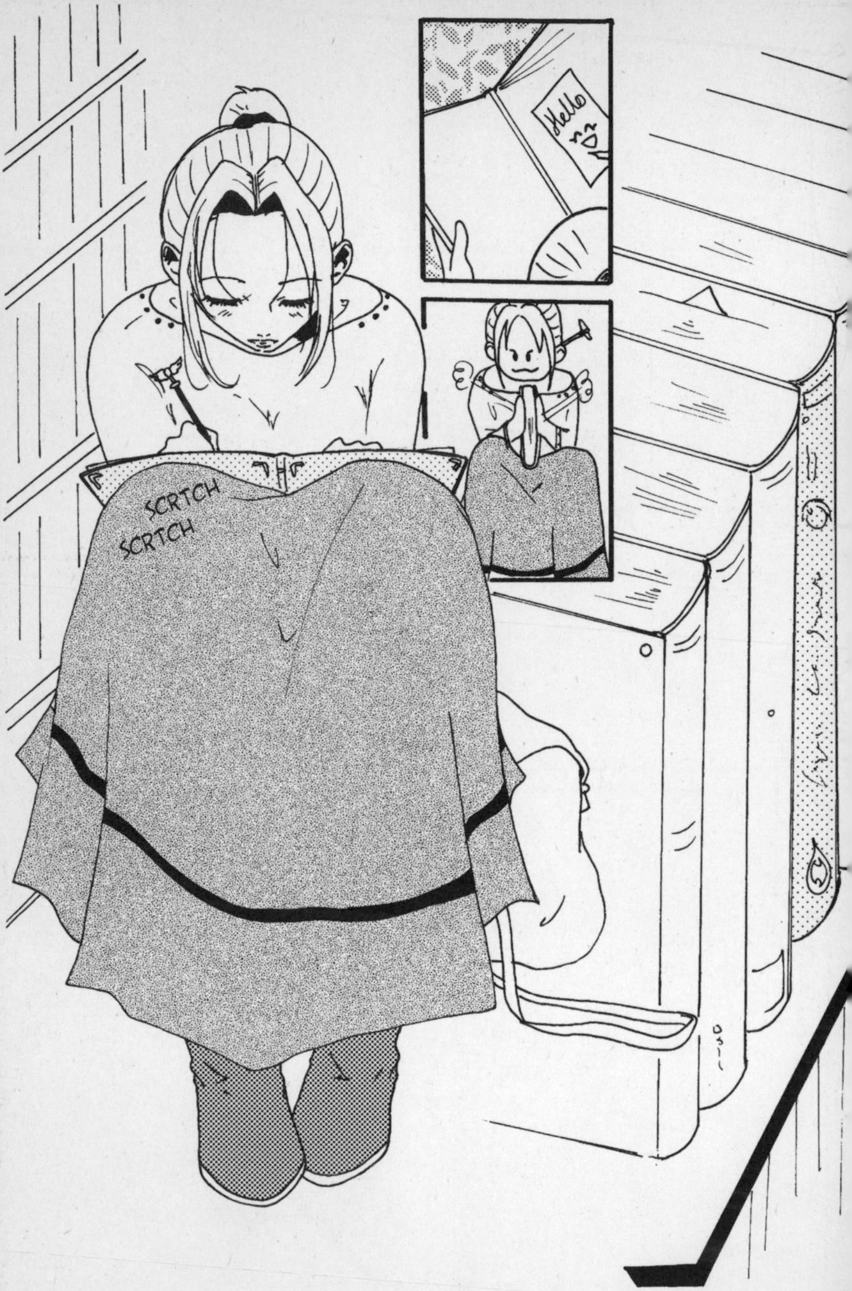
SCRTCH
SCRTCH
Hello

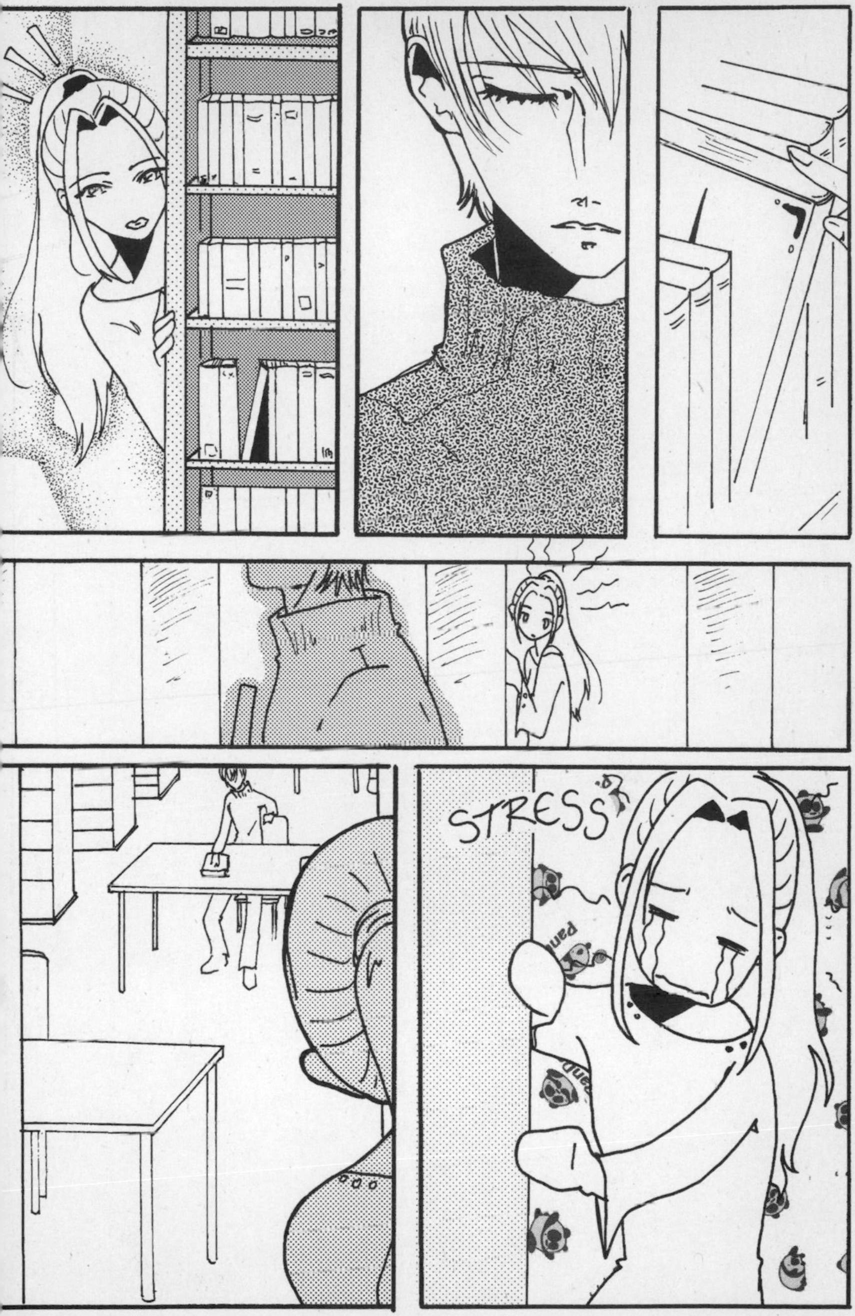
STRESS

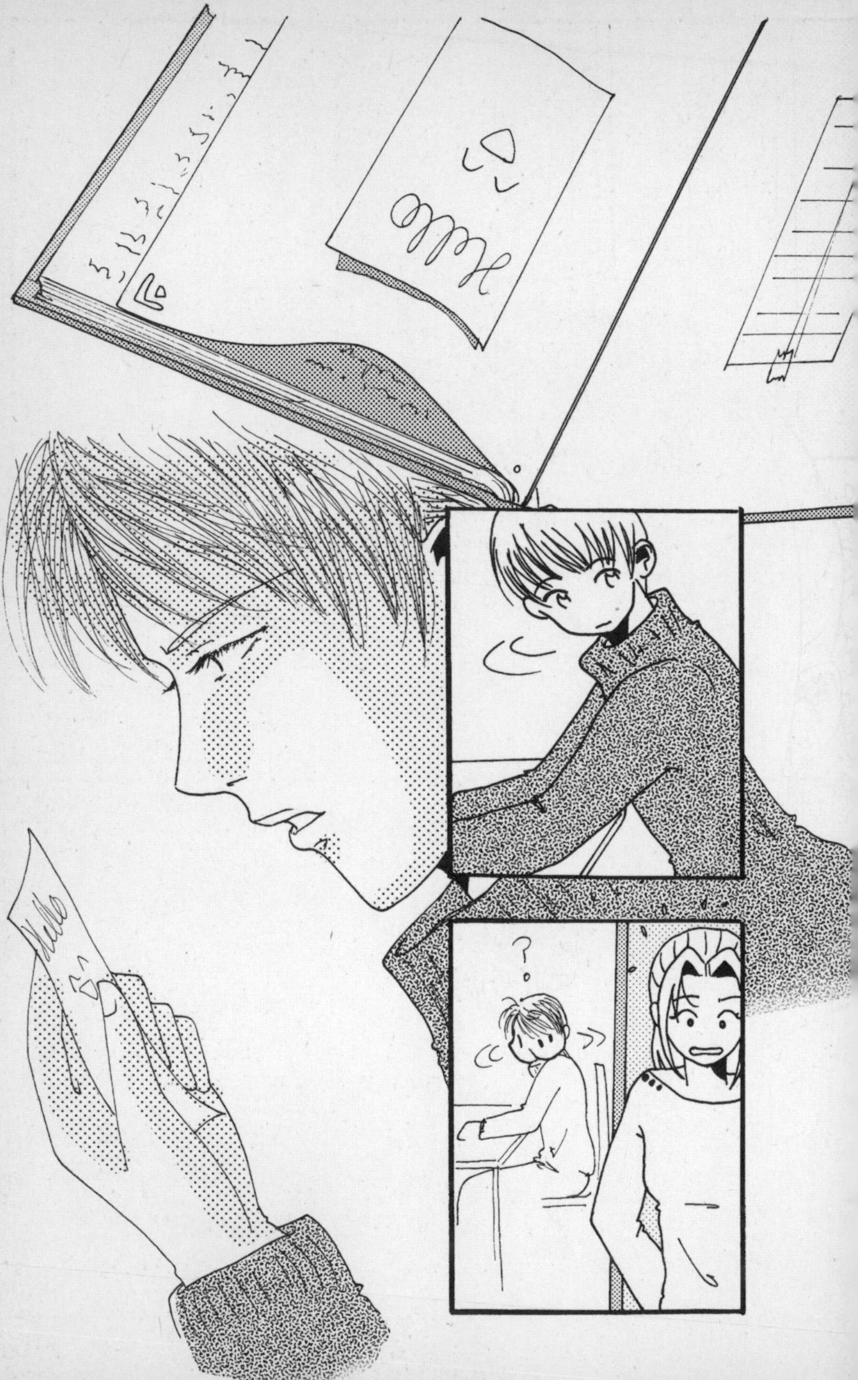
Hello
Hello
?

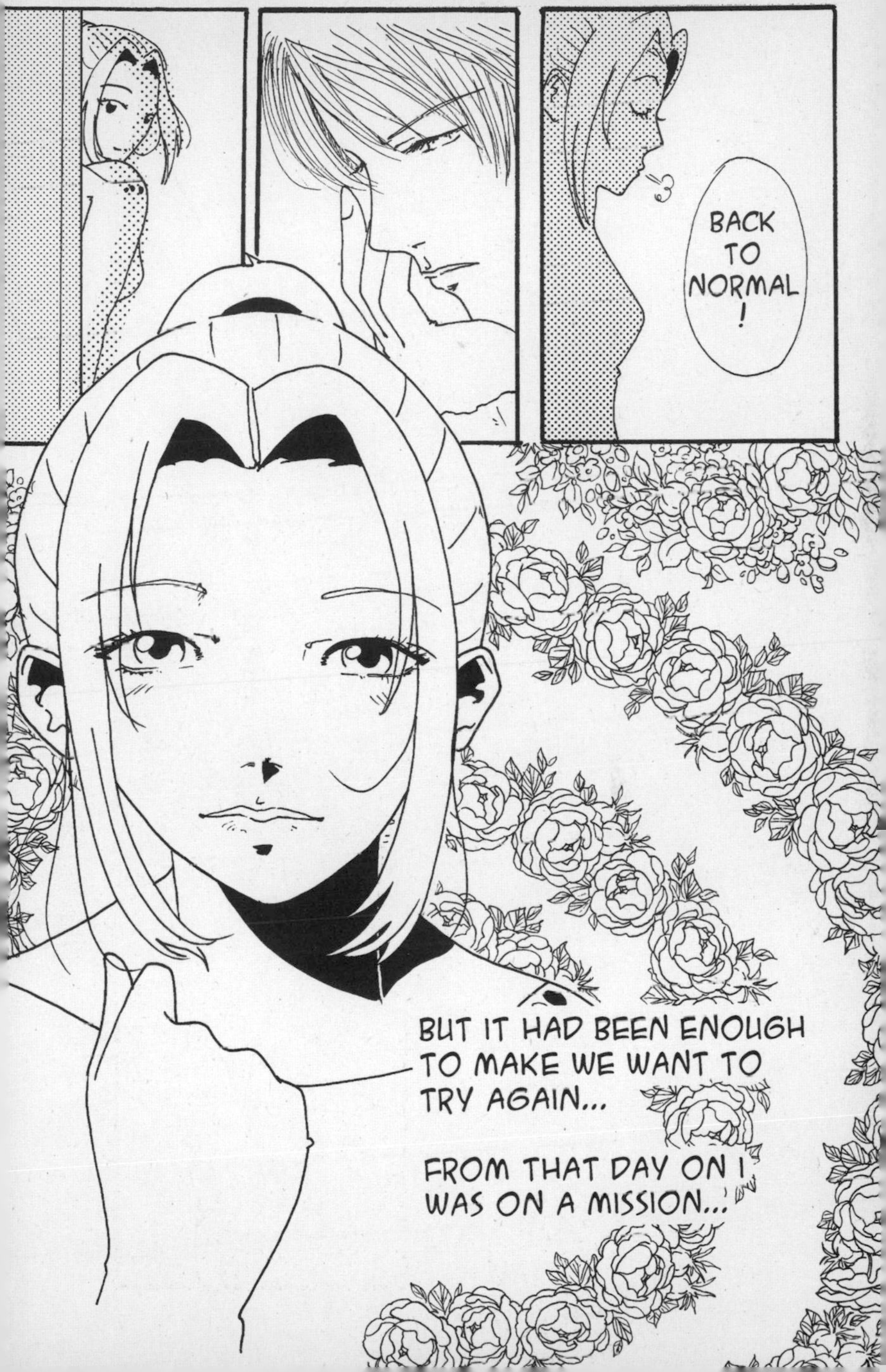
BACK TO NORMAL !
BUT IT HAD BEEN ENOUGH TO MAKE WE WANT TO TRY AGAIN...
FROM THAT DAY ON I WAS ON A MISSION...

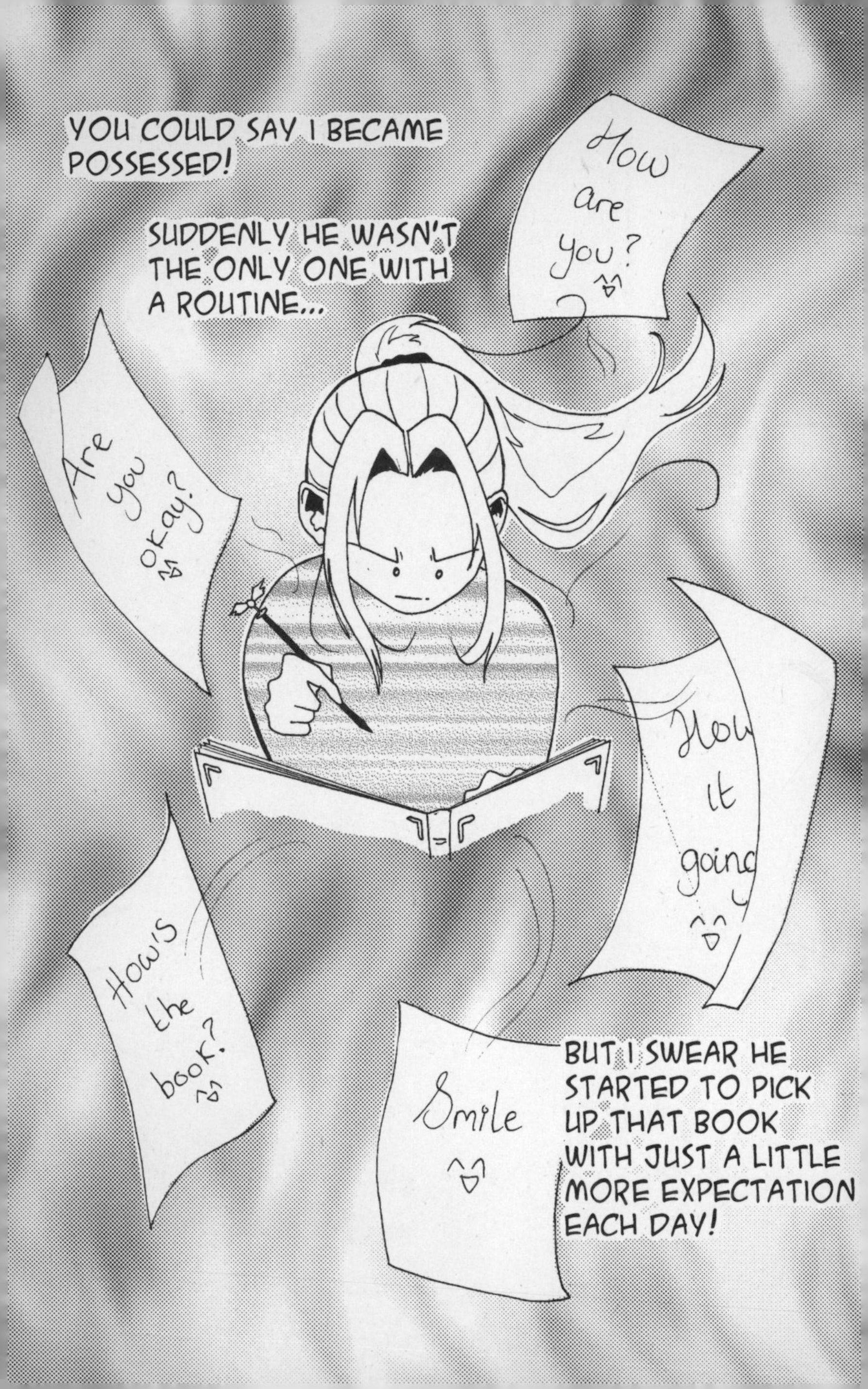
YOU COULD SAY I BECAME POSSESSED!
How are you?
SUDDENLY HE WASN'T THE ONLY ONE WITH A ROUTINE...
Are you okay?
How it going
How's the book?
Smile
BUT I SWEAR HE STARTED TO PICK UP THAT BOOK WITH JUST A LITTLE MORE EXPECTATION EACH DAY!

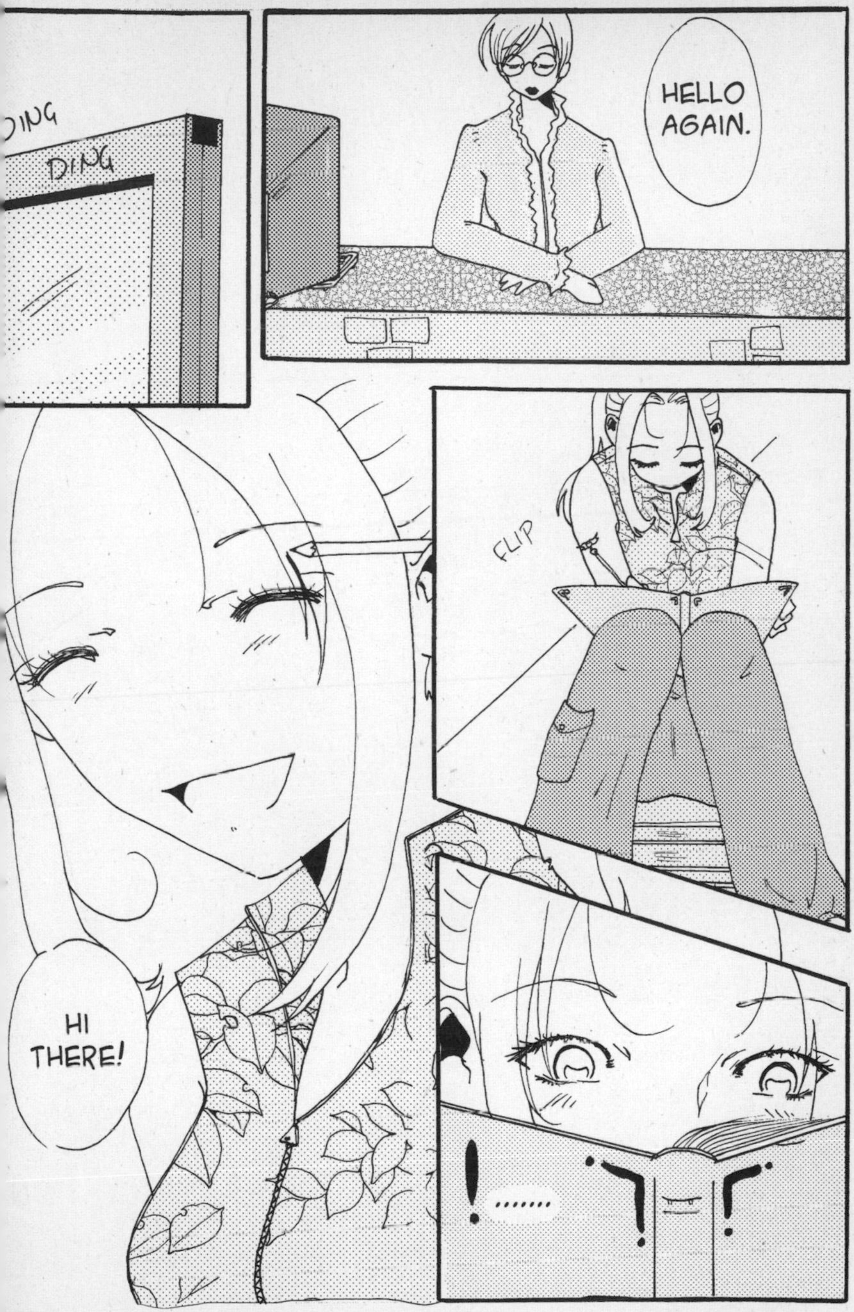
DING
DING
HELLO AGAIN.
HI THERE!
FLIP
!
....
!

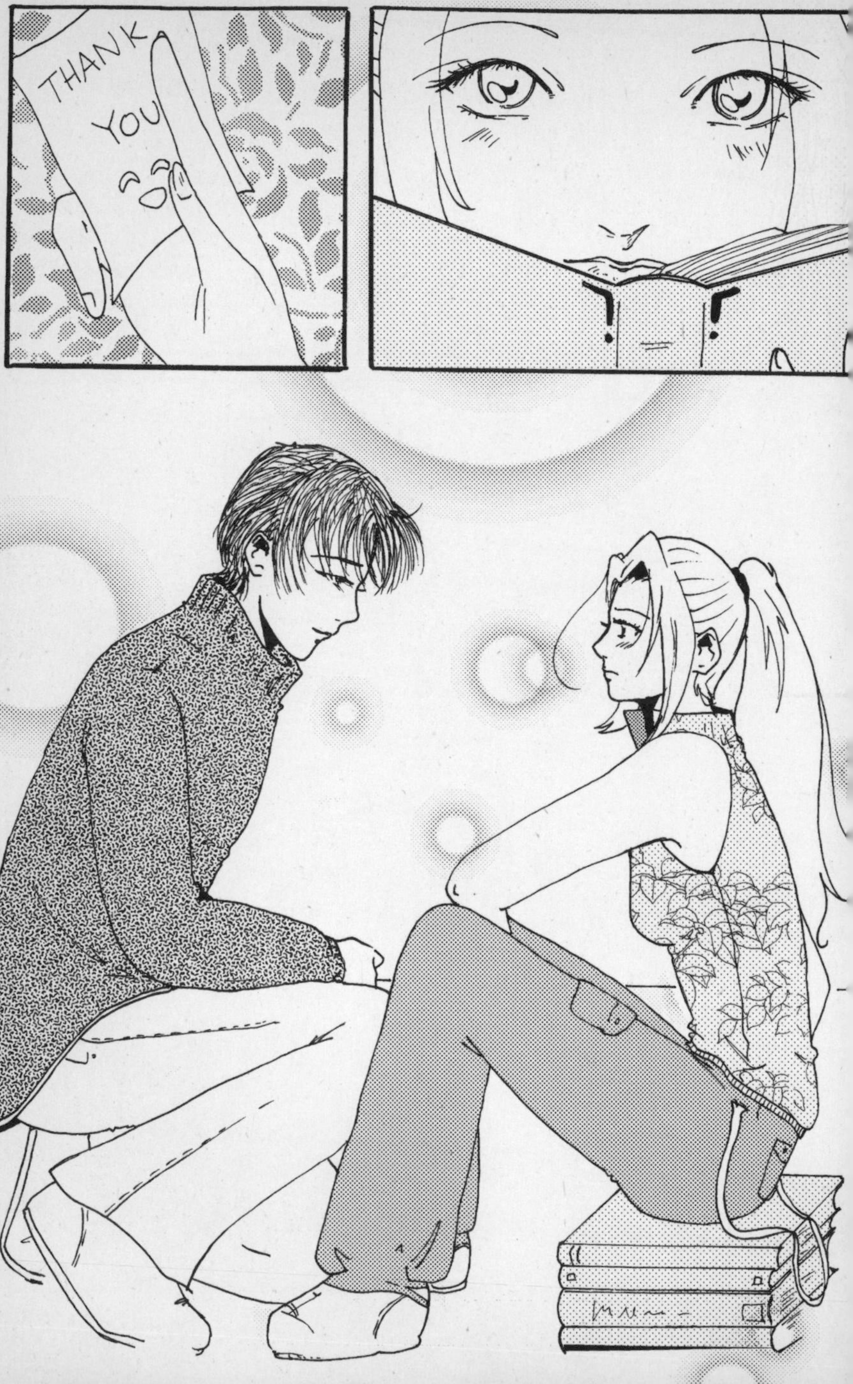
THANK YOU

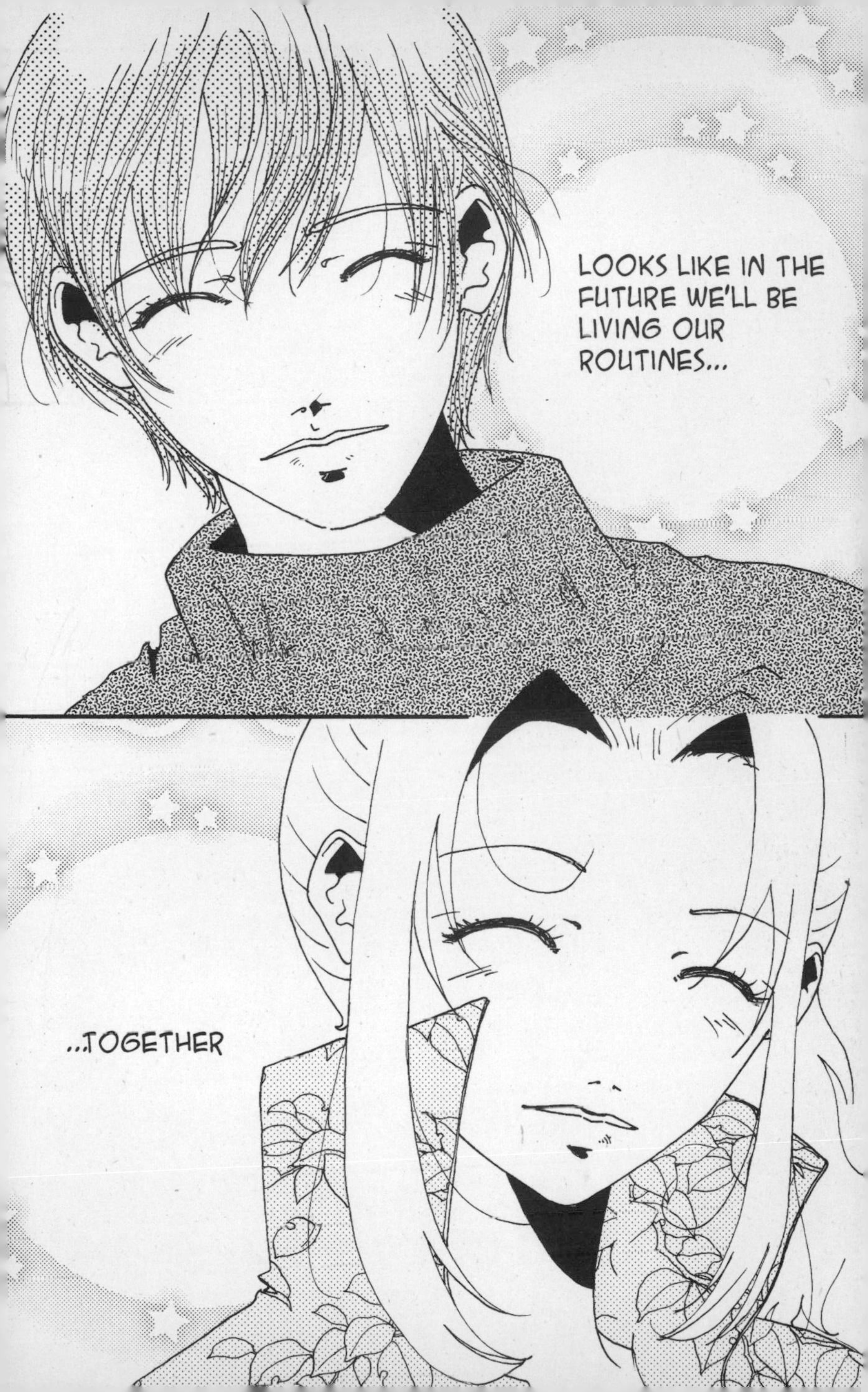
LOOKS LIKE IN THE FUTURE WE'LL BE LIVING OUR ROUTINES...
...TOGETHER

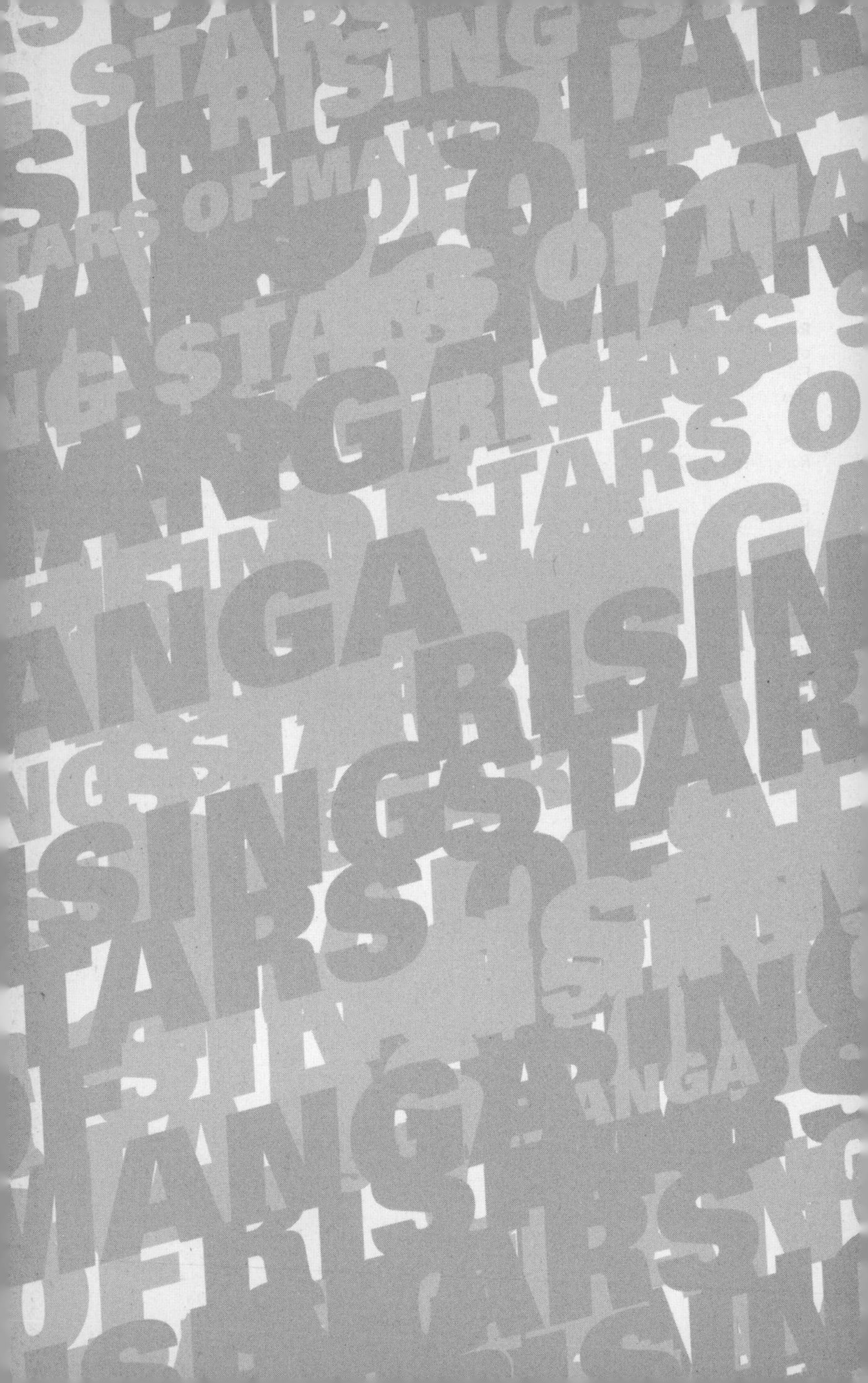

::

PRINCE OF CATS :: Runner Up ::

....

Roxanne Chen was born in London in 1988 where she lived until the age of 11. She currently lives in Bradford, West Yorkshire where she's a Sixth Form student.
chensterrain.cjb.net

Favorite manga:
Ranma 1/2, .Hack, Akira, Fullmetal Alchemist

Favorite manga artist:
Katsuhiro Otomo, Kosuke Fujishima, Akihiko Yoshida, Yi Lee, Tetsuya Nomura and Masaru Gotsubo.

....

Author's Comments:
I'd originally had much bigger plans for this manga—epic battles, car crashes, huge summons (complete with battlecries), you name it! But... uh...it didn't quite work out, and in the end I toned down the story and action quite a bit. There might also be the tiniest hint of RPG influence in there, but I'm sure it's unnoticeable. Really.
—Roxanne Chen

::

PRINCE OF CATS

RUNNER UP

RISING.STARS.OF.MANGA.2006

::

PRINCE OF CATS :: Runner Up ::

Judge's Comments:
Roxanne's story instantly won me over with its charming character designs and highly entertaining dialogue. Snappy writing is always a point in your favor in my book, and I got a particular kick out of the conversation between Elnine, the Prince and Pils, the descending gate guardian. It was neat to see the story come full circle too, with the confusing beginning being fully explained in a fun way by the end. As a judge, I did have a sense that there was a lot more going on in the world than the creator really had time to fully elaborate on and explain, and it's always tough to fit a budding epic into twenty short pages.

While inconsistent in places, I really liked Roxanne's artistic style, and especially the costume designs she came up with. They went a long way in setting the scene of the story. One of the biggest flaws in my mind though, was the lack of detailed backgrounds. A lot of love went into rendering the characters, but especially for a story about crossing worlds, I found the lack of environments to be more than a little confusing. I especially found the Edge of the World, which was supposed to be an impressive sight, to be a bit underwhelming and visually confusing. Throwing in some bishonen "fates" to guide our characters along was a great touch, not to mention the cute kitty familiars, but the story would have cohered just that much more if the setting was rendered in a bit more detail.
—Lillian Diaz-Przybyl

Judge's Comments:
I'd estimate that we've received hundreds of fantasy entries since the first *Rising Stars of Manga* contest, and most of them have failed as entries. There are many reasons, but usually it's a simple matter of knowing your page limit. Twenty pages just isn't enough space to tell a fantasy epic, but that hasn't stopped many people from trying.

That's why "Prince of Cats" is so refreshing. It's a fantasy tale, but it's not an epic. It hints at an elaborate world of Fates and magic, but it never bothers explaining it to us, and for good reason—we simply don't need to know. The story is an imaginative one, and it's well told by Roxanne Chen's superb visual storytelling. Granted, it's not a perfect entry. Parts of the story are a little unclear and some plot twists are resolved too conveniently. Inks are generally thicker than they need to be, backgrounds are pretty sparse, and the toning tends to look muddy in places, giving the art an overall flat appearance. It also must be said that while Roxanne draws her characters in a unique style, if the wildly mixed reaction it received from the judges is any indication, it's not a style that appeals to everyone.

Even with its flaws, "Prince of Cats" is a stellar debut, and is certainly deserving of inclusion in this collection. Only in this case, the reason has nothing to do with fate, but with talent.
—Tim Beedle

::

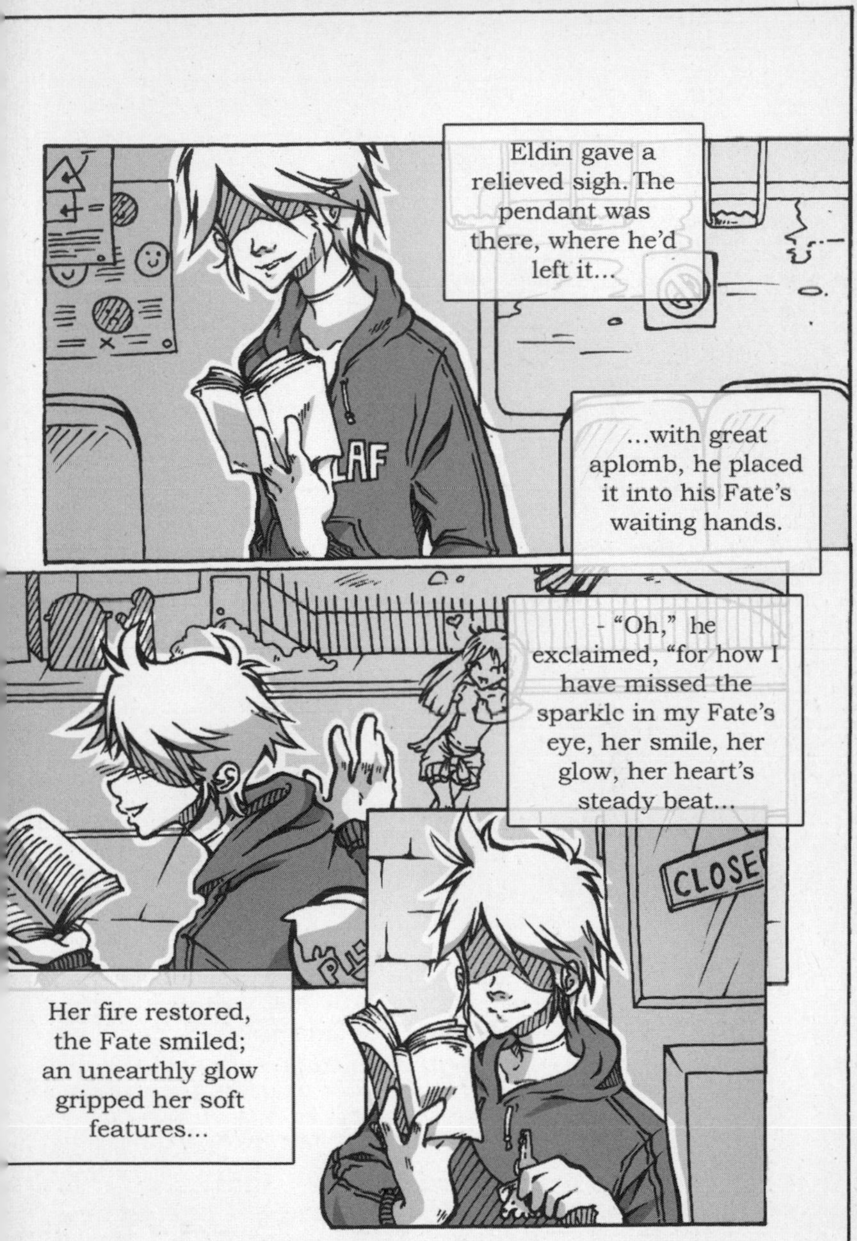
Eldin gave a relieved sigh. The pendant was there, where he'd left it...
...with great aplomb, he placed it into his Fate's waiting hands.
- "Oh," he exclaimed, "for how I have missed the sparklc in my Fate's eye, her smile, her glow, her heart's steady beat...
CLOSE
Her fire restored, the Fate smiled; an unearthly glow gripped her soft features...

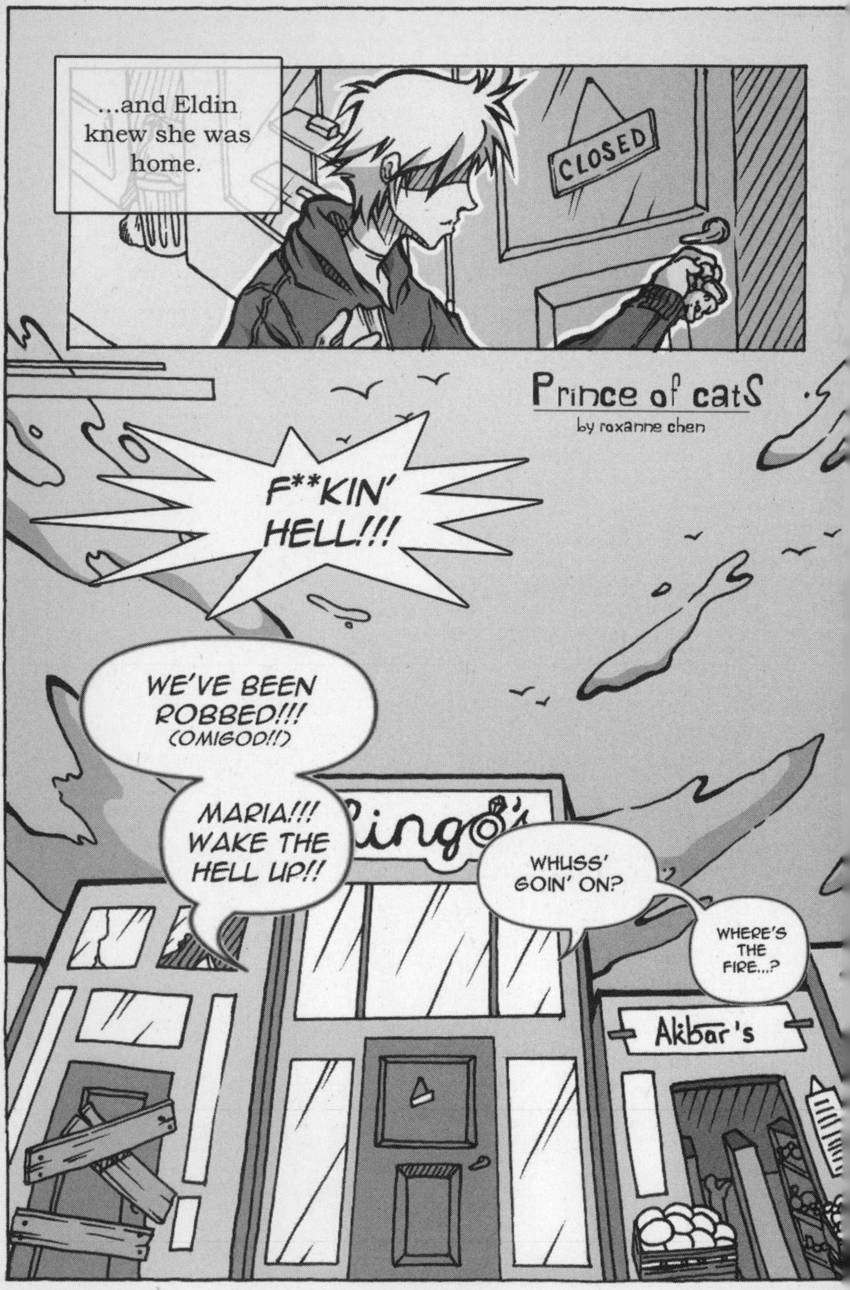

...and Eldin knew she was home.
CLOSED
Prince of catS
by roxanne chen
F**KIN' HELL!!!
WE'VE BEEN ROBBED!!! (OMIGOD!!)
MARIA!!! WAKE THE HELL UP!!
Ringo's
WHUSS' GOIN' ON?
WHERE'S THE FIRE...?
Akbar's

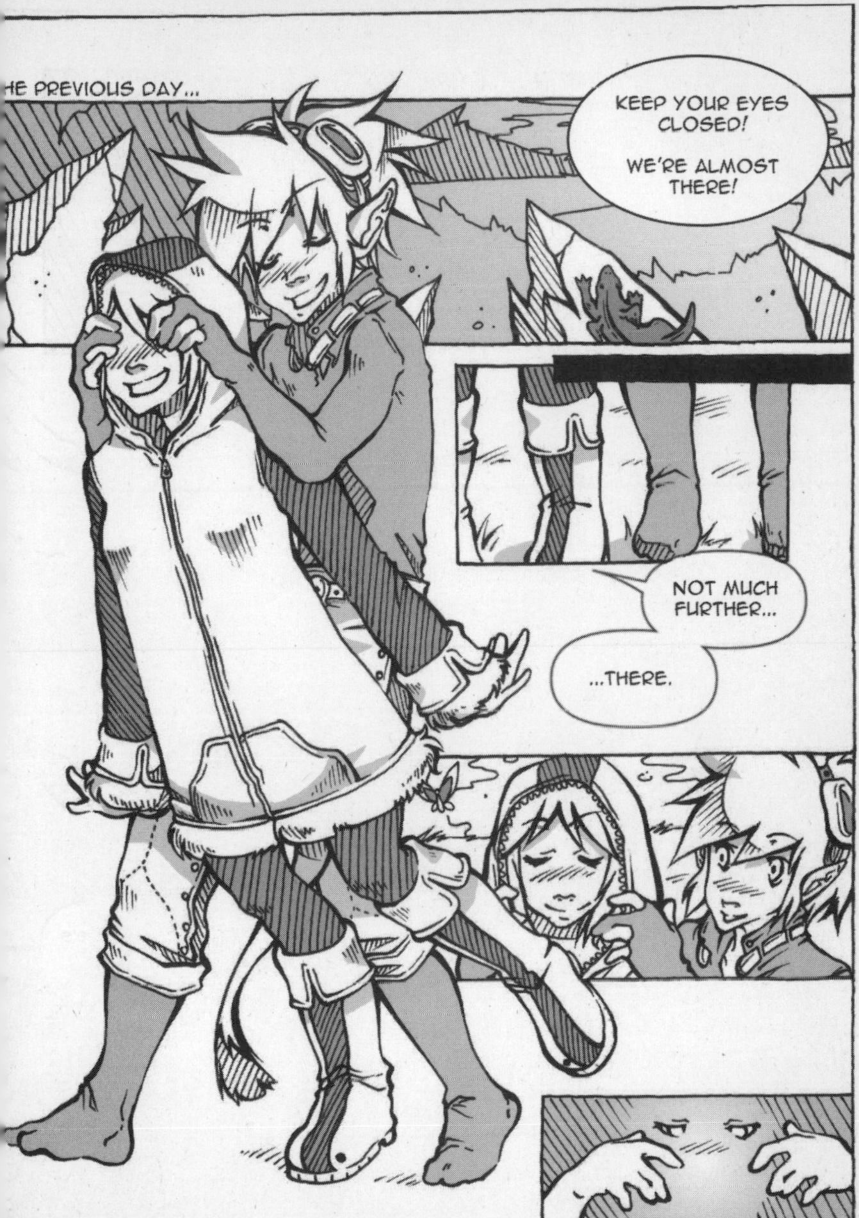
HE PREVIOUS DAY...
KEEP YOUR EYES CLOSED! WE'RE ALMOST THERE!
NOT MUCH FURTHER...
...THERE.

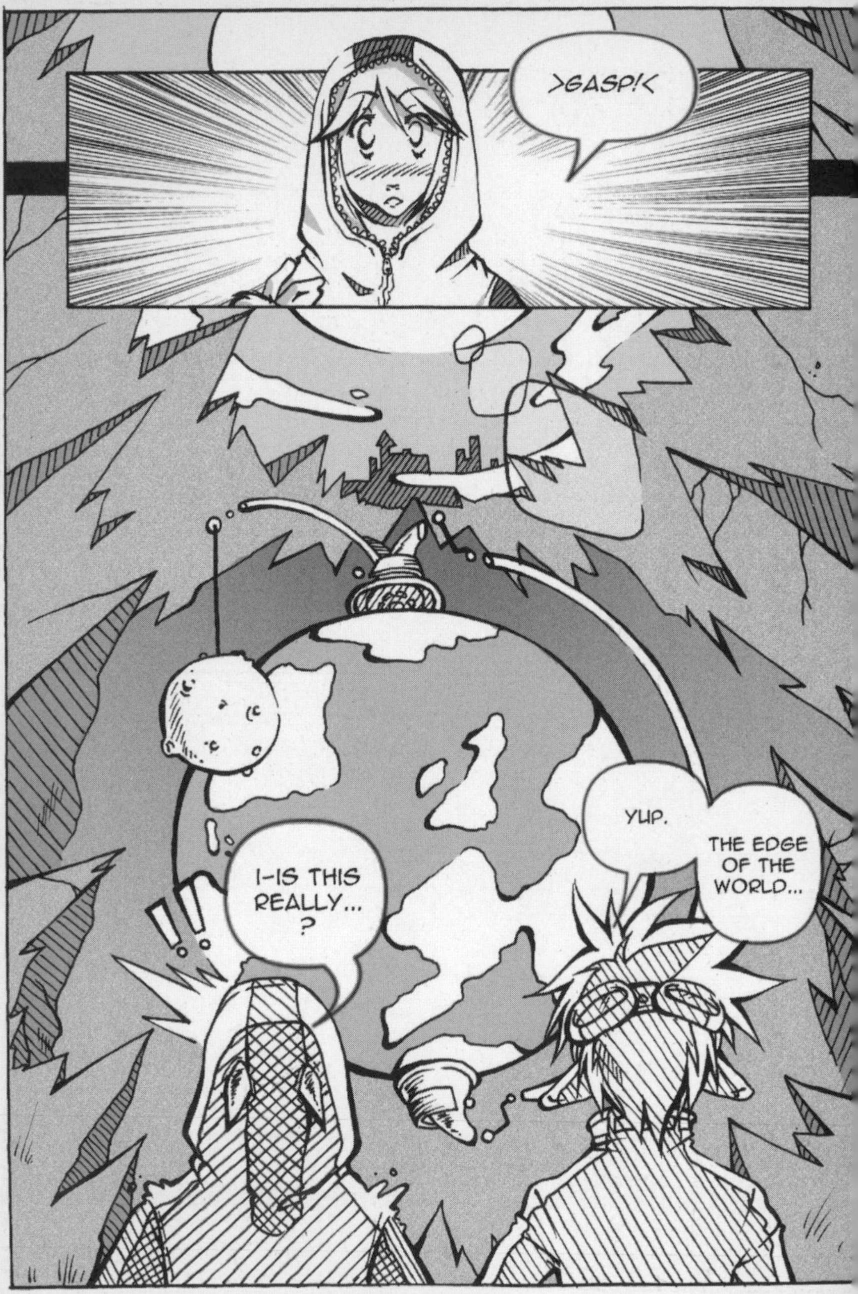
>GASP!<
I-IS THIS REALLY... ?
YUP.
THE EDGE OF THE WORLD...

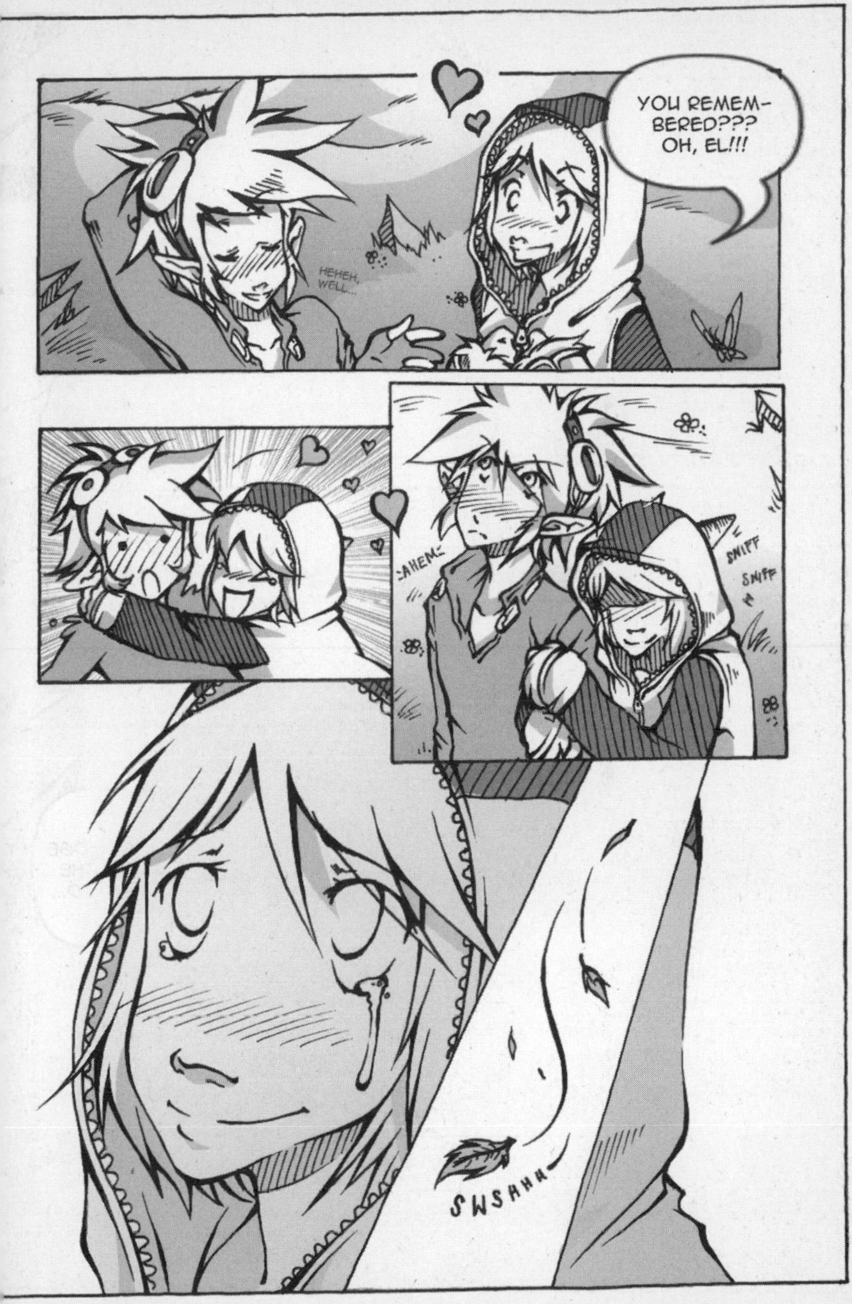
YOU REMEMBERED??? OH, EL!!!
HEHEH, WELL...
AHEM
SNIFF
SNIFF
SWSAHH

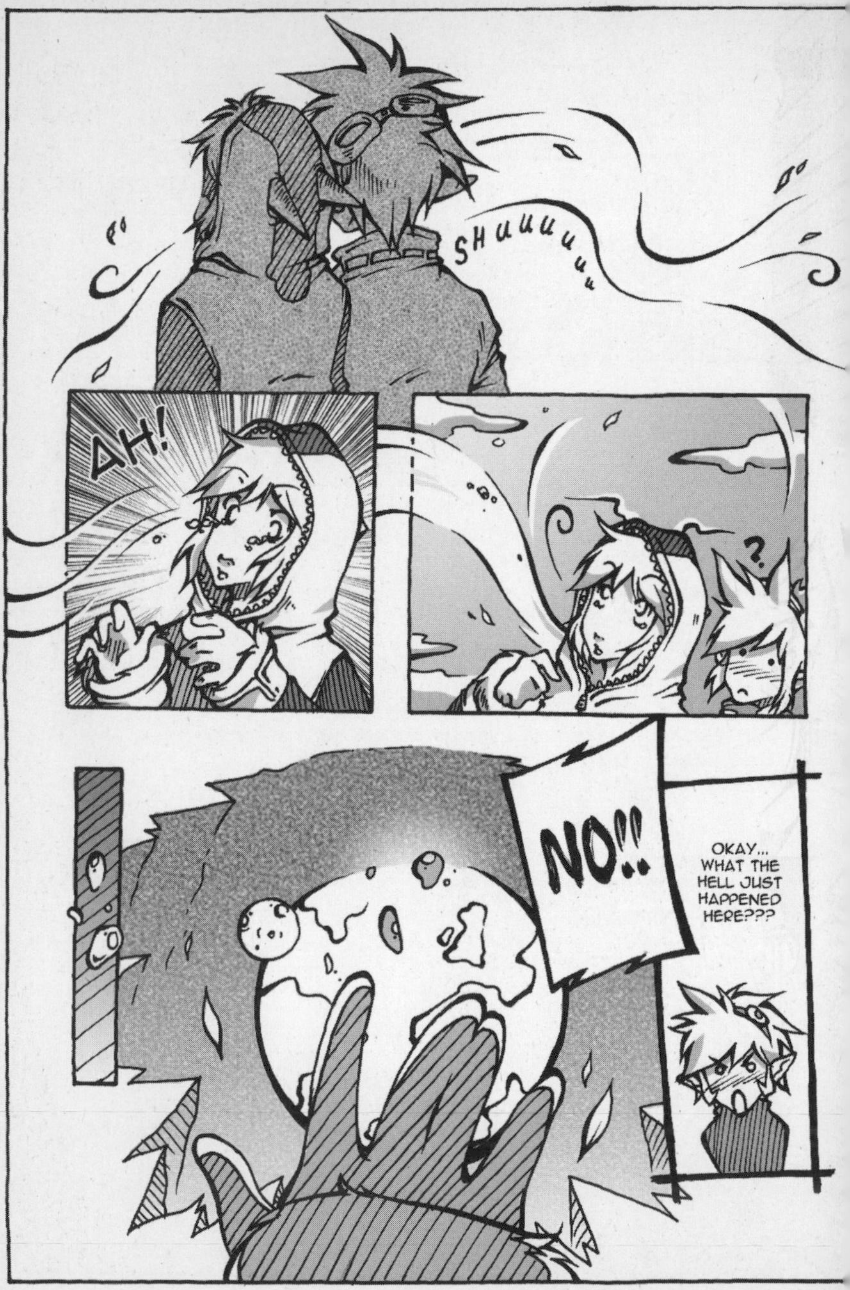
SHUUUUUUU
AH!
?
NO!!
OKAY... WHAT THE HELL JUST HAPPENED HERE???

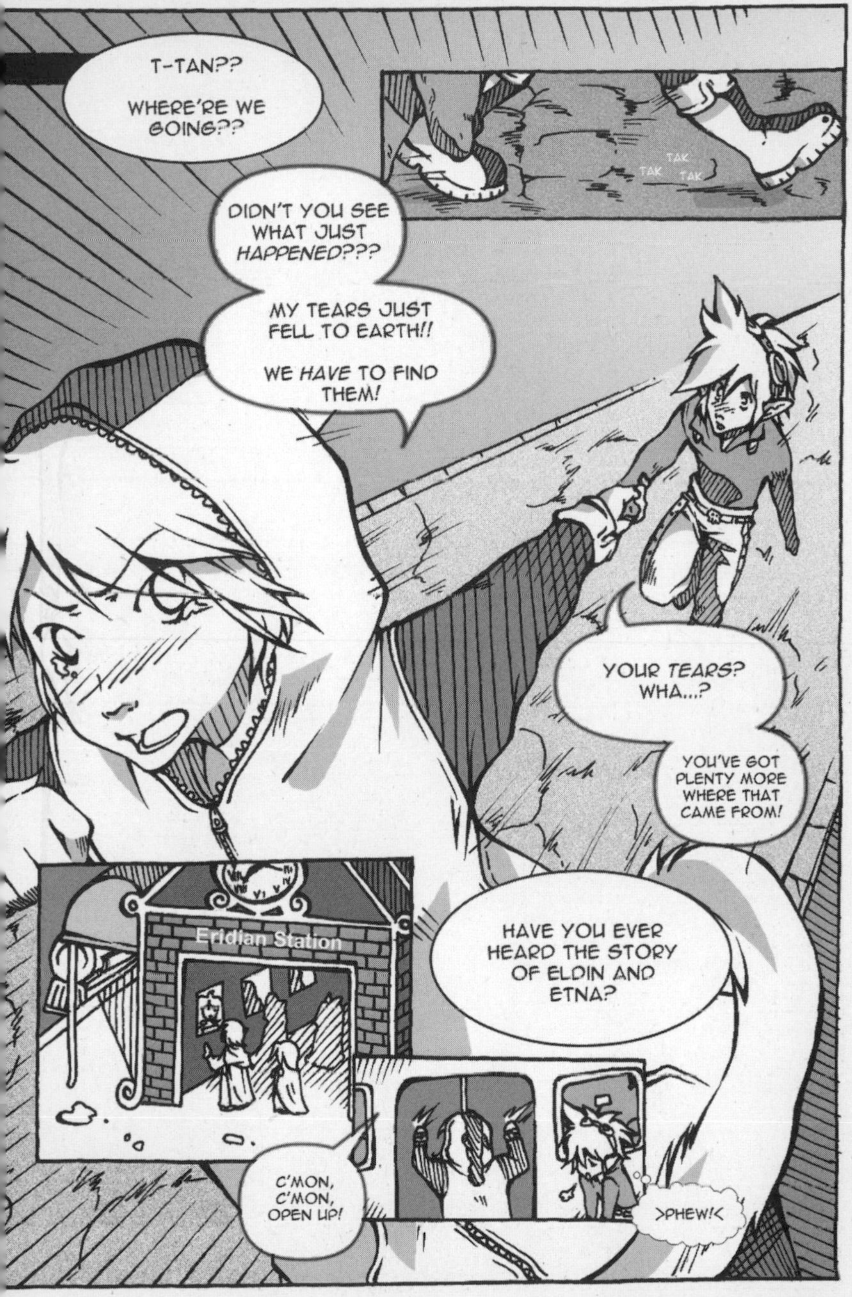
T-TAN??
WHERE'RE WE GOING??
TAK
TAK
TAK
DIDN'T YOU SEE WHAT JUST *HAPPENED*???
MY TEARS JUST FELL TO EARTH!!
WE *HAVE* TO FIND THEM!
YOUR *TEARS*? WHA...?
YOU'VE GOT PLENTY MORE WHERE THAT CAME FROM!
Eridian Station
HAVE YOU EVER HEARD THE STORY OF ELDIN AND ETNA?
C'MON, C'MON, OPEN UP!
>PHEW!<

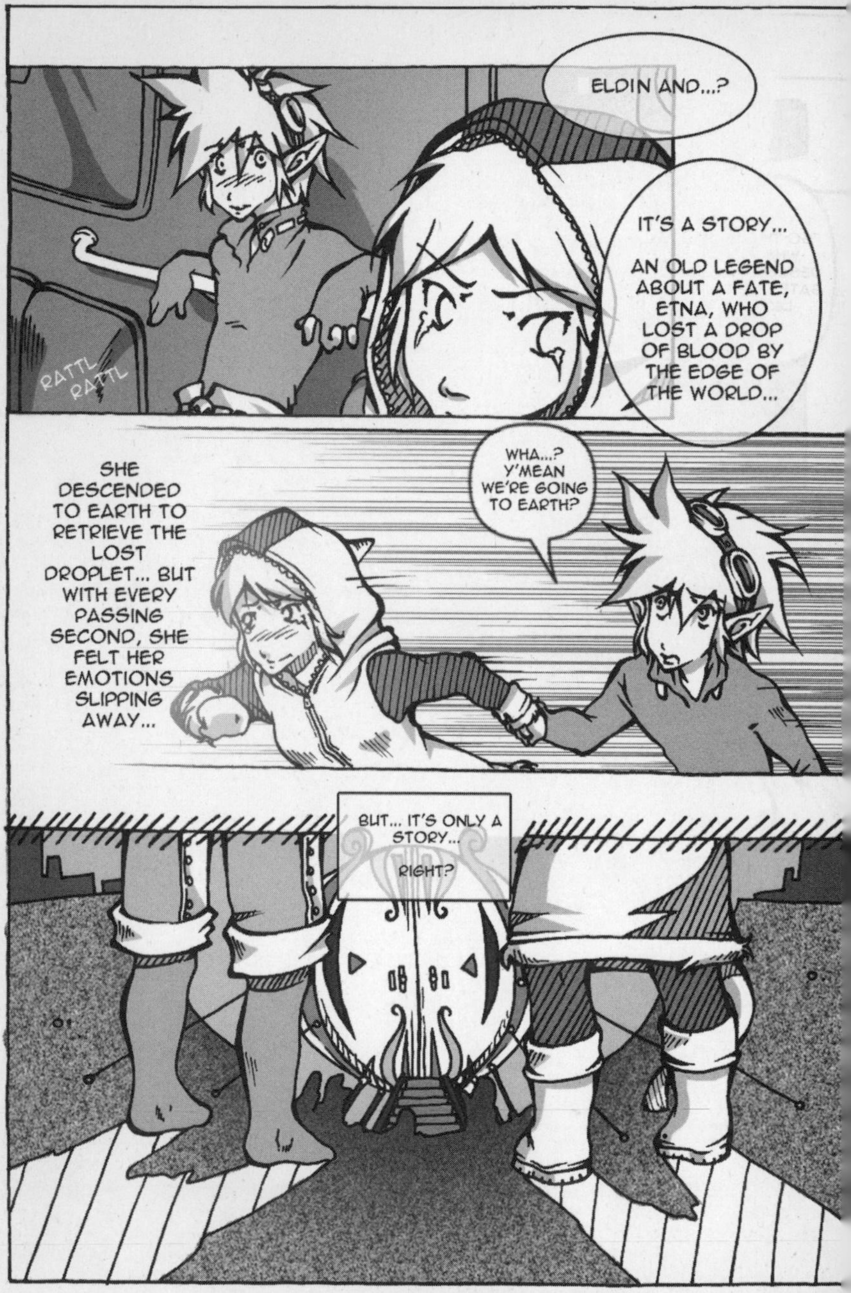
ELDIN AND...?
IT'S A STORY...
AN OLD LEGEND ABOUT A FATE, ETNA, WHO LOST A DROP OF BLOOD BY THE EDGE OF THE WORLD...
RATTL RATTL
SHE DESCENDED TO EARTH TO RETRIEVE THE LOST DROPLET... BUT WITH EVERY PASSING SECOND, SHE FELT HER EMOTIONS SLIPPING AWAY...
WHA...? Y'MEAN WE'RE GOING TO EARTH?
BUT... IT'S ONLY A STORY...
RIGHT?

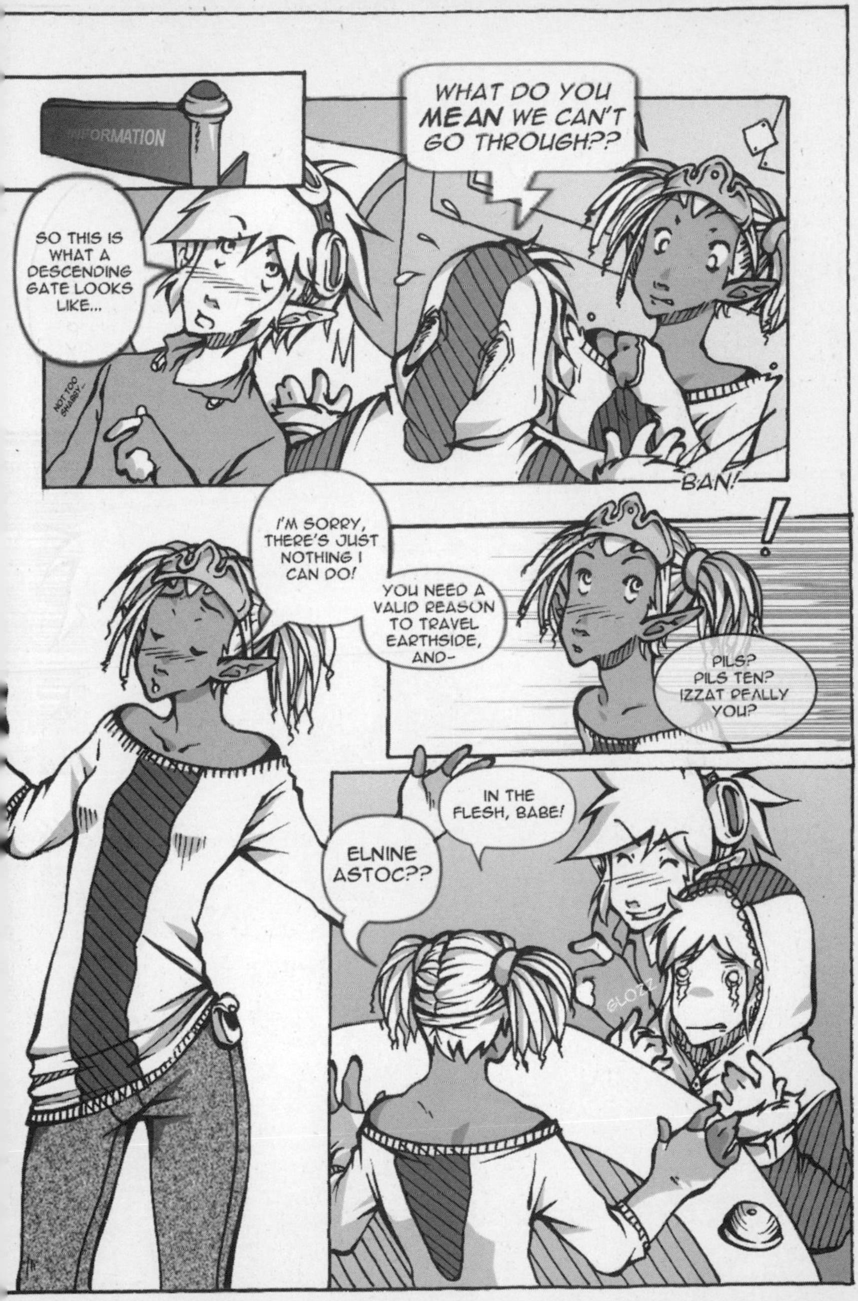
INFORMATION
SO THIS IS WHAT A DESCENDING GATE LOOKS LIKE...
NOT TOO SHABBY...
WHAT DO YOU MEAN WE CAN'T GO THROUGH??
BAN!
I'M SORRY, THERE'S JUST NOTHING I CAN DO!
YOU NEED A VALID REASON TO TRAVEL EARTHSIDE, AND-
!
PILS? PILS TEN? IZZAT REALLY YOU?
ELNINE ASTOC??
IN THE FLESH, BABE!
GLOZZ

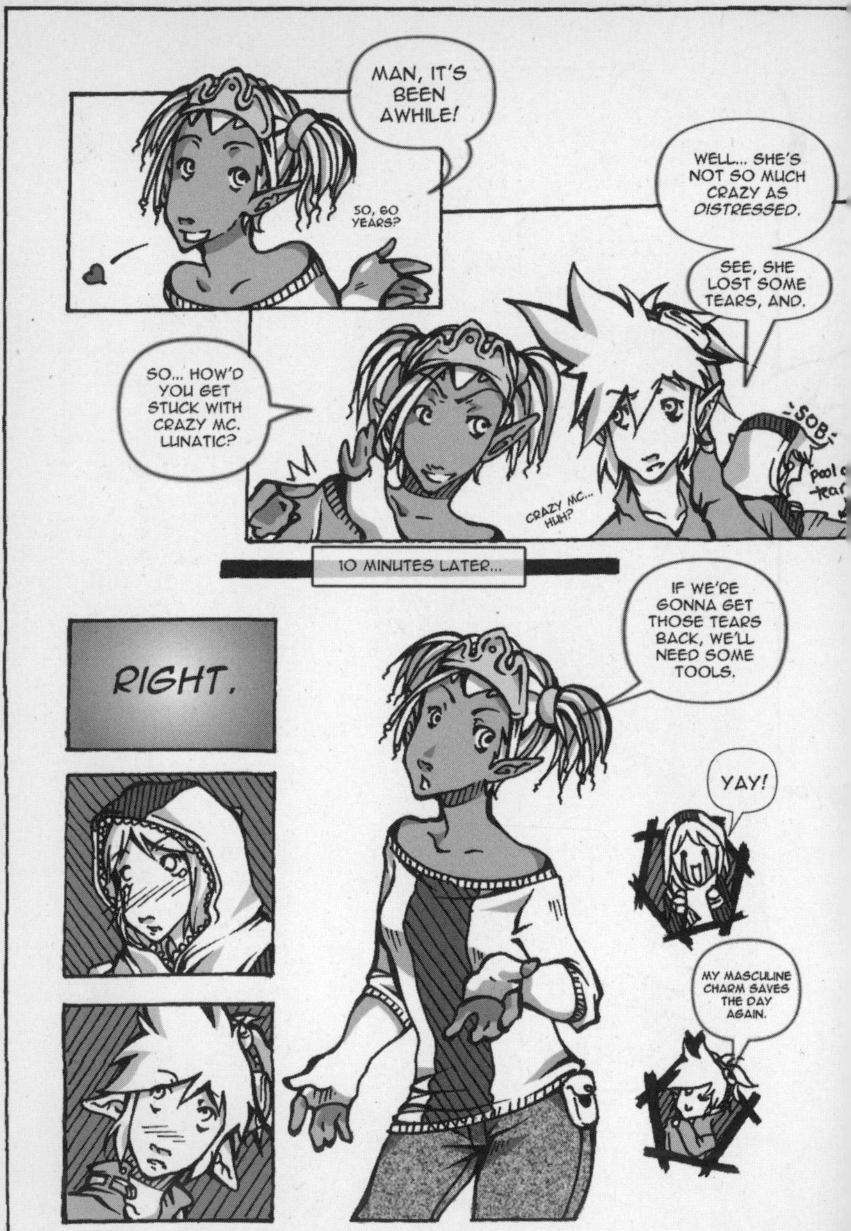
MAN, IT'S BEEN AWHILE!
SO, 60 YEARS?
SO... HOW'D YOU GET STUCK WITH CRAZY MC. LUNATIC?
CRAZY MC... HUH?
WELL... SHE'S NOT SO MUCH CRAZY AS DISTRESSED.
SEE, SHE LOST SOME TEARS, AND.
SOB
10 MINUTES LATER...
RIGHT.
IF WE'RE GONNA GET THOSE TEARS BACK, WE'LL NEED SOME TOOLS.
YAY!
MY MASCULINE CHARM SAVES THE DAY AGAIN.

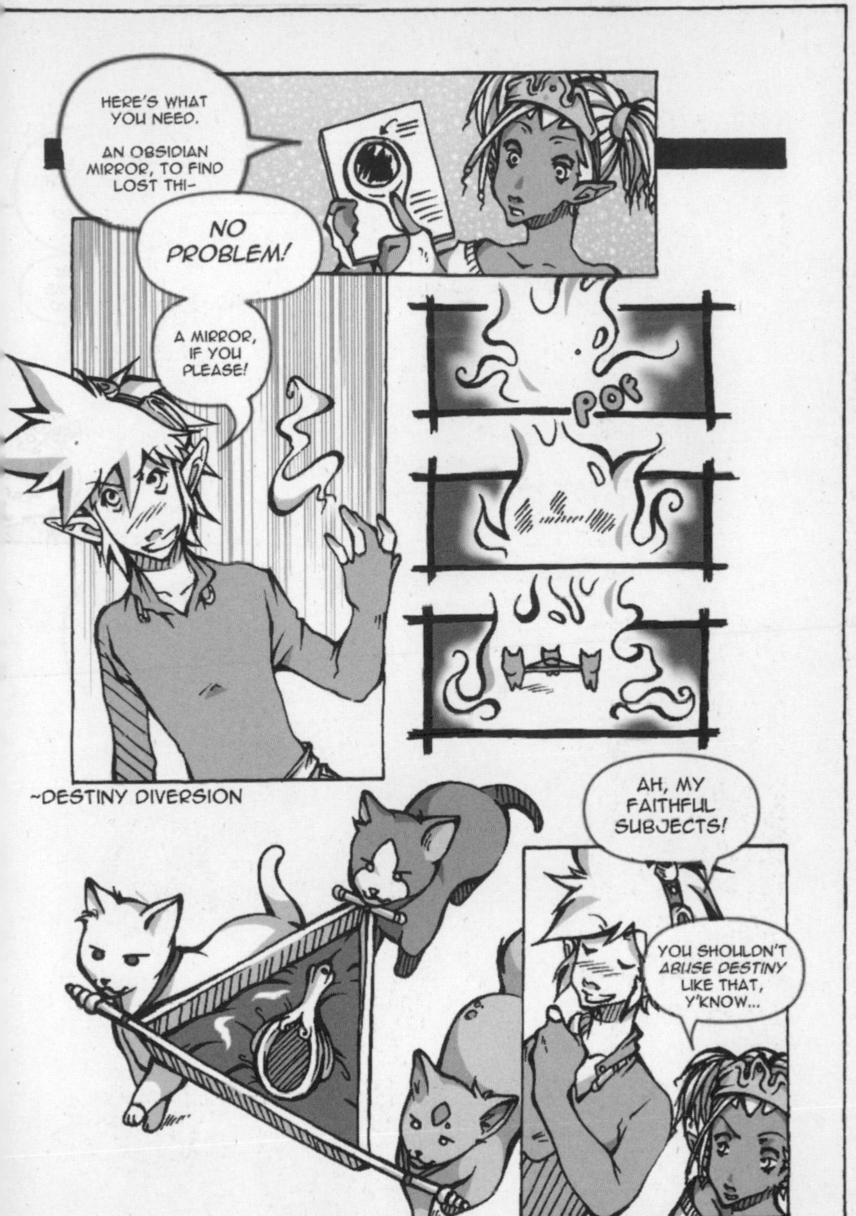
HERE'S WHAT YOU NEED.
AN OBSIDIAN MIRROR, TO FIND LOST THI-
NO PROBLEM!
A MIRROR, IF YOU PLEASE!
POP
~DESTINY DIVERSION
AH, MY FAITHFUL SUBJECTS!
YOU SHOULDN'T ABUSE DESTINY LIKE THAT, Y'KNOW...

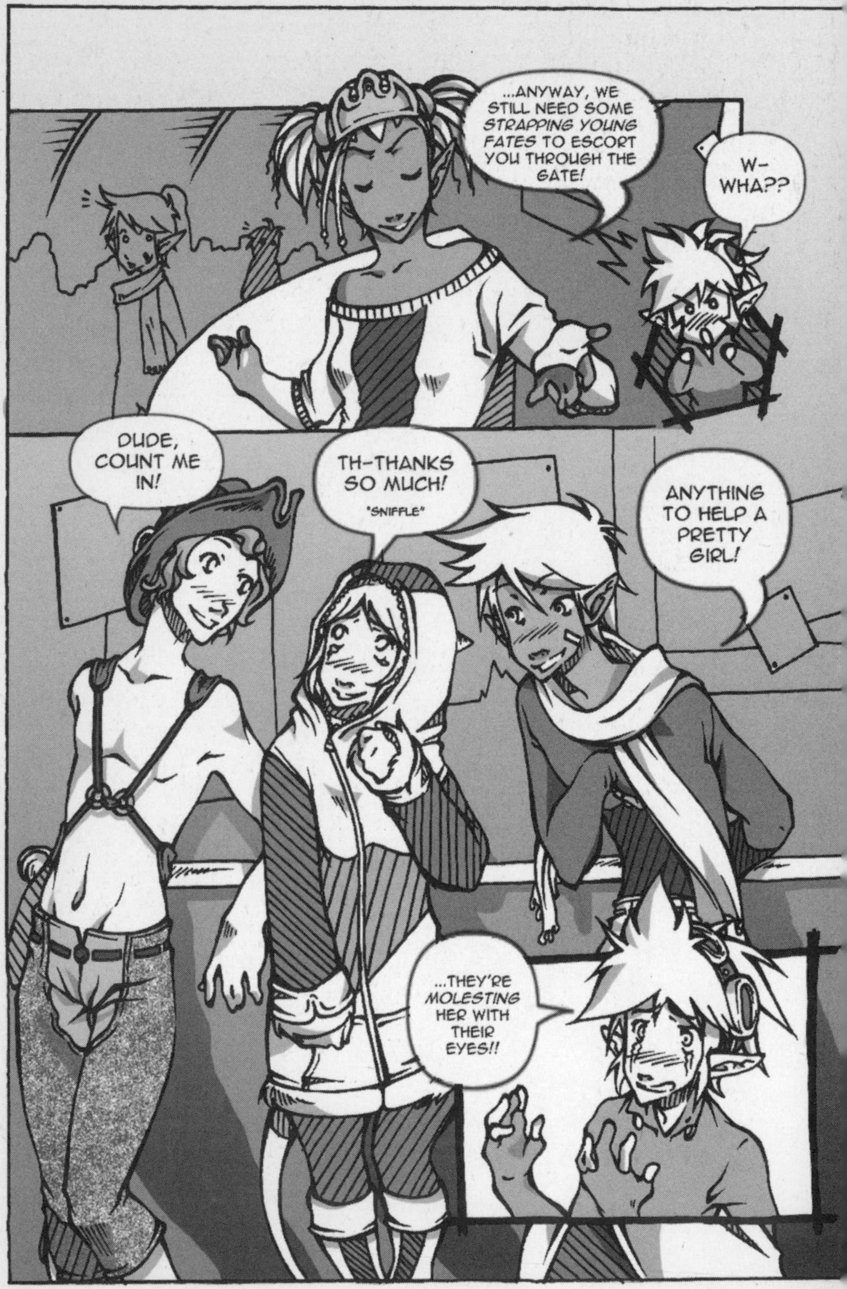
...ANYWAY, WE STILL NEED SOME STRAPPING YOUNG FATES TO ESCORT YOU THROUGH THE GATE!
W-WHA??
DUDE, COUNT ME IN!
TH-THANKS SO MUCH!
SNIFFLE
ANYTHING TO HELP A PRETTY GIRL!
...THEY'RE MOLESTING HER WITH THEIR EYES!!

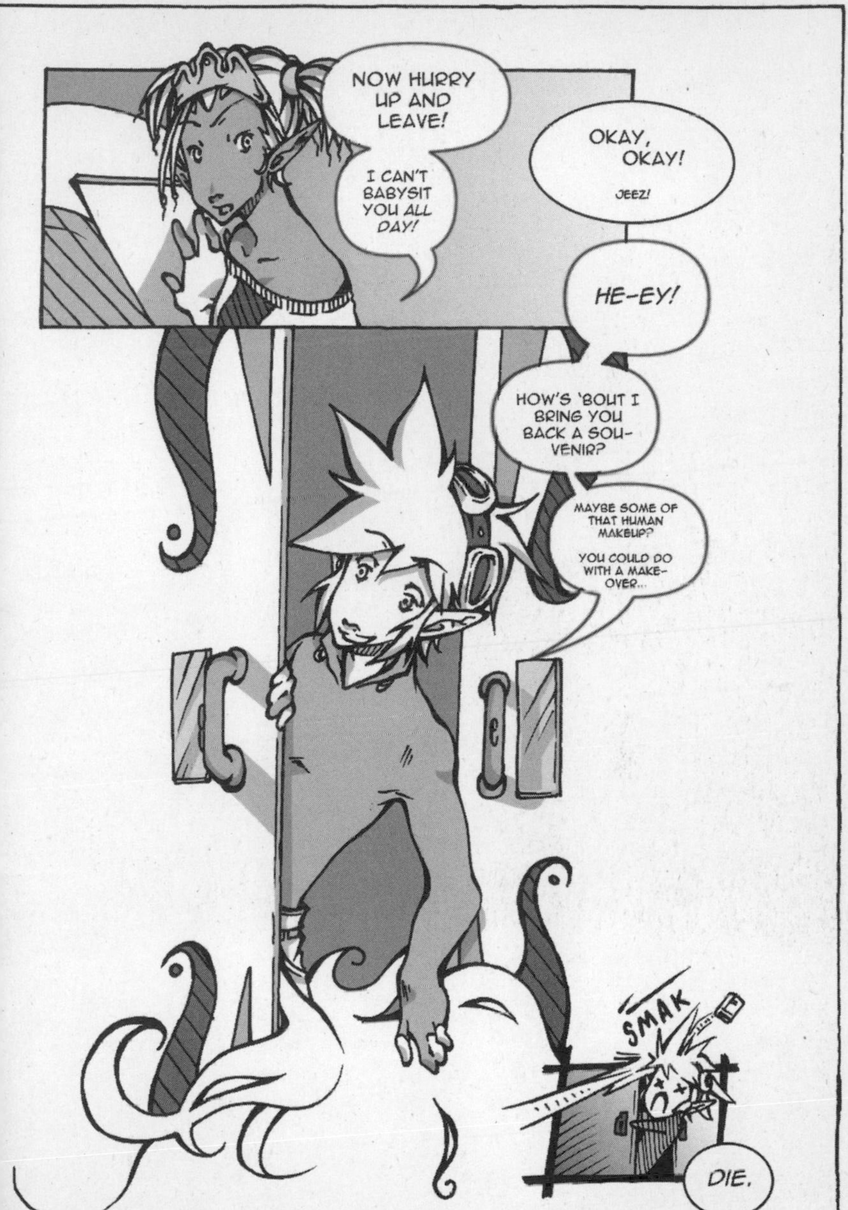
NOW HURRY UP AND LEAVE!
I CAN'T BABYSIT YOU ALL DAY!
OKAY, OKAY!
JEEZ!
HE-EY!
HOW'S 'BOUT I BRING YOU BACK A SOU-VENIR?
MAYBE SOME OF THAT HUMAN MAKEUP?
YOU COULD DO WITH A MAKE-OVER...
SMAK
DIE.

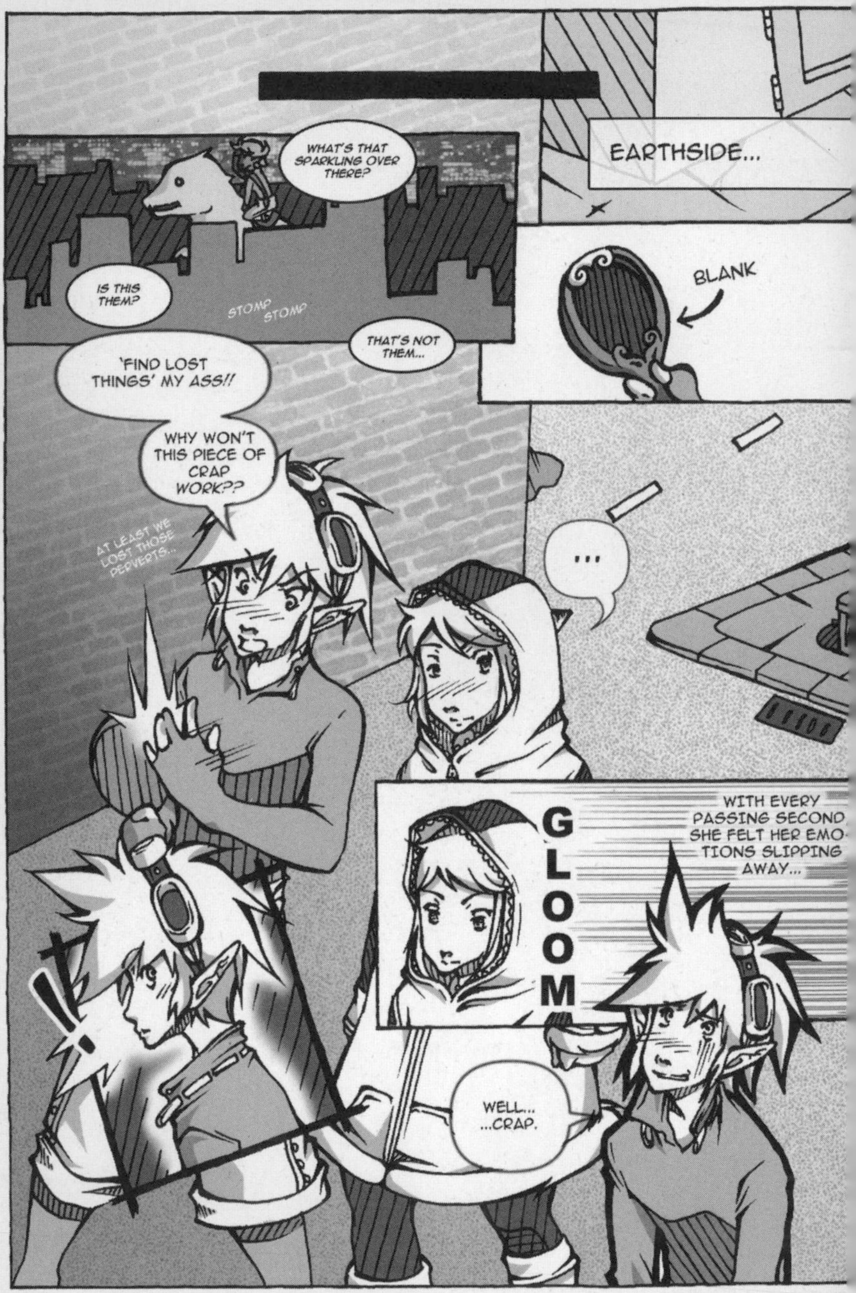
WHAT'S THAT SPARKLING OVER THERE?
IS THIS THEM?
STOMP STOMP
THAT'S NOT THEM...
'FIND LOST THINGS' MY ASS!!
WHY WON'T THIS PIECE OF CRAP WORK??
AT LEAST WE LOST THOSE PERVERTS...
EARTHSIDE...
BLANK
...
GLOOM
WITH EVERY PASSING SECOND SHE FELT HER EMO-TIONS SLIPPING AWAY...
WELL... ...CRAP.

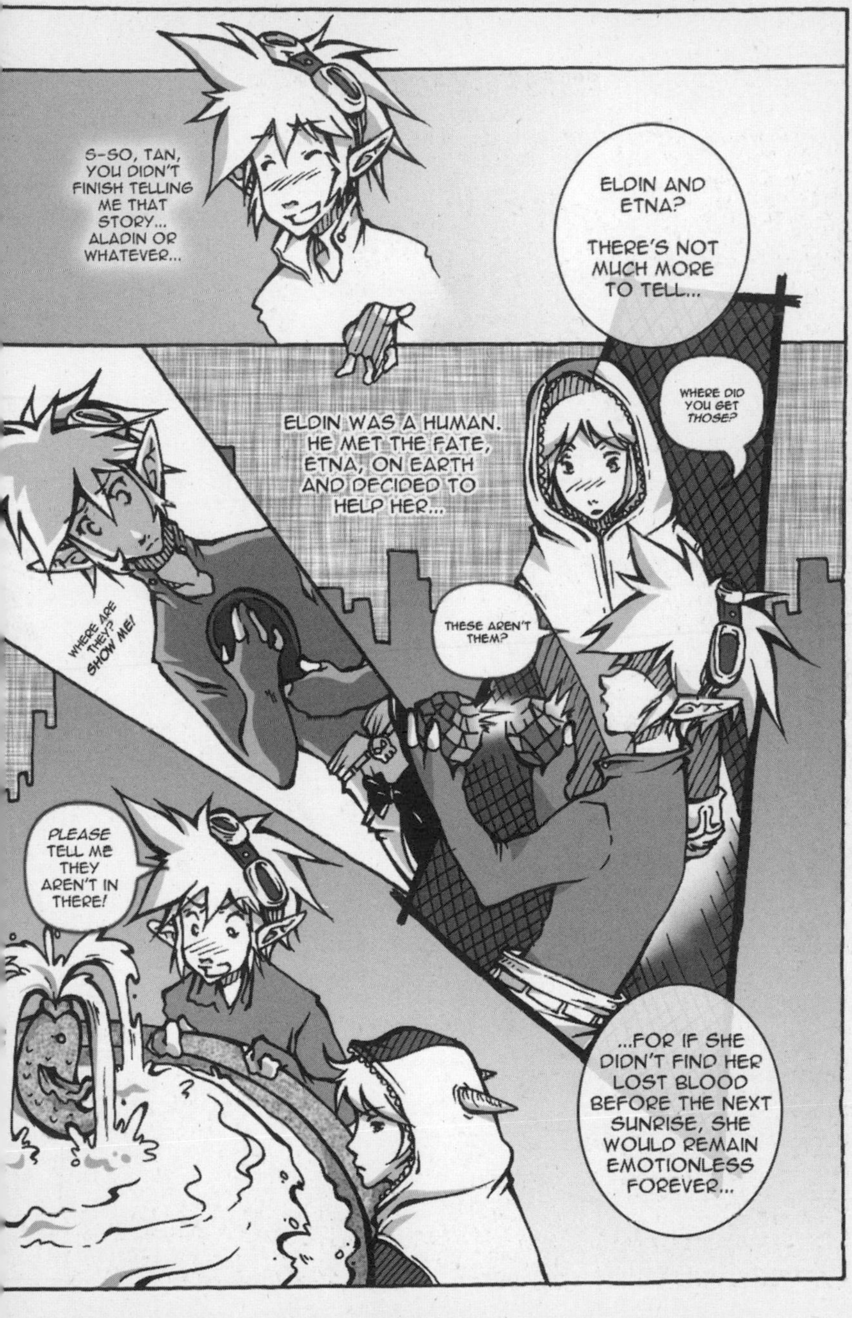
S-SO, TAN, YOU DIDN'T FINISH TELLING ME THAT STORY... ALADIN OR WHATEVER...
ELDIN AND ETNA?
THERE'S NOT MUCH MORE TO TELL...
ELDIN WAS A HUMAN. HE MET THE FATE, ETNA, ON EARTH AND DECIDED TO HELP HER...
WHERE DID YOU GET *THOSE?*
WHERE ARE THEY? *SHOW ME!*
THESE AREN'T THEM?
PLEASE TELL ME THEY AREN'T IN THERE!
...FOR IF SHE DIDN'T FIND HER LOST BLOOD BEFORE THE NEXT SUNRISE, SHE WOULD REMAIN EMOTIONLESS FOREVER...

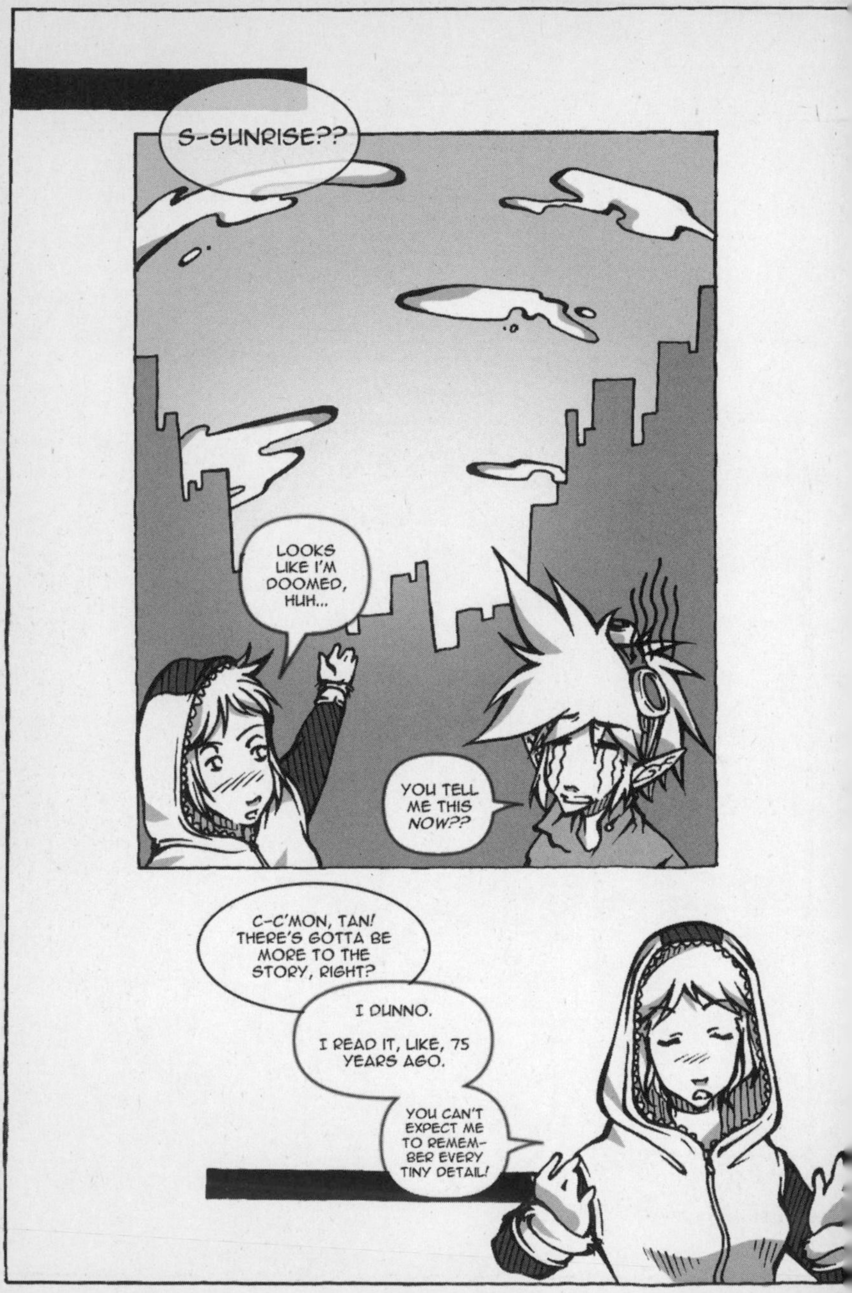
S-SUNRISE??
LOOKS LIKE I'M DOOMED, HUH...
YOU TELL ME THIS *NOW*??
C-C'MON, TAN! THERE'S GOTTA BE MORE TO THE STORY, RIGHT?
I DUNNO.
I READ IT, LIKE, 75 YEARS AGO.
YOU CAN'T EXPECT ME TO REMEM-BER EVERY TINY DETAIL!

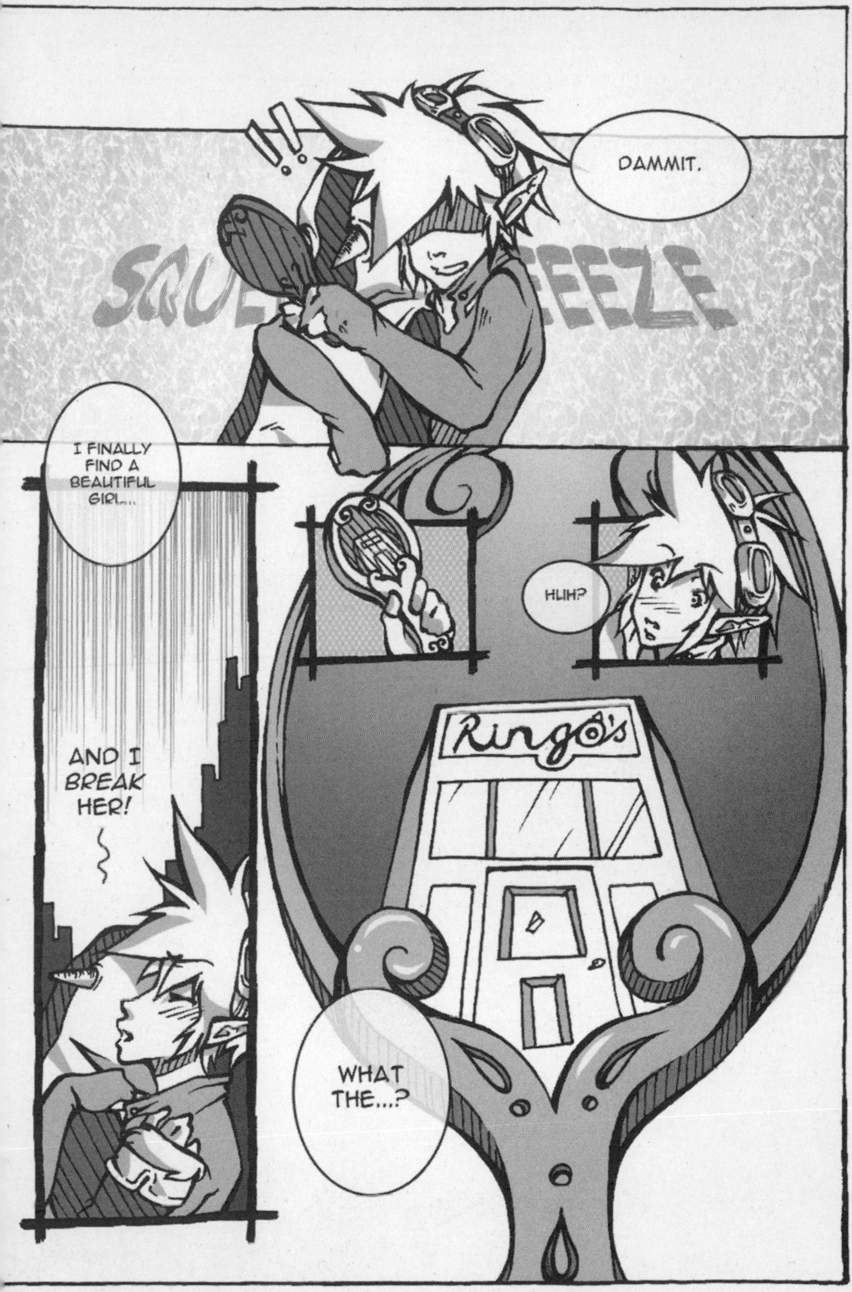
!!
DAMMIT.
SQUEEEEEZE
I FINALLY FIND A BEAUTIFUL GIRL...
AND I BREAK HER!
HUH?
Ringo's
WHAT THE...?

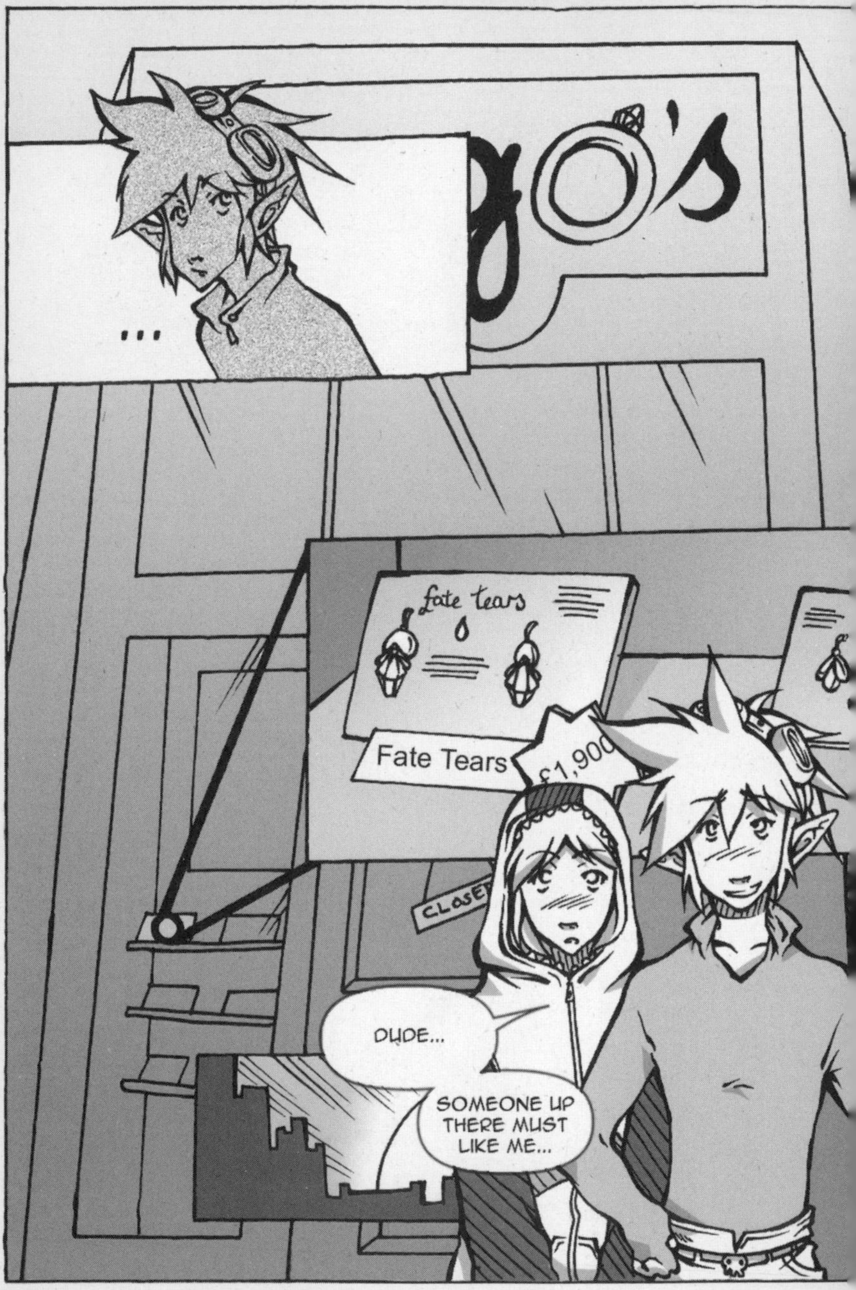
...
go's
fate tears
Fate Tears
£1,900
CLOSE
DUDE...
SOMEONE UP THERE MUST LIKE ME...

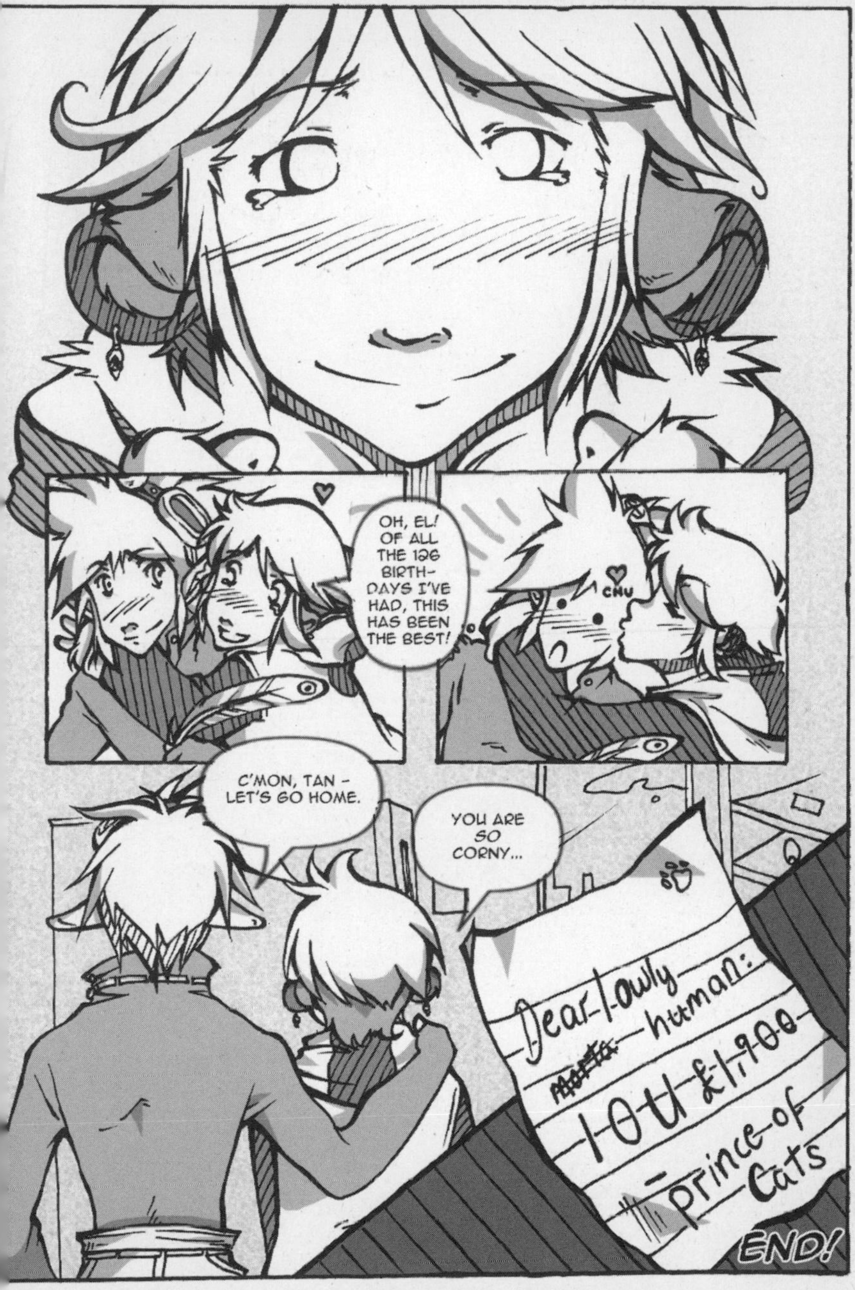
OH, EL! OF ALL THE 126 BIRTHDAYS I'VE HAD, THIS HAS BEEN THE BEST!
CHU
C'MON, TAN - LET'S GO HOME.
YOU ARE SO CORNY...
Dear lowly ~~mortal~~ human:
IOU £1,900
- prince of Cats
END!

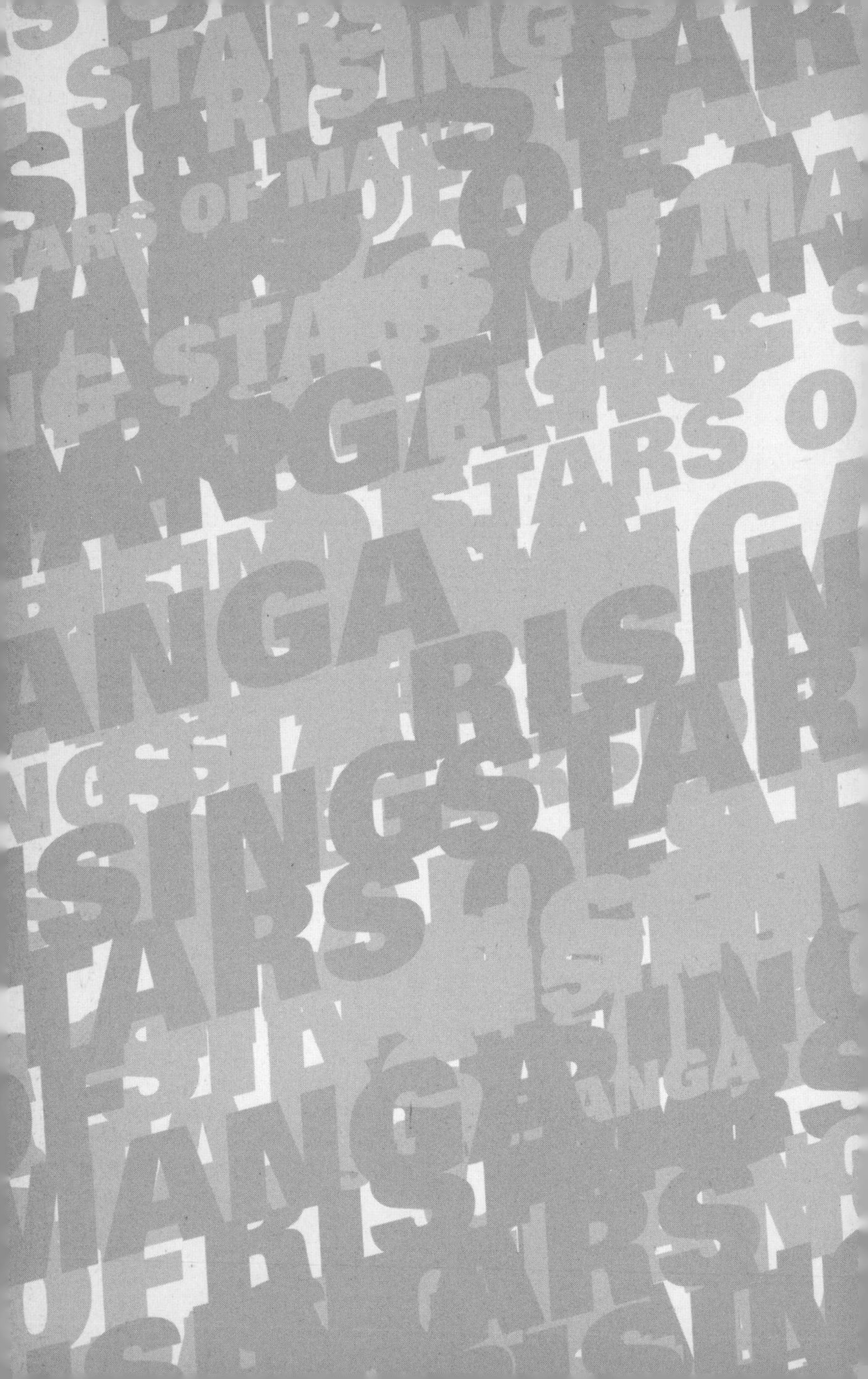

::

MODERN DAY CATASTROPHISTS :: Runner Up ::

....

Vee Chayakul was born in Bangkok, Thailand in 1980. He currently lives in Leicester and is a student at the University of Leicester.

Favorite manga:
Berserk, 20th Century Boy, MPD Psycho, Hunter X Hunter

Favorite manga artist:
Sho-U Tajima, Tsutomu Nihei

....

Author's Comments:
Sarah and Richard originated from a concept of a pair of siblings that a friend and I came up with a long time ago. Over many years, our versions of Sarah and Richard become more and more different from each other. Sarah and Richard are actually nice people. Unfortunately, their good (but inappropriate) intentions often lead to catastrophic outcomes—hence the name "Modern Day Catastrophists."
—Vee Chayakul

::

MODERN DAY CATASTROPHISTS :: Runner Up ::

Judge's Comments:
My initial reservations about this piece included its empty backgrounds, thick though well-intentioned inks, stumbled lettering and weak language. In no way, I thought, was this ready for prime time.

But underneath the surface flows an invigoratingly intense undercurrent of a story that tackles belonging, expectations and disappointment, the causes and results of violence, and how people become unfit to live in the world. And although the set-up of a kid who can't make himself conform to the low expectations of society is nothing new, the way Vee's story unfolds, disgrace upon disgrace, it is as unexpected and browbeating to the reader as it is to the characters.

What is perhaps relieving about the piece is that no one character seems to have a blameless or right way to deal with life (not even the overly-philosophic main character). But much like this manga, their desire to exist is so apparent and compelling that they validate their own continuation.
—Hope Donovan

Judge's Comments:
Vee Chayakul tells an interesting tale with a serious message—while using just enough humor to keep it light and fun. I find the contrast between Richard's primal behavior and highbrow commentaries on life to be refreshing, though at times it seems like writer may be struggling with a minor language barrier. Visually, the story is told quite well and is easy to follow and the characters are very expressive. The character designs are appealing, if not original (Onizuka, anyone?). The lack of tones leaves some of the pages rather flat looking, though I believe this stark look was a conscious choice and works well with the narrative. The page layout and panel composition are well thought out, making for easy readability. Overall, "Modern Day Catastrophists" is a solid and entertaining entry, making Vee Chayakul a rising star to look out for.
—Aaron Suhr

::

The last temptation is the greatest treason:
To do the right deed for the wrong reason.

-TS Eliot

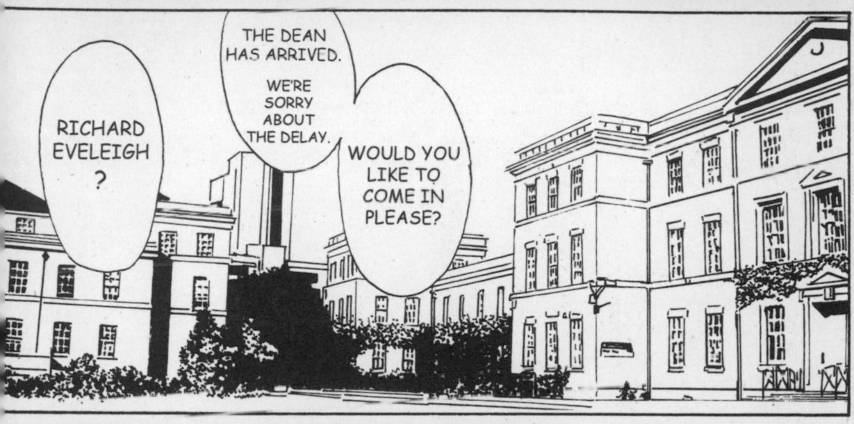
RICHARD EVELEIGH ?
THE DEAN HAS ARRIVED.
WE'RE SORRY ABOUT THE DELAY.
WOULD YOU LIKE TO COME IN PLEASE?

I HATE INTERVIEWS.

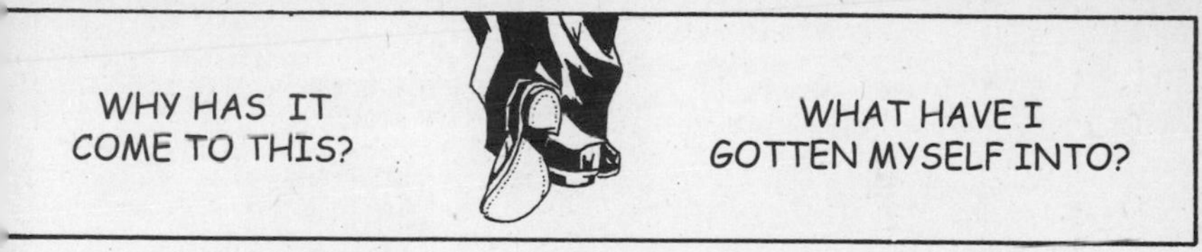
WHY HAS IT COME TO THIS?
WHAT HAVE I GOTTEN MYSELF INTO?

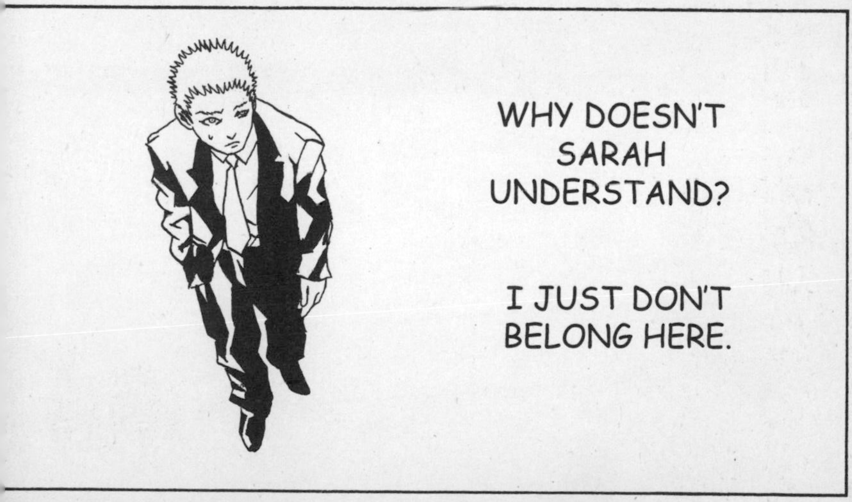
WHY DOESN'T SARAH UNDERSTAND?
I JUST DON'T BELONG HERE.

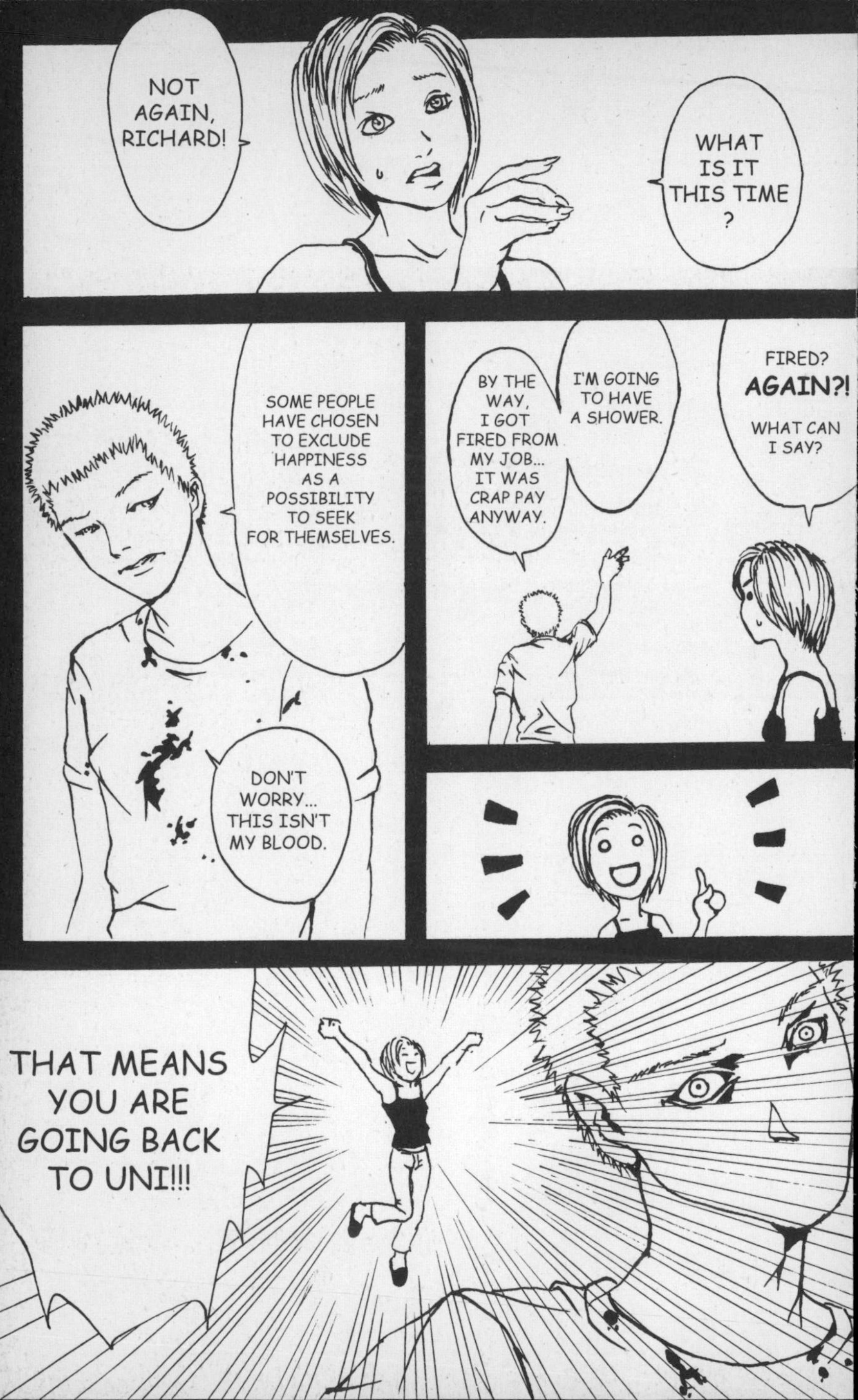
NOT AGAIN, RICHARD!
WHAT IS IT THIS TIME ?
SOME PEOPLE HAVE CHOSEN TO EXCLUDE HAPPINESS AS A POSSIBILITY TO SEEK FOR THEMSELVES.
DON'T WORRY... THIS ISN'T MY BLOOD.
BY THE WAY, I GOT FIRED FROM MY JOB... IT WAS CRAP PAY ANYWAY.
I'M GOING TO HAVE A SHOWER.
FIRED? AGAIN?!
WHAT CAN I SAY?
THAT MEANS YOU ARE GOING BACK TO UNI!!!

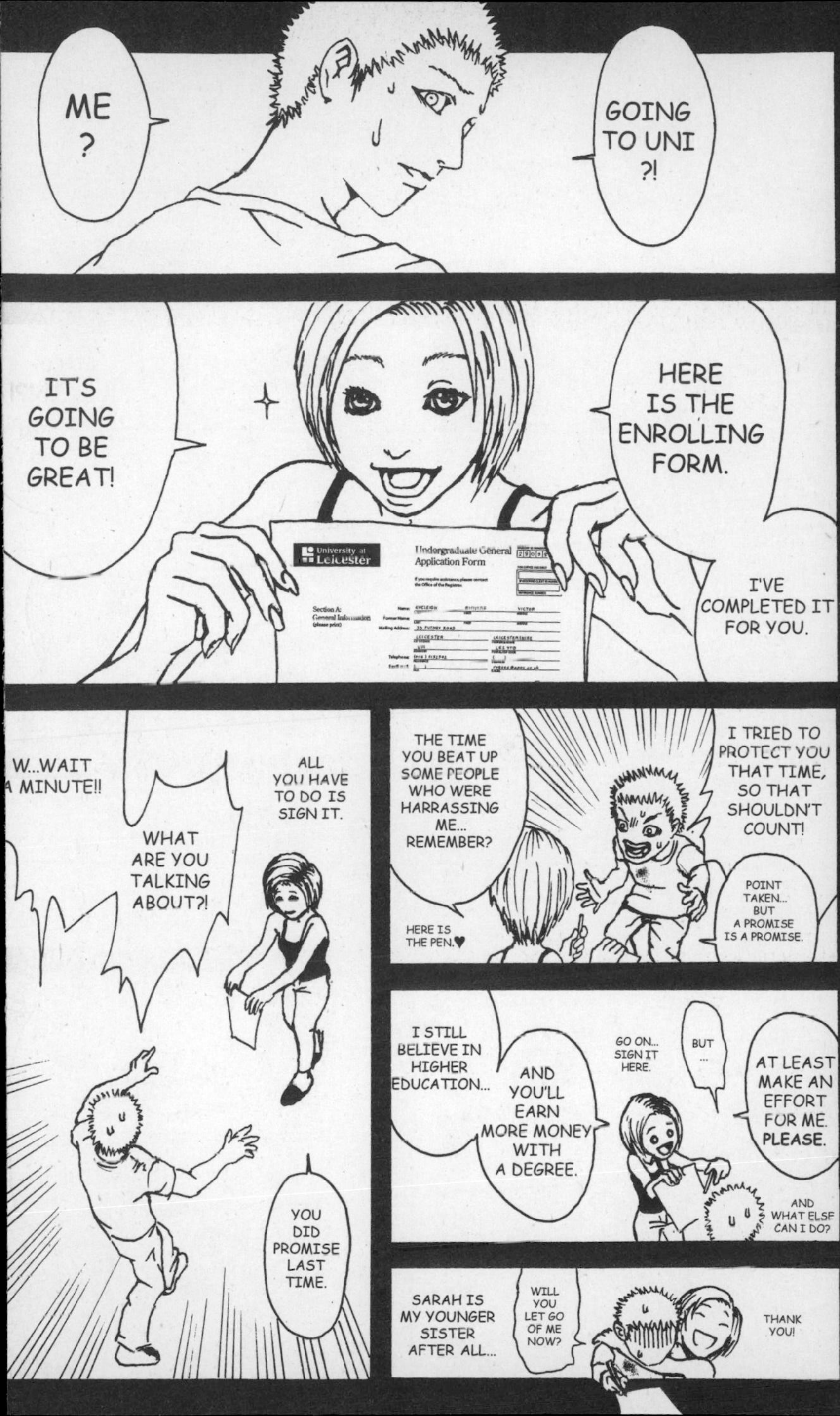
ME ?
GOING TO UNI ?!
IT'S GOING TO BE GREAT!
University of Leicester
Undergraduate General Application Form
HERE IS THE ENROLLING FORM.
I'VE COMPLETED IT FOR YOU.
W...WAIT A MINUTE!!
WHAT ARE YOU TALKING ABOUT?!
ALL YOU HAVE TO DO IS SIGN IT.
YOU DID PROMISE LAST TIME.
THE TIME YOU BEAT UP SOME PEOPLE WHO WERE HARRASSING ME... REMEMBER?
I TRIED TO PROTECT YOU THAT TIME, SO THAT SHOULDN'T COUNT!
POINT TAKEN... BUT A PROMISE IS A PROMISE.
HERE IS THE PEN.♥
I STILL BELIEVE IN HIGHER EDUCATION...
AND YOU'LL EARN MORE MONEY WITH A DEGREE.
GO ON... SIGN IT HERE.
BUT ...
AT LEAST MAKE AN EFFORT FOR ME. PLEASE.
AND WHAT ELSE CAN I DO?
SARAH IS MY YOUNGER SISTER AFTER ALL...
WILL YOU LET GO OF ME NOW?
THANK YOU!

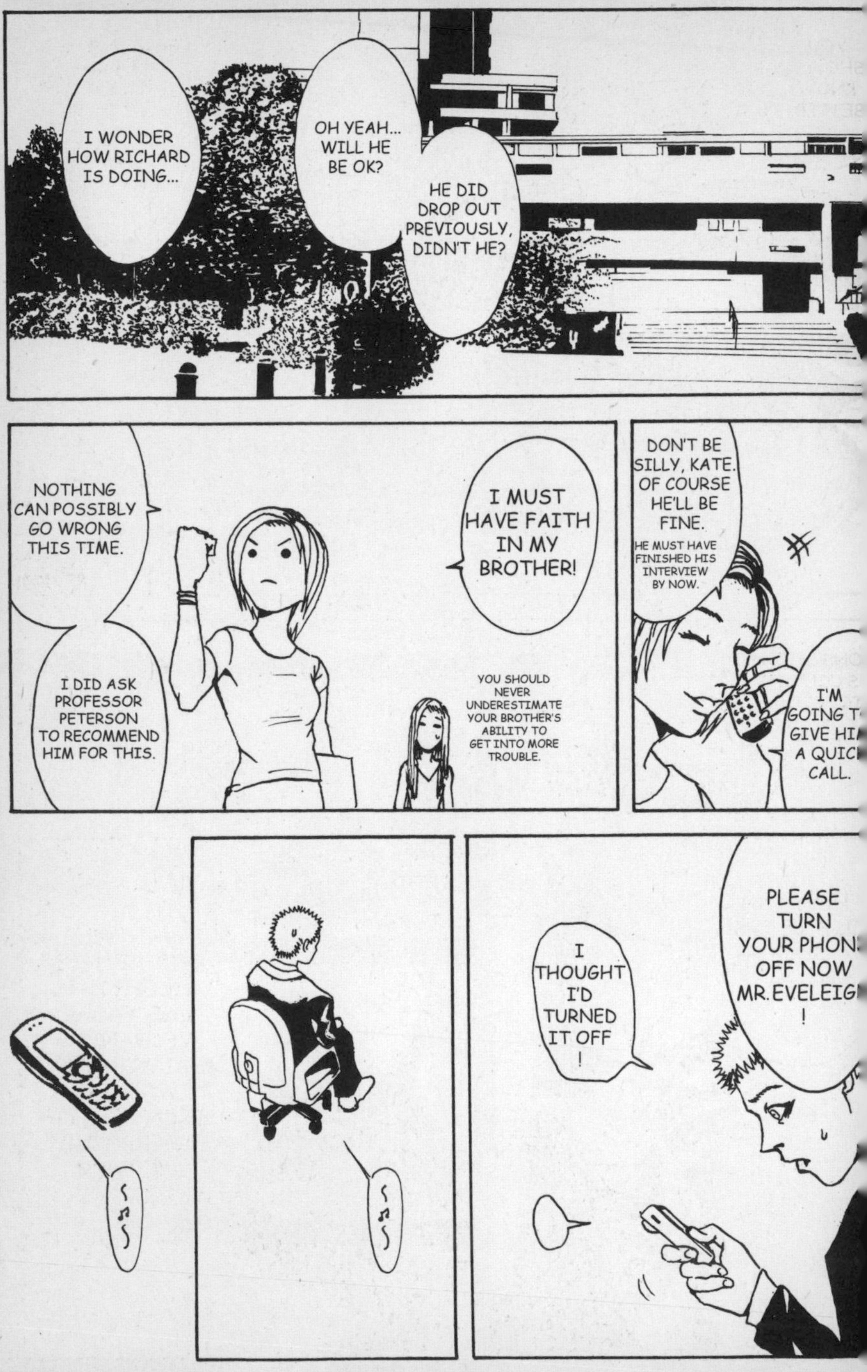
I WONDER HOW RICHARD IS DOING...
OH YEAH... WILL HE BE OK?
HE DID DROP OUT PREVIOUSLY, DIDN'T HE?
NOTHING CAN POSSIBLY GO WRONG THIS TIME.
I DID ASK PROFESSOR PETERSON TO RECOMMEND HIM FOR THIS.
I MUST HAVE FAITH IN MY BROTHER!
YOU SHOULD NEVER UNDERESTIMATE YOUR BROTHER'S ABILITY TO GET INTO MORE TROUBLE.
DON'T BE SILLY, KATE. OF COURSE HE'LL BE FINE.
HE MUST HAVE FINISHED HIS INTERVIEW BY NOW.
I'M GOING T GIVE HI A QUIC CALL.
I THOUGHT I'D TURNED IT OFF !
PLEASE TURN YOUR PHON OFF NOW MR. EVELEIG !

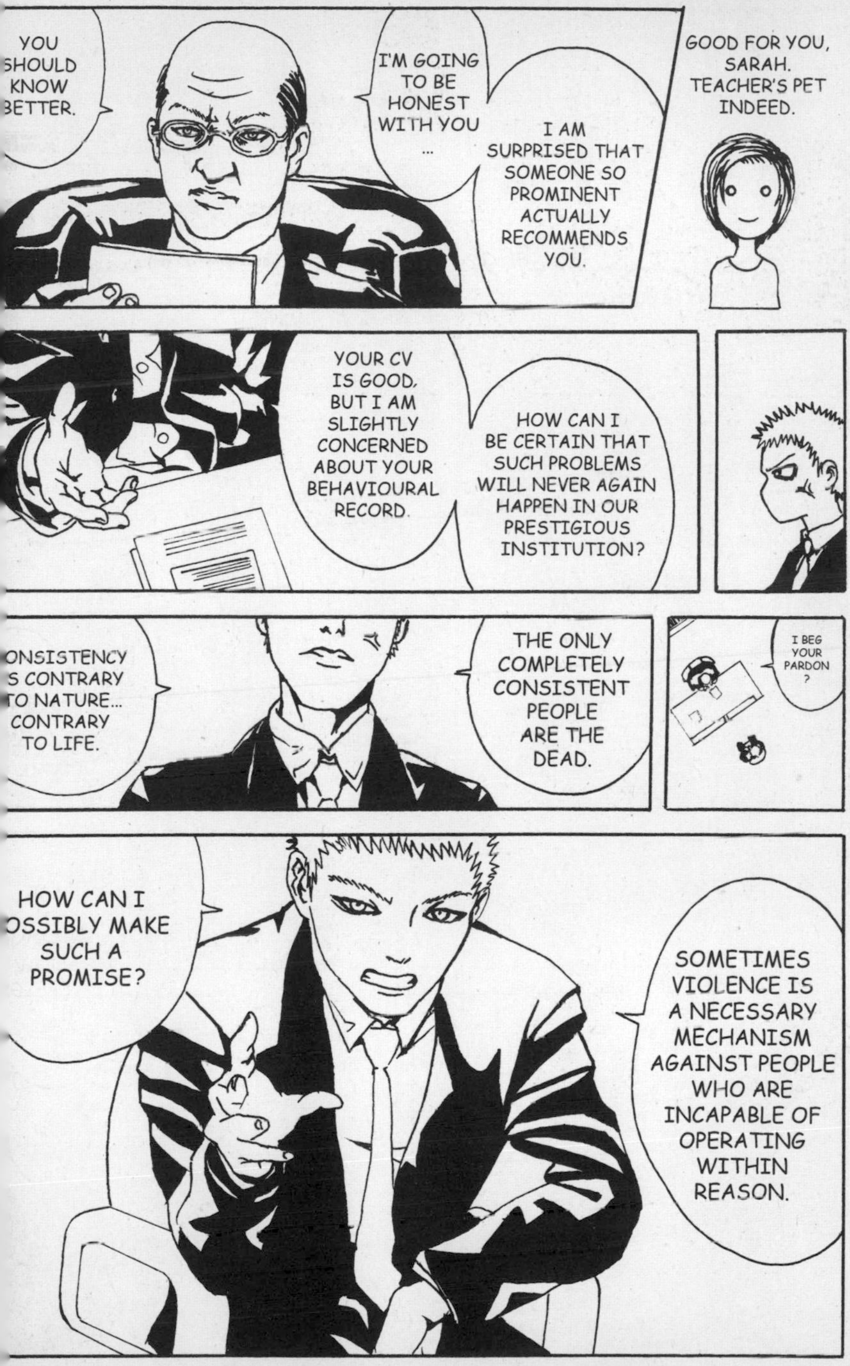
YOU SHOULD KNOW BETTER.
I'M GOING TO BE HONEST WITH YOU ...
I AM SURPRISED THAT SOMEONE SO PROMINENT ACTUALLY RECOMMENDS YOU.
GOOD FOR YOU, SARAH. TEACHER'S PET INDEED.
YOUR CV IS GOOD, BUT I AM SLIGHTLY CONCERNED ABOUT YOUR BEHAVIOURAL RECORD.
HOW CAN I BE CERTAIN THAT SUCH PROBLEMS WILL NEVER AGAIN HAPPEN IN OUR PRESTIGIOUS INSTITUTION?
ONSISTENCY S CONTRARY TO NATURE... CONTRARY TO LIFE.
THE ONLY COMPLETELY CONSISTENT PEOPLE ARE THE DEAD.
I BEG YOUR PARDON ?
HOW CAN I OSSIBLY MAKE SUCH A PROMISE?
SOMETIMES VIOLENCE IS A NECESSARY MECHANISM AGAINST PEOPLE WHO ARE INCAPABLE OF OPERATING WITHIN REASON.

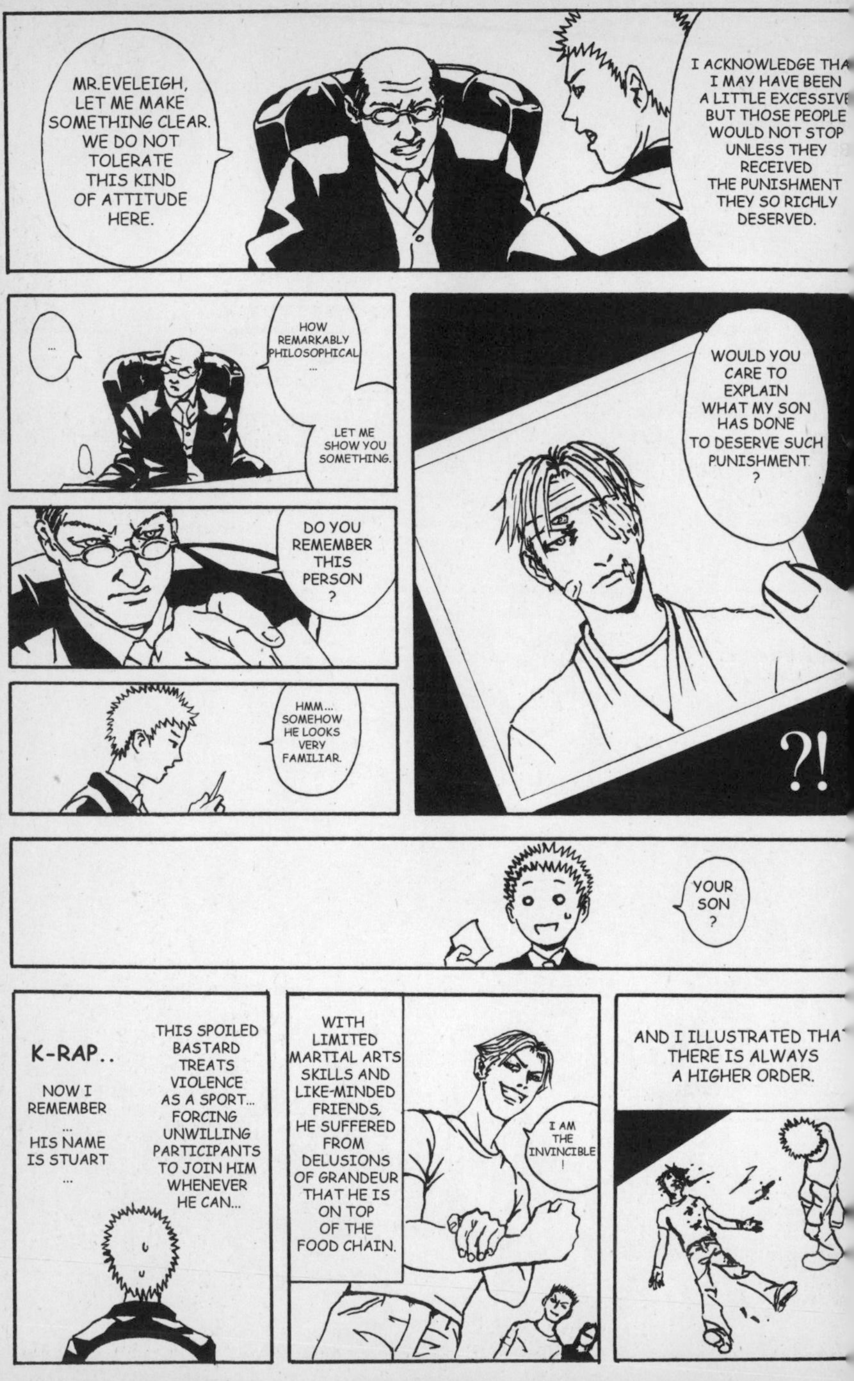

MR.EVELEIGH, LET ME MAKE SOMETHING CLEAR. WE DO NOT TOLERATE THIS KIND OF ATTITUDE HERE.
I ACKNOWLEDGE THA I MAY HAVE BEEN A LITTLE EXCESSIVE BUT THOSE PEOPLE WOULD NOT STOP UNLESS THEY RECEIVED THE PUNISHMENT THEY SO RICHLY DESERVED.
...
HOW REMARKABLY PHILOSOPHICAL ...
LET ME SHOW YOU SOMETHING.
DO YOU REMEMBER THIS PERSON ?
HMM... SOMEHOW HE LOOKS VERY FAMILIAR.
WOULD YOU CARE TO EXPLAIN WHAT MY SON HAS DONE TO DESERVE SUCH PUNISHMENT ?
?!
YOUR SON ?
K-RAP..
NOW I REMEMBER ... HIS NAME IS STUART ...
THIS SPOILED BASTARD TREATS VIOLENCE AS A SPORT... FORCING UNWILLING PARTICIPANTS TO JOIN HIM WHENEVER HE CAN...
WITH LIMITED MARTIAL ARTS SKILLS AND LIKE-MINDED FRIENDS, HE SUFFERED FROM DELUSIONS OF GRANDEUR THAT HE IS ON TOP OF THE FOOD CHAIN.
I AM THE INVINCIBLE !
AND I ILLUSTRATED THA THERE IS ALWAYS A HIGHER ORDER.

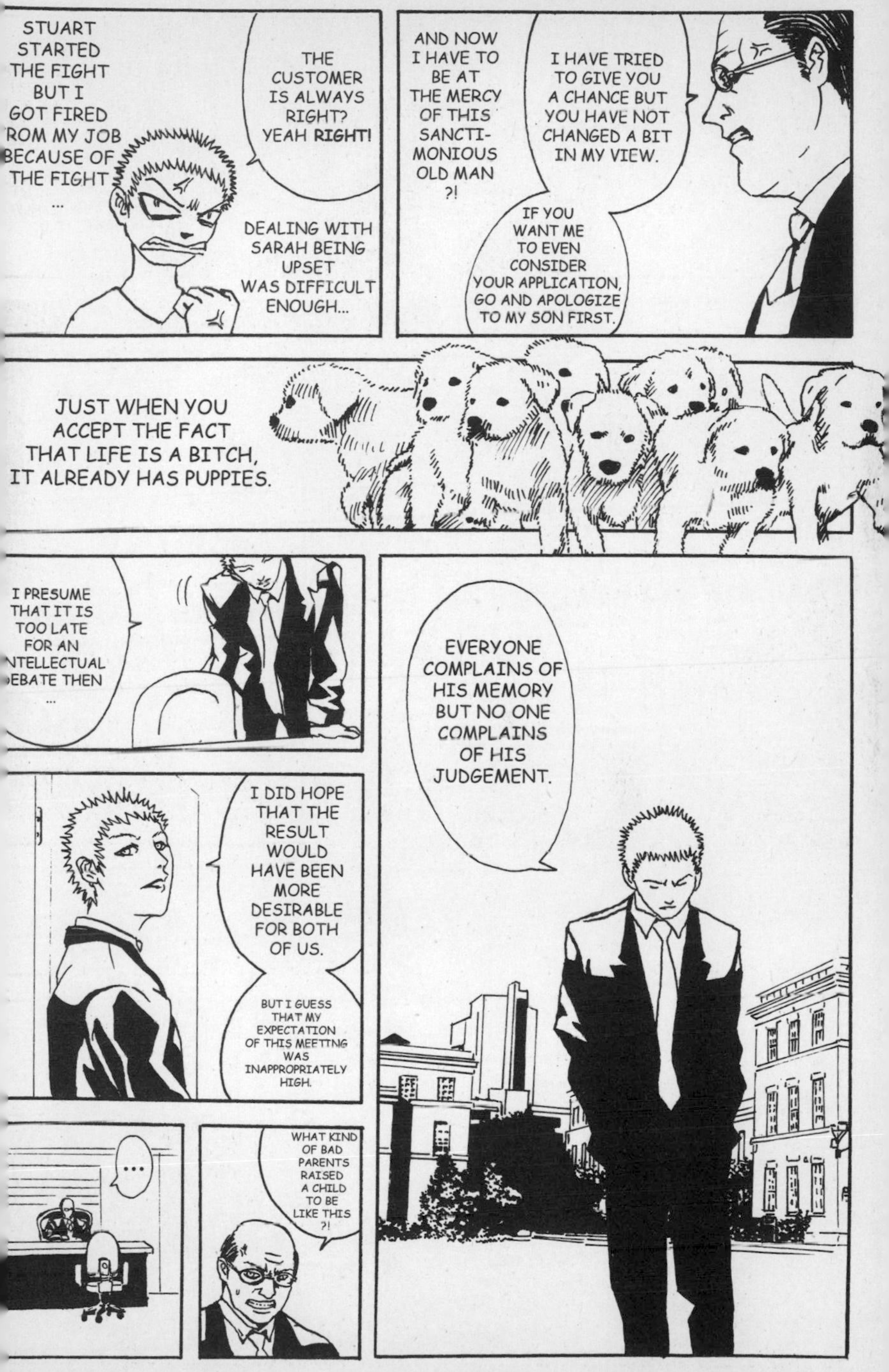
STUART STARTED THE FIGHT BUT I GOT FIRED ROM MY JOB BECAUSE OF THE FIGHT ...
THE CUSTOMER IS ALWAYS RIGHT? YEAH **RIGHT**!
DEALING WITH SARAH BEING UPSET WAS DIFFICULT ENOUGH...
AND NOW I HAVE TO BE AT THE MERCY OF THIS SANCTI-MONIOUS OLD MAN ?!
I HAVE TRIED TO GIVE YOU A CHANCE BUT YOU HAVE NOT CHANGED A BIT IN MY VIEW.
IF YOU WANT ME TO EVEN CONSIDER YOUR APPLICATION, GO AND APOLOGIZE TO MY SON FIRST.
JUST WHEN YOU ACCEPT THE FACT THAT LIFE IS A BITCH, IT ALREADY HAS PUPPIES.
I PRESUME THAT IT IS TOO LATE FOR AN NTELLECTUAL EBATE THEN ...
I DID HOPE THAT THE RESULT WOULD HAVE BEEN MORE DESIRABLE FOR BOTH OF US.
BUT I GUESS THAT MY EXPECTATION OF THIS MEETING WAS INAPPROPRIATELY HIGH.
...
WHAT KIND OF BAD PARENTS RAISED A CHILD TO BE LIKE THIS ?!
EVERYONE COMPLAINS OF HIS MEMORY BUT NO ONE COMPLAINS OF HIS JUDGEMENT.

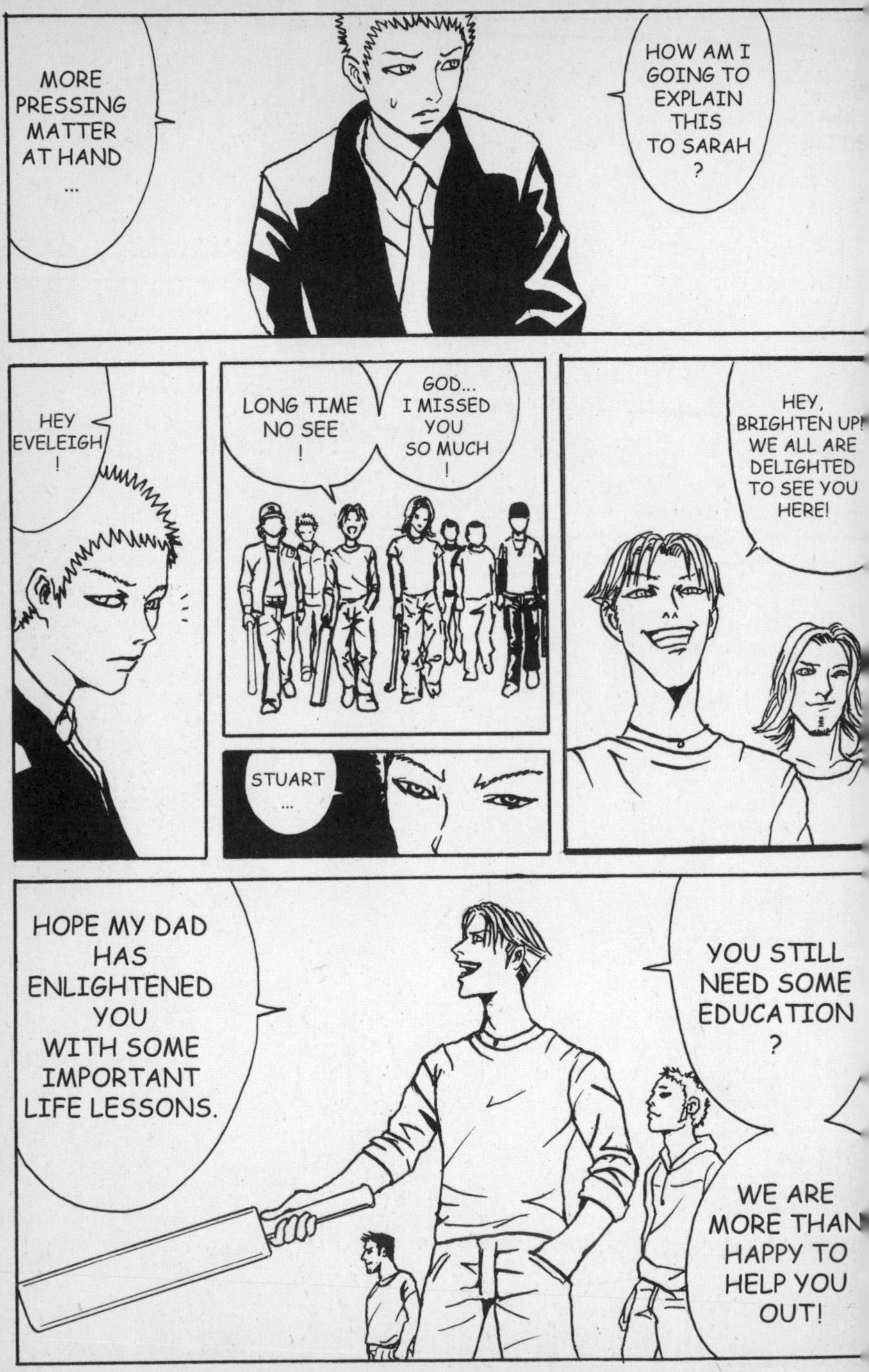
MORE PRESSING MATTER AT HAND ...
HOW AM I GOING TO EXPLAIN THIS TO SARAH ?
HEY EVELEIGH !
LONG TIME NO SEE !
GOD... I MISSED YOU SO MUCH !
STUART ...
HEY, BRIGHTEN UP! WE ALL ARE DELIGHTED TO SEE YOU HERE!
HOPE MY DAD HAS ENLIGHTENED YOU WITH SOME IMPORTANT LIFE LESSONS.
YOU STILL NEED SOME EDUCATION ?
WE ARE MORE THAN HAPPY TO HELP YOU OUT!

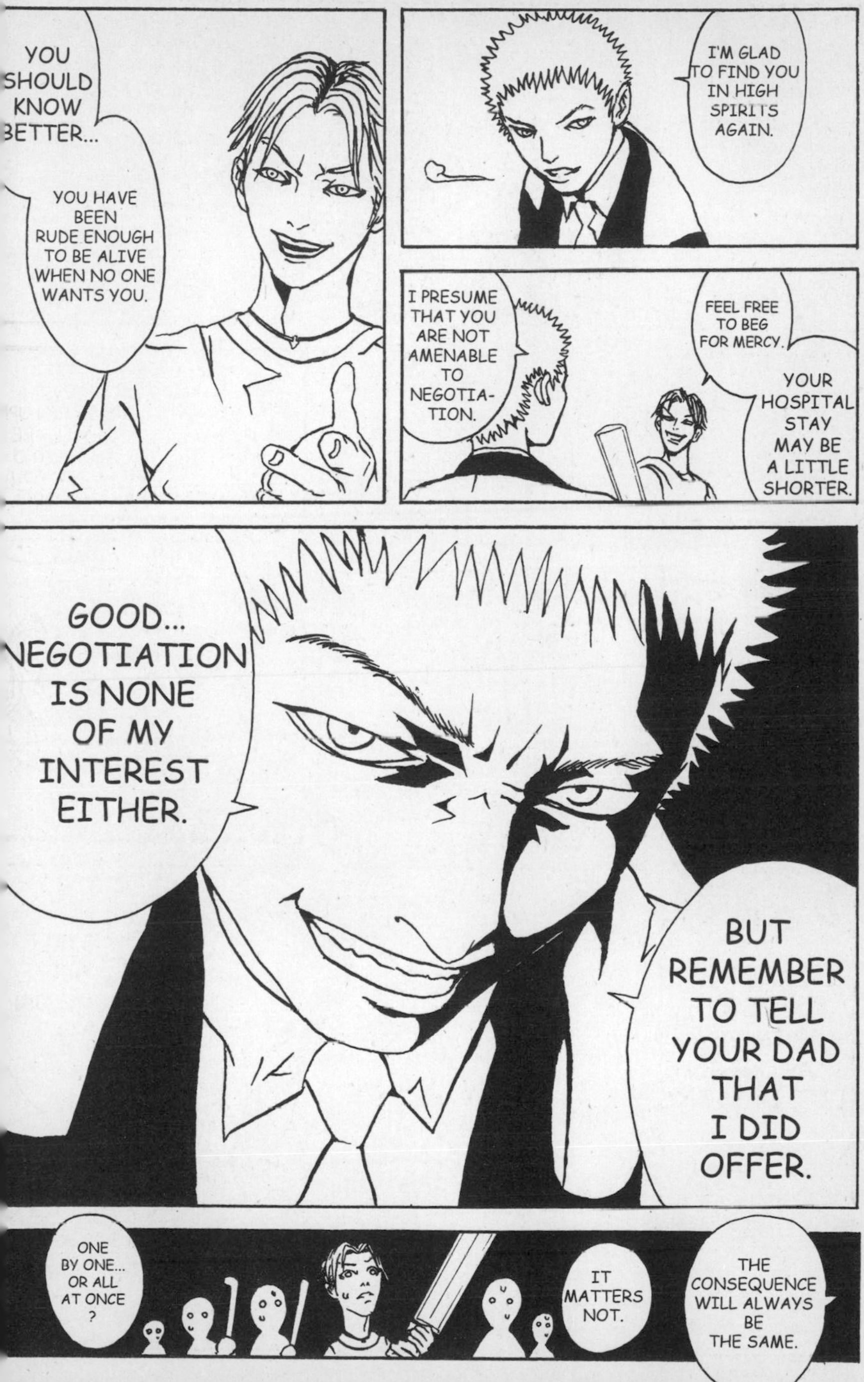
YOU SHOULD KNOW BETTER...
YOU HAVE BEEN RUDE ENOUGH TO BE ALIVE WHEN NO ONE WANTS YOU.
I'M GLAD TO FIND YOU IN HIGH SPIRITS AGAIN.
I PRESUME THAT YOU ARE NOT AMENABLE TO NEGOTIATION.
FEEL FREE TO BEG FOR MERCY.
YOUR HOSPITAL STAY MAY BE A LITTLE SHORTER.
GOOD... NEGOTIATION IS NONE OF MY INTEREST EITHER.
BUT REMEMBER TO TELL YOUR DAD THAT I DID OFFER.
ONE BY ONE... OR ALL AT ONCE ?
IT MATTERS NOT.
THE CONSEQUENCE WILL ALWAYS BE THE SAME.

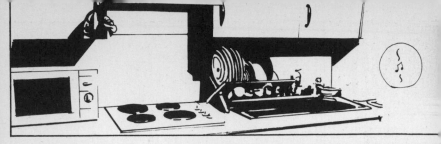

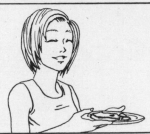

ROAST DUCK WITH PORT GRAVY... RICHARD WILL LOVE IT.
HE DESERVES A TREAT AFTER ALL THE HARD WORK.
SARAH ...
YOU'RE JUST IN TIME FOR DINNER.
I'VE GOT A SURPRISE FOR YOU ...
ERR... BEFORE YOU SAY ANYTHING LET ME EXPLAIN ...

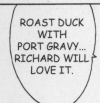

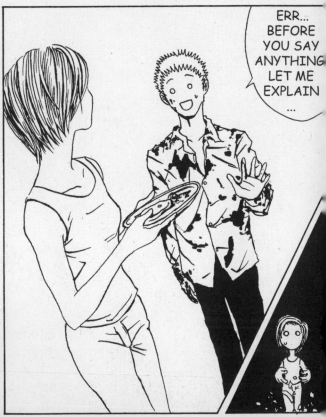

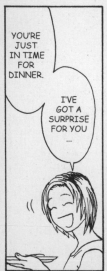

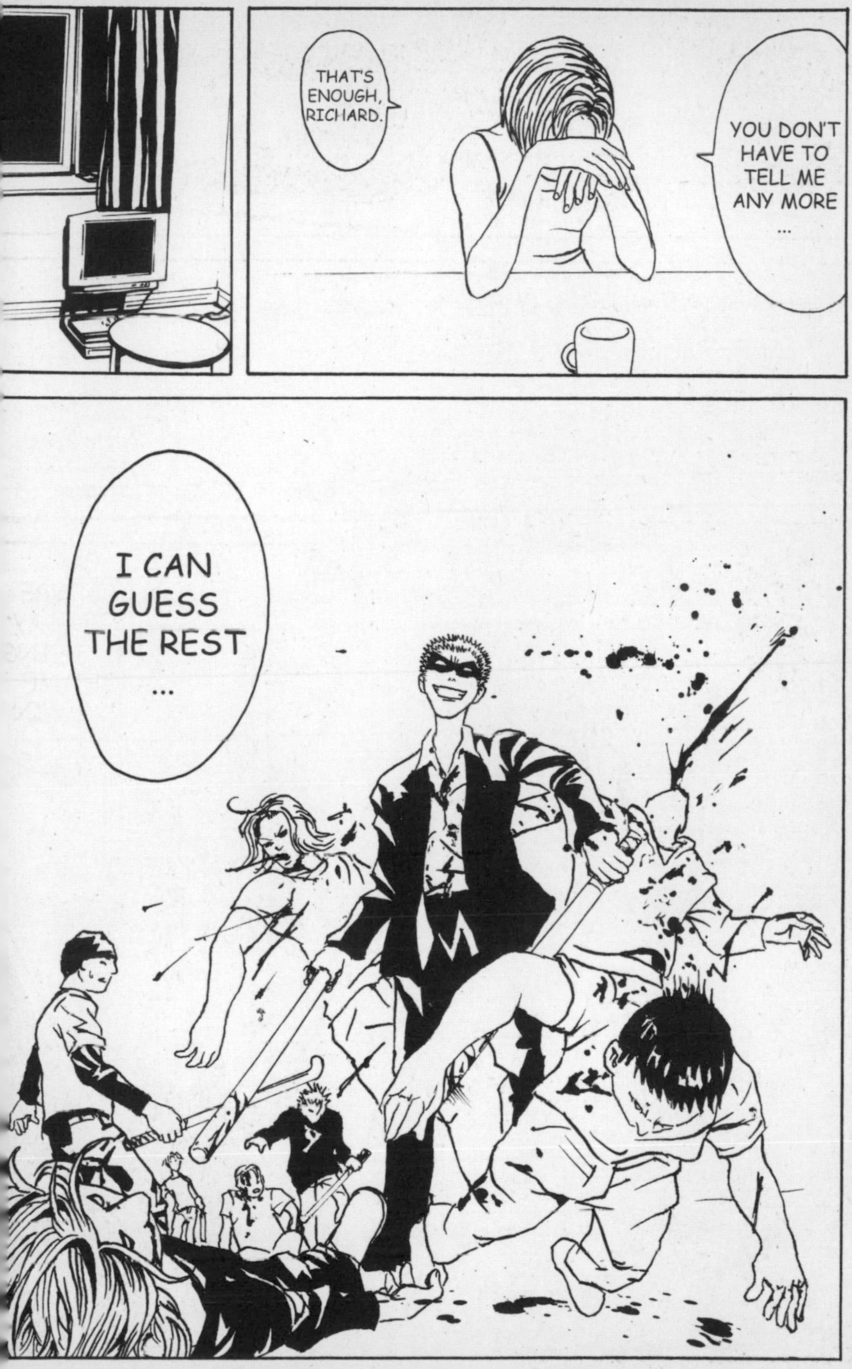
THAT'S ENOUGH, RICHARD.
YOU DON'T HAVE TO TELL ME ANY MORE ...
I CAN GUESS THE REST ...

I PRESUME THAT YOU HAVE SENT THE DEAN'S SON BACK TO THE HOSPITAL, HAVEN'T YOU?

DOES LIVING A LIFE LIKE THIS MAKE YOU HAPPY?

WHAT DOESN'T DESTROY US MAKES US STRONGER.

I EMBRACE ALL OF LIFE'S EVENTS FOR THE SAKE OF EXPERIENCE.

WHY DON'T YOU JUST ACCEPT THAT THIS IS THE WAY I AM?

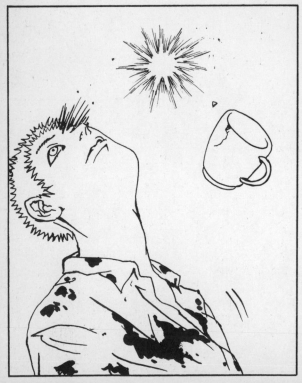

OW...

WHAT THE HELL IS WRONG WITH YOU?!

THAT REALLY HURTS!!

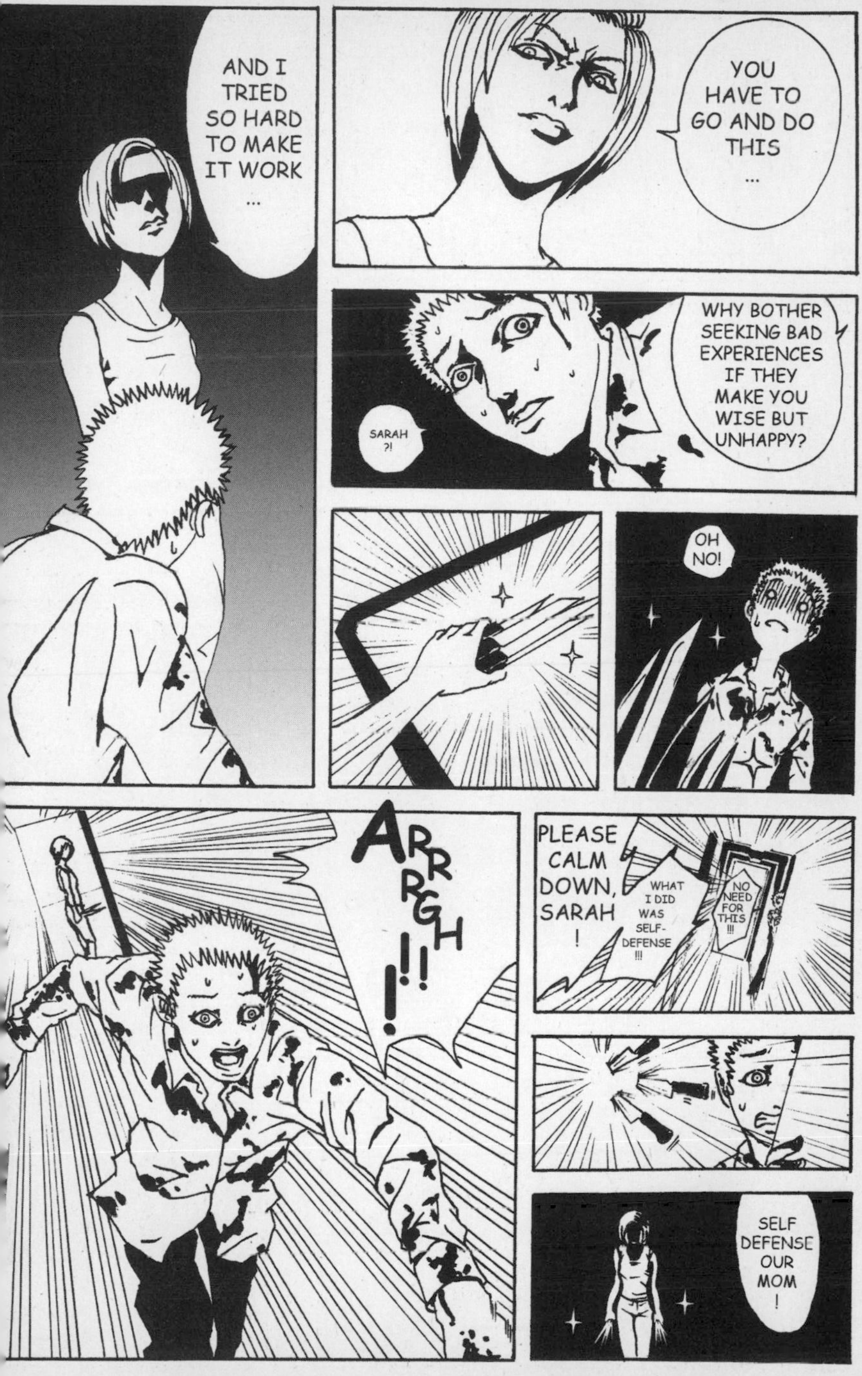
AND I TRIED SO HARD TO MAKE IT WORK ...
YOU HAVE TO GO AND DO THIS ...
SARAH ?!
WHY BOTHER SEEKING BAD EXPERIENCES IF THEY MAKE YOU WISE BUT UNHAPPY?
OH NO!
ARRRGH !!!
PLEASE CALM DOWN, SARAH !
WHAT I DID WAS SELF-DEFENSE !!!
NO NEED FOR THIS !!!
SELF DEFENSE OUR MOM !

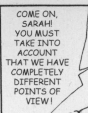
COME ON, SARAH! YOU MUST TAKE INTO ACCOUNT THAT WE HAVE COMPLETELY DIFFERENT POINTS OF VIEW!

I HAVE TRIED MY BEST!

...

HAVE YOU EVEN TRIED?

OR ARE YOU JUST LOOKING FOR SYMPATHY?

NOT GOOD ENOUGH IS NOT GOOD ENOUGH!!!

OK. OK. I AM SORRY.

WHAT I DID WAS NOT GOOD ENOUGH.

I WILL TRY AGAIN.

YOU PROMISE?

YES! YES! YES!

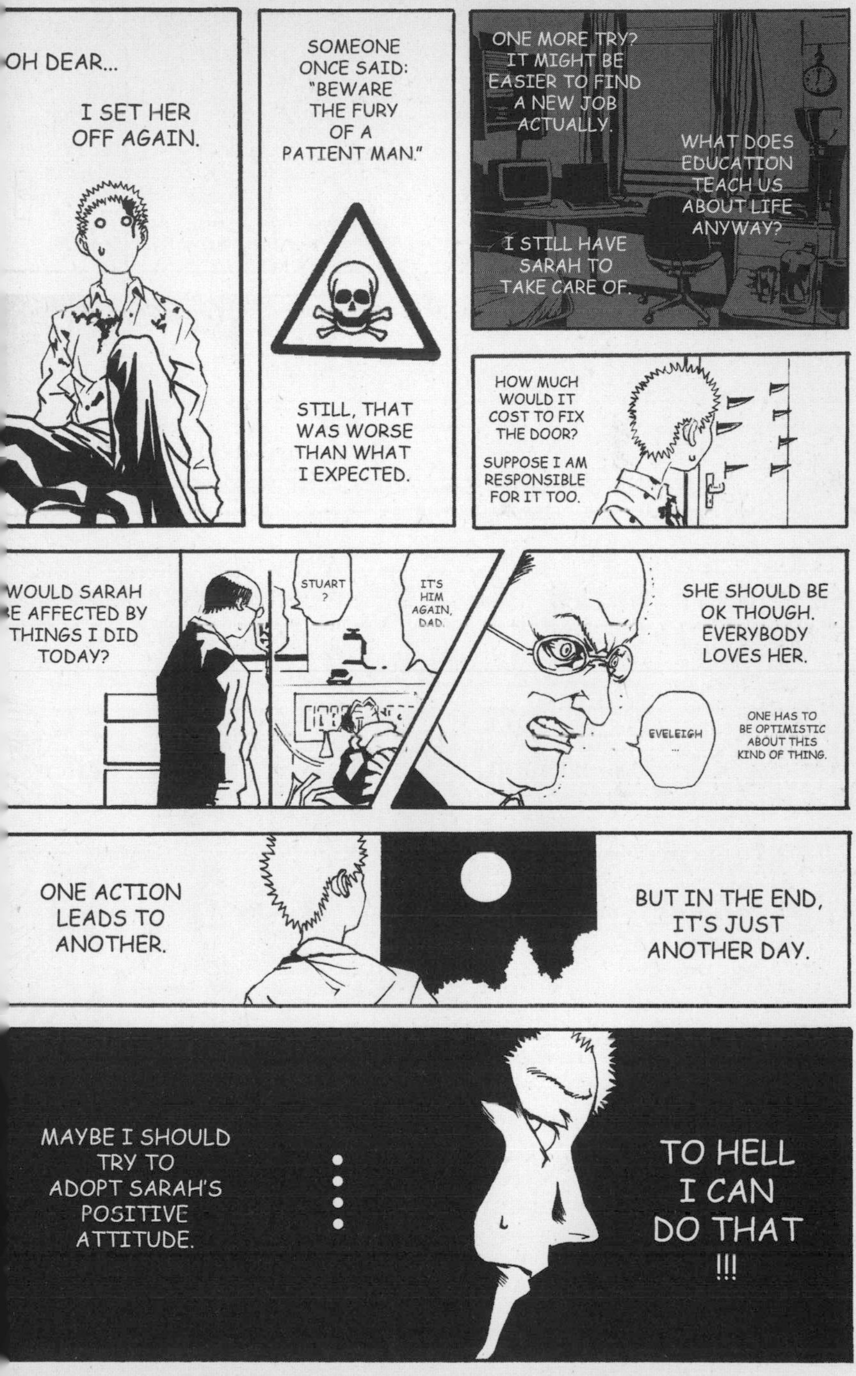

OH DEAR...

I SET HER OFF AGAIN.

SOMEONE ONCE SAID: "BEWARE THE FURY OF A PATIENT MAN."

STILL, THAT WAS WORSE THAN WHAT I EXPECTED.

ONE MORE TRY? IT MIGHT BE EASIER TO FIND A NEW JOB ACTUALLY.

WHAT DOES EDUCATION TEACH US ABOUT LIFE ANYWAY?

I STILL HAVE SARAH TO TAKE CARE OF.

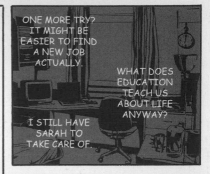

HOW MUCH WOULD IT COST TO FIX THE DOOR?

SUPPOSE I AM RESPONSIBLE FOR IT TOO.

WOULD SARAH BE AFFECTED BY THINGS I DID TODAY?

STUART?

IT'S HIM AGAIN, DAD.

EVELEIGH...

SHE SHOULD BE OK THOUGH. EVERYBODY LOVES HER.

ONE HAS TO BE OPTIMISTIC ABOUT THIS KIND OF THING.

ONE ACTION LEADS TO ANOTHER.

BUT IN THE END, IT'S JUST ANOTHER DAY.

MAYBE I SHOULD TRY TO ADOPT SARAH'S POSITIVE ATTITUDE.

...

TO HELL I CAN DO THAT !!!

OH DEAR... I LOST MYSELF AGAIN.

NOTHING CAN GET WORSE AFTER YOU'VE LOST YOUR TEMPER.

I WONDER IF RICHARD IS ALRIGHT.

HOPE HE'S NOT TOO ANGRY WITH ME.

I WILL COOK A NICE MEAL TO MAKE UP.

...

IN ANY CASE, I'M DOING ALL THIS FOR HIS FUTURE...

I CANNOT JUST GIVE UP NOW.

ROUND TWO...FIGHT!!

NO MATTER WHAT HE SAYS.

ONE DAY HE WILL APPRECIATE IT!

ANGELS CAN FLY BECAUSE THEY TAKE THEMSELVES LIGHTLY.

TOMORROW IS GOING TO BE A BEAUTIFUL DAY.

(AND THE CYCLE STARTS AGAIN

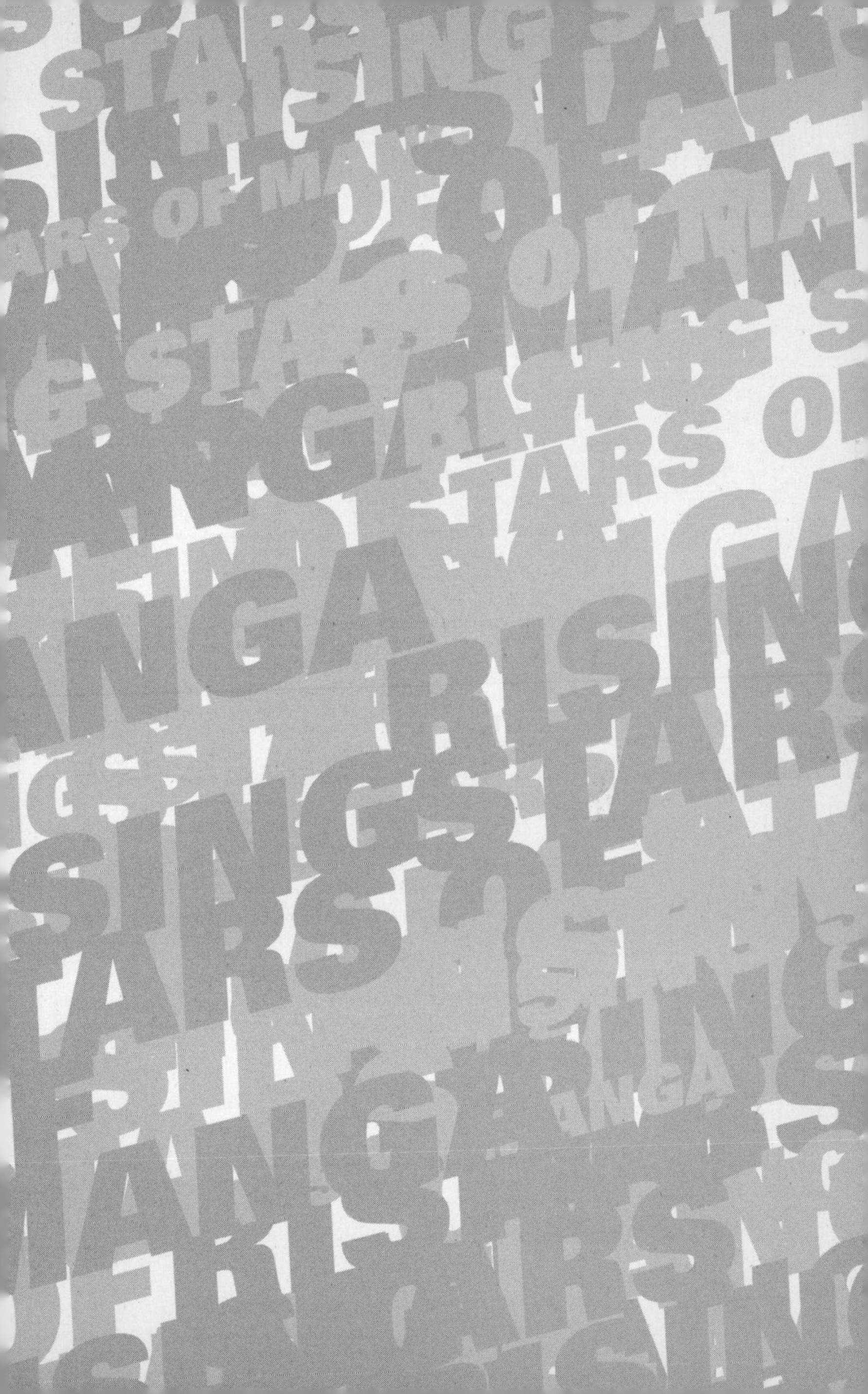

:WHERE ARE THEY NOW

the RISING STARS of MANGA
United Kingdom and Ireland

A rare image of the specimen in his natural habitat:
The RSoMbie.

ILLUSTRATION BY
PSEUDOME STUDIOS, LLC

::

"Want to be a manga artist? No one makes it easier than TOKYOPOP!"
-WIZARD

The grind of producing a complete 20-page manga is no small matter. Sleep deprivation, intense focus, and the absence of sunlight and outdoor air has contributed on numerous occasions to the RSoMbification of many fresh-faced manga-ka. Those that do not expire in the endeavor, however, face even greater challenges as they move onto professional projects with TOKYOPOP and other publishers. We are constantly seeking talented new manga-ka to both create and collaborate on original graphic novels. *Rising Stars of Manga* has not only exposed the talents of its finalists to the world, but has been also the proving-ground where we discover the best and brightest creative talent.

We thought it would be fun to catch up with these past winners, and preview some of their upcoming projects. These names are only the beginning. There are other finalists with whom we are working that cannot be announced at this time, and we trust that this success will continue with the winners from the volume you hold now in your hands. Hopefully these manga-ka will prove to be an inspiration to all the RSoMbies of future contests
—Brandon Montclare

::

::
Wes Abbott
RSoM 2: "Dogby Walks Alone"
It's been a long, lonely walk for the fan favorite Happy Place mascot. At long last we are proud to announce that Wes is working on a *Dogby Walks Alone* Original Manga series.
::

::
George Alexopoulos
RSoM 5: "Can I Sit Here?"
George can be seen applying his artistic skills to the upcoming Original Manga series *Go With Grace*.
::

::
T Campbell & Amy Mebberson
RSoM 5: "Pop Star"
T and Amy have been working on an expanded story based on their winning "Pop Star" entry. This series, now called *Divalicous!*, will be available from TOKYOPOP in 2007.
::

::
Lindsay Cibos
RSoM 2: "Peach Fuzz"
RSoM 2 Grand Prize entry "Peach Fuzz" is now an Original Manga series. Fun for all ages continues as we explore further the epic struggle inherent in the relationship between man (well, a girl) and beast (here, a ferret). *Peach Fuzz* is also serialized in many U.S. and Canadian newspapers. **Available Now!**
::

::
Tania Del Rio
RSoM 2: "Love Sketch"
We all loved her *RSoM* entry, and so did the editors at Archie Comics. Tania has picked up both the writing and art duties during her critically-acclaimed run on *Sabrina*.
::

173

the RISING STARS of MANGA United Kingdom and Ireland

::

Joshua Elder & Erich Owen
RSoM 5: "Mail Order Ninja"
Top prize winners in *RSoM 5*, Erich and Josh build upon the *Mail Order Ninja* mythos is their new ongoing series for TOKYOPOP. Volume 1 is scheduled for release this summer.

::

::

Irene Flores & Ashly Raiti
RSoM 3: "Life Remains"
Irene and Ashly wowed us with their touching relationship story in *RSoM 3*. The creators evidence a broad artistic range as they delve into the gothic genre with the Original Manga series *Mark of the Succubus*. **Available Now!**

::

::

Amy Kim Ganter
RSoM 4: "The Hopeless Romantic and The Hapless Girl"
Amy proved she could handle the ups and downs of love in her *RSoM 4* Third Place entry. Fans can look forward to new misadventures in romance in the full-length Original Manga series *Sorcerers & Secretaries*. **Available Now!**

::

::

Shane Granger
RSoM 2: "Possessions"
The reader feels immediately the impact of Shane's pencils in his RSoM entry. His skills and creativity in penciling are now being applied to the ongoing Original Manga series *Psy-Comm*. **Available Now!**

::

::

Andy Helms
RSoM 4: "Bombos versus Everything"
It turns out that everything is—well—a lot, so be on the lookout for more bat-smacking action in the full-length Original Manga series *Bombos versus Everything;* based on Andy's Grand Prize entry.

::

the Rising Stars of Manga
United Kingdom and Ireland

::

Dave Iseri

RSoM 4: "Down"

Although off studying architecture in Italy, Dave promises to get started on his new series *Dystopia* as soon as he gets a chance.

::

::

Marty LeGrow

RSoM 2: "Nikolai"

Marty's vision of manga impressed us with its innovative style and uncompromising attitude. Her unique flair is being applied to the new Original Manga series *Bizenghast*.

Available Now!

::

::

Christy Lijewski

RSoM 3: "Doors"

After her *RSoM* entry helped her land a gig at Slave Labor Graphics on the creator-owned *Next Exit* series, Christy returns to the TOKYOPOP fold with the full-length Original Manga *Re:Play*.

::

::

Maximo V. Lorenzo

RSoM 4: "Hellbender"

Maximo has come to the aid of fellow *RSoM 4* winner Andy Helms by taking over artistic duties on *Bombos versus Everything*.

::

::

Morgan Luthi

RSoM 5: "Seed"

Morgan has taken on the challenge of creating a whole new series for TOKYOPOP called *Snow*. Keep an eye open for this Original Manga series when it hits stores in fall 2006.

::

the RISING STARS of MANGA™ United Kingdom and Ireland

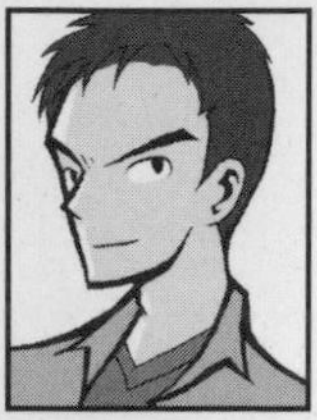

::

Nathan Maurer

RSoM 3: "Atomic King Daidogan"

A mix of wild hilarity, over-the-top action, and lovable characters made "Atomic King Daidogan" the top entry in *RSoM* 3. Readers will continue to be blown away as Nathan expands his Grand Prize entry into an Original Manga series. Anticipation is the high.

::

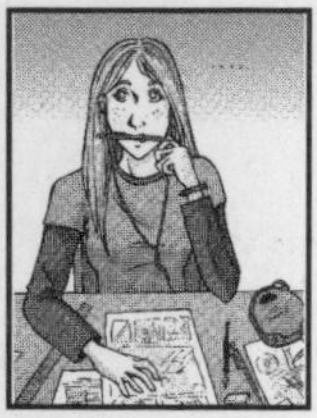

::

Karen Remsen

RSoM 4: "Le Masque"

Slightly more challenging than her 20 pages of manga in RSoM was probably Karen's recent graduation from high school. Look for her original "Chronicles of Koryo" back-up feature in *Threads of Time*.

::

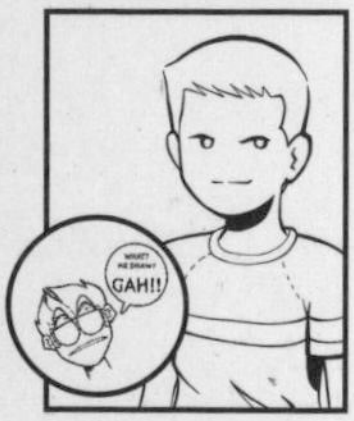
GAH!!

::

Michael Schwark & Ron Kaulfersch

RSoM 1: "Van Von Hunter"

Elder statesmen to RSoMbies everywhere, Mike and Ron continue to sponsor *RSoM* hopefuls on the forums at www.pseudome.net. And keeping up the street cred, their Second Place entry from RSoM is now the Original Manga series *Van Von Hunter*. **Available Now!**

::

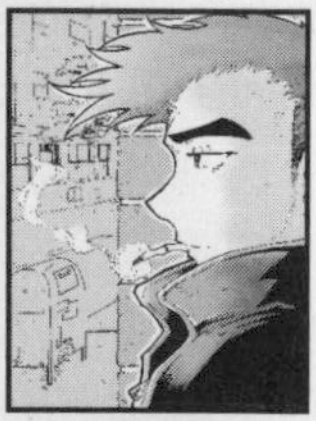

::

Michael Shelfer

RSoM5: "Blue Phoenix: No Quarter"

RSoM 5's online People's Choice winner has taken on the artist duties for an original story in TOKYOPOP's new *Star Trek* manga anthology.

::

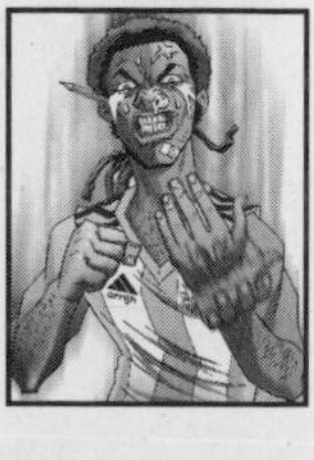

::

Felipe Smith

RSoM 3: "Manga"

The Second Place entry in *RSoM* 3 made every editor fear slightly for our lives. Luckily, it turns out that Felipe is really a nice guy. Check out his latest manga creation: *MBQ*. **Available Now!**

::

the RISING STARS of MANGA United Kingdom and Ireland

::

Jess Stoncius

RSoM 4: "Work Bites"

Work still bites. Catch up with the dark tribulations of the wannabe-lord-of-the-night-yet-stuck-in-my-crappy-job-at-the-mall vampire Lars in the forthcoming full-length Original Manga series *Work Bites*.

::

::

Jimmy Van

RSoM 4: "Beyond the Bird"

Jimmy puts badminton behind him as he joins forces with veteran comic book writers Jimmy Palmiotti and Justin Gray for his first ongoing manga series, *Zeroes*.

::

::

Jueng Mo, Yang

RSoM 5: "Modus Vivendi"

Jueng Mo once again finds himself alongside fellow *RSoM* 5 alumni Michael Shelfer in TOKYOPOP's *Star Trek* anthology due out later this year.

::

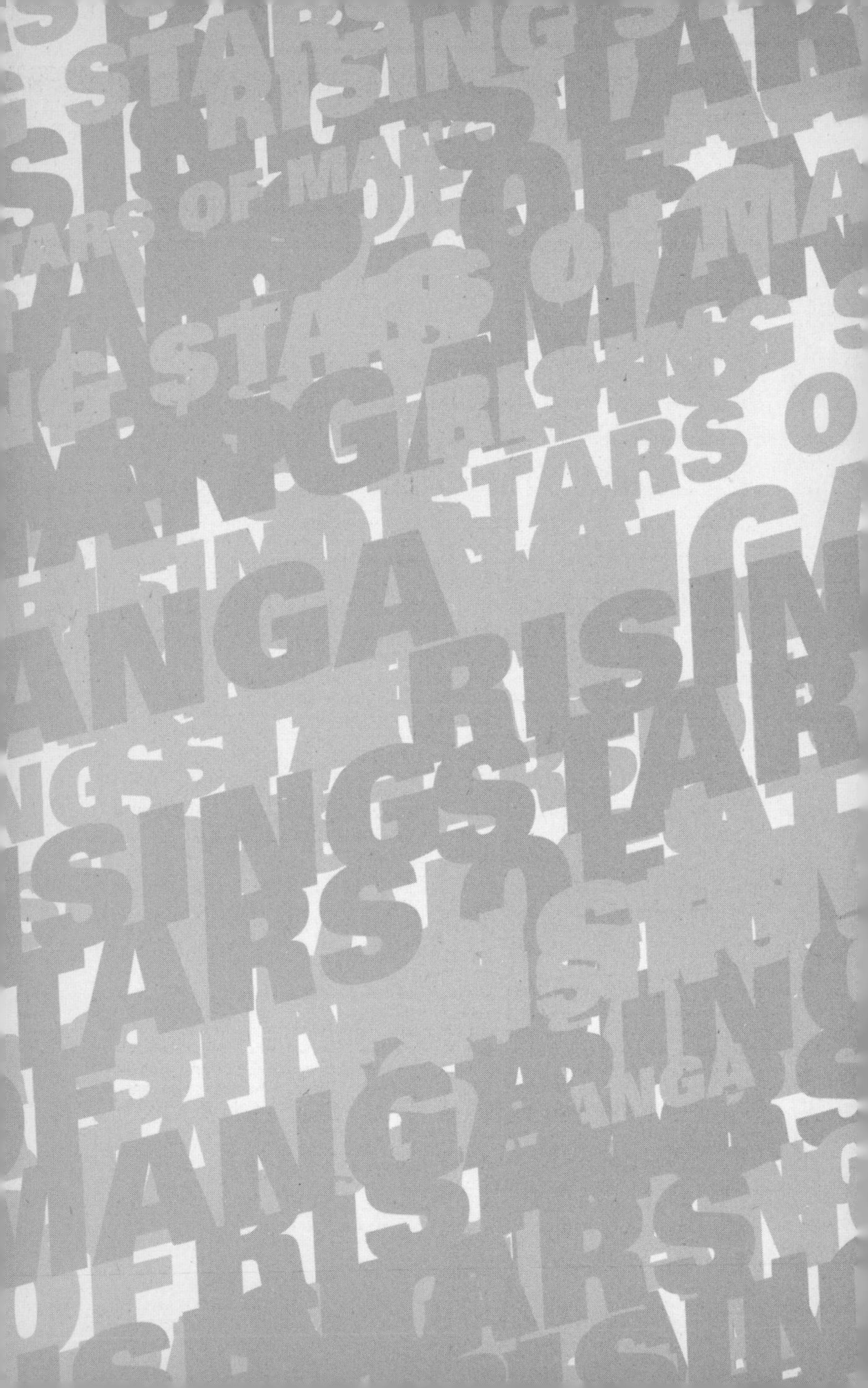

::

TIPS FOR MANGA-KA

Maybe this volume of *Rising Stars of Manga* has inspired you to take a hands-on approach in the manga revolution. Or perhaps you are one of the thousands of aspiring creators who have already entered one of our previous competitions. Either way, if you want your own manga star to rise, it's best that you review the following tips provided by our editors.

LAYOUT:

Before you begin your pencilling, you should map out each page in very rough thumbnails. Plan ahead as to how you want to establish the panels, and where you will place the objects and characters within the panels. Also remember to leave enough room for appropriately-sized word balloons. Having a solid plan of attack ensures that your manga will not get out of control. More importantly, it forces you to think about your storytelling—make sure every panel has an individual attitude as well as a direct purpose to the story as a whole.

Advanced Layout Tips:
★ Be sure to vary the reader's viewpoint from panel-to-panel. Zoom in or out with panel depth; and employ worm's eye and bird's eye perspectives. Maintaining a steady, unmoving camera throughout will make your manga appear stagnant and slow, so have fun and be creative!
★ Keep the pacing of each individual page moving forward. More so than in other sequential art mediums, manga is meant to have a fast and even pace. Generally, you want your manga to be a "page-turner" where the reader's eye never stops.

SCRIPT:

It has been our experience that most RSoM creators are artists first and writers second. Therefore, recognize your limitations and work within them. Try to tell uncomplicated stories that do not depend on excessive amounts of exposition or development. Also be sure that your story is complete, with a begining, a middle, and an end. Yes, there have been winning entries in RSoM without a satisfying ending. But nothing infuriates a judge more than a "to be continued" tagged onto the last page, or a story that has no ending at all. Your manga stands a much better chance of being published if it is definitive and understandable; rarely will you lose points for being too simple. Also, add the dialogue and narration to your thumbnail layout. You can always go back and tweak the script after your artwork is finished, but it is good to nail down a narrative pace early in the creative process.

Advanced Scripting Tips:
★ Write what you know. This axiom of creative writing survives because it is efficient more often than not.
★ Consider collaborating with a writer. Find someone who shares your passion with manga storytelling and with whom you can work comfortably. Work together and pool your strengths toward creating the very best entry.

PENCILS:

Here your raw talent will carry you. The best thing you can do to improve your rendering is repeated practice. As you draw, be mindful of the nuances particular to manga aesthetics. More so than other sequential art mediums, manga favors simplicity in art. You should not include meticulous, minute detail as it tends to slow down the pace of your manga. For the same reason, your art should fit into fewer panels per page. While the visual pace is often faster, manga artists usually need to concentrate more on character rendering—including body language and character expression—than other sequential art mediums. Also, remember to keep your manga consistent between panels. Make sure anatomy, clothing, and objects remain visually constant throughout.

Advanced Pencilling Tips:

★ Study Life Drawing. Most communities will have affordable Life Drawing classes available for every level of student. These classes will help refine all of your pencilling skills, especially in perspective and anatomy.

★ Learn to draw backgrounds and show us your ability to have characters interact with their environment. You are not fooling anyone when you set all your scenes in a room with four blank walls, an inter-dimensional void, or at night.

FINISHES:

Finishes refer to the inking and toning of your manga. Both of these are done to embellish your pencils, as well as to add depth and texture to the pages. As with layout and pencilling, your finished art should be informed by traditional manga aesthetics. Manga inking is primarily a technique for defining your line-work. Manga inkers should avoid cross-hatching or other shading methods. Don't think of your manga as black-and-white. Rather, you should approach finishes as coloring in grayscale. As in inking, tones add to the depth and definition of your art. The infinite patterns and shades can also be used to facilitate storytelling by setting moods, establishing contrasts and contributing purely to the beauty of the work.

Advanced Finishing Tips:

★ Vary your line-weight when inking. Varying the width of your lines will add dimension and depth to finished pencils. Invariable line-weight tends to flatten your rendering and stall any sense of the object's or character's motion.

★ Use digital tones. While the use of zipotone is a noble profession, it is a difficult and often heartbreaking endeavor that is being replaced, even in Japan, by digital tones. Digital tones are easier to manipulate, allow for greater experimentation, and are more cost effective. Be sure to tone your art at final size and save your pages as layered files.

LETTERING:

Just remember that it counts! Interesting fonts are great, but make sure they are crisp and clear. You can use different fonts for different characters or narrative situations, but don't go overboard with variation. Don't use fonts with serifs, as they are often unclear and do not reproduce well inside word balloons. Remember not to crowd panels with script, and be certain not to cover up important areas

of your art with word balloons. Don't forget to incorporate your word balloons and lettering into the thumbnail layout. And, please, **remember to proofread your manga.**

INSIDER INFO:

So, you have your entry for the next *Rising Stars of Manga* and you are sure it will blow our mind. To reward those who make it this far, the judges want to offer a few helpful hints.

★ Shoot for 17 pages. One of the most common problems is poorly paced manga (sometimes even appearing unfinished after 20 pages). When you plan your manga, pace it for 17 pages. This allows you room to either add or remove pages as it develops on the drawing board.

★ Send it in early. As soon as we receive a qualified entry it goes into a pile that can be read by our editors. While every entry is reviewed by at least one judge, entries that are around longer naturally have an increased chance of being read by several editors (and the more people who read it, the greater the chance that someone will recognize your genius). Also, if you plan to send it in early, you allow yourself more time to correct any last minute mistakes that may arise.

★ Less story is more. Another common problem is entries with so much story squeezed into them that the final product is convoluted and indecipherable. Save your complex tales for a multi-volume project down the road, and don't use *RSoM* to pitch your personal magnum opus. Focus instead on a short, easy-to-tell manga where you can exhibit your skills as a visual storyteller.

★ Enter *Rising Stars of Manga*. This is really not as dumb as it sounds. Even if you aren't a finalist, you should approach every competition as preparation for a future in manga. You will notice that each entry will improve upon the last, and that you are progressing toward a level of professional talent. And you know who else notices? We do. With four competitions now on the books, our editors often notice new manga from previous entrants. While we can't offer personal feedback to every *RSoM* manga-ka, there are creators for whom we are silently rooting, and we look forward to their entries in each competition.

This is just a small sampling of the resources that can be accessed on the TOKYOPOP Submissions and *RSoM* webpages. Be sure to review carefully the online material, and keep checking back for periodic updates. Also, don't forget that each volume of *Rising Stars of Manga* is another excellent source of information. Each of the four volumes contains judge's comments on every story. Study these critiques alongside the winning entries and try to anticipate the expectations of a *RSoM* judge. Above all, stay passionate about the art and dedicated to the craft. Good luck, and welcome to the indefatigable order of the RSoMbies.
—*Brandon Montclare*

::

TOKYOPOP SHOP

LIFE
BY KEIKO SUENOBU

Ordinary high school teenagers...
Except that they're not.

© Keiko Suenobu

OT
OLDER TEEN
AGE 16+

READ THE ENTIRE FIRST CHAPTER ONLINE FOR FREE:

Ayumu struggles with her studies, and the all-important high school entrance exams are approaching. Fortunately, she has help from her best bud Shii-chan, who is at the top of the class. But when the test results come back, the friends are surprised: Ayumu surpasses Shii-chan's scores and gets into the school of her choice—without Shii-chan! Losing her friend is so painful for Ayumu that she starts cutting herself to ease her sorrow. Finally, Ayumu seeks comfort in a new friend, Manami. But will Manami prove to be the friend that Ayumu truly needs? Or will Ayumu continue down a dark path?

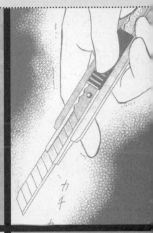

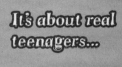

It's about real teenagers...

It's about real high school...

It's about real life.

LIFE
Volume 1
Keiko Suenobu

BIZENGHAST

Dear Diary, I'm starting to feel

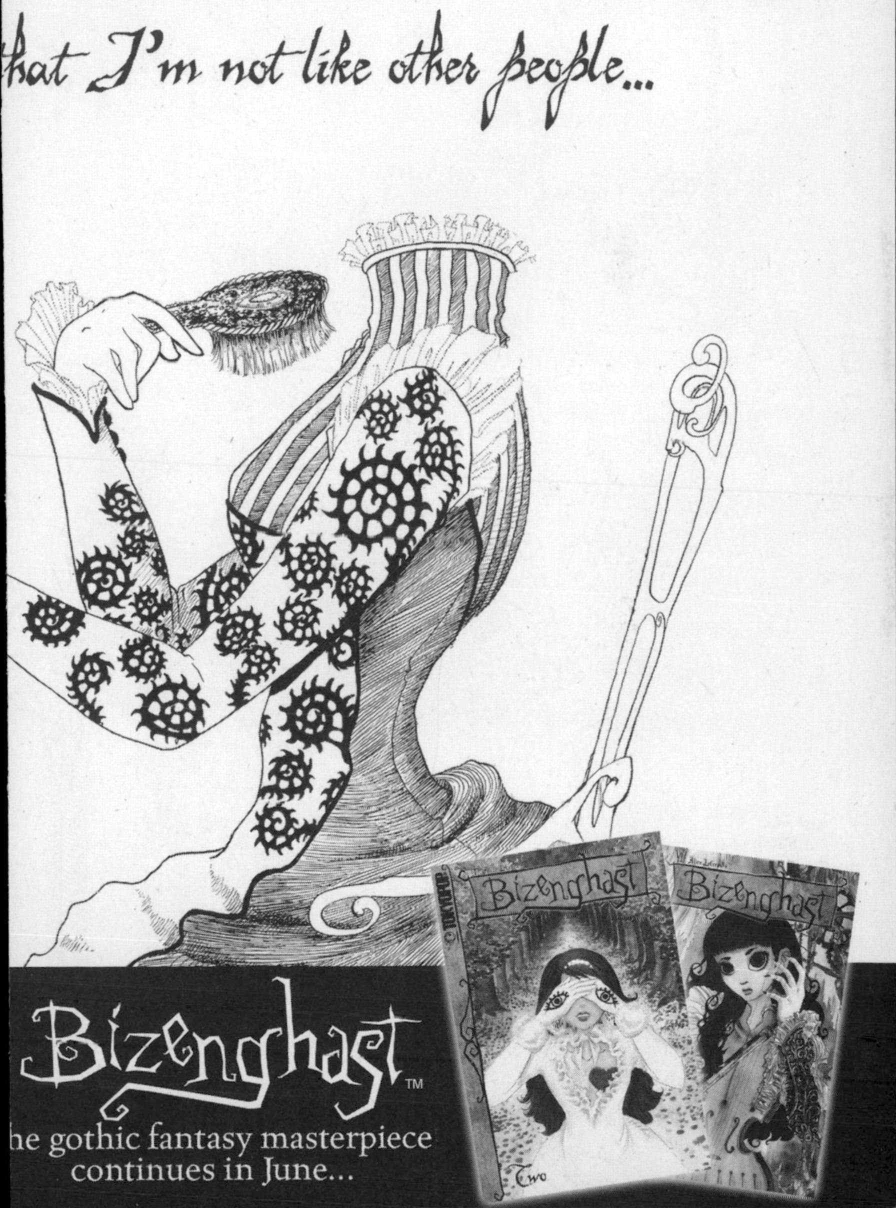
hat I'm not like other people...
Bizenghast
Bizenghast
TOKYOPOP
Two
Bizenghast™
he gothic fantasy masterpiece
continues in June...

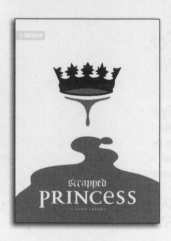

THIS FALL, TOKYOPOP CREATES A FRESH, NEW CHAPTER IN TEEN NOVELS...

For Adventurers...
Witches' Forest:
The Adventures of Duan Surk

By Mishio Fukazawa
Duan Surk is a 16-year-old Level 2 fighter who embarks on the quest of a lifetime—battling mythical creatures and outwitting evil sorceresses, all in an impossible rescue mission in the spooky Witches' Forest!

BASED ON THE FAMOUS
FORTUNE QUEST WORLD

For Dreamers...
Magic Moon

By Wolfgang and Heike Hohlbein
Kim enters the enigmatic realm of Magic Moon, where he battles unthinkable monsters and fantastical creatures—in order to unravel the secret that keeps his sister locked in a coma.

THE WORLDWIDE BESTSELLING FANTASY
*THRILL*OGY ARRIVES IN THE U.S.!

SPOTLIGHT TOKYOPOP MANGA SUPPLEMENT

THE DREAMING

BY QUEENIE CHAN

T
TEEN
AGE 13+

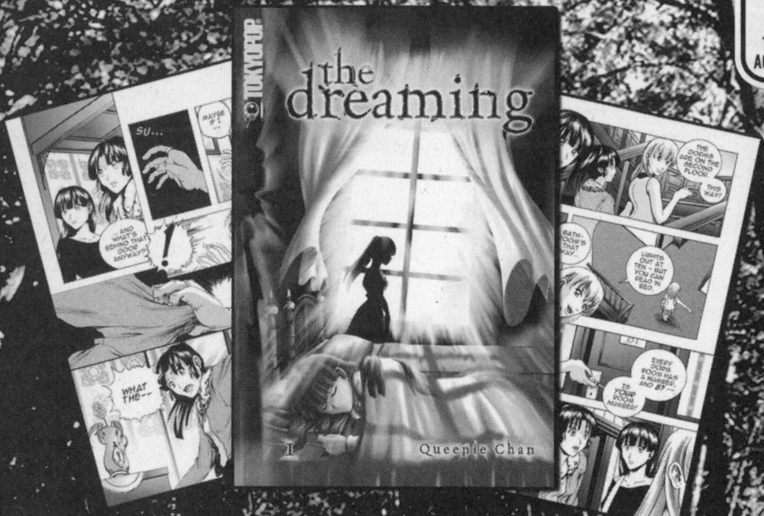
SU...
...AND WHAT'S BEHIND THAT DOOR ANYWAY?
WHAT THE--
TOKYOPOP
the dreaming
Queenie Chan
THE DORMS ARE ON THE SECOND FLOOR.
THIS WAY!
LIGHTS OUT AT TEN - BUT YOU CAN READ IN BED.
EVERY DORM ROOM HAS A NUMBER, AND 87 --
IS YOUR ROOM NUMBER!

ALL OF THEM VANISHED...WITHOUT A TRACE.

When twin sisters Amber and Jeanie enroll in an Australian boarding school, they soon uncover a dark, unexplained secret: Students have been known to walk off into the surrounding bushlands, where they have vanished completely! Few know how the girls disappeared...fewer yet know why. Amber and Jeanie soon realize that the key to unlocking a secret that has been hidden for years may lie in the world of their dreams!

SUSPENSE-HORROR SHOJO FROM THE CREATOR OF THE HIT WEB COMIC *BLOCK 6.*

FOR MORE INFORMATION VISIT: WWW.TOKYOPOP.COM/THEDREAMING

Kat & mouse

Bonus Lab Experiment

1 teacher torture

Story: Alex de Campi
Art: Federica Manfredi

When Kat moves to a posh private school, things seem perfect--that is, until a clique of rich, popular kids frame Kat's science teacher dad for stealing school property. Can Kat and her new friend, rebellious computer nerd Mouse, prove who the real culprits are before Kat's dad loses his job?

SPECIAL LOW MANGA PRICE: $5.99

YOUT AGE 10

© Alex de Campi and TOKYOPOP Inc.